VOICES FROM THE LANDWASH

11 NEWFOUNDLAND PLAYWRIGHTS
Edited with an Introduction by Denyse Lynde

PLAYWRIGHTS CANADA PRESS
Toronto • Canada

Voices from the Landwash © Copyright 1997
Playwrights Canada Press
Copyright of each play resides with authors (see opposite page)

54 Wolseley St., 2nd fl. Toronto, Ontario CANADA M5T 1A5
Tel: (416) 703-0201 Fax: (416) 703-0059
e-mail: cdplays@interlog.com   http://www.puc.ca

CAUTION: These plays are fully protected under the copyright laws of Canada and all other countries of The Copyright Union, and are subject to royalty. Changes to the scripts are expressly forbidden without the prior written permission of the authors. Rights to produce, film, or record, in whole or in part, in any medium or any language, by any group, *amateur or professional*, are retained by the authors. Those interested in obtaining amateur or professional production rights, please contact:
Playwrights Canada Press at the above address.

No part of this book, covered by the copyright hereon, may be reproduced or used in any form or by any means - graphic, electronic or mechanical - without the prior written permission of the *publisher* except for excerpts in a review. Any request for photocopying, recording, taping or information storage and retrieval systems of any part of this book shall be directed in writing to The Canadian Copyright Licensing Agency, 6 Adelaide Street East, Suite 900, Toronto, Ontario CANADA M5C 1H6 tel: (416) 868-1620

Playwrights Canada Press publishes with the generous assistance of The Canada Council - Writing and Publishing Section and the Ontario Arts Council.

Cover design by Tony Hamill.

Canadian Cataloguing in Publication Data
Main entry under title:
    Voices from the landwash : eleven Newfoundland playwrights
ISBN 0-88754-527-0
I. Canadian drama (English) - Newfoundland.* 2. Canadian drama (English) - 20th century.* I. Lynde, Denyse C. (Denyse Constance) 1955- .
PS8315.5. N5V64 1997   C812'.5408'09718   C97-930073-8
PR9198.2.N52V64   1997

First edition: May, 1997.
Printed and bound in Winnipeg, Manitoba, Canada.

ACKNOWLEDGMENTS

Caution: The plays in this volume are protected under the copyright laws of Canada and all other countries of the Copyright Union and all performances are subject to royalty. Rights to produce, film, or record, in whole or in part, in any medium and in any language, by any group, amateur or professional, are retained by the authors.

End of The Road © 1980 Michael Cook.

West Moon © 1980 Al Pittman.

Young Triffie Been Made Away With © 1985 Ray Guy.

Hanlon House © 1988, 1991 Greg Thomey and Bryan Hennessey.

Flux © 1993 Pete Soucy.

Catlover © 1990 Janis Spence.

The Only Living Father © 1991 Tom Cahill.

Tomorrow Will Be Sunday © 1992 Des Walsh.

Woman In A Monkey Cage © 1993 Berni Stapleton.

ALIENation of Lizzie Dyke © 1994 Liz Pickard.

CONTENTS

Preface   ix

Introduction   xi

End of the Road   1
  (1980) Michael Cook

West Moon   49
  (1980) Al Pittman

Young Triffle Been Made Away With   103
  (1985) Ray Guy

Hanlon House   143
  (1988, 1991) Greg Thomey & Brian Hennessey

Flux   165
  (1993) Pete Soucy

Catlover   217
  (1990) Janis Spence

The Only Living Father   257
  (1991) Tom Cahill

Tomorrow Will Be Sunday   303
  (1992) Des Walsh

Woman In A Monkey Cage   349
  (1993) Berni Stapleton

ALIENation of Lizzie Dyke   369
  (1994) Liz Pickard

PREFACE

One recurring lament at the Newfoundland Theatre Research Workshop held in St. John's, Newfoundland, in 1992 was the substantial number of unpublished plays that had received production and high praise. It was felt by everyone present that the plays needed to be published and that clearly an audience existed for them. With funding from the Canada/Newfoundland Cooperation Agreement on Cultural Industries and the advice of a local advisory board, playwrights were approached and the project was underway.

Each and every playwright represented in *Voices from the Landwash* worked very hard with me to prepare their scripts. Patience, good will and cooperation were characteristic of all relationships and I am deeply indebted to each of them. With Michael Cook's untimely death in the early stages of the project, I would like in particular to gratefully acknowledge his widow, Madonna Decker, and her generous assistance.

The project would not have been completed without the assistance of the Department of English, Memorial, and specifically Renee Husk, Department Secretary, and Graduate Students Louise Gravelle and Lisa Stowe, who all placed material on disk and helped with proofing and research. The theatre community of St. John's was always supportive and helpful in research and I gratefully acknowledge the assistance of Lois Brown of the Resource Centre and Donna Butt of Rising Tide Theatre. Always available for assistance was Gail Weir of the Centre for Newfoundland Studies and her research is gratefully acknowledged. A major contribution was made by colleague Dick Buehler who proofread all of the plays in various stages. This project would never have been completed without the support and advice of my husband, Peter Ayers.

Of course, at the heart of this project are the playwrights who created and now offer their work. *Voices From the Landwash* would never have been completed without their creativity and generosity. As an editor and as a student of theatre, I acknowledge and thank Al Pittman, Ray Guy, Bryan Hennessey and Greg Thomey, Pete Soucy, Janis Spence, Tom Cahill, Des Walsh, Berni Stapleton and Liz Pickard. To the memory of Michael Cook, a dear friend and colleague who will not see his play finally published, I dedicate this collection.

Michael Cook
1933-1994

INTRODUCTION

For centuries, Newfoundland has enjoyed a vibrant cultural climate with amateur and professional theatre as part of its history. By the mid twentieth century, there are two basic traditions, distinct but related: a deeply rooted concert tradition in the rural areas and strong amateur companies in the urban centres. In both, theatre, playmaking, performance and entertainment are dominant forces. Throughout the 1960's these two traditions thrive, but by the end of the decade other factors begin to refashion theatrical patterns. Perhaps the real turning point can be marked by the year 1967 — Canada's Centennial and Newfoundland's eighteenth birthday. In this year the Dominion Drama Festival, the cornerstone of amateur dramatic activity in Newfoundland as well as elsewhere in Canada, established an all-Canadian play mandate for the centennial's competition; companies across Canada were sent scurrying to find suitable plays and frequently turned to local poets, novelists or theatre practitioners to provide them. In St. John's, local companies scrambled for appropriate play texts to perform in the newly opened Arts and Culture Centre. At the subregional festival Michael Cook directed Gelinas' *Bousille and the Just*, which competed against local products, Cassie Brown's *The Wreckers* and Tom Cahill's *Tomorrow Will Be Sunday*. Cahill's play went on to the regional festival in Grand Falls, where it was victorious over the production of *Holdin' Ground* by local writer Ted Russell and those of the two mainland plays, Reaney's *The Killdeer* and Joudry's *Teach Me How To Cry*. Following the National Dominion Drama Festival Competition held in St. John's that centennial year, Newfoundland theatre, entertainments and playmaking again begin to be refashioned.

By the early seventies Michael Cook and Al Pittman join Tom Cahill as playwrights. These three writers are, of course, by no means the first nor the only playwrights; earlier examples are Grace Butt, founder of the St. John's Players, Cassie Brown, another major figure in the amateur tradition, and Ted Russell, humorist and radio and television writer. But the shifting cultural forces of the late sixties and early seventies seem to create an appropriate forum for these particular writers. Tom Cahill's *Tomorrow Will Be Sunday*, based on the novel by Harold Horwood, is chosen to be produced at Expo in Montreal. Following the local Open Group's production of Michael Cook's *Colour The Flesh The Colour of Dust*, it opens at the National Arts Centre in Ottawa in a production by Halifax's Neptune Theatre. Al Pittman's *A Rope Against The Sun* sees productions across the island. And an explosion of playmaking and play producing erupts against the backdrop of yet another emerging wave of artists, characterized by the very distinct CODCO company and the Mummer's Troupe, while Summer Festivals and Shakespearean productions continue to thrive.

The plays of Michael Cook and Al Pittman share many similarities as these two artists respond to their island home; *The End of the Road* and *West Moon* illustrate some of these similarities as well as each artist's own unique perspective. Michael Cook, who arrived in St. John's from the U.K. in 1966, quickly established himself as a radio dramatist, actor and director and then, in 1971, his first play, *Colour the Flesh the Colour of Dust*, was produced by the Open Group in St. John's. In 1973, the Open Group produced *Head, Guts and Soundbone Dance*, followed by *Jacob's Wake* in 1974. Termed his Newfoundland trilogy, these three plays are all set in Newfoundland; what is interesting is that the first, *Colour the Flesh The Colour of Dust*, is a bleak and brutal story of the past while *Head, Guts and Soundbone Dance* and *Jacob's Wake* are equally bleak and brutal fables of the not so distant future. Always a prolific writer, Cook continues to write for the stage and radio until his death in 1994. *The End of the Road*, written in 1980 and workshopped at the Banff Centre, is the only play in this collection that has not seen a full production. Reasons for its inclusion are several: Cook's work obviously deserves a place in such an anthology; the date and nature of this play work well with the companion pieces; the script itself is ready for production. Like Michael Cook, Al Pittman turns to his island for his stories but, unlike Cook, he responds with a bittersweet nostalgia to an apparently heart-rending loss. Compare *A Rope Against the Sun* with any one of Cook's early plays and a stark and immediate contrast is felt. *A Rope Against the Sun* becomes at once a tribute and lament for a lost community and a lost way of life. While Cook is relentlessly brutal in his attack on the 'old' ways, Pittman celebrates his community with poetry and song and allows the mini dramas of his outport communities their own place. Cook exposes; Pittman mourns.

In *The End of the Road*, Cook moves away from his usual Newfoundland setting and explores the experiences of a Maritime couple who move to Toronto. The shifting of focus from the prophetic present so dominant in several of his plays, seems to allow him greater freedom to explore fully a larger social issue. Here, the plight of the aged is set against the angst of youth but the exploration is handled with gentle humour and delicate sensitivity. While Cook's plays have always been highly theatrical, *The End of the Road* is, perhaps, his most self-consciously so. From the demanding scene changes to each and every mini performance piece to the sounding of the last post, *The End of the Road* becomes, not only a plea for the homeless but a celebration of the pure art of theatre.

Lizzie, Liander, Brigit and Greg are characters and performers; *The End of the Road* is both realism and theatrics.

Not unlike *The End of the Road*, *West Moon* challenges our perceptions of the physical stage. First produced by the Mummer's Troupe in 1980, *West Moon* defies easy definition but it is the lazy reader who terms it radio drama. Set on All Souls Night in a graveyard in St. Kevins, an imaginary community in Placenta Bay, *West Moon* is a most disquieting response to the fact of resettlement. Here the dead, who, according to superstition, can rise on this special night, discover that they are fully alone; their community has been resettled. As each individual responds to his/her loss of family, loved ones, friends and community, the emotional and tangible consequences of resettlement are firmly marked. For these members of the community, there is no resettlement; for them, there is no understanding of the awful 'why'. They only know they alone remain and now their memories, like their rotting corpses, will be neglected and forsaken just as their tombstones lie abandoned with their deserted community. While Dylan Thomas and Thornton Wilder's influence can be detected, Al Pittman uses his fine poetic skills and sharply defined characters to question fully the implications and costs of resettlement. The resulting play is a powerful and painful experience.

Ray Guy's *Young Triffie Been Made Away With*, first produced in 1985, is, perhaps, closest to the plays of Michael Cook and Al Pittman. Set in a fictional outport community, Guy's play examines the inhabitants and their relationships. While Pittman's perspective is often romantic and Cook's eerily prophetic, Ray Guy's approach is sharply satirical and relentless in its condemnation. Not one of the people of Swyers Harbour escapes his sharp knife and, while the response is to ache with laughter, one also ruefully shakes one's head.

In *Young Triffie Been Made Away With*, a young girl is found murdered and sheep are mysteriously mutilated while the local pastor preaches fire and brimstone against his corrupt community. The Ranger is called in to investigate and investigate playwright Guy does, the medical, religious and social aspects of this community where incest, rape and murder appear to be in the air. Like his other plays, *Swinton Massacre* and *Frog Pond*, satirist Guy lets nothing escape his cutting wit. While fashioned as a classic 'who done it', Guy's chief aim is to expose and ridicule the corruption and rot of this small community. From the alcoholic Doctor and his doped wife to the deranged Bible thumper, all are, one way or another, implicated in young Triffie's death and, finally, outport Newfoundland is itself the clear target of Guy's satire. Using dialect, recognizable but distinct character types and realistic but bizarre circumstances, *Young Triffie Been Made Away With* is a marked departure from the predominantly romantic view of earlier writing. It is an irreverent, biting, *Alice Through the Looking Glass* fractured view of outport life.

The late eighties brings not only productions of *Hanlon House*, 1988, *Flux*, 1989, and *Catlover*, 1990, but also another shift in focus. In each of these very different plays, characters reassess, negotiate and confirm a new awareness of self and those who surround them. Playwrights Thomey and Hennessey, Pete Soucy and Janis Spence do not follow Cook's despair, Pittman's nostalgia or Guy's satire; it is as if this group of writers choose to view their world in predominantly comic terms, and consequently with positive and hopeful eyes. With this new confidence is a new milieu; these playwrights all write from and reflect an urban setting. The outport has been put aside. History has been replaced with contemporary tales of city life. Not withstanding the careful negotiation and reassessment these characters or individuals must undergo, in each instance the play closes with an affirmation or the hint of a new beginning.

Hanlon House, first produced in 1988, explores a father and son relationship. Gary has come home to St. John's for a short visit and is preparing to return to his own place on the mainland. In this apparently understated one act, writers Hennessey and Thomey draw a poignant picture of this familial relationship that moves from the particular to the generational with the use of objects like the John F. Kennedy Memorial Album and the Dust Buster. The two men appear miles apart, but the son's parting gift confirms their inherent closeness. Through detailed action, sparse dialogue and sharply drawn characters, *Hanlon House* is an affirmation of familial ties and the often taken-for-granted but pure bond of blood ties.

Like *Hanlon House*, Soucy's *Flux* is centred on the nuances and complexities of relationships, but here we have an unusual triangle where issues of perception and art are central. Self perception and artistic perception become intertwined as each character examines his and her values and goals in relation to another. At the centre of the setting, the characters' lives and the play is a statue, a statue that is adjusted, reworked and examined until, at the close of the play, the two remaining members of the triangle reach a consensus on what this piece of art says. The departure of the pipefitter and the artist as the play closes marks the possibility of a new relationship where further interpretation could be the key.

A new beginning, a new direction, another way of seeing, is also at the heart of Janis Spence's *Catlover*. With the unexpected return of her absent husband of nineteen years, Hester, chief caregiver of her father-in-law and her husband's ancient cat, reassesses her life during her apparent widowhood and, comparing it with her husband's adventures, decides it is her turn. Hester, while valuing her past life and loves, decides that she too can leave for a time. Just as her architect son is preparing to begin a new life with his fiance, Hester, while not rejecting her husband's planned reunion, decides to postpone decision by leaving for her 'adventure'. Leaving the ending deliberately ambiguous, with the aged father-in-law on the streets again, Spence asks us to consider and conclude with her that life and our responsibilities are complex and never ending but always rich and full of potential.

In all three plays, characters are asked to reassess and question themselves and those around them. Gary and Dad in *Hanlon House* do this unconsciously, almost casually but nonetheless seriously as Dad probes his son, his life, his job and his values. Gary, apparently used to this, steadily negotiates his visit and leaves unruffled; however, with his father's use of his gift, the Dust Buster, following his exit, the strength and depth of this relationship is confirmed. The two men not only know and understand each other, they care deeply. In *Flux*, art, specifically sculpture, becomes the focus for ways of seeing, for ways of 'interpretation', for ways of living which include work choices and life style choices. Again, while the original couple is not reunited, a new relationship is confirmed between the two men at the close; when they share expressions of art, a new friendship is confirmed. In *Catlover*, Hester alone is able to reassess her world of father-in-law and aged cat and, like the tiny foetus in her hands which her husband misinterprets as guilt, Hester is able to free herself from the morass of responsibility that her world has become; guilt free but not reckless, her last words in a note are "Edwin. I'll call you. Me". She doesn't run away or escape. She will stay in touch.

Tom Cahill, who had written a play based on Harold Horwood's *Tomorrow Will Be Sunday,* turned to Newfoundland history for *The Only Living Father*, a play written in 1991. A year later, poet/screen writer/playwright Des Walsh returned to the Horwood novel and wrote his own version of *Tomorrow Will Be Sunday*. The two plays, while markedly different in style, approach and tone, share an unsentimental but not cynical viewpoint. It is as if both playwrights shared a concern for giving an unedited perspective on the major but substantially different topics they found as their subject matter. In the former, Cahill paints a portrait of the man, Smallwood, and the turbulent and provocative times he lived. Walsh, on the other hand, unflinchingly dramatizes the sensitive material of Horwood's novel.

The Only Living Father is Cahill's memory play of Joey Smallwood. A one man *tour de force* that relies on simple setting, sound and music, this play, appropriately, has the character of Joey downstage centre throughout the play. Beginning with reminisces of his birth and childhood in Gambo, Cahill dramatizes the up-and-coming politician's career, from his meeting at the age of nine with Sir Robert Bond, to his early infatuation with William Coaker, supplanted by Richard Squires and followed by escape to New York and so on. Using coat rack, desk, microphone, telephone and simple costume changes, the performer, with the assistance of sound and lights, traces Smallwood's path back to another Christmas, Smallwood's birth date, the Christmas following his retirement with plans as the only living father of confederation, to travel, collect honorary degrees and start work on the Newfoundland encyclopaedia. Smallwood's life is, of course, drama itself, and Cahill's memory play is both a dedication to the man and his times and compelling drama of power and politics. The one performer form fits neatly with the subject, granting the flamboyant politician unshared limelight in order to tell his story.

Walsh uses the image of the eagle as the governing motif in his version of the novel, *Tomorrow Will Be Sunday*. Structuring the play around a series of short scenes, Walsh economically and sensitively retells the painful story of broken trust and abuse of power when a teenager, Eli, finds those that surround him fail him. From his parents who refuse to see, to his peers, to Virginia, the woman he comes to love, to his educators, one from the church and one from the education system, all, in one way or another, misinterpret, reject or abandon him. Walsh effectively compresses this novel into a taut and moving drama of the many faces of love. Love, sex, friendship and trust are the complex issues that lie behind the soaring eagle; once broken, Walsh questions whether the powerful bird can ever fly again. The ending of Walsh's *Tomorrow Will be Sunday* leaves us with great doubt.

While Cahill centres his play in the one figure and consequently on one character, Walsh peoples his play with the inhabitants of this outport community of the 1940's. The preacher, teacher, local congregation and urban court play their part in this drama of basic human failings. Both playwrights, however, use simple but evocative settings to create their many places and passing time. Cahill uses the symbols of the rising politician's life, phone and desk, to move from event to event. Walsh uses the symbols of the outport, the wharf, a twine loft, the chapel and the landwash, to create stark contrasts between the natural world and the community. Likewise, both playwrights rely heavily on sound to support and comment on action. While Cahill uses sound to fill out Smallwood's eventful life, Walsh uses it to create atmosphere and maintain the constant tension between the natural world of the soaring eagle and the particular world of this outport community.

While Walsh and Cahill return to older forms to create their play texts, the former to the Horwood novel and the latter to history, Berni Stapleton and Liz Pickard move in markedly different directions with their play texts, *Woman in A Monkey Cage* and *The ALIENation of Lizzie Dyke*. Although both are single performer scripts centred on a female figure in some unidentified future, the two plays are remarkably different in subject matter, tone and style. It is as if the shared choice of the future allows each playwright the opportunity to explore deeply the limits and variety of the physical stage while commenting on a range of female and societal concerns.

Woman in A Monkey Cage, written in 1993, is a disturbing story of entrapment and imprisonment. In a series of short numbered scenes, Woman is in a monkey cage. By beginning the play on Day

30, Stapleton signals to the audience that this figure has been caught in this trap for some time already. Moving from dancing to music and counting to ten, *Woman in a Monkey Cage* charts this prisoner's efforts to understand her predicament and her unseen watcher/s. The audience is quickly implicated in this situation as Stapleton has the woman speak directly to us as she desperately tries to make sense of her situation. Early in the play, the elephant dies and she is put into a larger cage, the monkeys' cage, and, from this point on, Woman has an overwhelming need to assert self. However, her stories of her ex-husband, her mother and her father cannot contain the growing panic, epitomised by the dead elephant that apparently stalks her. The dead elephant and the silence cause her great distress and she counts to expell the terrifying images that fill her head. Increasingly, it is who she is that fills her with fear.

Woman in A Monkey Cage uses a single performer, Woman, and lighting to chart a terrifying journey. In the past the woman had defined herself in relation to others, as someone's daughter or wife; now her isolation prevents such comfort and, although she interprets her imprisonment as the consequence of some alien life form, she increasingly feels compelled to assert her identity. Because of the cage, she believes her captors have misidentified her as a monkey, but when she tries to articulate her name, she cannot. The play closes with the woman unable to complete a naming sentence.

By placing this female in this horribly isolating position, Stapleton explores issues of identity and self. By creating this cage through bars of lights and only allowing the woman to peer out into the darkened auditorium, the playwright forces the audience to become unwittingly captor and judge. We cannot release her; we cannot even answer her desperate pleas for human contact. The audience, like the woman,is also captive, and must wait until the lights blackout for the last time.

In *The ALIENation of Lizzie Dyke*, 1994, Liz Pickard turns to a world of the future where aliens are a part of the everyday landscape but, while Stapleton sees this world as potentially dangerous and a place of prisons, Pickard's future is a brave new world where Lizzie will escape from the corruption and rot of her own society. Pickard uses video, music, puppets and special effects to create a multimedia text that spans Lizzie's life as a mother of triplets, Andromeda, Electra and Persphone (Percy). Lizzie recounts her childhood at the Little Sisters of Immaculate Heart Convent School for Girls where she met her first love, Sister Rosa, through her life as a single parent when she makes a living singing in a bar. With her daughters' preoccupation with space shows and Percy's growths and protrusions and arrests for cheating the welfare system, Lizzie becomes increasingly militant. At the close of Act One, just as Lizzie is about to be arrested yet again, she is mysteriously saved by a swirl of changing lights and a voice. The voice identifies itself as from the Planet Karundia and offers escape.

Act Two traces Lizzie's reunion with her growing daughters as she awaits the return of Magenta, her saviour. Safely hidden from the corrupt world, she helps her daughters come to realize that Percy is different. With Magenta's return, her daughters begin their education in other worlds. Lizzie, however, feels that she has a responsibility to educate her world and uses television to send out her message. From the broadcasts, she receives countless invitations to speak and her influence widens. Spinning from such publicity to depression to grandmotherhood, Pickard keeps the fable spinning until, in a final video image, an aged Lizzie meets Mag on the other side.

While Stapleton sharply focuses the bright light on a solitary figure caged by bands of unrelenting lighting, Pickard peoples her play with voices from this and other worlds by video, sound and performance. Lizzie's world is a world of prisons, media, performance and strange new planets. Pickard achieves this with a sophisticated and demanding blend of music, song, dance, puppetry, video and lighting. Always in the centre is the rebel and renegade, Lizzie, who rejects the rules and unkindness of her childhood, the laws and structures of a rigid society, and concentrates on protecting and saving her triplets. Her efforts land her in prison and finally away from the only world she knew to a place where her children could grow beyond the limitations of the human race. As her children and grandchildren evolve further, Lizzie confidently awaits her own death and final reunion.

The ALIENation of Lizzie Dyke is a fantasy of love and betrayal with a fairy tale happy ending. It squarely challenges society's vision of lesbianism and single parenthood and places political motherhood at centre stage. Lizzie's devotion to the triplets leads her to escape from a corrupt world and create a new place, a type of utopia, for them; this 'ALIENation' is clearly an empowerment and a means of freedom for both mother and triplets. Berni Stapleton's *Woman in a Monkey Cage* is a nightmare tale of imprisonment, unbelievable loneliness and, perhaps, finally, loss of self. While Lizzie finds strength, support and love in her new world, Woman finds emptiness and silence. Perhaps Lizzie's independence, fighting spirit, and refusal to be opted into the system gives her the strength to find a new world and, likewise, it is Woman's inability to define herself independently of others that finally confines her. Regardless, the two portraits are startling in their contrast and clearly indicative of new directions in Newfoundland drama.

The work in *Voices From The Landwash* spans fifteen years of playwrighting and playmaking. However, when considering these ten plays, there are several similarities. All but one are single-authored texts from a province frequently associated with collective theatre. But while collectives clearly dominated for a time, playwrights were working independently of this phenomenon and within this tradition creating a substantial body of plays. Some of these playwrights participated directly in collectives as actors, writers or directors but in some way all are influenced and perhaps shaped by the dominant collective tradition, either by direct involvement, the make-up of first production teams or the background of production houses. Despite this clear heritage, however, each of these plays clearly confirms or introduces major voices from the landwash where the craft of playwrighting has clearly come of age.

While not all of these plays are specifically set in Newfoundland, all speak in some way for the Newfoundland experience. Clearly, *West Moon*, *Young Triffie Been Made Away With*, *Tomorrow Will Be Sunday* and *The Only Living Father* are deliberate reflections and/or refractions of an aspect of Newfoundland life. *The End of The Road*, with the young people returning East, *Hanlon House*, *Catlover* and *Flux* all move away from the specifically local, native, historical, but atmosphere, confidence and the predominantly comic affirmation link each to the local community. With *Woman In the Monkey Cage* and *The ALIENATION of Lizzie Dyke*, two dominant trends are intertwined; each playwright uses Newfoundland for the character's specific background, with alien forces either imprisoning or protecting the character from her native land. The specific is carefully translated. Despite similarities, these ten plays are also illustrative of the complexity and diversity of these voices from the landwash. Each voice speaks from his/her particular perspective, which results in a myriad of different styles, approaches and genres. *Woman in a Monkey Cage*, *The Only Living Father* and *Tomorrow Will be Sunday* have markedly different responses to their specific community. Although the urban plays, *The End of the Road*, *Hanlon House*, *Catlover* and *Flux* conclude with the exit of the main character as a consequence of a homecoming, again, each is distinct. *Hanlon House* concludes following a leave-taking, not an exit; the son will return and their visit will be played again. In *Flux*, the two men leave to celebrate prior to the leave-taking of one of them. Each voice speaks with her/his own timbre.

With the publication of these plays, productions and debate can begin. Due to geography and economics among other things, many of these voices have only spoken on Newfoundland stages. They look forward to and deserve stages elsewhere on which to tell their stories. Newfoundland drama over the last fifteen years, while influenced in some degree by earlier traditions, clearly breaks new ground. The Collective is an obvious reference point, but to move beyond the most recent past leads to questions of amateur vs. professional, urban vs. rural, concert vs. 'Play' and, most importantly, of post-colonialism and the watershed year of 1949. The tides and storms that occur between 1949 and 1967 are significant and clearly helped shape the theatrical landscape that allows these voices from the landwash to emerge. What line, if any, can be drawn from these plays to pre-1967 and pre-1949? What role, if any, do companies have in shaping the final play script? Theatre, playmaking, performance and entertainment remain major forces; *Voices From the Landwash* is a tribute to these strong and clear voices and an invitation for future production and continued debate.

The End Of The Road

1980

Written by
Michael Cook

CAST

LIZZIE	60-70, Ex-Stripper
LIANDER	60-70, Veteran (possibly.), Frustrated Entertainer
LANDLORD	30-35
GREG	20's
BRIGIT	18-20
DUMMY	Indeterminate

THE END OF THE ROAD

Act One

Scene 1:

(The lights rise on a ramshackle, derelict room, the top of a run down tenement off Queen Street in Toronto. The single door opens onto a dingy corridor which runs backstage right and then turns, giving the impression of leading to a staircase.

A couple, LIZZIE and LIANDER, are discovered in bed. The bed is a collapsing iron structure which barely supports an ancient mattress. The couple are covered with newspapers and some old rags. In the room there is also a rusty chrome table, a cracked washbasin, and a dresser with only two back legs, supported in the front by old telephone directories. A solitary gas burner holding a tin kettle stands on the table. Scattered about the table and the top of the dresser are the accoutrements of their diet: the makings for tea, discarded Kentucky Fried Chicken boxes, assorted plastic debris, a couple of empty forty ounce rye whiskey bottles.

LIANDER is a small, visibly desiccated, mousy man with a hacking cough, occasional crazy vitality, and a penchant for singing Vera Lynn songs. He is about sixty. LIZZIE is an ex-burlesque chorus girl turned stripper, somewhat older than LIANDER. They are fully clothed beneath their newspaper coverings—their clothes are castoffs, picked up from a Goodwill Centre. LIZZIE doesn't give a damn about her appearance but LIANDER, pathetically, tries to maintain an air of respectability.

As the lights rise, LIANDER is coughing, horribly.)

LIZZIE: *(Stirring beneath the paper.)* Here. Give over.
LIANDER: *(His coughing becomes worse.)*
LIZZIE: *(Sitting up.)* Sit up, Liander. Sit up and I'll pat your back.
      (LIANDER sits up. LIZZIE whacks him mightily.
      He falls forward across the bed.)
LIANDER: My God, I'm done for.

LIZZIE: It's stopped yer coughing.
LIANDER: Has it?
LIZZIE: Well—you ain't coughing.
LIANDER: I'm not. (*He tries to cough. Nothing happens.*)
LIZZIE: Rothman's.
LIANDER: What?
LIZZIE: It's them damned Rothman's. Tears yer apart. I've told you before.
LIANDER: Ah—but they're a good company. I'd go so far as to say a great company.
LIZZIE: How do you know? When was you last at a board meeting.
(*LIANDER glares as LIZZIE chuckles at the image.*)
LIZZIE: I can see you now, addressing the shareholders. (*Imitating LIANDER's wheeze.*) Ladies and gentlemen.
LIANDER: Do they have ladies at shareholder's meetings?
LIZZIE: Jesus, boy—what time are yer living in? We are in everything now. Didn't you know?
LIANDER: Well, of course—I mean, I've heard rumours. Spotted the occasional headline in a newspaper. Woman takes over bank. Woman runs for mayor. Women burn (*Coughs delicately*) undergarments. I confess, the significance hadn't really struck me. It's not as if one lives in these times.
LIZZIE: Oh, no. It's not as if one lives in these times. (*She stares off into space. Shivers.*)
LIANDER: Here. Are you cold? Would you like another *Globe and Mail*?
LIZZIE: No. There's no warmth in that newspaper, never was. Have you got an old *Star*. Now that's a newspaper.
(*LIANDER rummages among the papers, comes up with an old* Star.)
LIANDER: 14th February 1973. Will that do?
LIZZIE: You couldn't have done better.
(*With the gallantry of a courtier, he drapes the paper about LIZZIE's shoulders.*)
LIZZIE: Do you think we should get up today?
LIANDER: I've been thinking about that same question. I wonder what's it doing outside.
LIZZIE: What it always does.
LIANDER: Moving a little. Passing on.
LIZZIE: Passing by.
LIANDER: Poor devils.
LIZZIE: Who?
LIANDER: Them. Out there. Rushing here, rushing there, buying this and that. There's no—(*Pauses.*) They don't have any—
LIZZIE: Peace.
LIANDER: That's what I was going to say. No—peace.

(A pause. Outside a streetcar is heard rumbling down the street. The sound fades.)

LIZZIE: What time is it?

LIANDER: I'm afraid I don't know. I haven't heard the church clock today. Perhaps it's frozen.

LIZZIE: It must have stopped.

LIANDER: But it never has since we've been here. *(Pause.)* Perhaps I'm losing my hearing. It happens. One day, the world's noises assaulting the senses, the next, silence. Would you care to—would you think it indelicate of me if I asked you to shout in my ear?

LIZZIE: Oh, no, sir. Not at all. I've been asked to do things much more indelicate than that. Are you ready?

LIANDER: *(Shutting his eyes, bracing himself.)* Yes.

LIZZIE: *(Screams.)* Shit!
(LIANDER almost jumps off the bed.)

LIANDER: You didn't have to be so loud.

LIZZIE: That's what you asked me to do. Shout in your ear.

LIANDER: *(Grumbling.)* There's shouting and shouting, you know. *(A pause.)* But, you know, for your age you have a remarkable set of lungs. I'd say they were in very good condition.

LIZZIE: That's what the doctor said.

LIANDER: What doctor?

LIZZIE: I had to have a medical once. Couldn't get the job unless I had a medical. It was hard work, you see. On me—*(She pauses, sly)*—feet all day. Laid his head on me breast to hear me heart, he said. *(She laughs.)* He wouldn't do it now.

LIANDER: The last time I had a medical was when I joined the Army. They expected us all to undertake strenuous functions, you see.

LIZZIE: Is killing people strenuous?

LIANDER: Oh ... that's only part of it. You had to march. You had to eat well. You had to climb bars and walls and swing on ropes. Oh, yes. You wouldn't have recognised me in those days.

LIZZIE: I have trouble recognising you these days.

LIANDER: And then, of course, you had to sing. Oh, how I sung.
    (Sings.) There'll be blue birds over,
              The white cliffs of Dover,
              Tomorrow, just you wait and see.
              There'll be love and laughter
              And joy ever after ...
    (He stops, struggling for the line. LIZZIE claps.)

LIANDER: Thank you. I used to be able to do it better than that.

LIZZIE: You did it better than that yesterday.

LIANDER: I did?

LIZZIE: Before you consumed three packs of Rothman's.

LIANDER: But I like them, and, as I believe I said, they're a good company. They're involved in the arts. I like to think I'm supporting something that promotes the finer things in life. There was an exhibition once—did I tell you this before?

LIZZIE: I don't think so. Perhaps I don't remember.

LIANDER: I just happened to be passing. A gentleman who had kindly stopped to put a quarter into my outstretched hand turned into the building. There were tall colonnades and a revolving door and acres of black stone. I found myself drawn past those pillars to the door—the revolving door. I became unsure of myself then. I had never been through a door like that. And then, too, it acted as it were, like a mirror. Staring back at me was this broken down old face—I hardly recognised it and yet it looked like an old friend, an old enemy. Peering thus, I was suddenly propelled through, as a person of some size pushed out. An American I think.

LIZZIE: How d'you know it was an American

LIANDER: Well—I didn't know exactly. It was just his size. And he was wearing a suit striped like a street crossing.

LIZZIE: (*Snorts derisively*.) You wouldn't know an American if you saw one. That was a Canadian, alright. One of us. I know'em. Toronto's full of 'em. And Calgary.

LIANDER: I didn't realize you were such a student of human nature.

LIZZIE: You don't find it in the art galleries, boy. It's in the clubs where I worked. Where I was the only exhibition. And there's not much that's human about it. I remember one once, might have been the same person you just described. He tried to burn my breast with the butt end of his cigar.

LIANDER: He knocked me down.

LIZZIE: Who.

LIANDER: The one who burnt you. I remember—from my vantage point on the floor, seeing a large pair of boots. The guard, I think. Without ceremony I was propelled back through the doors. The memory is painful.

LIZZIE: So is mine.

LIANDER: Yes. It must have been.

LIZZIE: I wonder if it could have been the same one. How long ago was it?

LIANDER: I don't remember.

LIZZIE: Did he walk—(*Chuckles*)—upright? Or a little bent?

LIANDER: I told you I don't remember.

LIZZIE: What's the use. You've got a head like a colander.

LIANDER: You're right. My memory isn't what it was. That's understandable. I lie awake at night sometimes, trying to remember what I've learnt during the day. Yesterday for instance—it was in a *Globe and Mail*, I think, (*He struggles for recollection*) somebody had sold some orchards.

LIZZIE: So what's so remarkable about that. Everybody's selling these days. Nobody's planting. It's the way things are.

LIANDER: But these were special. I had been amongst them as a boy. Crushing the windfalls underfoot. And now, they've gone.

LIZZIE: Poor old bugger. You still let childhood torment you and that's foolishness. I flushed mine down the john at seventeen, together with thoughts of motherhood, martyrdom, God and the Queen.

LIANDER: (*Shocked.*) Lizzie, how could you.

LIZZIE: Easy. They're just millstones around yer neck to keep yer bowed and dumb, like any beast of the field. When I was a stripper, I tell yer, I looked the world square in the face. Yes, and even if I didn't like what I saw it weren't of any consequence. It was out there, and I was up on that stage and we had to take each other as best we could. Mother spoke to me just once after she found out. I think that Doctor told her because I wouldn't let him go all the way. But it didn't matter. "Naked before strangers," she sobbed, like some poor old ewe seeing the butcher's knife for the first time. "Naked." And I said, curious, "have you never been naked, mother?" And she said proudly, "Never. Never." That's what she said. "Your father has never seen me naked and never will." I felt sorry for her. And worse for me father. But the time of children's stories was done. Once upon a time, there were three bears, bear tits, bear ass, bear cunt ...

(*LIANDER begins to have another horrible coughing spasm.*)

LIZZIE: Oh dear. I've upset you again, haven't I. I'm always forgetting you was well brought up. At least, you claim to have been.

(*LIANDER is still coughing. She goes to smite him on the back. Adroitly, almost nimbly, he leaps out of bed.*)

LIANDER: Oh no. Not this time. You don't catch me this time.

(*LIZZIE laughs and hurls herself across the bed trying to grab him. LIANDER leaps away.*)

LIANDER: No you don't. You'll have to wait now until I'm ready.

LIZZIE: And when will that be.

LIANDER: When I decide to give up on all this—(*Waves his arm.*)—magnificence. Then, maybe, just one swift blow, the heart in the mouth, the film of days unrolling in the mind's eye.

LIZZIE: And the soul soaring up through the dark to the gentle arms of Jesus. (*She laughs.*) Christ! A flea-bitten romantic to the end.

LIANDER: What's wrong with it? What's wrong with it, eh? You've got to admit, it's a nice thought. Something to sustain—to make possible the leap from the light to the dark.

LIZZIE: I can see yer now, drifting past the sun on the wings of the cherubim and seraphim. And they're all singing "The White Cliffs of Dover."

LIANDER: (*With great dignity.*) You seem to be very well informed for someone who flushed the heavenly host down the toilet.
LIZZIE: (*Baiting.*) Horny bunch, them angels used to come down to see me in dreams, they did.
   (*LIANDER snorts derisively.*)
LIZZIE: I wasn't like I am now, you know. I had pink nipples thrusting upwards like wild roses and a bush, soft and fine, like new green grass. That was long before the fat faces, the butt ends of cigars. I'd lie in bed of nights and stare through the window at the stars and pay attention to the hunting owl and listen to the sea making love to the pebbles on the beach.
   (*LIANDER has been listening with increased amazement.
   She stops to check his reaction.*)
LIANDER: And then ... what happened then.
LIZZIE: There'd be a rushing of wings, and a light, and a bright majesty filling the room.
LIANDER: Yes.
LIZZIE: Then they would lie with me, one after the other.
   (*LIANDER throws up his hands in disgust.*)
LIZZIE: And after they'd all had their fill, or vice versa, there'd be choirs of larks ...
LIANDER: They haven't been for some time, now, I suppose?
LIZZIE: Bastard. Do I always spoil your stories.
LIANDER: Most of the time. But I don't really mind.
LIZZIE: I wish you would, on occasion.
LIANDER: (*Briskly.*) Well ... as we're being religious, I think I should do "In a Monastery Garden."
LIZZIE: Oh, my God.
LIANDER: Shall I do it over here?
   (*He crosses to the chest of drawers and leaning upon it,
   adopts a nonchalant, almost jaunty air.*)
LIZZIE: I don't give a shit where you do it. I don't even care if you do it.
LIANDER: (*Hurt.*) The first time I did it you said it reminded you of home. The farm, you said.
LIZZIE: You say things to strangers you'd never say to friends.
LIANDER: And what's that supposed to mean.
LIZZIE: I didn't realize I'd become yer permanent audience.
LIANDER: Good enough for you at the time. "Go on," you said. "Nobody's sung to me in years. Nobody's whistled at me for years. It'll be a treat", you said.
LIZZIE: Some treat. There you were, poised at the corner of Queen and Yonge in yer rags like some shrunken Fred Astaire waiting for any poor fool to stop, to be drawn in, to take on another misery.
LIANDER: You didn't have to, you know. This is a free country.

Everyone's free to make their own decisions.
LIZZIE: If I had walked out on you, if I'd walked away during your recitation, you would have died.
LIANDER: Oh, so that's what happened to you, is it. When the cigar wielders, the money jugglers walked out on you ...
LIZZIE: Fool. I was dead long before that happened.
LIANDER: *(Petulant.)* I'm sorry. I didn't realize how boring this was for you. I suppose I should go out—leave you to your thoughts, if any. Perhaps the Archangel Gabriel might pay you a visit.
(He goes rapidly to the door. Opens it. Steps outside, slams it shut behind him. Pauses. Inside, LIZZIE falls back on the bed. LIANDER opens the door, pokes his head in.)
LIANDER: I said I was going out.
(LIZZIE sits up.)
LIZZIE: For the love of God, Liander, leave me alone.
(His courage, his hurt, his anger, drain away. He wilts before our eyes. It is unbearable.)
LIZZIE: I'm sorry, Liander. I didn't mean that. Go on, if you must. Do it. One more time.
LIANDER: *(Recovers immediately—steps into room, closing door behind him.)* May I, really?
LIZZIE: Just this once. Ok.
(LIANDER jumps on to the edge of the bed. Poses.)
LIZZIE: Not there, you fool. I'm not one of yer modern theatre goers. I need a proscenium, a sense of distance ...
(LIANDER rushes across to the dresser. Jumps up and sits on it. Picks up a used Kentucky Fried Chicken box and places it on his head. Despite herself, LIZZIE laughs.)
LIANDER: There ... I've got you. The audience, enraptured, waits for Liander Clegg's famous interpretation of "In a Monastery Garden". The lights dim. The spotlight illuminates his features. All eyes are riveted to his mobile, sensual mouth.
(LIZZIE lets out a muffled peal of laughter.)
LIANDER: *(Cross.)* Well, if you feel like that.
LIZZIE: No. Go on, please. I was just passing wind.
(LIANDER makes a few tentative bird calls, then, speaking in a hideous facsimile of, say, Richard Burton or John Gielgud, begins.)
LIANDER: It is early dawn on the edge of a great forest. Behind me, the fields stretch away, hill upon rolling hill, the golden corn vying with the green meadow, the dewy tops of beet ...
(A snort from LIZZIE.)
The first cock crows. *(He imitates a cockerel.)* As if in response, a fox barks clear and cold from yonder bosky hill. *(He barks like a fox.)* Out there, on the distant meadow, the first cow turns and with a dainty tread leads her sisters towards the warmth and

sweet smelling comfort of the milking shed. (*He moos, several times.*) On the distant mountains, the twitching lamb nuzzles the patient ewe. (*LIANDER bleats several times. LIZZIE tries to control her mirth by stuffing paper into her mouth.*) But, in the forest, all is astir. There breaks, from the top of a stately oak, the sound of a thrush. (*He whistles.*) A lesser spotted Grebe drifts o'er the marsh (*He croaks*) and is answered by a quivering yellowhammer (*He whistles. It is the same sound that he has made for the other birds.*) And above all, a cloudful of larks proclaims the beginning of another glorious summer day.
   (*He whistles, and then, after several abortive tries, gets into the tune for "In a Monastery Garden" which he whistles shrilly, with gusto. Half way through he becomes aware of LIZZIE, who is rolling about the bed. He stops.*)
LIANDER: Is anything wrong? Are you ill?
LIZZIE: Oh, no. No. (*She falls off the bed, cackling. Raises one arm feebly.*) Pray continue.
LIANDER: I find it impossible to continue in these circumstances. Never in my career have I been so abominably treated.
LIZZIE: Oh, shut up, you silly old bugger. (*Tries to control herself.*) That's the funniest thing I've heard in years.
LIANDER: But it's not meant to be funny. You didn't laugh the last time.
LIZZIE: It's because I've never listened properly before, you see. Never ... but (*She wipes her eyes on a piece of newspaper.*) You've made my day. You really have. And to think I tried to stop you.
LIANDER: Do you really mean that?
LIZZIE: Of course. You were ... you were ... (*She breaks out again but controls herself.*) Superb. Quite magnificent. Thank you.
LIANDER: Well, that's nice of you to say so. Of course, it does take people different ways. I do know some who have cried all the way through it, they have been so affected.
LIZZIE: I'm sure—I understand exactly how they feel. Now, come on, Liander, after that I think we should go out.
LIANDER: D'you have any money left?
LIZZIE: The last of me pension. It'll buy a packet of cigarettes and a bottle or two.
LIANDER: Well ... that's very nice. Very nice, I must say. You don't mind?
LIZZIE: Consider it payment for the entertainment.
   (*They cross to the door.*)
LIANDER: By the way, did you recognize Sir John? I've been working on that for years ...
   (*LIZZIE opens the door. As she does so, the sound of a Christmas carol drifts into the room from a radio down the hall. It is "Oh Little Star of Bethlehem".*)
LIANDER: My goodness. Is it that time again.

LIZZIE: Does it make any difference?
LIANDER: It stirs—memories, inclinations of hope, bedtime prayers, cattle kneeling in the fields ...
   (The carol reaches the line "the hopes and fears of all the years". LIANDER sings with it softly. The carol stops.)
LIZZIE: I told you before, Liander. We ain't children no more.
LIANDER: May I not dream, a little?
LIZZIE: I like us as we are now. Now, are we going? Attention. *(LIANDER snaps to attention.)* By the right, quick march.
   (LIANDER marches smartly through the door, turns, marches down the corridor, singing in time with his march "Roses are Blooming in Picardy". LIZZIE smiles. As she turns to shut the door, she surveys the hovel. The smile fades into a bleak mask. Then she shrugs, closes the door, and follows LIANDER.)

End Act One Scene 1

Act One
Scene 2:

(The stage is bare for a moment. Up the stairs and down the landing comes the LANDLORD. He pauses outside the door. Looks backward. Looks at the door. Looks backward. Looks at the door. DUMMY rushes up the landing. Gesticulates. The sense is that others are coming.)
LANDLORD: I know. I know. Didn't I advertise. Now get down there and make sure that they've gone.
   (DUMMY rushes back down the landing and, presumably, down the stairs. The LANDLORD takes a mess of keys from his pocket. Tries one, then another. Finally finds it. The door opens. He steps inside. The LANDLORD is a young man, thirty or so. He has about him the look of a hungry ferret.)
My God. *(He surveys the mess.)* Look at it. Just look at it. Filth. Dirt.
   *(He crosses to the dresser and sweeps off the debris.
   Goes to the bed and begins to knock off the papers,
      tramples about them in a fine frenzy.)*
Respect the old, they say. Honour thy father and mother. Take a senior citizen to lunch today. If it's not starving little bastards coming at you out of Brazil or Cambodia or Vietnam, it's some doddering old coot with a walrus moustache, bleating about saving the country only to be treated like a leper. Why not, I say. Why not. *(He snatches up a sheet of newspaper.)* You see. *(Stabs at page. Reads.)* "Eighty-four year old Thomas Gaunt was found today by a shocked neighbour, dead in the hallway of his lodging

house on Queen Street. His gnarled hand, the hand that had once fixed bayonets and pointed towards the grim lines of grinning Huns, was clasped about the grimy neck of an empty bottle. And in his left hand, the hand that once hauled fallen comrades back over the duckboards in the morass of the Marne, was a note to his landlord. It was a simple request, begging that he be not thrown onto the street for non-payment of rent. The last painfully scribbled words he wrote were, please ... please ... It is a symptom of the social disease crippling this country that we treat those who sacrificed themselves like dirt ... " Bah! *(He crumples the newspaper and throws it to the floor. Goes to the door and shouts.)* Come on, there. Hurry up. We haven't got all day. They'll be here in a minute.

(The stage hands rush down the landing and into the room. First they clear away the debris, carrying away the battered furniture, the bed, etc. During the LANDLORD's monologue, they cover the flats with wallboard or similar new coverings: hang modern bright kitsch pictures on the wall—a Manhattan skyline, a naked black girl on a white background. They furnish the new flat with a decent little gas stove, a rollaway bed, easy chairs, a small breakfast table and chairs, carpet, standard lamp—by the time they have finished the place looks like a small but reasonably clean and cosy bed sitter of the kind sought after by many young couples just starting out in life, in the big city. Throughout, the LANDLORD talks to them as they work at feverish speed. Never do they give an indication that they have listened to or heard anything. The LANDLORD dodges amongst them as they work.)

It's a conspiracy, that's what it is. Bloody blackmail. This pair, now, they haven't paid their rent for five weeks. Five weeks. And the pair of them on pensions. Christ. They're rich. Seventy a week, that's all I asked. That's cheap. That's little enough for a roof over your head in winter, for warmth and security. And what do they do. Wreck it, that's what. They're all alike. Well, let me tell you, I've had it with the aged. I'm on a new venture now, young marrieds, that's where it's at, I can see that. They try. They've got guilt feelings; they can be intimidated, but these old buggers ... Look. I've got thirty of them. Thirty! You imagine. And me like a father to them all. And then that silly old bastard goes and dies under me roof and the press crawling about like wood lice. Critical they were. Well, that's it, I told 'em. They're all going out on the street. Once they're through that door, you take the responsibility, I told 'em. Sharp little bitch from the *Star*, there, all tits and no brains, crying, she was. Look, I said. Who else would have 'em. Eh? You? Their kids don't want 'em, no way. You don't find daughters these days prepared to spend their days changing the sheets every hour on the hour, taking them to the toilet, spoon feeding them, putting up with their dirty habits. And as for the state. The state don't want 'em, no, sir. But if they come here and die ... what am I? I'm a monster. What am I supposed to be? A charity? A Bronfman Foundation? Well, I don't get no tax relief. And look, some of them, now, the morals of alleycats. Take these two, now, Mr. and Mrs. Clegg. That's how they're registered. Mr. and Mrs. ...huh. The nearest they've ever been to a licence is when they go to the liquor store on pension day. That's where their money goes. She drinks like a fish. He smokes like a tilt. They piss in the corridor and, you might not believe this ... I know it's a bit hard to believe, but they have sex. Oh, I know, I know, I've got a conscience, you know. I come up to check the fire escape on occasion—some old bastard is always trying to hang himself on the rope—and I've heard them. It's enough to make a civilized man puke. And him. Liander or whatever his name is ... you'd think butter wouldn't melt in his mouth. *(Savage.)* Fucking veterans. They're all the same. Keep the Home Fires Burning. Pack up yer troubles in your old kit bag. Vera Lynn all the way up and down the stairway—all the old bastards joining in as he goes up and down. You'd think they'd all fucked her, the way they carry on. Well, no more. I've had it. That's it. It's young marrieds from now on. I can stand a bit of rock and roll. A bit of folk music. I can tolerate the music of bedsprings between decent young folks. But the desiccated scrapings of a couple of old coots sounding like a belt sander? No. Believe me, I'm liberal enough in me own way. I don't even object to a couple of gays here and there. They're alright these days. Civilized. Everyone to their own thing, that's what I always say. But the old ... Euthanasia, that's what we ought to have in this country. Euthanasia. Keep the country clean. Keep it fresh. I mean, we all know that human nature is rotten. But watching it rot—now that's something else.

(The stage hands have finished. One by one they leave.)
Very nice. Very nice, indeed. Still a bit of a smell though. *(He takes an aerosol can from his pocket and sprays it liberally. While he is doing this, DUMMY rushes in, gesticulates wildly.)* Oh. So they're here already. Well, keep 'em busy signing the book. Go on. Go on.
(He chases DUMMY out. Then, once again begins to spray in the corners.)
That'll keep it down for a spell, at least. Until they've settled in. Once they've come in from out of the cold, had their first piece of tail, it'll be just like home. They'll settle for what they know, the familiar, rather than leave. *(Laughs.)* Oh, the worlds full of 'em. People prepared to put up with the worst as long as they believe one day they'll do better. That's what was wrong with the old buggers, see. They knew they had nowhere to go but down. Six feet down. The monster, they called me. The Scavenger. The

Parasite. Is that fair, I ask you? I'm human, too. I hurt. Somebody has to make a living out of misery, I said to her, the one with the big tits. And I don't do very well at it, I said. Not as well as the doctors and them, I said, in the hospitals and homes, making their fortunes and their reputations by cutting them up. Dissecting them. Publishing papers on every disease known to man because, believe me, they've got 'em. Developing drugs for sale, it's a whole industry out there. And every time they cry out, they shut them up with a needle. Well, when they cry out here, they cry out, believe me, you can hear 'em. I'm proud of that. And, at least if they suffer, they feel the suffering. They're alive. Just look at those two, now. They've just gone out. Singing. Singing! How d'you like that. I mean, I've thrown them out—although they don't know it. I mean, I just can't take anymore—but you must admit, eh, they've got spunk, spirit, a kind of style. He wouldn't be singing "Roses of Picardy" in no damn hospital, no, sir. He'd be doped out of his mind. That's what I done for them. I gave them a place where they could be their selves to the end. (*He goes to the door.*) In a way, you know, I'm kind of sad they drove me to this. Fixed bayonets. Grinning Huns ... Scavenger. I'd like to ram the whole edition of her newspaper right up her arse ... (*DUMMY rushes down the landing again.*) I know, I'm coming, I'm coming. You know, that's what I like about this business, the variety.

(*The LANDLORD exits at speed and re-appears almost immediately with GREG and BRIGIT. GREG carries two suitcases, BRIGIT a shoulder bag. They could come from any small depressed rural community in the Maritimes. Both in their early twenties, BRIGIT has about her an aura of latent, almost perverse sexuality—she has a face of strength rather than good looks. GREG is dark, good looking, dangerous—he has an instinctive capacity for violence, developed, rather than inherited. Both, in terms of their experience, are older than their years. They are the inheritors of a world without values, that generation which succeeded the flower children, knowing that there can be no change for them—that the world of self interest and instinct will be the only one they will ever know. The LANDLORD opens the door with a flourish.*)

Here we are, then. A home away from home.

(*GREG dumps the suitcases in the middle of the room.*
BRIGIT, weary, sits.)

And you're from the Maritimes, eh? Great place. Great people. Hospitality, yes, sir, that's what I always remember about the Maritimes. Friendliest people on earth. I was in Halifax once. Everybody smiling. Everybody saying hello. That's worth a lot these days.

GREG: Is it?

LANDLORD: Of course it is. You don't get that in the city. Smile at someone and they think you're queer or something. (*Laughs.*) But, of course, don't get me wrong. There are advantages—I guess you know that, eh, else you wouldn't be here. Yes. Everybody comes to the city to make a buck or two. But they go home, eh? Yes, sir. There's no place like home.
BRIGIT: You didn't say how much.
LANDLORD: Didn't I? D'you know. You're lucky. The builders were just leaving when you came. You saw my ad, eh?
GREG: That's right.
LANDLORD: Apartments are hard to find these days, you know. Why, when me and the old lady were starting out ...
 (*The LANDLORD is having trouble keeping his eyes off BRIGIT.*)
BRIGIT: (*To GREG.*) What do you think?
GREG: It's okay, I guess. Where's the bathroom?
LANDLORD: Bathroom? Oh, yes. The bathroom. Well, we haven't finished all the renovations yet, you know. The bathroom's on order. It'll be—let me see. (*Walks about the room. Bangs on the wall.*) There. Right there. Have to put a door through, of course. A day's inconvenience–
BRIGIT: When will that be?
GREG: Yeah. How soon?
LANDLORD: Let me see. I was speaking to the contractor only this morning. It'll be within the week. Yes. Definitely within the week. He's been waiting for the fittings for weeks now, but you know how things are these days. You get a bath and no taps. Get two cold when they do come and no hot. They send you a toilet and no flush box. I tell you, the building industry's in chaos and they don't give a damn, no, sir, for the poor property owner ...
BRIGIT: Where do we go?
LANDLORD: What.
BRIGIT: The john. Where is it?
LANDLORD: Its just outside, round the corner. You can't miss it. Perhaps you'd like me to show you.
GREG: No, thanks.
LANDLORD: Oh. Well—I'll leave you two young lovebirds to settle down. Just married, eh? I can always tell. Starting out on the 401 of life ...
BRIGIT: The rent? You didn't say how much.
LANDLORD: Look—I'm not going to harass you the minute you walk in, tired out and weary from God knows what journeying. And there's this business of the bathroom—If it's ok with you, I'll see you tomorrow. You are taking it?
GREG: Brig?
BRIGIT: It'll do for now, I suppose.
LANDLORD: Great. Just great. I know we're going to get on like

a house on fire. And look—you're as free as the birds, you know, there's no house rules—you can come and go as you please ...
(He moves towards the door. Stops.)
LANDLORD: Oh. There is something else.
GREG: Yeah?
LANDLORD: Perhaps I shouldn't mention it but, you being new to the city.
BRIGIT: What is it?
(LANDLORD advances back into the room, lowers his voice, addresses his remarks, confidentially, to BRIGIT.)
LANDLORD: Its this old couple, you see. They live out on the street. Vagabonds really, a few marbles loose here and there, well, living like that, what can you expect, but they're as harmless as a pair of sparrows ...
GREG: What the hell's that got to do with us?
LANDLORD: They keep coming into the building at all hours. *(Laughs.)* They've got this crazy idea that they live here. Generally, I stop 'em, you know, or Dummy does—he's my night watchman. Can't speak a word but he understands everything you say and these days that's a blessing in an employee, let me tell you. But if they do manage to sneak through, don't let 'em in, that's all. They'll go away. They're harmless.
BRIGIT: But how will we know?
LANDLORD: Know what?
BRIGIT: That it's them and not someone else?
LANDLORD: Oh, that's simple. He'll be singing. Always singing, he is. Got a voice like a chain saw in a basement. Vera Lynn songs, mostly—don't suppose you know her. If he's been into the hair tonic, he does "Mademoiselle from Armentieres." And when he's gloomy, it's "Fare Ye Well Ye Banks of Sicily"—an old veteran, you know. Should be in a home.
(DUMMY rushes down the corridor and gesticulates in the open door.)
LANDLORD: Well. I must be off. More tenants, you know. A landlord's day is never done.
(Pushing DUMMY before him, he exits down the landing, whistling "Mademoiselle from Armentieres." GREG goes to the door, watches LANDLORD disappear, then closes and locks it.)
BRIGIT: Well?
GREG: We got here.
BRIGIT: It looks like it.
GREG: How d'you feel?
BRIGIT: Worn out. Did you see the way he looked at me?
(She shudders, hugs her breasts. GREG goes back to door. Opens it. Looks down the landing. Closes it again.)
GREG: I thought the creep might be snooping about outside.
BRIGIT: He had one eye on each nipple. Cross-eyed bastard.

The End Of The Road

GREG: Should've pushed his teeth down his throat.
BRIGIT: What good would that do? At least we've got a place to stay.
GREG: I don't trust him.
BRIGIT: Neither do I. I'd better start unpacking.
(She puts one of the suitcases on the bed and begins to sort things out.)
BRIGIT: What do you think he'll charge?
GREG: Too much, that's for sure.
BRIGIT: Be serious. $200?
GREG: Two hundred? For this? Go on. There's no bathroom and hardly enough room to swing a cat.
BRIGIT: It's done up nicely, though.
GREG: Not bad, I suppose. *(Spots the picture.)* Here. Just look at this. I wouldn't mind meeting her in the dark.
BRIGIT: You'd have trouble seeing her in the dark.
GREG: I'd feel me way.
BRIGIT: *(Sighs.)* Is that all you can think about? No. Don't answer. Your brain is one permanent hard on.
GREG: Are you complaining? *(Drops on all fours.)* Okay, kitten. *(Growls.)* Old Tom is coming to get you. Old Tom is coming to stroke your fur and nibble your ears and make you purr ...
BRIGIT: Old Tom can fuck off.
GREG: *(Hurt.)* What?
BRIGIT: You heard. Old Tom's already had it once today, so let's give it a rest, okay? Let's try and get ourselves organized. You didn't say what you think he'll charge.
GREG: *(Getting up, sulky.)* Oh, about a hundred and fifty. It's not worth more, that's for sure.
BRIGIT: Well, I'm going to allow two hundred. Just in case. You're making $380 unemployment, and mine is $260—that'd leave us $440 a month.
GREG: That's pretty good, I'd say. We can live like lords on that.
BRIGIT: I don't want to live like a lord. I just want us to survive, that's all. And don't forget, my cheques run out in two months. Then what do we do?
GREG: You get a job.
BRIGIT: Oh. I see. What as?
GREG: Anything you can find.
BRIGIT: I don't want a job as a waitress.
GREG: Jesus, Brig, you've become damn choosey all of a sudden. What's wrong with it for eight weeks.
BRIGIT: It's sixteen now. Probably more here. In any case, I'm sick of it.
GREG: Alright. You're sick of it. I bet the tips'd be bigger here though.
BRIGIT: I don't believe what I'm hearing. Christ, I've really come

a long way, haven't I? From the A & W to cocktail waitress—or professional prick teaser, whichever they prefer—and six years living with a guy who's turned into an animal. An unfeeling animal.

GREG: (*Shouting.*) But that's all there was at home. Is that my fault? Shit, I'm not running the country. That's why we came, isn't it. There'll be better jobs here—that's what you said.

BRIGIT: You don't have to shout. I know I said it. It's easy to dream back there. But I was thinking, on the way down, what am I going to say down to Manpower? (*She paces agitated.*) You know what the fuckers are like. (*Mimics.*) "And what was your last job, Miss?—or do we have to call you ms, snicker?" Oh, I know you don't have to curtsy when you walk in but, Christ, you do in your head. And if you tell them you've been a cocktail waitress, they think you're a whore and if you say you slung burgers and root beer they think you're stupid. And d'you know something? They're right. I'm not going to do it any more.

GREG: Alright, alright. No more A & W.

BRIGIT: And no more lousy bars lit by a five watt bulb so that the slobs can feel you up as you pass by.

GREG: (*Frustrated.*) But what if that's all there is? (*He tries to embrace her. She pushes him away.*)

GREG: Let's not kid ourselves, eh. We're never going to get good jobs. Either of us.

BRIGIT: Speak for yourself. I can try.

GREG: Go ahead and try, then. Me? I can put up with anything as long as I get enough stamps. Work for a few months, then sit back and enjoy life. That's the way it is now. For people like us, anyway.

BRIGIT: No, it isn't. You can go to night school here. You can learn a trade. It'd make all the difference.

GREG: For Christ's sake, we've been over that. The records worn thin, Brig. I'm not cut out for it, that's all. Bunch of arseholes putting you down. I left school once, and I ain't going back.

BRIGIT: Too damn stubborn, that's your trouble. Know all the answers, don't you. Shit. You don't know anything, least of all about yourself.

(*BRIGIT is close to tears. GREG is confused, agitated. He tries the only solution he knows and puts his arms round her, strokes her hair.*)

GREG: Hey. This is no way to start, is it. What's wrong, eh? Are you coming up for your period?

BRIGIT: (*Pushes him away again.*) It's not me period, you fool. It's you.

(*GREG looks blank.*)

BRIGIT: This morning. On the train. You forcing me like that. It was all wrong.

GREG: Okay. Okay.
BRIGIT: You listen. I didn't want it. All the other people in the bunks listening.
GREG: They couldn't see anything.
BRIGIT: Oh, no. They couldn't see anything. But they've got ears, I presume. Jesus, Greg, I mean if we're going to keep it together, we've got to allow each other a little privacy—a little dignity. The rest of the world doesn't and there's no hope for us if we don't. Do you know what I mean –
GREG: I think so.
BRIGIT: Thinking's not enough. You've got to know.
GREG: (*Exasperated.*) Jesus. You know what. We're beginning to sound like me mother and father on a good day. Nag, nag, nag. You nagged me to come here and now I'm here.
BRIGIT: Alright. But d'you know why I nagged you to come.
GREG: To get out of the god damn place, for one thing.
BRIGIT: That's right. But it was you I wanted to get out of the place. I could have stood it. For a bit longer, anyway.
GREG: You could have fooled me.
BRIGIT: You've become a stranger, Greg. I don't know you. I was—well all the anger of the guys out of work down at the beer parlour seemed to get to you. I thought you'd kill someone one day.
GREG: (*Astonished.*) Hey, Brigit. You're not serious.
BRIGIT: You've never seen yourself in a fight.
GREG: Fights. That's nothing, Brig. Gets rid of a bit of frustration, that's all.
BRIGIT: There you are.
GREG: But that's crazy, Brigit. Kill someone? Me? You're talking to the original Big Tom, remember, the one who walked you home from school, fought off the boys, stroked you to sleep night after night. (*A pause.*) I love you, Brigit. I always have.
BRIGIT: (*Through tears.*) That's what you say.
GREG: Hey. You remember the big storm. Boxing Day, it was. And I saw you coming back from the store, head down, pushing your way through the snow, panicky, like some bird trying to escape before the snow froze to its wing. That's when I knew. Funny. I couldn't do anything to help you. Just stood by the corner of the barn and watched as you blew by.
   (*BRIGIT goes to him, puts her arms round him. They stand hugging, reaching for understanding, comfort.*)
BRIGIT: I was so proud of you, those days. I had the handsomest boy in the school, and all the girls chasing after you, and you never looked at them, not once. You were mine, all mine. And what we did together, that was our secret. It was always to be our secret, wasn't it?
   (*GREG nods.*)

BRIGIT: No swapping notes with the girls or the boys. What does he do, or what does she do and how often. It was all we had, and we had to keep it—clean. And then—on the train ...
GREG: A mistake, Brig. Honest. I was so god damn tense.
(BRIGIT puts a finger to his lips to stop him.)
BRIGIT: No one else ever to know.
GREG: No one. I promise.
(A pause—BRIGIT's emotional exhaustion resolves itself into a need for purging, for sex. She begins to play their game.)
BRIGIT: What about the birds. They talk.
GREG: Big Tom will scare them away. They won't harm you.
BRIGIT: But he mustn't hurt them. If he hurts them, then he'll be taken away from his kitten. He'll be put into a cage, and his kitten will pine away and die, with no-one to love.
GREG: Kitten—it's only when you're hurt that Big Tom gets mad. Something snaps and he becomes big like a tiger. As cruel as a tiger.
(He drops on all fours again and snarls. BRIGIT runs across the room, covering herself with her hands. GREG begins to stalk her.)
GREG: It's dark in the woods.
BRIGIT: Pecks of snow drifting down.
GREG: The paths have all vanished.
BRIGIT: No light. No moon. No stars.
GREG: Big Tom smells something. There's something else, another creature, ahead of him, crouched against a rock.
BRIGIT: It's a small, furry kitten. Far from home. Lost. Frightened. And all the birds are looking down at her from the trees, waiting.
GREG: Big Tom sees her.
BRIGIT: The first bird moves down from the upper branches. Its eyes gleam red.
GREG: As it moves to strike, Big Tom pounces.
(He does so, flailing his arms like cats claws. Growling, he buries his teeth in an imaginary bird.)
BRIGIT: Don't kill it. Don't kill it.
GREG: Its blood is warm.
(But he lets go of the imaginary bird.)
BRIGIT: The other birds whisper in the trees.
GREG: Big Tom snarls again. There is a rushing of wings.
BRIGIT: Silence.
GREG: Big Tom begins to stroke the little kitten, stroke and stroke her.
BRIGIT: Until she stops trembling.
(GREG is stroking her. His stroking becomes urgent. She pulls him towards the bed.)
GREG: She begins to purr ...

(Off stage we hear LIANDER's singing.)
LIANDER: Mademoiselle from Armentieres, parlez vous. Mademoiselle from Armentieres, parlez vous.
GREG: Shit!
BRIGIT: What is it?
GREG: It must be them. That crazy pair Creepy said might come around.
BRIGIT: Oh. Perhaps the night watchman will throw them out.
GREG: If he doesn't, I will.
(LIANDER, still singing, in tandem with LIZZIE, appears on the landing and moves towards the door. DUMMY rushes up behind them, gesticulating. He grabs LIZZIE.)
LIZZIE: What are you doing, Dummy. Take yer hands off me.
(LIANDER gallantly, if feebly, struggles with DUMMY.)
LIANDER: That's right. *(Belches loudly.)* You leave my woman alone. I've handled better men than you in my day. In the army.
(DUMMY is still wrestling with LIZZIE.)
LIZZIE: Touch me again, you snivelling wreck, and I'll do for you.
LIANDER: *(Trying to get hold of DUMMY's arm.)* I'll try the old unarmed combat trick ... *(DUMMY hurls him against the wall. He subsides in a heap, groaning.)*
LIZZIE: You bastard. Can't you see that he's sick. Can't you see that he's ill. Take that.
(She kicks him in the nuts with remarkable force. DUMMY, making strange, inhuman sounds falls slowly back down the landing and disappears from view.)
GREG: What the hell is going on out there. *(He moves towards the door.)*
BRIGIT: Greg. Be careful. Please.
LIZZIE: Here, my love. Let me help you up.
(She lifts LIANDER up. He feels himself for broken bones.)
LIANDER: Where is he? I'll pound him to pulp. I'll have his guts for garters. I'll ...
LIZZIE: Silly old bugger. He's back down there. *(LIANDER walks cautiously back down the landing. Peers down the stairs.)*
LIANDER: Oh, my God.
LIZZIE: I got him right where it hurts. *(Laughs.)* Last time I did that was to that cigar chewing bastard. You know, the one who burnt me here. *(She holds her breast.)*
LIANDER: Beast.
LIZZIE: I got him straight between the legs. He swallowed his cigar. Probably burnt his balls, too, 'cos they couldn't have been that far from his throat.
LIANDER: *(Peering.)* He's very still. Do you think he's alright?
LIZZIE: What do I care if he's alright. Does anyone care if we're alright? Where's the key?
LIANDER: The key ...

BRIGIT: What are they talking about? The key?
LIZZIE: (*Mimicking.*) Key. Key. You sound like a bloody parrot. Where is the key?
LIANDER: (*Rummaging.*) Here it is.
GREG: What the fuck ...
BRIGIT: Must be a different door.
LIANDER: (*Struggling to insert key.*) I can't find the hole.
LIZZIE: Christ. You never can.
LIANDER: I try. Give me that. You can't say that I don't try. I'll try again tonight, if you like.
LIZZIE: (*Laughs.*) It's like being tickled by a cocktail sausage. But when it's all you've got... (*LIANDER has found the hole. He turns the key. The door opens. LIZZIE and LIANDER confront GREG and BRIGIT.*)
LIANDER: Here. Who are you?
GREG: (*Belligerent.*) Never mind about that. Fuck off. Go on.
LIZZIE: (*Puzzled.*) This isn't ours. What's happened?
GREG: I'm warning you.
LIZZIE: Don't worry, son. We're going. I'm sorry. Come on, you. (*She grabs LIANDER by the arm. LIANDER resists.*)
LIANDER: Wait a minute.
LIZZIE: This isn't our room. And we've disturbed these nice young people. Now, come on.
LIANDER: But this is our room.
LIZZIE: Since when have we ever lived in anything like this. (*To GREG.*) Don't mind him. When he's had a few in, he don't know where he is.
   (*She succeeds in dragging LIANDER back from the door
      but he wrestles free and runs inside, triumphantly
         pointing at the number.*)
LIANDER: There you are. 107. This is our room.
LIZZIE: (*Taken aback.*) That's funny. Then it must be the wrong building.
LIANDER: What about Dummy?
LIZZIE: That's right. Then ...
GREG: Look. I don't know what all this is about except that we live here and you don't. Now get out before I throw you out.
BRIGIT: Wait a minute, Greg. The key.
GREG: (*Misunderstanding.*) That's right. I was forgetting. I'll take that key. You can't go running around with keys that fit other people's places. Give me that key.
LIANDER: (*Backing into the middle of the room.*) No. No, I won't. It's our key and this is our room.
   (*GREG moves swiftly to LIANDER, picks him up bodily
         and moves toward the door.*)
BRIGIT: Greg, wait a minute.
LIZZIE: Go on, young feller. Be a hero. Throw out an old man

with bones like driftwood. What's he done to you.
GREG: (*Frustrated. Puts LIANDER down.*) You walk into my apartment and you ask me what's wrong. Shit!
LIANDER: (*With sudden illumination.*) It's him.
GREG: Who?
LIANDER: The landlord. He's done it. When our backs were turned. Oh, perfidious wretch.
BRIGIT: But what has he done?
LIANDER: It was ours, you see. But now it's yours. He changed things the moment our backs were turned. Moved the papers.
LIZZIE: Threw out the bed, of course.
LIANDER: Redecorated.
LIZZIE: Turned a perfectly comfortable home into a funeral parlour.
LIANDER: Look. (*Pointing at the nude.*) Look at that. That's indicative of the man's taste. I always knew he was a sex maniac.
(*GREG and BRIGIT are by now totally confused. LIZZIE explains.*)
LIZZIE: It's because we didn't pay the rent, you see. So he's changed it and gone and sublet. Without saying a word. Hateful man. No sense of humor. And after all we've done for him.
LIANDER: (*Surprised.*) What have we done for him?
LIZZIE: Given him something to bitch about these past months, that's what. We've performed a perfectly valuable social function, I'll tell you. D'you know what those types do when they go home frustrated? When they've nothing to complain about? No one to shout at or despise or hate?
(*She pauses. Expectant.*)
BRIGIT: No. What do they do?
LIZZIE: They go out and kill people.
LIANDER: Or rape. That's the very least they'd do. Rape.
BRIGIT: They're right, you know, Greg. Remember what I told you about him.
GREG: I don't know what's happening.
LIZZIE: Some poor little creature walking home from ballet lessons, sucking a popsicle.
LIANDER: Snap. Something goes snap in his head, like a elastic band.
LIZZIE: Or a garter belt.
LIANDER: He grabs her.
LIZZIE: Pulls her into a darkened alley.
LIANDER: Tears off her little knickers, the ones with frills. Her dancing knickers.
LIZZIE: Should be shot. That bastard. I'd do it meself if I had a gun. You could do it. You're big enough. (*To GREG.*)
LIANDER: Hanging's too good for types like that.
LIZZIE: He pleads before some bloody wasp magistrate—that is, if

he ever gets caught.
LIANDER: And that's unlikely.
LIZZIE: Gives out a few backhanders here and there.
LIANDER: Tickets for the police ball.
LIZZIE: Well known charities. Liberal Party funds.
LIANDER: Gets a psychiatrist to certify that he was depressed.
LIZZIE: Pleads pressure of business.
LIANDER: An unsympathetic wife.
LIZZIE: Hasn't had it for ten years. Not even a feel.
LIANDER: Is an outstanding citizen, helper of the poor, the deprived.
LIZZIE: The aged.
LIANDER: Us.
LIZZIE: Gets fined two hundred dollars and is told not to do it again.
LIANDER: Triumphant, comes home and abuses his wife ...
LIZZIE: Fucks the cat ...
LIANDER: Do you always have to be so vulgar.
LIZZIE: I was only trying to illustrate a point.
LIANDER: But our young friends here aren't used to you like I am. They look well brought up.
GREG: Jesus, will somebody please tell me what's going on?
LIZZIE: Nobody's well brought up these days, so come off your middle class posturing. (*To GREG.*) He always had a wish to be refined, you know. Like the English.
BRIGIT: My parents were a bit like that.
LIZZIE: Its commonplace, my dear. It's a terrible Canadian affliction.
(*DUMMY appears in the corridor. Rushes up and in the door. Makes for LIANDER. BRIGIT screams.*)
BRIGIT: Greg.
GREG: Here ... what the hell d'you think you're doing.
(*He goes for DUMMY. DUMMY aims a blow at GREG. GREG ducks, lands him a blow in the midriff. DUMMY doubles up. GREG hoists him on his shoulder. Trots through the door, down the landing and heaves him down the stairs. A loud, inhuman wail from DUMMY. GREG comes back in, dusting his hands.*)
LIANDER: Well ... thank you. Thank you very much. Er—is he alright?
GREG: Yeah. He's only hurt.
LIANDER: Oh. Good. Did you see what our young friends did, Lizzie?
LIZZIE: Of course, I did. And we're grateful. Honestly. But the truth is, old bugger, that we've been thrown out on the street, and we've got to be going. It's a pity, though ... had some good times here, eh ...

(She moos loudly several times ... laughs ...)
LIANDER: To say nothing of the occasional cocktail sausage.
LIZZIE: Old bugger. Ah, well, I think we're on the last lap this time. Will you take my arm.
LIANDER: May I sing?
LIZZIE: Sing? Jesus, boy. If you didn't, I'd do to you what I did to Dummy down there.
LIANDER: Well ... *(To GREG and BRIGIT. Bowing to the latter.)* It was nice meeting you—and we're sorry to have bothered you.
LIZZIE: Yeah, it wasn't your fault. And it weren't ours. *(To LIANDER.)* Together, now. *(They line up their feet and begin to cross towards the door, marching in time.)*
LIANDER: *(Sings)*   Fare ye well, ye banks of Sicily,
   Fare ye well, ye banks and braes,
   There's no Jock will mourn the loss of ye,
   Poor bloody soldiers are weary ...
(BRIGIT has been whispering urgently to GREG.)
BRIGIT: We've been thinking. It doesn't seem fair, does it, Greg?
GREG: It isn't.
LIZZIE: Nothing is these days, my dear—we're used to it.
BRIGIT: No. Wait. It's not as simple as that. He threw you out without telling you, and got us to come in. He tried to make us responsible.
GREG: Creep. I'd like to break his neck. *(A warning look from BRIGIT.)* Alright, alright. But who does he think we are.
BRIGIT: We think you should stay. Tonight, anyway.
GREG: And I'll speak to him in the morning.
LIANDER: Well—I can't speak for my partner here, but personally, I'd be most honoured. Most honoured. *(He bows.)* And the weather outside, to say the least, is inclement.
LIZZIE: He means that it's snowing. Look, dears, it is nice of you, but—oh dear, Liander. I don't know.
BRIGIT: He did tell us about you. He lied, though.
GREG: Yeah. Said you were crazy.
LIANDER: The scoundrel.
BRIGIT: He said you'd be singing. We recognized you by your song.
LIANDER: You did? That's thoughtful of you to say so. "Mademoiselle from Armentieres" is one of my favorites, of course. Sometimes I think it's the "White Cliffs of Dover" and then ...
LIZZIE: There are others, dears, and I'm quite sure you'll hear them all before the night's out.
BRIGIT: You will stay then.
LIZZIE: It's not as if we have that many invitations, dear. *(She laughs.)* Alright, Liander, shut the door, in case our friend returns.
GREG: He won't, if he knows what's good for him.

LIZZIE: Proper tiger you have there, my dear. The kind I used to like when I was younger. But that's a long time ago. Now—I'm reduced to that.
LIANDER: Lizzie, dear, let me remind you that we are guests. I'm sure these fine young people aren't interested in our personal problems.
LIZZIE: Is that what they are? (*Laughs.*) But you're right. As we're guests in our own home, we must behave ...
    (*She fishes in her bag and comes up with a forty ounce bottle of rye.*)
LIZZIE: Allow us, at least, to offer a little something in return.
    (*She holds the bottle aloft. BRIGIT takes GREG by the hand and draws him back to sit down.*)
LIANDER: (*Clearing his throat.*) Well ... (*An embarrassed pause.*)
BRIGIT: We brought some glasses.
    (*She gets up hurriedly, rummages in a case and produces some glasses wrapped in newspaper. She unwraps them, one by one, and hands them to LIANDER, who fills them and dispenses them, one by one.*)
LIZZIE: (*Glass in hand.*) Coke. I've got some coke.
    (*She puts the glass down, feels in her bag and comes up with a bottle of Coke. Pours some into her own glass and passes it on. All glasses are eventually filled. They pause, and look at each other. LIANDER whistles softly, "Fare Ye Well Ye Banks of Sicily."*)
    (*The lights fade.*)

End Act One

Act Two
Scene 1:

(*The lights rise on the scene as before. The bottle, on the table, is half empty. BRIGIT is sitting on GREG's knee, her arm around him. They are watching as LIANDER, standing on one of the chairs, hand to mouth, is attempting to hum the music of "The Stripper" making a sound like an emasculated kazoo. LIZZIE is parading about the apartment, throwing off items of clothing until she is clad only in a bra and skirt. Despite her age and size, her bump and grinds still show us the old pro she once was.*)

LIZZIE: (*To imaginary audience.*) There you are, my darling. (*Throwing a shawl.*) The next pasty is for you. (*LIANDER continues. LIZZIE continues her routine.*)
LIZZIE: If you want me tonight dear, it's going to cost you. I've already been offered one hundred and champagne. (*LIANDER and the routine continue.*)

LIZZIE: Drum roll.
LIANDER: (*Stops playing.*) What?
LIZZIE: Drum roll, drum roll. It's the moment they've all been waiting for. Their eyes are glazed. Their tongues are hanging out. The ladies are sitting cross legged and the guys have their hands deep in their pockets ...
LIANDER: Looking for money?
LIZZIE: (*Ignores him.*) One old farmer is so excited he stands up, puts out his arms, stumbles towards me and trips ...
LIANDER: Poor old devil.
LIZZIE: He pole vaults through the window. But no-one hears the smashing of glass. All eyes are riveted ... Drum roll ...
LIANDER: (*Worried.*) Lizzie ...
LIZZIE: I'm waiting.
  (*She is poised on one foot, hand on brassiere.*)
LIANDER: Lizzie. Don't get carried away. Our guests ... I mean, our hosts ...
GREG: (*Whispering.*) She wouldn't.
BRIGIT: I bet she would.
LIZZIE: (*Screaming.*) Where is my drum roll?
  (*LIANDER leaps off chair, jumps up on table. Begins to tap out a drum roll with his feet. LIZZIE simulates taking off her bra. Relieved, LIANDER beats louder. She simulates taking off her skirt. LIANDER beats louder. Simulates removing a G string ... Poses, reminiscent of Venus de Milo. LIANDER brings the sequence to a close with a veritable burst of heel drumming on the table. GREG and BRIGIT applaud.*)
BRIGIT: You were marvellous, wasn't she, Greg?
GREG: Not bad. I'd love to have seen you when you were younger.
BRIGIT: Greg. That's not fair.
GREG: Well— she knows what I mean.
LIZZIE: Of course I do, dear. And it's real nice of you to say so.
  (*She sits and sighs, pours herself another drink. Notices LIANDER still standing on the table.*)
LIZZIE: What are you doing up there?
LIANDER: Waiting to be recognized.
LIZZIE: What the hell for.
LIANDER: It's customary for the stars to indicate their accompanists. To include them in the applause.
LIZZIE: You don't honestly think that my audience would have taken any notice of a desiccated old thing like you.
LIANDER: (*With quiet wounded dignity.*) I wouldn't have been desiccated then. I was just out of the army then. Chest pushing against the rough serge. Biceps like melons. (*He flexes his muscles.*) Legs like young maples. Oh, yes, they'd have noticed me.
LIZZIE: Silly old bugger. Come down.

BRIGIT: I bet you were handsome then, Mr. Clegg. Why—I bet you were really sexy. I can see it in your face.
LIZZIE: Don't flatter him, dear, for God's sake. He'll start to sing next, and we don't want that.
LIANDER: Did you speak. (*He folds his arms and turns his back to them.*)
LIZZIE: Oh, for Christ's sake, not again. Alright, then. Alright. (*She gets up and poses again. GREG and BRIGIT clap. She indicates LIANDER, who turns. GREG and BRIGIT clap. LIANDER bows. But as he does so, LIZZIE goes and lifts him bodily down.*)
LIANDER: Here. Hang on. You don't have to choke me to death.
BRIGIT: I wonder if I could do that?
GREG: What? Strip? In front of a bunch of guys.
BRIGIT: Why not?
GREG: I don't think I'd like it very much.
BRIGIT: Is that any reason why I shouldn't do it?
GREG: Alright, then. What about the secret?
BRIGIT: It's not the same. It might be in your mind but not in mine. (*She gets up.*) Play, Mr. Clegg. I'm going to dance for you.
LIANDER: What?
LIZZIE: Play, you old goat.
LIANDER: D'you think I should. I mean ...
(*LIZZIE digs him hard in the ribs. LIANDER feebly begins to play. BRIGIT bumps and grinds, in an awkward, but highly sexual variant of LIZZIE's dance, shedding her clothes and speaking at the same time. LIANDER, while squawking away, keeps a wary eye on GREG.*)
BRIGIT: I don't see too much difference between this and waiting on a bunch of drunks, do you? The only thing is that this is up in the open, nobody's pretending, and I'd get well paid for all those prick proud fantasies. (*She has reduced herself to bra and panties. Stops in front of GREG.*) Well?
LIANDER: (*Trying to change the tone.*) She's right, you know. Who was it said, "Fifteen arms went round her waist, and then men say, are barmaid's chaste?"
GREG: Who's side are you on?
LIANDER: Sides. Oh, I never take sides. I was quoting somebody—an artist, I think.
BRIGIT: (*To LIZZIE.*) How was I?
LIZZIE: Nice. But a bit awkward, my dear, if you know what I mean. You're trying to tell yourself, or tiger there something. I don't know. And to do it properly, you have to be detached. It's very difficult. The best ones I knew hated men. And them that didn't soon learned.
BRIGIT: Oh. I don't think I'd like that.
GREG: That's a relief.

LIZZIE: You mustn't mind, Tiger. There's not too many women haven't wanted to dance naked in the world, at some time. But on their own terms. For themselves, for each other, maybe, a lover even or an artist who'll paint you whole, with dignity. Even me poor mother must have dreamed, once.
BRIGIT: Was it hard for you, the first time?
LIZZIE: You know, I don't remember now. I don't think it was. I didn't care much for men meself in them days. Bunch of foolish, selfish buggers from top to bottom, and all stops in between. Thought they were brilliant when they flung 'emselves on top of yer like a steam train and charged away fer four minutes. Thought they were gods when they filled yer with kids and left yer day in and day out to go and create the business of the world. Or so they thought. Thought they were martyrs when it went wrong, back there in the Thirties. Thousands of 'em, angry, hurt, hungry. Turned back by a few bullets, a few blows. Could've taken back what was theirs if they'd a mind, but see, they're not like women, dear. They ain't rooted in pain and reality, and never enough of 'em could agree. No. I give up on 'em then, dancing out there, their poor little lust like steam and about as useless. I used to think—Christ, how the hell can you grow anything if you don't know what a woman is.
(There is a loud knocking at the door.)
GREG: Now, who the hell is that?
LIANDER: *(Whispering.)* It must be him.
BRIGIT: Who? The Dummy?
LIANDER: No. The landlord. What will we do?
BRIGIT: Here. Get down behind here.
(The knocking continues. BRIGIT hustles LIANDER and LIZZIE behind one of the easy chairs. They crouch down. She arranges herself in the chair, legs crossed, hitching up her skirt a little.)
BRIGIT: *(Whispering.)* Greg. Get rid of him.
(GREG strides to the door. Opens it. The LANDLORD is poised outside, ready to knock again.)
GREG: Yes.
(The LANDLORD peers over GREG's shoulder, takes in the glasses. The bottle.)
LANDLORD: Understand you've had a bit of trouble. Just came up to see if you're alright.
GREG: We're fine.
BRIGIT: Just fine.
LANDLORD: Oh, they've gone then.
GREG: Who?
LANDLORD: That pair of—the old couple I told you about.
GREG: They've never been.
(LIANDER sneezes. The sneeze is strangled as LIZZIE

claps a hand over his face.)
LANDLORD: What was that?
BRIGIT: What?
LANDLORD: I could have sworn I heard a noise.
(Another strangled sneeze from LIANDER.)
LANDLORD: There it is again. Here ... you don't have a cat?
GREG: No.
LANDLORD: You're sure.
GREG: I think I'd know if I had a cat.
LANDLORD: I suppose you would ... er ...
(He is being distracted by BRIGIT who is trying to divert his attention by giving him a glimpse of her thighs.)
LANDLORD: Sometimes a little pussy will ...
GREG: If you don't mind, we're tired. *(BRIGIT rises, stretches, yawns.)*
BRIGIT: Yes. I think I should get ready for bed.
LANDLORD: And you definitely haven't seen ...
GREG: No.
LANDLORD: You didn't wait for me to finish.
GREG: We haven't seen anybody.
LANDLORD: Oh, well. Now about the rent. Look—I'd better come in for a moment.
(He tries to push past. GREG blocks him.)
GREG: You said you'd talk about it in the morning.
BRIGIT: *(Sweetly.)* We don't mind if you want to leave it for a few days until things are fixed.
LANDLORD: A good point. But I'm concerned about you, you see. You'll probably want to budget, want to know how much you'll have left to live on. Sensible couple, I said to myself. I can always tell a sensible couple. Get to know people by instinct in this business.
(Loud sneeze by LIANDER. Muffled grunt and blows.)
LANDLORD: There it is again. *(Tries to push past GREG again.)* That was definite. You must have heard that. It must be a cat. One of the builders left it. It's trapped in the wall somewhere ... I'll just ...
GREG: *(GREG holds him firmly by the shoulder.)* You'll just nothing. I've told you. We don't have a cat. And if you don't take your eyes off my woman ...
LANDLORD: What? Look, young feller. You might think you can bully me. You might think you can forcibly stop me from coming into an apartment I own—for which you haven't paid any rent yet. You might think you can fool me into thinking that stupid pair of buggers aren't in here. But if you think you can question my morals—
BRIGIT: What morals?
LANDLORD: *(Indignant.)* I'm a Rotarian.

GREG: I don't give a fuck if you're a vegetarian.
LANDLORD: And a Grand Master.
GREG: (*Topping.*) You were pawing her when we came in, and now you're eyeing her as if she's a stripper or something—and I don't like it. Now—git.
LANDLORD: You can't tell me to leave.
GREG: No?
(He turns LANDLORD, propels him back through the door.)
LANDLORD: You won't get away with this. There are laws in this country, you know. My God, what protection does a landlord have, eh? I trusted you. Gave you a roof over your head. But you're worse than they are, yes, sir. Much worse. But don't think you can set that woman up as a call girl in my house, no, sir ...
(GREG roars with rage, the LANDLORD, pursued by GREG, rushes down the landing, disappears down the stairs. GREG stands at the top looking down.)
LANDLORD: (*Off.*) I'm going this time. But I'll be back. I have friends. Big friends. (*His voice trails away.*) Shit. From fucking veterans to a brothel in one day. I'm going to get out of this business.
(BRIGIT runs round the chair, lifts LIZZIE and LIANDER up, hugs them, laughing. As GREG re-appears in the door, she crosses to him, kisses him. As she does so ...)
LIZZIE: Shut up, you old fool.
LIANDER: (*Dusting himself down.*) Well, thank you very much, young man. That's the second time you've come to our rescue.
LIZZIE: Don't be so bloody formal. His name's Greg. You handled him well, I must say. And you had one hell of a handicap. Cat!
(She glares at LIANDER.)
LIANDER: But it was dusty behind there.
LIZZIE: Dust. It's them damn Rothman's. Tearing you apart.
LIANDER: You didn't have to sit on me.
LIZZIE: So what was I to do? Introduce each sneeze with a fanfare. No. Don't tell me, you'd have liked that. I'm sorry, dears. We've brought you nothing but trouble.
GREG: It's no trouble. Really.
BRIGIT: He can't do anything to us.
LIANDER: He can put you out. You haven't paid any advance, you see.
GREG: And I'm not going to.
BRIGIT: What?
GREG: Come on, Brigit. We can't stay here. (*Grinning.*) You brought me all the way here to protect me, you said. And I've already had one fight, and it looks as if we're all set for another. I think we should go home.
LIZZIE: I think that's very sensible. Even if you left here, he'd

find some way to screw you, one way or another.
LIANDER: A vindictive man. He'd get his own back. You humiliated him, you see. But I must confess ... (*Chuckles*) I enjoyed it.
GREG: Ok, then. We'll all go tomorrow. We'll march down the stairs singing. We'll show the bastard.
LIANDER: (*Sings.*) Mademoiselle from Armentieres, parlez vous, Mademoiselle from Armentieres, parlez vous ...
    (He takes LIZZIE's arm and they begin to parade about the room.)
GREG: Come on, Brigit. *(He takes her arm and they fall in behind the other two, whistling.)*
GREG: Straight past him and his dummy.
LIANDER: Eyes right ... Salute—eyes front.
BRIGIT: We'll flush the keys down the john first.
LIANDER: And on, out into the bright freedom of the day.
    (LIANDER suddenly comes to a stop.)
LIANDER: Where will we go, Lizzie?
LIZZIE: Oh, I dunno. The station. We can go to Union Station.
LIANDER: The proper place to start a journey.
GREG: You can see us off.
BRIGIT: Are you serious?
GREG: I'm serious.
LIZZIE: And once you've gone, we'll wait until we get arrested.
LIANDER: No, Lizzie. Didn't you know. They don't do that anymore. They throw you out onto the street and hope for a blizzard to come and blow you away.
BRIGIT: But that's horrible. They can't do that.
LIZZIE: (*Sadly.*) But they do, my dear. The world's too full of us, you see. From Hastings Street in Vancouver and Main Street in Winnipeg all the way here, you can see us propped up in doorways, poor old scarecrows just waiting for the starlings to come and peck out our eyes.
BRIGIT: But I thought there were homes.
LIANDER: All full.
GREG: Well, what about hospitals?
LIZZIE: They don't want us. Anyway, I tried that once.
LIANDER: When?
LIZZIE: Before you, dear. *(She sits down slowly. To BRIGIT.)* I was bleeding and it wouldn't stop.
GREG: Where? What happened?
BRIGIT: It's a woman's thing, Greg. That's what you mean, isn't it?
LIZZIE: That's right, love. Huh. It's a woman's thing.
BRIGIT: What happened?
LIZZIE: Nothing. Nothing at all. I sat there in emergency and a little thing full of starch and self importance came and asked me name, that was at seven. Came back at nine and asked if I had

me card. I never had no card. Came back at eleven to ask how old I was, where was I born, had I ever been there before. Went off duty at twelve and was replaced by another piece of starch. When she came over at one to ask me name, I gave up. I didn't mind really ... I had a bit of a doze. (*Laughs.*) Left blood all over one of their shiny new chairs. So I got me own back, in a little way.
  (*LIANDER reacts with disgust.*)
LIZZIE: Come on, not you, too. Men, my dear, spend their lives trying to crawl back into the hole they come from but don't want to know anything about how it functions. The price of the Fall.
BRIGIT: Did you get better?
LIZZIE: Well, I had to, dear. No-one else was going to do anything about it. And what did it matter, I said to meself, how I go, whether from loss of blood or just heartsick, with nowhere to go anymore. We've run out of roads, Liander.
  (*LIANDER has been following LIZZIE's comments with anxiety and distress.*)
LIANDER: Come on, Lizzie. That's not like you. Remember Harry Lauder, eh. (*Sings.*)
    Keep right on to the end of the road,
    keep right on to the end,
    though the way be long yet your heart be strong,
    keep right on round the bend ...
(*He watches LIZZIE for reaction. After a pause, she smiles.*)
LIZZIE: Ah, well, it's not your problem, dears. Come on, let's finish up the bottle. Let's go out in style.
LIANDER: I've got it.
LIZZIE: (*Snorts.*) By George, he's got it.
LIANDER: We'll do it at the station.
LIZZIE: Do what?
LIANDER: (*Excited.*) It's a stroke of genius. My last performance.
GREG: What are you talking about. What performance?
LIANDER: We—(*Pauses dramatically*)—will commit suicide. (*A blank silence.*)
LIANDER: Well, what d'you think of it?
BRIGIT: I think it's crazy.
LIZZIE: He's had one too many. Here, have another and come back to normal. (*Fills his glass.*)
LIANDER: No, no. You don't understand. Any of you. It's a way of getting our own back, me and Lizzie. For the butt ends of cigars—and the hospitals, and the landlord, and the boots that were always kicking me out of places–
GREG: So you kill yourself to get your own back. Do you think anyone will care, except us?
LIZZIE: (*Intoning.*) O, death, where is thy sting? Grave, where is

thy victory.
LIANDER: You're not listening to me. See, Lizzie and I make this suicide pact —
LIZZIE: Go on ahead, boy. You can send me a wire to tell me what it's like.
LIANDER: We write a note.
LIZZIE: You write the note. I can't write.
LIANDER: (*Triumphant*.) And we say it's all his fault.
BRIGIT: Whose?
LIANDER: The landlord's.
GREG: Hey, I see what you're getting at. That'd put a dent in his business, alright. Serve him right, eh, Brig. (*Whispers to her*.) It's ok. I'm only kidding.
LIANDER: (*Adopts a pose*.) Old couple removed from lodgings. Love birds to the end, they were found in Union Station, locked into a last, despairing embrace.
LIZZIE: Oh, no, you don't. If you think I'm going to pass on from this world to find meself saddled with you in the next, you've another think coming. I want more than a cocktail sausage as my heavenly reward, let me tell you.
LIANDER: (*Stamping his foot*.) You're not taking me seriously. You never take me seriously. It's not fair.
LIZZIE: Alright. How are we going to do it? (*LIANDER sulks*.) Well, come on. What do we do? Throw ourselves under the feet of galloping commuters? Strap ourselves to the rails in front of the Transcontinental? Eat a Canadian National sandwich ... ?
LIANDER: I confess ... I haven't thought out the details yet.
GREG: Last feller down home to commit suicide, hanged himself with nylon rope.
LIANDER: (*Shudders*.) Oh, I couldn't do that. It's barbaric. It would hurt.
LIZZIE: Of course it would hurt. Dying's not easy, you fool. It's painful.
LIANDER: It doesn't have to be that painful. Anyway, it's banned in this country.
GREG: (*Laughing*.) Dying?
LIANDER: No. Hanging. (*To BRIGIT*.) I can see I'm not going to get any help from those two. Do you have any suggestions?
BRIGIT: No, I don't.
LIANDER: Ah. I thought, perhaps, you might have read. In school, you know. The ancient Greeks, the Romans.
GREG: (*Helpful*.) The Japanese cut their intestines out. I read about that.
LIANDER: Oh, my God.
(*He clutches his stomach. LIZZIE and GREG laugh.*)
BRIGIT: (*Crying out*.) Stop it. All of you.
GREG: Hey, Brig, what's the matter?

BRIGIT: I don't like it, that's what the matter is. I don't like the thought of you going out into the cold tomorrow on your own, and you go on about committing suicide and all you can do (*To GREG*) is to encourage him. Don't you understand? He's serious.
(She begins to cry. LIZZIE crosses to her and comforts her.)
LIZZIE: There, there, don't take on so. He was only joking. Only playing a game. We always play games, him and me, it helps to pass the time. Stops us thinking too much. We're so used to being on our own, you see, we forget that other people mightn't understand. See what you've done. (*To LIANDER*.) She's real upset.
LIANDER: Oh, dear. Foolish. How one forgets. It's been so long, you see, since anyone cried—shed tears for us.
GREG: She's soft hearted, my Brigit. Always was. Same with animals as with people. Used to get upset when I went birding. Worried about the blood on me hands.
LIANDER: Birding? I'm not familiar with the term.
GREG: Shooting, you know. Ducks, murrs, things like that. I used to walk for miles across the salt flats, four o'clock in the morning, the light coming off the water at you like an outsize street lamp, pink and gold. And the wind smacking your face and birds rushing at you out of the East. That's what I liked most, anyway. The walking and the wind. The birds rushing. We'll go, eh, Brig? When we get home. I'll leave the gun.
LIANDER: She has a gift. A real gift. I knew when I first saw her. Like my Lizzie. She has it, too, you know, but pretends not to.
LIZZIE: Don't you try analysing me, you old goat. You may entertain me, but don't try and educate me. It's too late for that.
LIANDER: Feeling. That's a gift. Out there, it's dying. I know. I've felt it for years.
LIZZIE: It was never there.
LIANDER: It was so. If one fell down, somebody would stop, extend a hand. Lift one up into the day ...
LIZZIE: (*To BRIGIT*.) There he goes again. Dressed in the rags of dreams like some old actor—the house is empty, Liander. It was always empty, for the likes of you and me. I been turning into dust since the day I was born, and at every corner there was someone waiting with a broom to sweep up the remains and dump them in the garbage truck.
BRIGIT: But you make everything sound so hopeless.
LIZZIE: But it is, my dear. Not for you, no. We made our choices long ago and this is where they led us. You make sure you make the right ones.
LIANDER: I've never seen her so happy. Listen to her. A happy cynic, that's what she is. I sing to keep my spirits up. She sifts through her days ... (*He chuckles*.) The garbage of her days— (*LIZZIE snorts*.) Your words, your words. Looking for the

dirtiest scraps she can find, then she trots them out with all the relish of a gourmet sitting down to a ten course dinner.
LIZZIE: What do you know about ten course dinners? You've never got past MacDonald's in your life.
LIANDER: I have looked through windows. I have observed—the wine glittering like blood in candlelight, the crystal shimmering, a single rose splashed against linen—Oh, I have seen ...
LIZZIE: Second hand. Why, when I was in my prime, that was the time ...
GREG: When you were a stripper?
LIZZIE: That was the only prime I knew. They would come for me in their cars ...
LIANDER: Don't you mean limousines.
LIZZIE: *(Ignoring him.)* They would send a chauffeur to the stage door, staggering beneath champagne, gentians ...
LIANDER: I have never seen anyone staggering beneath the weight of a gentian.
LIZZIE: It would always be dinner for two. Why—I remember now. Once I looked out through the window and saw this wizened little tramp, peering in, nose pressed to the plate glass.
LIANDER: *(Annoyed.)* I told you before, I wouldn't have been wizened then.
LIZZIE: Alright, tramp, then?
LIANDER: I might not have been too elegantly dressed. But wizened. Never.
(After a pause, LIZZIE grins.)
LIZZIE: Alright, wizened—never. Just a slightly buffeted, ragged little sparrow.
(LIANDER is taken aback at the tenderness in her voice. After a pause ... he bows.)
LIANDER: Thank you.
LIZZIE: You see, my dear. Things aren't that hopeless, even between us. They only look hopeless.
BRIGIT: Its funny, really. Before you came, things looked pretty hopeless between us. We played games, too, but they didn't seem right any more. We had to hurt each other first, you know, to try and get things going again. I don't think we need that game any more, Greg, do you?
GREG: No. No more Big Tom. Just Greg. Seems like we came all the way here just to find that out.
BRIGIT: And you really want to turn straight round and go home.
GREG: I think so. Well, not home, but Halifax, say, something like that. We'll get it together before we try again. If we need to try again.
LIANDER: You love each other. We knew that. Spotted that the minute we came in. It's difficult to hide it from other people.
LIZZIE: But easy to hide it from each other.

BRIGIT: That's true enough. I never knew it could be such hard work.
LIZZIE: Ah, my dear, you must take love where you find it, and hang on to it like grim death and not care. Only time will tell if it will grow into age so that you don't notice yer body collapsing like some building down for demolition. But, you two will be alright. Give each other a bit of room, you'll survive. *(She sighs.)* I swore it would never happen to me. I wanted none of it. I'd seen it all. And what happened?
BRIGIT: You met Liander.
LIANDER: I swept her off her feet. At least, what was left of the dust.
LIZZIE: No, dear, that's not correct. I picked him up and carried him home.
LIANDER: To our mansion.
LIZZIE: Right here.
LIANDER: We were just like you.
LIZZIE: I think there's a difference, Liander.
LIANDER: It's never too late for beginnings, you see.
GREG: Did you get married?
LIZZIE: Whatever for. Are you?
BRIGIT: No.
LIZZIE: There you are. You get married, love, for two reasons. To cheat the income tax or to please your parents. Now—believe it or not, we don't pay taxes.
LIANDER: And our creators are long gone.
LIZZIE: According to me mother, I must've been a near miracle.
LIANDER: That's it.
LIZZIE: What is?
LIANDER: That's why I wanted to do it. You know, the love pact.
LIZZIE: Oh, not again.
LIANDER: Don't you see. It would turn dying into a wedding. If we could only get put down—have the benefit of a certain ceremony, a little dignity, it would be a miracle.
LIZZIE: He's worse than usual tonight, much worse.
LIANDER: *(Agitated.)* No. Listen, Lizzie. You too. It's important. What will happen to us out there? Come on, what? *(LIZZIE shrugs.)* Oh, we might last a day or two. Might beg the odd coin or two. Might last another pension cheque, perhaps. But when January comes—Lizzie, I don't want to be gone from you—I don't want a cot in some Salvation Army Hostel and you somewhere else. They'd never let us be together, you see ... we're not married. We're just a pair of vagabonds. *(Crying out.)* Lizzie, I don't want to be gone from you.
GREG: Hey, come on, Liander, take it easy. She's not going to leave you. She said that.
BRIGIT: And something might turn up. Another place. We can

leave you a bit of money ... can't we?
GREG: Yeah. We don't have much but—well, it's more than you've got, that's for sure.
LIANDER: No. I don't want that.
LIZZIE: (*Soft.*) What do you want then, old fool. Dear old fool.
LIANDER: I want, for you and me, Lizzie, a decent funeral.
GREG: Funerals cost a lot of money. When Aunt Kate died last year, it cost fifteen hundred dollars.
BRIGIT: And she hardly had any flowers.
LIANDER: (*Hasn't heard.*) Cadillacs, with lights on, slowing down traffic in the streets, the thoroughfares of the city.
LIZZIE: It would be a laugh, wouldn't it.
LIANDER: Passers-by turning, taking off their hats, whispering.
LIZZIE: I wonder who that is ...
LIANDER: Somebody important, look at the parade.
LIZZIE: But why are there two coffins?
LIANDER: A tragedy, don't you know. A latter day Romeo and Juliet.
LIZZIE: Oh, my God.
LIANDER: Society is to blame, sir. Society—unfeeling, unthinking, killed them.
LIZZIE: (*Soft.*) It would be a laugh.
LIANDER: Cadavers in mourning dress paid to lift us out of the hearses.
LIZZIE: Paid weepers weeping.
LIANDER: Paid mourners singing.
BRIGIT: There'll be blue birds over ...
LIANDER: Of course.
GREG: Hey. The graves'd be side by side, and all around 'em nothing but flowers.
LIANDER: A Bishop for the service.
LIZZIE: Go for the Archbishop.
LIANDER: Alright. The Archbishop.
GREG: What about soldiers?
LIANDER: What?
GREG: You know, the songs you sing. They're all from the war, aren't they? Don't you get a bodyguard or something?
LIANDER: Brilliant. Of course. The Last Post.
LIZZIE: That'd be nice.
LIANDER: Trumpets against the sky. The old banners furling. Heads bowed then—the walnut coffins poised at the mouth.
LIZZIE: A light rain—a little drizzle perhaps. Nothing hard. A soft rain.
(*LIANDER leaps centre, snatching a cover from the rollaway bed. He begins to intone the funeral service.*)
LIANDER: Man that is born of woman is of few days and full of trouble, He cometh forth like a flower and is cut down, he flees

a shadow and continueth not. Oh, God ... in thy infinite wisdom look down upon these thy humble and obedient servants, Liander and Lizzie Clegg—
LIZZIE: Lizzie and Liander Clegg.
LIANDER: Does the order matter?
LIZZIE: It does to me, though whether it does to Him is another matter.
BRIGIT: You'll be hand in hand anyway.
LIZZIE: Yes. I suppose so. A knight and his lady. Done with the Crusades.
LIANDER: We ask not that you remember their frailties, their sins. But only that ... only that ... (*He begins to break down.*)
LIZZIE: Well, don't stop now. It's the best performance you've ever given.
LIANDER: I am moved.
LIZZIE: For Christ's sake, get on with it. I need a bit of earth to warm me up.
LIANDER: Only that they never, wittingly, with intent, harmed any other living thing.
LIZZIE: You old bastard.
BRIGIT: That was beautiful, Liander. If I was going to die, I'd like you to say the words over me. What do you say, Greg?
GREG: Well, if it had to happen, I suppose it'd be alright.
LIANDER: Lower the ropes.
LIZZIE: Slowly, they disappear from view.
LIANDER: The walnut ...
LIZZIE: The heavy brass, polished.
LIANDER: You—and me.
LIZZIE: Flowers—they strew flowers.
    (*BRIGIT and GREG move about throwing flowers into the imaginary grave.*)
LIANDER: Then the first handful of earth. The weight of the earth.
LIZZIE: The pain of the earth.
LIANDER: The warmth of the earth. The darkness.
LIZZIE: The peace.
    (*GREG mimes shovelling. BRIGIT strews flowers.*)
LIANDER: Here lies the body of Lizzie Clegg,
Too poor to live, too proud to beg,
May God protect her little dust,
Who only did what she thought she must.
    (*LIANDER bows to LIZZIE. Slowly she goes and looks down at his imaginary grave.*)
LIZZIE: Stranger, when you're passing by,
Don't be surprised if from the sky,
A sparrow looking gaunt and thin,
Begins to sing like Vera Lynn.

(*LIZZIE and LIANDER go to each other, take hand, kneel slowly, they lie down together, grizzled crusader and his lady. GREG shovels, BRIGIT grieves. Sound, very faint, as if one is imagining it ... the Last Post from the auditorium, not the stage area. Hold the scene for a few seconds. Suddenly the door bursts open. LIZZIE and LIANDER don't move. DUMMY rushes in.*)

GREG: Oh, no. You again.
(*He goes for him. DUMMY falls into foetal position. Makes inhuman sounds.*)

BRIGIT: Leave him alone, Greg. Leave him. He's not come to harm us.
(*Seeing that he is not to be molested, DUMMY rises cautiously. His face is a mess. He has been beaten. With fear, he crosses to LIZZIE and LIANDER. Looks at them both, arms folded, touches them. Jumps back when he feels that they are warm. Runs and cowers in the corner. LIZZIE rises slowly. DUMMY is paralysed with fear.*)

LIZZIE: Ah hah. That fooled him.
LIANDER: (*Rising slowly.*) I nearly fooled meself.
BRIGIT: What does he want?
GREG: I dunno. I'll ask him. He can hear, remember? (*Crosses to him.*) What do you want?
(*DUMMY makes sounds, pointing to LIZZIE then LIANDER, then downstairs. There follows a dumb show in which it must be obvious that he is showing that, because of LIZZIE and LIANDER and his failure to throw them out, he has been beaten and fired. The dialogue between his gestures is as follows:*)

LIANDER: He's talking about us.
GREG: But what's he saying?
BRIGIT: I think he means that he was told to throw them out.
(*DUMMY nods vigorously.*)
BRIGIT: (*Reading him.*) Because of you (*To GREG*) he didn't.
(*DUMMY pantomimes beating.*)
BRIGIT: The coward. Attacking a person who can't speak.
(*DUMMY mimes throwing himself into the street.*)
BRIGIT: He's been thrown out, too.
(*DUMMY nods vigorously. Makes signs.*)
BRIGIT: He doesn't know what to do. He needs our help. Is that what you want?
(*DUMMY nods vigorously. He then pantomimes a scene in which three or four big men will come in the morning to throw them all out. He runs in and out of the door to simulate the number—this game resembles nothing so much as that old party game when one has to guess what the other does ...*)
BRIGIT: There's men coming.

(DUMMY nods.)
GREG: How many?
(DUMMY holds up four fingers.)
GREG: Jesus, Brig, I can't handle that many.
LIANDER: We'll have to go.
GREG: Wait a minute. When?
(DUMMY mimes sun rise.)
BRIGIT: In the morning.
GREG: Well ... that's a relief. We've got till morning.
LIZZIE: It nearly is morning. What time?
(DUMMY holds up eight fingers.)
LIANDER: Eight o'clock.
(DUMMY gets very excited. Mimes boxing. Bodies flying.)
LIANDER: Now what's he saying?
BRIGIT: I don't know. It's a fight.
(DUMMY nods vigorously. Indicates them.)
GREG: He wants us to fight.
(DUMMY nods.)
BRIGIT: Revenge. That's it. He wants to get his own back.
LIANDER: Well, it's a nice thought. But it won't work. We'll have to go quietly.
BRIGIT: I hate fights.
GREG: I'm not that keen when the odds are four to two.
LIANDER: I can handle myself, you know. I've done unarmed combat.
GREG: I was talking about her.
(Indicates LIZZIE. LIZZIE laughs.)
LIZZIE: Thank you, tiger.
GREG: Hey, I didn't mean that badly, you know. I wouldn't want you to get hurt, that's all.
LIANDER: Well, I suppose it is thoughtful of you.
LIZZIE: Here, dummy, here. (She pours him a drink.) You deserve a drink. He came to warn us, after all we've done to him.
(DUMMY guzzles drink.)
BRIGIT: That was brave. After the beating.
LIANDER: A true comrade. Who would have thought it. (He crosses and shakes DUMMY's hand.) I'm prepared to let bygones be bygones. You have made a truly heroic gesture.
(DUMMY guzzles another drink.)
LIZZIE: You know, I'm half inclined to sit it out.
LIANDER: What?
LIZZIE: I'm tired, Liander. I'm tired of going in and out of doors.
LIANDER: But, Union Station.
LIZZIE: I don't want to go to Union Station. Liander, I don't want to go anywhere.
LIANDER: And the funeral.
LIZZIE: It was—a fine funeral.

*(DUMMY is making strange noises. He is drunk
and very excited.)*
LIZZIE: What on earth is the matter with him?
BRIGIT: I think he wants to stay with you. Do you want to stay?
(DUMMY nods ...)
LIZZIE: After what I did to him. He must be a masochist.
*(DUMMY shakes his head, implying that it doesn't matter.
He tries to communicate with BRIGIT.)*
BRIGIT: You're his family, that's what he's saying.
*(DUMMY nods emphatically. Runs to LIZZIE. Embraces her.
Runs to LIANDER. Hugs him. LIANDER is taken aback.
DUMMY imitates LIANDER's walk, mimes him singing.
Claps his hands.)*
BRIGIT: He was always happy when he heard you sing.
LIANDER: Well ... after all this time, thinking I was unappreciated. It's amazing how, sometimes, an affliction can sharpen, as it were, the artistic perceptions.
LIZZIE: *(Laughs.)* You could milk a sterile goat.
(DUMMY kneels, holds out his hands, pleading.)
LIANDER: Well, under the circumstances, dear ... I mean he has no home either, and it would appear to be our fault ... I think we should adopt him.
LIZZIE: Increase your audience to two. *(DUMMY beseeches LIZZIE.)* Oh, alright. *(Laughs almost hysterically.)* Me first son. After all this time.
*(DUMMY jumps for joy. Runs round shaking
everybody's hand.)*
LIZZIE: It's too much, it really is. *(Pours herself a drink.)* Afflicted of the world—unite.
*(She sits. DUMMY crosses and sits at her feet, making
contented sounds. She strokes him, absently.)*
LIZZIE: So, now we are three.
GREG: Hey. There's five of us.
BRIGIT: I think we should go, Greg.
GREG: What?
BRIGIT: We should go.
GREG: I can't leave them to Creepy and his thugs.
BRIGIT: You can. You must. It's not our fight.
GREG: Yes, it damn well is. If it's not our fight, who's is it?
LIZZIE: Ours.
(She continues stroking DUMMY, who has gone to sleep.)
GREG: *(Frustrated.)* That's great. After all this, you expect me to walk away from you. How the hell can I do that? How could I live with myself after doing that?
LIZZIE: You've got a mother and father?
GREG: Yeah. So what?
LIZZIE: You walked away.

GREG: Oh, come on. No more games, eh? That's not the same.
LIZZIE: No. Perhaps it's not. I'm tired, son. You wanted to go home. You said so. I wish you'd leave.
BRIGIT: Come on, Greg. Let's start packing.
GREG: Hell, no. He's right—that landlord. You are crazy, the pair of you.
BRIGIT: Alright, I'll pack.
GREG: Brigit, what's got into you?
LIANDER: The truth is, Greg—we don't need you now.
GREG: Great, I suppose you'll fight to the bitter end, eh? I can see the mess, now.
LIANDER: I don't know what we'll do, yet. But Lizzie and me, we'll think of something. It's too late now. We can't hide behind anyone anymore.
LIZZIE: Harry Lauder ...
LIANDER: That's right. (*Sings.*)
    Keep right on to the end of the road,
    Keep right on to the end
    Though the way be long, let your heart be strong ...
(*BRIGIT is throwing things into the suitcases. Snaps them shut. LIZZIE gets up, steps carefully round the sleeping DUMMY. Puts a hand across LIANDER's mouth to stop him.*)
LIZZIE: (*To GREG.*) You've given us something, son. You and Brigit. You cared. And you shared. It was a gift we didn't expect. And if you stay now—it'll spoil. Don't spoil it for us.
LIANDER: We really appreciated your help with the funeral. (*GREG is still not sure.*)
BRIGIT: They want to do it their way, Greg. They don't want to be guilty about us. They don't want to be guilty about anything. That's what you're trying to say, isn't it? And we mustn't be, either. About anything. Ok?
GREG: Alright, alright. (*He picks up the suitcases.*) Is this it, then?
BRIGIT: Yes.
LIZZIE: No good-byes. You know.
BRIGIT: Yes. I do.
LIZZIE: You've got a diamond there, Greg. I'd put a ring round it. For you—it might work. Go on, now. (*She crosses to him, gives him a little shove. Suddenly laughs—the old LIZZIE.*)
LIZZIE: My, what a romp I'd have had with you, forty years ago.
GREG: (*Grinning.*) You wouldn't have been so bad yourself.
LIANDER: (*Coughing to attract attention.*) If it would not be considered indelicate of me ...
(*BRIGIT Crosses. Give him a big hug that leaves him breathless. She whispers something in his ear.*)
LIANDER: (*Pleased.*) Really. How nice of you to say so. Of

course, I was never one to take advantage.
LIZZIE: A pity.
(BRIGIT opens the door. GREG, after a moment's pause, goes out with the cases. BRIGIT follows. GREG walks towards the 'staircase'—pauses, waits for BRIGIT.)
GREG: Hey. D'you know what, Brigit. It's Christmas Eve.
BRIGIT: *(Holding on to herself.)* So?
GREG: So—oh, shit. I don't know.
(He drops the cases. Feels in his pocket. Comes up with a packet of Rothman's.)
GREG: Just a minute. *(He goes back to the door.)*
GREG: Here, Liander. *(He throws the pack to him. LIANDER catches it.)*
LIANDER: My dear boy. What a comfort. My favourite brand. I'd go so far as to say ...
LIZZIE: Liander!
(GREG turns and goes back down the landing. Picks up the cases. LIANDER scuttles to the door.)
LIANDER: It's probably still snowing. *(GREG and BRIGIT exit with LIANDER and LIZZIE following.)* You can get a cab on the corner. An all night stand. You can't miss it.
(They have gone. After a beat LIANDER comes in slowly. Shuts the door.)
LIANDER: Funny. How empty the place seems now.
(LIZZIE does not answer.)
LIANDER: We had quite a family for a while, didn't we?
(LIZZIE does not answer.)
LIANDER: You know, I think I could get used to having a family. It's really quite pleasant. Shared concerns. A little laughter on occasion. Celebrations at the year's turning. How foolish. To turn one's back upon such experiences.
(He lights a cigarette, puffs furiously. Into the silence comes the sound of a distant church clock. It chimes the hour, then strikes five.)
LIANDER: *(Excited.)* Did you hear that, Lizzie? My hearing is unimpaired. The clock is not frozen.
LIZZIE: And God's in his Heaven, all's right with the world. *(They stare at each other.)*
LIANDER: Lizzie!
LIZZIE: The time for children's stories is done, Liander. They learnt that quicker than us, didn't they?
LIANDER: Do you think we helped them, in some way?
LIZZIE: Perhaps they'll think of us when things look bad.
LIANDER: I'm scared, Lizzie.
LIZZIE: So am I.
LIANDER: You? Even you? It must be bad then. *(A pause.)* There have been so many of these moments. Apparently insur-

mountable. Apparently definite. But always, we have moved on.
LIZZIE: Toward other such moments.
LIANDER: Yes. You will not come to Union Station?
LIZZIE: No. You can go.
LIANDER: For whom would I sing? You were right. If you had left me then—how long ago?
LIZZIE: I don't know.
LIANDER: It doesn't matter. I would have died.
LIZZIE: No, Liander. Don't say that. I shouldn't have said it. You'd have gone on, as you put it.
LIANDER: Perhaps then. But not now.
LIZZIE: And him? (*Indicating DUMMY.*)
LIANDER: Ah, yes. I was caught up, the revelation you know, excited me. Pleased me. We did not need another responsibility.
LIZZIE: No.
LIANDER: Well. May I get you something?
LIZZIE: Is there any water in the kettle?
(*LIANDER crosses to the stove. Shakes the kettle.*)
LIANDER: Yes.
LIZZIE: A little rye and hot water will be fine, dear. I think there is a spot left.
(*LIANDER turns the stove on. Puts the kettle on the ring.*)
LIZZIE: My father would always drink that on bitter mornings, before going out to feed the animals. It will keep the frost out, he'd say. Then it got to two drinks. Then three. Poor old bugger. Frost in the house too—everything my mother touched turning white—white outside. I found him once, leaning against a calf, face pressed to its neck. He was trying to feed it, see, with two fingers. It was sick or something. And the tears pouring down his face like a spring thaw. But it was the middle of January. Shit. This is a cold country. (*The kettle whistles shrilly. LIANDER mixes LIZZIE's drink. Takes it to her.*)
LIANDER: I never seemed to mind the winter, as a boy, that is. The orchards black against the snow, deer tracks, branches scrabbling against the pale, Okanagan light. I think, you know, that was why I was drawn, impelled, to that exhibition, those revolving doors so long ago. There might have been there a picture or two, something to remind one that one once existed as a child ... the blossom, the light. But I was not permitted. I often think of that. And yet one should not, I suppose, have regrets.
LIZZIE: She asked me, you know, Brigit, if I felt anything, that first time.
LIANDER: Yes.
LIZZIE: I lied to her.
LIANDER: You don't have to speak of it.
LIZZIE: But I do. That first time—it was a small place. Full of farmers with broken hands, eyes full of dust. Like my father.

They were all my father. And I danced for them, my fathers, danced to make the rain come, danced to make the corn green, danced wild and naked about the tables amongst those who had never seen nakedness, from whom women and nature hid their faces. And not one hand reached out to touch me. And there was not one laugh. And when I had done, I was assailed by silence, and I was ashamed, because they were my fathers. And then one said: 'Jacob's daughter?' And I nodded. And he said, 'Thank you', and he was crying. It was after that I left home. And yet one should not, I suppose, have regrets.
    (She laughs, drinks. DUMMY groans, stirs.)
LIANDER: My goodness. I had forgotten. Are you alright?
    (DUMMY sits up, holding his head in his hands.)
LIANDER: I said, are you alright?
    (DUMMY feels himself ... nods slowly, affirmatively.)
LIZZIE: They will be here soon.
    (DUMMY makes sounds. Gets up. Shadow boxes feebly.
    Falls back on the bed.)
LIANDER: I don't think he'll be very effective, do you? Of course, if I could just remember one or two moves ... one could paralyse with the point of the little finger. I forget where ... *(He trails off ... A pause.)* The snow, perhaps, might impede them. *(LIZZIE shakes her head.)* Perhaps, then, the spirit of Christmas might prevail. Yes. That's it. There will be footsteps on the stairs. A joyous pounding on the door. And a small boy with rosy cheeks will shout: "Mrs. and Mr. Clegg—a turkey, compliments of the landlord. Merry Christmas." And we will eat gloriously, stuff ourselves on the golden bird and then go out, to walk light footed through the throng, carols and greetings crisp in the air, the trees aflame, and there will be strangers thrusting brightly wrapped gifts into our hands, and the church doors will be open, hands beckoning—join us, join us ... and I might—might even be asked to sing at some festive gathering, as I was wont to do.
    (DUMMY claps. Excited. LIZZIE says nothing.)
LIANDER: May I not—dream?
LIZZIE: You will ... whatever I say. Old fool. Dear old fool.
LIANDER: Is there not then, one gesture, one thing to bind–
    (LIZZIE closes her eyes. LIANDER and the DUMMY look
    at her anxiously. She opens them. Rummages in her
    handbag. Opens a purse. Takes out five dollars.)
LIZZIE: Dummy, can you hear me? *(DUMMY nods.)*
LIZZIE: You must go to the all night drugstore. D'you know where that is? *(DUMMY nods again.)*
LIZZIE: Here. Take this. *(She hands him the five dollars.)* You must go there and find the biggest Christmas Card in the store. Can you write? *(He indicates a little.)* Good. Then write on the card—from Lizzie and Liander. Can you do that? *(He nods*

again.) And then you will come back here and mount guard outside the door. (*DUMMY strikes guard pose.*) That's right. And when he comes, the landlord with his friends, you must give him the card.
LIANDER: Lizzie, you never cease to amaze me.
LIZZIE: Me neither.
LIANDER: There is hope, then. You do believe. The old magic might work its spell. All may be well. (*He sings.*)
>There'll be blue birds over ...
>The white cliffs of Dover ...

LIZZIE: Wait, Liander. (*To DUMMY.*) D'you know what to do? (*DUMMY nods.*) Off you go.
>(*DUMMY obediently rushes off.*)

LIZZIE: (*Sighs.*) Alone at last.
LIANDER: Yes. I must admit. Company of any kind is exhausting. Do you think this is the beginning of a busy social season?
LIZZIE: It could be.
LIANDER: (*Yawning.*) Amazing, isn't it. The prospect of a New Year. Hope. The lightening of the dark. (*He goes to bed and lays down.*) I feel, you know, that even he will respond. There is good in all of us. Haven't I told you that before?
LIZZIE: Yes, you have. Often.
LIANDER: (*Sits up suddenly.*) I wonder ...
LIZZIE: What?
LIANDER: The lateness of the hour. This unaccustomed luxury. The lack of newspapers. Would you think too badly of me ...
LIZZIE: No cocktail sausage.
LIANDER: The spirit is willing, you understand. But the day has been wonderfully full ...
LIZZIE: And the flesh.
LIANDER: Falls and folds. Exactly. (*Laughs.*) You know, perhaps it was not so significant after all. If I had once seen, had some unknown artist's vision inflicted upon me, been made aware of the terrible fragility of life, things might have become unbearable.
LIZZIE: Yes. That is possible.
LIANDER: You will wake me when they call.
LIZZIE: Of course. (*LIANDER relaxes, folds his arms. After a moment begins to snore, gently. LIZZIE looks about her. Finds a cover, crosses to him, covers him with infinite tenderness.*) So it comes to this. After all the hurt. The despair. My little, desiccated old man. My own sparrow. If only you had been my audience, long years ago. A gentle man. (*She goes to the stove. Turns on the gas. Blows out the flame. It hisses on in silence. She goes and sits at the foot of the bed.*) Liander. I never did tell you, did I? I love you. Can you hear me? No. Everything comes too late to us. Jesus! I hope Christmas is better on the other

side. (*Anguished.*) You'd better be there, old bugger, old fool. (*LIZZIE leans back on the wall. Tears stream down her face. The gas hisses. LIANDER has stopped snoring. Bearing a large envelope, DUMMY comes on to the landing and takes up his place, standing guard against the door.*)
(*The lights fade.*)

The End

West Moon

(a play)

Al Pittman

**For Mary
who lived a lot of it**

Author's Note

The characters are dead and in various states of decay. Their bodies are buried. They recline in coffins beneath the ground. On All Souls Night their voices, their memories, their mental faculties, their personalities, their emotions are returned to them. So for a while they are, to some degree, resurrected. The play itself does not suggest any kind of bodily resurrection and, in fact, denies such in its references to 'eyeless skulls' etc. How to portray them on stage? Certainly not as skeletons and rotted flesh. Certainly not entirely as they were in real life. Somewhere in between these two extremes. Perhaps as they were in death at the time of burial, but with the ability to move. Clothed perhaps in their burial clothes. Not, God-forbid, in sou'westers and rubber boots, not with pipes and chewing tobacco, not with knitting needles and kidney pills. Funeral clothes. The fact that these people are dead and confined to the grave cannot be forgotten, must always be emphasized. Their movements must be punctuated by their confinement. Nowhere in their recollections can they have access to the accoutrements of their former lives. As they move they are limited to movement within the perimeters of their own grave space. Nowhere can they move among one another. Nowhere can they touch one another. They can stand, sit, lie, slouch, jump, and so on in their own territory but they are forever frustrated in any inclination they have to move outside the boundaries of their death. The props they may use are the props at hand. The bushes, the gravel, the grass, the gravestones, and so on. Nothing that isn't present naturally in the graveyard and within reach of the resurrected corpses can be placed within their reach. Always they are dead and remain dead, always they are confined to the grave and remain so for the duration of the play. Within these limitations all liberties of movement, gesture, posture, and all else may and should be explored. An ingenious set combined with an ingenious approach to animation could be conducive to the intention of the play without in any way rendering it static or boring in its immobility. Then again, someone more creatively courageous or more courageously creative might see it differently. And that might make all the difference.

a.p.
Corner Brook
November, 1994

Cast of Characters

	Born	Died	Age
A Voice –			
Jack Leonard	April 11, 1900	September 2, 1955	55
Raymond Dwyer	June 6, 1908	October 13, 1960	52
William Sullivan	May 2, 1880	August 9, 1953	73
Rose Anne Hepditch	June 23, 1872	December 10, 1962	90
Margaret Green	November 9, 1925	November 21, 1961	36
Sheila Connors	July 19, 1940	April 15, 1951	11
Edward S. Shea	September 19, 1905	April 5, 1965	60
Bridget Sullivan	May 25, 1885	May 30, 1965	80
Aaron Leonard	August 6, 1936	November 22, 1964	28
Ignatius Rogers	January 12, 1914	September 8, 1965	51

Dead men, naked, they shall be one
With the man in the wind and the west moon.

Dylan Thomas

The Scene

The time is November 2nd, 1965. The place is a graveyard in a small isolated coastal community in Placentia Bay, Newfoundland.

Part I

This Side of Heaven

> I pray you ... please
> make in your mouths
> the words that were our names.
> *Archibald MacLeish*

A VOICE: In all the dark world, there is no darkness like the dark of an outport night. Here on the coast of Newfoundland, darkness comes in all seasons as sudden as sudden death, comes coasting unannounced from its hideaway over the hills, sweeps silently down upon the seaside settlement of St. Kevin's, and covers the quick-silver looking-glass sea like a shroud thrown from the sky to fall upon the face of the funereal earth.

No human eyes can pierce the eternal darkness as it lies like death upon the dead village. And in St. Kevin's now, this November All Souls Night, there are no human eyes alive and shining where once, not too dark a time ago, fishermen returning from their dreams upon the sea could see with blazing eyes the firebrands lighting the way for the livyers as they moved from house to house upon the hills, their bright kitchen visits over for the night, as they blinked their way, with caution and prayers, home to their bouncing beds.

Tonight, with no human eyes to see them, the only fires alive are the fires in the eyes of the animals as they go about their animal business in the dead dark, in a wilderness of ruins.

The sleek otter gliding over the cold stones of Middle Brook, a quiet gurgle splitting the village in two as it runs unseen down from the warm wooded hills, leaps at a quick spark of silver somewhere in the sound of the brook, and comes up with a tiny otter-appetizer of Eastern Brook Trout.

The rabbit, running erratically down the grass-grown road to or away from God-knows-what, stops suddenly at the grey decayed gate on the edge of Jack Leonard's hayfield, perceives some rabbit threat in the black breeze, and leaps—a silent flash of fur swallowed by the meadow in one grassy gulp.

A forlorn fox laps at the chill water of the spring at the foot of the scrape behind the cathedral ruins of Bill Sullivan's house and, by the light of his eyes, sees his amazed self in the gun-metal gleam of the pool. One look is enough, and away he races to the shelter of the woods pursued by his own vicious image of himself.

In Chapel Pond the arrogant frogs croak their solemn sermons to the night as the trout doze irreverently, a faithless congregation heeding only the dreams they inhabit as they lie suspended in sleep among the lily pads.

On the beach below the old beach road—below the grey-green skeletons of stages and stores standing like amphibian invaders from worlds beneath the sea, their crooked strouter legs wading in the shallows, their grotesque headless torsos thrust lumbering in the air—a million crabs crawl lopsided over the rocks rolled round and smooth by a million years of wave break, swish, and roll.

In the graveyard below the waterfall of Ladore the mice run hunting or playing hide-n-seek among the headstones which announce mutely to the living night all that matters concerning the dead decayed lives of the villagers buried in the sinking soil below.

(Thunder.)
(Silence.)
(Thunder.)
(Silence.)
(Thunder.)
JACK: Hello!
(Silence.)
(Thunder.)
   Hey!
(Silence.)
   Hello!
(Thunder.)
   Ray! Skipper Bill! Anyone!
(Silence.)
(Thunder.)
RAY: Hello!

JACK: Hello!
RAY: You, Jack?
JACK: Yeah! That you, Ray?
RAY: I s'pose it is.
JACK: We're still here then!
RAY: Looks like it.
JACK: Is it only us?
RAY: Don't know.
JACK: No sound of the women and them?
(Thunder.)
RAY: Can't hear 'em. Can't hear nothin' 'cept you and the thunder.
(Thunder.)
(Silence.)
RAY: P'rhaps they're all gone.
JACK: All at once?
RAY: P'rhaps they didn't all go at once. It's a year now since the last time.
JACK: I guess they could be gone by now. Some of 'em anyway.
(Thunder.)
RAY: Listen.
JACK: Just thunder.
RAY: No! Listen.
JACK: What then?
RAY: Listen.
(Thunder.)
BILL: Hello there!
RAY: See, they're not gone.
JACK: Hello!
BILL: Hello Jack!
RAY: Bill?
BILL: That you, Raymond?
RAY: Yeah! Me and Jack. We're still here.
BILL: Me too. And Rose is still here. I heard her groanin'.
ROSE: That's a terrible thing to say, Bill Sullivan. I certainly was not groanin'. Ninety years alive and at least twelve dead, and in all that time I haven't been heard to utter a single groan. It wouldn't hurt you to have a little respect for the dead, you know.
BILL: Sorry, Rose. I thought I heard you groanin', that's all.
ROSE: I was sayin' my prayers. Like the rest of ye ought to be instead of goin' on with your chatter.
BILL: Sounded like groanin' to me.
JACK: Just tryin' to find out which of us is still here, Aunt Rose.
RAY: We're wonderin' if there's any of us gone.
ROSE: So who is it haven't spoke up yet?
JACK: I guess it's just Maggie and Sheila now. There was ever only the six of us put down here. Up 'til this time last year, anyway.

ROSE: Well, I don't know about Sheila, poor child. Could be she's gone to Heaven. But I doubt very much if Maggie is. So if she's not gone to Hell, she must be hangin' around here someplace.

MAGGIE: I heard that, Rose Hepditch, you old bitch! Always holier than thou.

BILL: That's Maggie! That's Maggie for sure.

ROSE: A year deader and no better than ever.

JACK: Ah, Aunt Rose, that's just Maggie. You know what she's like.

MAGGIE: And what difference do it make? You're the saintly one, Rose, or so you think, and you're still here. I'm one of the devil's own, accordin' to you, and I'm still here. And the men, they're a fine lot aren't they? And they're still here. And if you ever thought we'd ever get out of here, I doubt if the grubs got fat eatin' your brains, maid.

RAY: Now, knock it off, Maggie. Besides, there's Sheila yet. She could be gone by now.

SHEILA: No, I'm not. I'm still here, still wishin' I wasn't.

JACK: Ah Sheila! It's good to hear your voice again.

MAGGIE: Misery likes company, I s'pose.

JACK: I don't mean it like that, child. It's just that I'd miss you if you was gone.

RAY: That's it then. Anyone who was ever here is still here.

ROSE: I hoped some of us, one of us at least, would be gone by now. What was it we did so wrong to keep us here like this?

JACK: That's not for us to say, Aunt Rose. We're here, that's all.

MAGGIE: Shouldn't we find out if anyone else's come? They can't live forever, that crowd up there. They got to perish sometime.

BILL: It'd be good to get a bit of news.

JACK: It's a sin to think it, but I almost hope someone's come.

ROSE: They all got to come sometime, sooner or later.

RAY: It's three years now, since anyone was buried here.

SHEILA: It'd be nice to hear something from Mom and them.

ROSE: If they was here, wouldn't they have spoke up by now?

JACK: Maybe not. Mind the year Maggie came? When we got our voices back, she didn't speak for the best part of the whole time. Scared to death, remember, afraid that the devil might get her.

ROSE: It's a wonder to me that he haven't got her yet.

MAGGIE: Oh, shut yer trap, Rose. Besides, who wouldn't be spooked out of their mind in a place like this, with corpses goin' on all around you?

JACK: That's what I mean. It isn't a easy thing to get used to. Whoever might be here might be a bit nervous about it. *(Loudly.)* If there's anyone besides us lyin' here in this graveyard, anyone who was buried here since this time last year, could you let us know?

RAY: All you got to do is talk. You got your voice now, for a little while at least.

JACK: And there's certainly no need to be afraid. I'll tell you who's here. All people you know, most likely. Sheila's here. Little Sheila Connors.

SHEILA: I drowned under the ice.

JACK: And Aunt Rose. Rose-in-the-bed, she's here.

ROSE: It's a fine bed I'm in now. Lovely linen, no mistake!

JACK: Ray Dwyer, he's here. Used to make up the songs, remember. Always makin' up songs and singin' all the time.

RAY: I sung all the way from the cradle to the grave. Got to the grave too quick.

JACK: And Maggie Green is here.

MAGGIE: Maggie Green, the old bag. Remember? What would they call me, if they could see me now? A old bag of bones I am now, the same as me betters.

JACK: And Skipper Bill Sullivan.

BILL: I should of drowned in The August Gale. A watery grave 'd be a damn sight better than this.

JACK: And me, Jack Leonard. Died in fifty-five, in the best of health. Been here ever since.

ROSE: We're all here ever since.

RAY: And we only get this time of year with voices. All Souls Night, that's all we got. Whatever we're allowed of it. So, if there's anyone else here, and you can hear us, then speak up for Godsake.

(Silence.)

ROSE: If there was any of them that did die these past three years, they mightn't be here anyway, because they could of gone straightaway to Heaven. Or to Hell.

MAGGIE: Even if they went to Hell, they'd be better off. Hell can't be no worse than this.

JACK: We got this spell at least.

BILL: Then back to nothin'.

ROSE: I'm beginnin' to think all my prayers is gone to waste. All the thousands of rosaries I said, and the novenas I made, and the advents and the lents, and all the fastin', and the penances, and all The Acts of Contrition. All gone to waste.

JACK: Maybe not, Aunt Rose. Time is different here. It seems so long in passin', seems like centuries. But it's only a few years we been here. That's all.

RAY: Sure we was always told that even a venial sin, the tiniest kind, could keep you in purgat'ry for a hundred years or more. God knows we all committed a scattered one. And who knows, but this might be purgat'ry. It could be.

JACK: It don't seem to be nowhere near the same purgat'ry I learned about in school.

RAY: Still, it wasn't more than fifteen years ago and there wasn't

nobody buried here at all.
ROSE: We used the old graveyard before that. The one up by the Church. A nicer place it was too. I bet the ones buried up there isn't in such a state as this.
JACK: Sheila was the first one put down here. I can mind the day we buried her. The first grave ever dug in the new cemet'ry. That was fourteen years ago. If time adds up at all.
SHEILA: I should of done what I was told. Mom told me not to go playin' out on the ice. But I went anyway, not thinkin' nothin' would happen outside of gettin' wet and gettin' bawled out for it. And then the pan went over, and I was under the water, and I couldn't breathe, and there was ice in my mouth chokin' me, and I got a awful pain in the head, and I tried to screech out, and the salt water came in and made me sick, and I vomited. And then it was like I was into a dream and all I could see was rainbows everywhere, and they was all broken into pieces, and the colours hurt my eyes, and I didn't remember to think of nothin'. Not even to say the Act of Contrition.
ROSE: Your poor mother nearly went out of her mind.
RAY: The cove was full of slob and we was out there tryin' to hook you up from the bottom. It was me that jigged you. The whole crowd of us was out there, and I kept waitin' for someone to shout out that they got you. I kept hopin' it wouldn't be me, but if it was me, that the jigger would be caught in your coat or something. But when I hauled you up and saw where the jigger was hooked, I passed out in the punt, and the line slipped out of me grip, and you went to the bottom again. The rest came over then and took hold, and hauled you in. But it was me that jigged you in the eye.
SHEILA: I got no eyes now, Mr. Dwyer. So it don't make no difference. (*Weeping.*) I got no eyes at all now.
(*Thunder.*)
JACK: Listen!
BILL: More weather, that's all.
JACK: No listen. It was a voice I heard.
NED: It's me you heard. Tryin' to get used to the sound of myself.
JACK: Who is it? Who are you?
MAGGIE: It's Ned Shea. I'd know him anywhere.
NED: It's me. Ned. You remember me Jack.
JACK: Ned Shea! I dare say I do.
BILL: Well, I'll be damned!
NED: Skipper Bill?
BILL: Yeah!
RAY: And me, Ray Dwyer. Sorry to see you here, Ned.
NED: Me too, Ray. Me too.
MAGGIE: Robbed from the poor 'til the day you died, I s'pose.
NED: That got to be Maggie.

ROSE: Don't pay no mind to her, Ned.
NED: And that must be Rose Hepditch.
ROSE: Rose-in-the-bed is what they called me. Remember?
NED: Sure I remember you, Rose.
SHEILA: Hello, Mr. Shea. I used to be Sheila.
NED: Ah, freckle-faced Sheila!
BILL: And yourself, Ned. How are ya, b'y? How ya doin'?
NED: It's dead is how I am, Bill. And not lookin' very good, I can tell you. Mostly bones is what I am now. Mostly bones.
MAGGIE: You'll be all bones, like the rest of us soon. The worms 'll see to that. How's my one and only? How's my Tom, Ned? How's he gettin' on?
NED: Damned if I ever thought I'd be talkin' to you again, Maggie. Contrariest customer I ever had.
MAGGIE: Well, you was the crookedest shopkeeper I ever dealt with.
JACK: Now, don't go gettin' on with that stuff. That's all over with, all past, that stuff.
MAGGIE: How's my Tom, Ned? How's my handsome one, he's self? Is he still mournin' over me?
NED: If he is, he's doin' it in fine company.
MAGGIE: What fine company?
NED: Tom got he's self a new woman, maid.
MAGGIE: No! That's a damn lie, that is.
NED: No, Maggie. No lie at all. Tom is all tied up now. Goin' on three years, I'd say.
MAGGIE: Tied up? To who? Who got my Tom now?
NED: Edna Leonard.
MAGGIE: That can't be. It couldn't be.
NED: It is, Maggie, maid. It's the God's truth.
MAGGIE: *(Wailing.)* Oh no! No. No. No.
JACK: Now, now, girl. No use gettin' yourself all upset about it.
MAGGIE: Edna Leonard! Tom and she? My Tom and the likes of that! I don't believe it. He couldn't stand her. Nobody could. She was always so stuck up. And all she was a streel, really.
NED: Well, whatever she might of been, she is proper enough now, since the wedding.
MAGGIE: Wedding? They went and had a wedding? In church and everything?
NED: The most beer I sold in six months.
MAGGIE: They celebrated it?
NED: The whole place was hung over for a week.
MAGGIE: White wedding dress and all?
NED: Yes. And a pretty penny it cost, too.
MAGGIE: And she about as much of a virgin as Tim Slade's cow.
ROSE: No cow I knows could hold a candle to you.
NED: She still owes onto it, too. Like they all owes me on one thing

or another. Now I'spose they'll just tear up their slips and be done of 'em. If I hadn't of died, I'd be in the poor-house.
ROSE: Yes, I allow now. So far as I could tell, you was every bit as crooked inside as you was out.
NED: I never dealt crooked with no one. And besides I'm not crooked anymore on the outside either.
BILL: You mean you got no more hump-back?
NED: I'm as straight as a whip now.
JACK: How come, Ned? How'd you get cured of that?
MAGGIE: You was bent near to the ground all your life.
NED: I guess they had to straighten me out to fit me into a coffin.
JACK: Christ! Couldn't they have built you one to fit?
NED: Oh, I'm sure they would've. But I bought me coffin off me ownself, out of me own stock. That way I got to keep the mark-up on it, see.
ROSE: What did you think? That you could take your ill-gotten gains to the grave with you?
NED: No gains I ever got was ill-gotten, Rose. And they wasn't what you'd call a wealth of money neither. But for what they was worth, I did take 'em with me.
JACK: Go on!
BILL: How?
NED: I got it sewed into the lining of my coffin. Every cent I had is buried right here with me.
MAGGIE: A lot of good it'll do to you here.
ROSE: Once a merchant, always a merchant.
NED: A man got to get along the best he can.
JACK: Is there others, Ned?
NED: Other what?
JACK: People. Ones that died the year. Any more besides yourself?
NED: I don't know. Aunt Bride was ailin' the same time I was. But I think it was just the flu she had. It was the damn cancer got me, so I was done for anyway. But you know Aunt Bride. She's liable to outlast the works, no matter what she got.
BILL: Eighty she'd be now. Time for Bride to give up on it. Time she took her place here alongside of her old man. I gets lonely for she betimes.
BRIDE: That's very nice now Mr. Bill, wantin' me to come to a place like this.
BILL: Bride! You is here. Thank God! I was beginning to think you was never goin' to die.
BRIDE: Well, I certainly didn't try to, you know, even though there was times I missed you bad enough.
JACK: It's too bad Bride, that we got to meet again in such a place as this.
BRIDE: It's not what I hoped for, Jack.

RAY: Not what any of us hoped for.
MAGGIE: We hoped to be out of here before you or anyone else ever come.
BRIDE: This seems to me to be a good place to get a chill. I hope you got your long underwear on, Bill.
BILL: Ah, no need for that here, girl. The cold can't do us no harm now. No more need for pills and hot-water bottles and beef iron wine. No need for none of that stuff now. The only thing can harm you here, love, is time. Thinkin' it might go on forever. Still, I finds it nice to hear your voice, Bride.
BRIDE: All the prayers I prayed to you, Bill, thinkin' you'd be up in Heaven, among the saints. Thinkin' you could do us poor mortals some good. Isn't no one at all gone to Heaven?
JACK: We're all here, Bride. All of us that got put down here in this place.
ROSE: I don't s'pose we're all in Hell, are we? Not that I never did nothin' wrong, mind you. But how much wrong can a body do that spent more than a lifetime in bed? I said enough prayers, God knows, and the priest came all the time and heard my confession and gave me Holy Communion. I saved up thousands of years worth of indulgences. Two hundred days indulgence for this, three months indulgence for that, and so on. "Sacred Heart of Jesus have mercy on us!". That alone was good for a hundred and fifty days indulgence. I used to lie there in my bed morning, noon, and night with my notebooks, the ones I kept special for that purpose, and for every prayer I said with indulgences attached to 'em, I'd mark 'em down in the book. How many days, or months or years I gained on each one. And then I'd add it on to the total. I had the total up to three million, six hundred and ninety-two thousand, seven hundred and fifty something years, before I passed away. And that's not countin' the perpetual indulgences I kept in a separate book.
JACK: Maybe all them indulgences you saved up went to someone else, Rose. Maybe God sort of scattered 'em around among the crowd that didn't have so much. Maybe a few Protestants got their souls saved on account of your prayers. Or maybe even someone up in the old cemet'ry went to Heaven on account of 'em.
ROSE: That'd hardly be fair, would it? Still this can't be Hell. Hell is for them that committed mortal sins and I can't imagine myself ever committing a mortal sin. I know I never.
MAGGIE: Maybe it was that business with the priest that time. Young Father Walsh. That would be a mortal sin, if you ask me.
ROSE: There was nothin' but lies in that. All lies.
MAGGIE: That's not what I heard.
ROSE: I got a good idea what you heard. I'm not stunned, maid. I might of been laid up most all me life, but I always knew what

went on around. Inside the house and out. I always knew.

MAGGIE: So, I s'pose there's not a bit of truth in it at all. About you and the priest.

ROSE: Not a speck. People got nothin' better to do than to go around makin' up stuff. That's all.

MAGGIE: How come you went to bed then, for the rest of your life?

BRIDE: And you only seventeen at the time.

NED: All we ever heard was the business about the priest. How you was s'posed to have designs on him, and how you hove yourself at him to tempt him away from he's vows. And to protect he's self he put a curse on you, and you went straight home and went to bed and never was able to get up again 'til the day you died. I can't say what truth is in it or what is not. It was all we heard though. And nobody never told us no different.

ROSE: Isn't that a lovely story now! A lot of nonsense is what it is. What stuff people will believe is beyond me.

MAGGIE: If it's all lies, then, Rose Hepditch, what was the truth of it?

ROSE: Apart from tellin' you it's none of your business, Maggie dear, I can tell you this much. And I wouldn't be bothered lyin', would I, mostly gone from dust to dust and hopin' to have my soul lifted out of this place one day. So I'll tell you this much about it and you can believe it if you like. That Father Walsh was only here for a short spell, only that one summer while he was fillin' in for Father Dormody who wasn't at all well that year. And yes he was a good lookin' man, I'll admit that. Enough to make any girl take notice to him if he hadn't of been a priest. And you can ask anyone and they'd tell you that I wasn't such a bad sight myself then. Oh, I was a picture to be seen, they say. With my hair down to my waist nearly. And I had manners too. Not like most in St. Kevin's. A coarse lot, most of 'em were. They'd go around with anyone at all, they would. Boys off of the boats from Buffet all covered with herring scales, stinkin' of fish. It didn't matter to them. But not me. I had more self-respect than that. I never went around with nobody. I used to sing in the choir. I had a lovely voice then. And I'd help out around the church too, help arrange the flowers on the altar and things like that. And that's all Father Walsh 'd talk to me about, the choir and the flowers. And that's all there ever was to it, until one Sunday in August. Lady Day it was. He told me before Mass that he wanted to see me after, about something. So after Mass I waited outside the twin gates by the belfry. And after everyone was gone on home, he came and asked me to walk with him around Chapel Pond. I went of course, thinkin' he wanted to talk about gettin' more people in the choir or something like that. But instead he started to tell me how he felt all cramped up living in the priest's house all by he's self in St. Kevin's. And he told me that I was the only one in the parish he never felt lonely with, the only one he could be comfortable talkin' to. And then he told me that he wasn't so sure he was cut out to be a priest afterall. And that he had feelings about me that bothered him a lot, and that he had a lot of trouble keepin' he's mind on the Mass when he'd be readin' the gospel or givin' out Communion because he could see me up in the choir and I took he's mind off of the Mass. Well, I can tell you, I was pretty puzzled at it all. He sounded like he was frightened. There was a shiver in he's voice that I never heard before, and when he took me by the hand to help me across Middle Brook, I could tell that he was tremblin'. And when we got across he just stood there holdin' my hand and lookin' at me like he couldn't let go, like something had took hold of him, like he was into some kind of spell or something. Then I got scared. Scared that the devil had something to do with it all. It was like I could feel Satan he's self at work inside of the both of us. And I got so scared, I ran away. Just turned and ran all the way home. When I got there I made out I was sick and I went to bed and shivered and prayed until I fell asleep. And when I woke up, sometime that afternoon, I couldn't move a muscle. I was paralysed from the waist down. Just seventeen that summer I was, and 'til I died at the age of ninety, I was never able to get out of that bed. In seventy-three years, the first move I ever made from that bed was to this place here. And that's the truth. You can believe it if you like. Suit yourself. But it's the God's truth. Cross my heart and hope to die, it is.

MAGGIE: You're already dead, my dear.

ROSE: Yes maid, I know. And there were times, believe me, I looked forward to it. Before I knew how terrible it would be. It was Heaven I looked forward to, not this.

NED: Well, I'll be damned!

MAGGIE: You might very well be damned already, Ned Shea. No less than the rest of us.

NED: I mean about the priest. Not that I believe it, mind, but a person could almost, to hear Rose tell it.

BRIDE: But if it went the way she tells it, then how come she got cursed to bed instead of the priest?

JACK: Might be there was no curse on anyone. I heard tell of people all-of-a-sudden couldn't walk. All-of-a-sudden paralysed. With rheumatic fever and stuff like that. Nobody ever said it was a curse or a punishment of any kind. Just a natural kind of crippleness, that's all.

RAY: Well, we're all laid up now, aren't we! And maybe there's more of us poor cripples yet, more come besides Ned and Aunt Bride.

MAGGIE: If there is, they're takin' their own sweet time about speakin' up.

BILL: They'd have a job to get a word in edgeways anyhow with all the gab goin' on here.

SHEILA: If there is anyone else come, I hope it isn't Mom or Dad or Robert or Julie or any of them. It's nice to think that they're alive and think about what they'd be doin' now, up there. Except I got 'em all pictured like before I got drowned. They'd all be older than that now, wouldn't they?

JACK: Pretty near fifteen years older.

SHEILA: I sees Robert, still a little thing, not nearly five and him goin' to the spring well with he's little buckets and he's little hoop that Dad made for him. Goin' along with the men to get he's turn of water, actin' just like he was all growed up.

JACK: He's well growed up, by now.

SHEILA: That's what I can't get into me head. Still, it's better to think of him alive and all growed up than to think he might be lyin' here like us.

BRIDE: He's a fine young man. A real blessing to your Mom and Dad. And Julia is married with two youngsters, two little girls. You didn't know you was Aunt Sheila now, did you? Oh, they're adorable little things, the both of them. Only one, Cecilia, I think it is, got a club foot. A sin it is really, because except for that, she's the prettiest little thing you ever laid eyes on. It run in the family of course. You was a pretty one yourself. I remember when you was all freckles and curls and quick to laugh. You used to laugh at almost anything then. And the way you had of laughin' used to set all hands laughin' along with you. Oh, you used to be a happy child before you died so sad.

SHEILA: But I'm not happy no more, Mrs. Sullivan. There isn't nothin' to be happy about, being dead.

AARON: That's for sure.

RAY: Who's that?

ROSE: It's someone.

AARON: It's me.

MAGGIE: Who is it?

AARON: Me. But I wish it wasn't.

BILL: But who the hell are you?

JACK: It's Peter! My son! One of my boys. It's he's voice. But it can't be him. Not Peter.

AARON: Not Peter, father. Aaron.

JACK: Aaron! What in God's name you doin' here? You and Peter, you're young strappin', healthy men. You can't be dead.

AARON: But I am all the same. Dead as I can get.

JACK: You'd only be twenty-eight yet. You and Peter. How come you're here, dead like me, like the rest of us?

AARON: I got shot.

JACK: Shot! How? Who shot you?

AARON: Me and Peter was out birdin'. Lookin' for turrs. Nothing on the go but a scattered bawk and a few pigeons. I was up in the bow, Peter was back aft. I was just goin' to let go at a pigeon. He was right on top of the lop, dead ahead. But just as I was goin' to fire, I heard Peter's twelve gauge goin' off behind me. And that's the last sound I heard 'till now.

JACK: It was Peter that shot you.

AARON: He was the only one could of. We was out there off the Redlands, and not another boat in sight.

JACK: But Peter knew how to handle a gun from the time he was ten. Always so careful, he was, when it come to guns and stuff like that. God, he must of felt awful, havin' that happen right before he's very eyes. And he's self to blame for it. How could such a thing happen?

AARON: I don't know, sir. Don't know what made he's gun go off like that. But it did and that was the end of me.

JACK: Such fine strappin' young fellows, ye were, the both of ye. Always together. Born together on a full moon and side by side ever since. I allow he'll miss you now Aaron, b'ye. I allow he'll be lost without you.

AARON: We shared everything, me and Peter. Everything except her.

JACK: Who's her?

AARON: Donna.

JACK: Who's she?

AARON: Donna Hennessey.

JACK: What did she have to do with ye?

AARON: We was goin' to be married.

JACK: That might of been good enough news once upon a time. Hennessey! From Marasheen?

AARON: Yeah. She came over to stay with her sister, married to Joe Collins. Joe's missus wasn't well at the time, and after she got better, had a boy, Donna stayed on. We got to be pretty good buddies, the three of us, me and her and Peter. We used to have a lot of fun together. Sometimes just playin' cards up at Joe's or down to the house. Other times we'd go swimmin' in Chapel Pond or go berry pickin' on the barrens. Or we'd just hang around, go walkin' in the road in the evenin's, doin' nothin' but havin' fun all the same. The three of us together all the time. Sometimes I wish it could of stayed like that. Me and Peter and her. But after a while it started to change. It got to be more of just me and Donna. We'd go on walks up Cradle Hill and row out to Manny's Cove and things like that, all by ourselves, without Peter in tow. And the more things we did like that, without Peter being a part of 'em, the more he took to broodin' over it. It wasn't the three of us anymore. It was me and Donna on the one side, and Peter, all by he's self, on the other. And there wasn't much could be done about it. You couldn't go around sharin' what me

and Donna had between the both of us by then.
JACK: So she got to be a trouble between ye?
AARON: We still did everything together, me and Peter. Rabbit catchin', birdin', the works. We even built a new punt together after that. But it wasn't the same, especially when me and Donna got engaged. We planned to be married within the year. I sent for a ring and everything. But it never came off, because I got shot. I misses her some though. I misses her something terrible.
JACK: I dare say you do, b'ye.
BILL: How's the fish?
(Silence.)
How's the fish above, young fellow? Any fish?
AARON: Fish? No, sir. Hardly worth goin' at. Inshore anyways.
BILL: Inshore. Offshore. What difference with ye young crowd at it? What did any of ye ever know about fish, for Christ's sake!
JACK: They were good men at it, Bill. The finest kind. Knew all about fish, my boys did. Peter and Aaron. Knew near as much as I did.
BILL: So they goes and kills each other off with guns. Arsin' around, I bet they was. The young crowd is good enough for that, certainly. Always foolin' around at things until, sooner or later, someone is bound to get hurted or killed.
JACK: Accidents happen to the best, Skipper Bill. And you know it got nothin' to do with young or old. Look how I died. Tripped in a bit of rope, not much more than a piece of sud-line. Fell off of the stagehead, plowso, right down into the skiff. Hit me head on a grapple and that was the end of it. Over, just like that. And I wasn't a youngster when it come to stages and flakes and boats. You know that yourself. But that didn't make no difference. When my time was up, the Good Lord didn't need no more than a piece of rope to bring 'er to a end. There I am, one minute whistlin' along the finest kind, the next minute lyin' in the bottom of the skiff, dead. It's the way of things. That's all.
ROSE: That's right. The Good Lord makes up He's own mind about when our time comes. And nobody can do anything that'll make Him change He's mind either.
MAGGIE: You're the very proof of that yourself, Rose, if you ask me.
ROSE: What do you mean by that?
MAGGIE: Only what every one knows. About when your father was dyin' and your mother already gone, how he give he's whole house and property over, lock, stock and barrel, to John Joe Callahan on condition that he'd look after you 'till the day you died. You was only twenty-four then and already bedridden for seven years, so nobody thought at the time that you was going to live much longer. But like you said, the Good Lord calls the tune,

so He went and let you lie there like the tyrant you was for sixty-six or some odd years while all around you was dyin' of this, that and the other thing.

ROSE: Lies!

MAGGIE: And only then, when the choice wasn't yours no more, did you give up and die. The length of time you lived on in that house never made no sense to anyone, least of all poor John Joe Callahan whose bargain backfired on him. But like you said yourself, maid, God got he's ways, and there isn't no way around what he intends for any of us.

ROSE: I'd tyrant you, Maggie Green, if I could lay a hand on you. For someone who never lived no better than a pagan, you got a lovely mouth on you. The things I know about you, my dear, I wouldn't even whisper to myself. I wouldn't abuse my own ears to let 'em hear what I know about you.

JACK: Now Rose, Maggie, that's no way to go gettin' on in this bit of time we got.

NED: Being dead don't seem to make no difference to some people, Jack, by'e. I could swear, listenin' to them two, that I was up above again, in the shop cuttin' up some salt meat or something and listenin' to the crowd goin' on while they was waitin' to be served. It was good as a concert most times in that shop. 'Specially with the likes of them around.

BILL: I mightn't have no stomach left, but by God, just thinkin' about salt meat is enough to make a man hungry. I know it wouldn't put no flesh back on me bones, but would I ever love to have a taste. A forkfull would do.

MAGGIE: That's just about what you'd get too, if Ned picked it out for you. If you picked it out of the barrel your ownself, you could get a fair piece, but if you left it up to Ned all you'd get 'd be fat and bone.

RAY: We don't need no more bones than we already got. But a bit of fat wouldn't go to waste here, would it?

SHEILA: Peppermint knobs.

BRIDE: What's that, child?

SHEILA: That's what I'd like if I could go down to Mr. Shea's shop. Peppermint knobs.

NED: If we were still alive, my dear, you could have all the peppermint knobs you could eat. And for free too.

MAGGIE: Some hope! Nothin' whatever went through the door of that shop went through free. Twice the price is what you'd pay, most likely.

BRIDE: Twice the price or not, I'd give anything to have some of that overseas tea you used to have, Ned. That was a lovely cup of tea. Put it on to steep in the morning, have a cup, shove the pot over to the side of the stove, and by bedtime, it'd still be good. Oh, what I wouldn't give for a nice cup of tea!

RAY: I could go for a dozen Dominion, myself.
BRIDE: To each he's own.
NED: Shea's General Store, Edward S. Shea, proprietor. Groceries, provisions, drygoods, hardware, rum and ale, milk of magnesia and other remedies, confectionary and sweet biscuits of all sorts. What's not in stock, we can order. Whatever your heart desires, at the best prices in St. Kevin's.
MAGGIE: The best prices in St. Kevin's? The only prices in St. Kevin's. What robbery!
NED: That's what it is to be a merchant. You're bound to be a scoundrel to some, no matter how quick you're bound for the poor house.
ROSE: I wouldn't go to your shop, even if I could. You can't get goods here like you can from away. I'd order out of the catalogue, the same as I always did. What wonderful things you could get out of the catalogue! I had a whole closet full of dresses come from away, you know. Oh, dozens of the loveliest clothes you ever saw. I never got to wear any of 'em. But they was nice to have, all the same.
MAGGIE: Pity! I had a nice bra once, come from the catalogue. Mae Rogers had it come for herself, only it came in the wrong size. You know Mae now, skinny as a rake and nothing much up top. But it fitted me perfect. Made out of black silk it was, and it had a little lace edge onto it. Wicked as sin. The first time I ever wore it, Tom broke the hapse. Oh, it'd be heavenly to get dressed up again. In something like that, with a bit of make-up to go with it. Tom'd be all eyes. And wouldn't that Edna Leonard go right up the wall!
BRIDE: You'd look a pretty sight, no mistake, Maggie, with your rib bones wrapped in lace.
MAGGIE: I know Bride, maid. Skeletons are a sorry lot when it comes to dressin' up. But there was a time, there was a time, when the men'd have trouble enough keepin' their eyes off of Maggie Green.
ROSE: The way I heard it, it was their hands they couldn't keep off of you, and only because you never asked 'em to.
MAGGIE: So much you knows about it, Rose. You who spent a lifetime in bed but never felt a man's hands on you, never felt the roughness or the smoothness of 'em. And even them built like barrels cryin' like babies in your arms. What would you know about that with all your high-falutin' notions? How could you know what it's like to have a man's tears flowin' down your body? There's more to it than you could ever know, maid. And not all fun either.
ROSE: Well, I wouldn't even want to know so much as you do about such stuff. But I know one thing for sure. What time you spent in bed certainly didn't do your soul much good.

MAGGIE: So far as I can see, we're both in the same boat when it comes to that.

ROSE: Yes! But only for the time-being, please God, only for the time being.

JACK: The time-being might be all we got, so quit your contrariness, the both of ye.

NED: And then they wonder how come I stayed a bachelor all my life. Not that the women'd have anything to do with me anyway what with the way I was bent so double, like I was a question mark. But how the women got on in the shop was enough to make a man keep he's distance anyway.

MAGGIE: More 'dn likely you was bent double the better for dealin' double with your customers.

BILL: Never mind your bad mouthin' Maggie. What I remember most about that old shop was all the good yarns what was told in there.

JACK: I'll never forget that night Tim Collins told about the August gale.

BILL: Tim was there when we rode 'er out.

JACK: Well sir, the way he told it afterwards, you could fair feel the shop shakin' in the wind and see the bye's gropin' their way up the rattlins, and the water, mountains high, breakin' over the side of 'er. And then choppin' away the spars and ridin' 'er out all night on nothin' but hope.

BILL: Well, he was there, so it wouldn't be no word of a lie.

BRIDE: I had you give up for lost.

NED: Everyone had you give up for lost.

AARON: I got her wedding ring give up for lost. What'll become of it now Ned, with your shop closed up and me not there to have it?

NED: Oh, it'll get sent back most likely, or someone else'll have it. If there's anyone left up there to wear a ring.

AARON: She didn't even know I went and ordered it. We never even had a date set for the wedding.

BRIDE: Mind the time we got married, Bill? In the old church it was, before the fire. Remember? I just adored that old church. It was so pretty, all pink coloured stones and lovely arches and everything. Not like the pile of junk they went and put up in its place. I mean it still might of been the house of God and everything, but it wasn't the same. Not nearly as nice as the old one we got married into. Remember, Bill?

BILL: I remember havin' one hell of a hang-over the next day.

BRIDE: And the flowers all over the altar. Fresh picked too, out of Mom's garden. Roses and marigolds and mums and bleeding hearts and, oh, all kinds. And the smell of 'em all through the church. Like a lovely perfume it was, comin' straight from Heaven. Remember, Bill?

BILL: I remember the brew I made went bad on me. Godawfullest stuff I ever did drink.

BRIDE: And the music! That was a wonderful organ they had in the old church. Not like the groaner they bought in its place. Beautiful it was. And Tom Sullivan's Joan played it like a angel.
BILL: Nothin' like Ben Foley on the 'cordian though. Back at the house after, Ben was playin' 'Stack o' Barley' and Pat Flynn was dancin' on top of the plate. Gatchin' was all it was 'cause he wasn't that much of a hand to dance anyway. And he slipped on the plate and busted he's head open on the kitchen floor. Said it was on account of grease on the plate.
BRIDE: And the guns, the long-Toms, goin' off all over the place when we were makin' the procession back to the Cove. Bang! Bang! Bang! All over the place. Everyone was so happy! It was a wonderful wedding, even if I do say so myself. Wasn't it, Bill?
BILL: And young Hepditch went and shot the weather vane off of me henhouse. Drunken little bugger! I promised him a boot in the arse for that. It was one of the few promises I never kept.
BRIDE: All the same though, it was a wonderful wedding.
AARON: Ours was goin' to be a wonderful wedding too. I wonder what she'll do now that I'm dead.
JACK: She'll be alright. She'll mourn for a while and then get on with the rest of her life. For you, it's a long sleep now. So much of nothing, except for this, this spell we got here. That's all there is to it until we get out of here, until we're taken up into Heaven. Until then, there's no need to worry. Everyone got to die sooner or later. And them that's left alive, well, they just got to get over it and carry on. And they usually do. I hope your mother is makin' the best of it now.
AARON: She's okay. Or she was anyways, up to the time I got killed. It took her a couple of years to get over it after you died. But she's alright now. Peter'll look after her.
JACK: She'd be goin' on sixty-two now, Maud would. I dare say she's beginnin' to show it, all she's went through. Fifty-two she was when I died, and didn't look a day more than forty. Always looked younger than her years, your mother did. But I allow it's all catchin' up on her by this time.
AARON: It never came to me about you missin' her. It was always how much we missed you our ownselves. Do you miss her more than anything else in the world? The way I misses Donna.
JACK: Now, that's no easy question to answer, Aaron. What do a dead man miss most out of the life he had? For myself, I can say I miss the whole of it, the works. I miss your mother, and everyone around, miss being with 'em. And I miss a bit of music now and then, and a game of cards, and a nap on the daybed come evening. I miss it all, the good and the bad. But what do I miss most of all, out of my whole life? Well, my son, let me put it this way. If I had one day back at it, just one day give back to do what I pleased, what would I want to do on that day? Just one

day given back, mind, and I could pick the day. I'd pick a day in July month, or maybe the first week of August. I'd be at the wheel of the Alice-Eileen. That was the first real boat I ever owned, outside of punts and skiffs. A nice little jack she was, the Alice-Eileen. And she'd be under sail, all fresh paint and good canvas. And I'd be at the wheel of 'er with a nice sou'west breeze blowin'. Just a nice enough breeze around fifteen knots, a nice easy breeze. And we'd be takin' her down past the Grey Gull in lee of the Ragged Islands. And the sun would be lovely on the water. And we'd be loaded down with fish. The best kind of salt fish from off of my own flakes in St. Kevin's. We'd be takin' 'em down to Spencer's Cove, to A. Wareham and Sons. Nothin' but Madiera on board and she loaded down to the gunwales. With the sun on the water, a nice sou'west wind, and me at the wheel of my own boat. Well, I guess if that's the way I'd want to spend one day with body and soul together again, one day if I had it, then I guess I got to say, that is what I miss most of all.

SHEILA: I misses my mom tuckin' me in, sayin' "goodnight, God bless," kissin' me on the cheek where I got none now.

ROSE: The wall paper in my room, the little purple flowers climbin' to the ceiling. Always there, always growin', always in full bloom, summer or winter.

RAY: Snow. Snow clung to the eaves like upsidedown waves, white like ... like snow.

MAGGIE: I misses my lookin' glass most. It was the nicest thing I ever laid eyes on.

BILL: It'd be the sound of the sea for me. The sound of the sea with a sea on.

NED: The smell of cinnamon, and cloves, and new leather. The smell of fresh dustbane. The smell of new things.

BRIDE: The sound of Bill's snorin'. You could always tell when Bill was in off the water. The house'd be shakin' with the snores comin' out of him. Oh, what a lovely racket!

AARON: The touch of her underneath her blouse. Soft like soft glass.

ROSE: Hmmph!

AARON: Donna. *(Loudly.)* Donna. Remember me? Remember the times you held on to me in the meadow, weepin' like a baby beneath the birches?

MAGGIE: No!

AARON: Remember the first time I kissed you, and you told me to get lost, and I said okay I would, and then you grabbed hold of me and made me kiss you again?

MAGGIE: No!

AARON: Remember how it was when we walked in the landwash and you told me there was ten things you wanted most out of life, and nine of 'em was babies, but you kept the tenth one secret to yourself?

MAGGIE: No!

AARON: Remember the last time we was together, and you told me that one of your wishes was comin' true, and every word you said was "wedding"?

MAGGIE: No! No!

AARON: Did you cry at my funeral, girl? Did you weep buckets? Did you swear never to love nobody else ever again so long as you lived? Do you still think of the touch of my hand on your body? Can you still feel it, and do it make you want to cry all over again?

MAGGIE: No! No! No!

AARON: God damn it! Who's that sayin' "No?"

MAGGIE: It's me. That's who.

AARON: Why?

MAGGIE: Because.

AARON: Because what?

MAGGIE: Because it's just the way it is, that's all.

AARON: What way?

MAGGIE: If she could answer you, that's what she'd say to all that. No! No! No! Unless she was a liar.

AARON: No she wouldn't and she got no reason to lie to me. Besides, you don't even know her.

MAGGIE: Don't have to know her to know the way things is. All lies and falseness. It's someone else's hand she's feelin' on her self now. And it won't be the last one either.

AARON: That's not true.

MAGGIE: If you think she's up there pinin' away in misery for the likes of you, my son, when she can have the likes of you in her bed any time she got a mind to, then your brains is rotted away good and quick.

AARON: *(Loudly.)* Is it true? What she's sayin'. Is it true?

MAGGIE: As true as you're lyin' there dead, sir. Yes, every bit as true at that.

JACK: You know, Maggie, sometimes you can be a real—pardon the language—bitch. There's no need to be gettin' on like that. Things is miserable enough here without addin' to the misery of it. And God knows, the bit of time we got don't allow no time for bad mouthin'.

ROSE: That's Maggie sure. Isn't that her all over!

BRIDE: Nice talk that is Maggie!

JACK: Don't you pay any mind to it, Aaron.

RAY: She's just gettin' on like that because Tom went and got married.

NED: Ray, there was a young fellow at that wedding who knew a lot of your songs, a fellow be the name of Walsh, from Isle Valen. Wasn't a bad hand at singin' 'em either. Sang right through the

night, one song after another, and most of 'em was Ray Dwyer songs.
MAGGIE: Singin' at such a wedding is a insult to music, if you ask me.
BILL: Golden Bay, b'y, that was the place for songs. In the sailin' days. In the night time when all the boats would be at anchor, and all the crews sittin' around on the hatches, and the lamps lighted all aboard. One fellow'd start up a song and then, when he finished, someone else'd take up another one, and so on it'd go like that, song upon song, sir, 'til we all turned in. I s'pose there wasn't hardly a song in the world that wasn't sung one time or another in Golden Bay.
BILL: How about one now, Ray?
ROSE: What!
NED: Why not?
ROSE: Because we don't have forever. Any minute now, just you watch, we'll be back to silence. Back to nothing. We might have enough time with voices to say the Rosary. And that's what we should be at, too. Our prayers. No wonder we're kept here the way we are. Every year comes and goes and we only get a little while each one being able to talk and all, to say a few prayers, to ask for God's mercy and forgiveness. And what do we end up doin'? Gabbin' the whole time away with no purpose to it. No wonder we're kept here like this, lyin' in our own rot. No wonder at all, when we should be at the Rosary, and not carryin' on like it was a garden party or something.
JACK: I don't think there'd be any harm in a song.
NED: No harm at all.
BILL: Come on, Ray, give us one, b'y.
RAY: I don't want my songs to get in the way of anything.
MAGGIE: So, who apart from Rose, got any objection.
BILL: What about "The August Gale"?
RAY: Oh, that'd be too long, Skipper. That's a long song, that one.
BRIDE: Bill always wants to hear "The August Gale" just because he's into it.
BILL: I'm not the only one likes it.
BRIDE: What's that one you used to sing about Cradle Hill? That was a lovely song!
AARON: That's where me and Donna was together for the first time. The first time for the both of us. Up there in the meadow on the side of Cradle Hill.
RAY: It's a long time since I sung that one.
ROSE: Well, ye might as well get on with it. As far as I can see, some people are no better dead than alive. But I'll have nothin' to do with any of it. Either your songs or your sins. So, if you'll excuse me, I'll be at my prayers.
RAY: *(Singing.)*

When the sun goes down on Cradle Hill
And darkness then fills up the sky
And memories fill up your mind
I hope you do not cry
I hope you do not weep for me
For I am always with you still
As on evenings long ago
We strolled up Cradle Hill

Oh do not weep my darling one
Oh no don't ever weep for me
For I'm far beyond the reach
Of the wild and the raging sea
For I'm far beyond the raging sea

Remember what it all meant then
The fragrant flowers blooming there
And birds whose summer song
Did fill the evening air

These are the things I keep with me
They are the constant joys of love
And they were ours and still will be
While stars shine up above

Oh do not weep my darling one
Oh no don't ever weep for me
For I'm far beyond the reach
Of the wild and the raging sea
For I'm far beyond the raging sea.

AARON: Damn it! I wish I was still alive.

A VOICE: So it goes!
While death lies buried deep beneath the foot-steps and voices of visitors who come loving and longing to the long remembered, the worms can go about their slow, busy feast, and it won't matter. While death decays no distance at all from the smells of fish frying, and outhouses freshly used, and savory hanging upsidedown in brown paper bags behind the stoves, the rivulets, running like tiny subterranean rivers to the sea, can carry their residue of flesh with them all their flowing lives, and it won't matter. While death sleeps deep in the soundless ground beneath the sighs and cries of babies buried in cribs full of blankets, and the sing-song sound of women weeping in beds full of husbands, and the tiny talk of big men rolling home from the fields of fish on the zillion acre ocean, the silent sleep can last forever, and it

won't matter. Nothing of death's desolation will matter as long as dead lovers are loved still in the wishes of lovers left alive and longing. Nothing of it will matter as long as the honoured dead are honoured still in the heart-felt toasts of drunk and drinking men, or as long as cursing men still curse their dead enemies, glad to be rid of them and their interventions. It won't matter how long the dead lie dying of hunger, as long as children remember the taste of their dead mom's milk and the feel of breasty flesh upon their cheeks. It won't matter as long as the living live and remember. Whether they thrive or endure, as long as the living live and remember, the dear deceased cannot be diminished by the frightening fact of death.

All this, and more, the ever-remembered of St. Kevin's have learned. However brief, however uncertain their time alive, they learned, before they died, that there is no survival this side of immortality, no final gladness this side of Heaven.

Part II
The Coming of Winter

> I shall say you will die
> and none will remember you.
>
> Archibald MacLeish

A VOICE: In all the measure of time's turning, it may not matter that the dead are dead as long as the living live and remember.

But what if widows were to forget the sweet smell of rubber boots that stood steaming by the stove once upon a time in the nights of their wedded and wife-long days? What if they were to forget the feel of their husbands' horny hands groping disobediently in the dark for their fistfuls of flesh? What if they were to forget the nervous joy those same aging fish-scaled hands trembled them into, in the days of their young and carnal courtships?

What if husbands, their soft wives gone from their rollicking beds, should forget the smell of soap and onions, the sound of breathing by their sides? What if they were to forget the almost inaudible noise of all the wives in the world tapping about in their own world's most comfortable kitchen, the insistent commands to the wind to stop blowing dust into the doilied houses? What if they were to forget their wives' bodies, wet with sweat, heaving beneath them, rising and falling like the swell of the sea in the worn-out hours of their tired, tide-borne love?

What if mothers, their children kidnapped out of their arms by kidnapping death, should ever forget the whimpers, whispers, weeping, wailing, shrieks, giggles, cries, barks, and bad language of their youngsters, alive once and blooming in the wind and the rain and the frost and the snow and the endless sun of their mother's love?

What if fathers, their sons given as gifts to the insatiable sea, should forget their blood-red pride on the day of birth, on the day of the first tom-cod brought slipping home from the stagehead, on the day of the first birch-cleaving axe stroke, on the day their sons' young hands first laid claim to the tiller? What if they were to forget their love for their sons growing from love to respect (the kind of respect reserved for the fraternity of men)? What if they were to forget their own brave tears on the day of death, the absolute vacancy of the guernsey hanging half-mast in the back kitchen?

What if ever, in the measure of time's turning, friends were to forget friendship, lovers forget love? Then the dead would be dead indeed. And death indeed would be their dominion.

ROSE: Holy Mary, Mother of God, pray for us sinners now and at the hour of our death. Amen.
BILL: The hour of our death is long past. So you might as well give up on it, Rose. It's too late for prayers here.
RAY: Besides, we mightn't have a lot of time left and I'd like to know what's goin' on up there.
JACK: It's three years now since we had anyone to bring us a bit of news.
MAGGIE: Wouldn't we be better off without it? There's no such thing as good news, so it seems.
NED: It's all resettlement up there now-a-days. Nothing good about that.
ROSE: Resettlement? What's that?
NED: The government got it up.
AARON: Centralization.
NED: Centralization, resettlement. It's a rotten scheme no matter what.
ROSE: So what is it all about?
NED: It's a plan the government got to shift everyone around. So much money for every family that moves.

ROSE: Moves where?
NED: I don't think it much matters so long as they move off of the islands and out of the coves. And lots of places are already emptied out. All the people belong to Toslow, St. Anne's, Big Bona, Little Bona, Clattice Harbour, all them places, they're all gone.
AARON: The gulls'll have the whole bay to theirselves one of these days.
ROSE: Not here though. St. Kevin's people won't want to move out of here.
NED: It mightn't matter a damn if they want to or not.
BRIDE: They were the next thing to it when I passed away. Don't know what went on since, but it was one awful fuss up to that time.
ROSE: No. No one in their right mind would want to shift out of here. Where could they go to that'd be any better place than here?
NED: Some of 'em seem to be ready for it. Don't know if they'll move or not but they're talkin' that way.
AARON: It was a racket and a half the last I saw of it.
JACK: Why? What was goin' on then?
AARON: Meetings. Meetings and more meetings. And some goin' around tryin' to talk the rest into signin' the petition.
BRIDE: They got to have a certain percent sign up sayin' they want to be shifted. Unless enough signs up the government won't pay no one to shift.
RAY: Why wouldn't they let the ones who wants to move, move? And let them that wants to stay, stay?
NED: Because they want the whole lot out of here and they isn't goin' to settle for anything less. They don't want no one left that'll make any demands on 'em. They want the whole lot cleared out or none at all. So if enough of 'em signs up, then it'd be all over for St. Kevin's. What stayed after that would have to stay at their own risk with no help from the government at all.
RAY; Are some of 'em signin' up? Enough of 'em I mean?
AARON: I'd say she was about half and half the last I saw of it. Half, or nearly half, already signed up and the other half sayin' they'd be damned if they'd ever sign.
RAY: I can't imagine half the people I know up there electin' to move some place else.
BRIDE: It's not so much that they want to. I don't know a single soul that really wants to move, but still I know lots that already signed up.
RAY: How come they're signin' up if they don't want to?
NED: They're forced to, b'ye.
BRIDE: Not really forced now, Ned. Nobody got to sign.

NED: But they're left no other choice, not really.
JACK: How come?
NED: Well, for one thing, the government is sayin' that they can't afford to keep all small settlements like St. Kevin's goin'. They say that it's no good for anyone in places like this to think that someday they'll have electric lights or a hospital clinic or anything like that, because they can't afford to put all them things in all such places around the coast. And another thing they're sayin' is that the fishery is done with, finished. That nobody will be able to make a living fishin' ever again. If a person wants to work from here on in, then they got to go to places where there's work to be had. Factory work.
JACK: But how come they wants to put a end to the fishin'?
AARON: They're goin' to knock off with the fish and build factories. Factories is the new thing.
JACK: I don't see no sense to that. Damned if I do!
AARON: But that's what's goin' on. One meeting I was at up to the school, the member he's self was there makin' a speech, and he went on the whole night about how Newfoundland was nothin' but a nation of squid jiggers, that that's all she ever was, and how the government was goin' to put a end to that.
NED: A lot of that kind of talk goin' on. Puttin' down the place. A meeting I was at, when they first come around, one of them fellows from the government got up and spouted off about what a awful disgrace it was that we had nothin' better than trunk-holes for toilets. And that's all we'd ever have, he said, unless we moved to places that had water and sewage in 'em. We were too cut off, he said, to be a part of the new age. The age of industry. And he said if the people here was goin' to share in the benefits of it, then they'd have to move, else they'd all end up on welfare. Oh, he went on and on with stuff like that, and I tell you it wasn't easy for anyone to listen to.
BRIDE: And God forgive me, the priest is just as bad. He got nothin' good to say for the place anymore. He says he can't get teachers to come here because they'd sooner be in bigger places. And he says they can't afford to keep up the school any longer, and that from now on no one will ever have the slightest chance of a job without their grade eleven. And what's more, he says, anyone who considers themselves a Catholic have got to move where their children can get a Catholic education. He puts it like it would be a mortal sin if you didn't shift some place else. Oh, it's a wonderful lot of pressure on 'em to sign up. And there's lots won't go against the priest, no matter what.
JACK: You figure they'll go then, Ned?
NED: I don't know, Jack b'y. I don't know. I can tell you it looked like it was gettin' awful close to that the last I seen of it. But still there was some sayin' they wasn't about to leave, ever; that

they'd live here by theirselves if they had to. So I can't rightly say how she's goin' to go.

AARON: I was right in the middle of it too, with me and Donna goin' to be married. I didn't know if it'd be best to stay in St. Kevin's at the fish after we got married, or what. I would of wanted to stay. She liked it here fine enough, and Mom certainly wasn't about to move, not at her age. She allowed she'd rather die before she'd move away from here.

JACK: Yes, I don't say Maud 'd be the first to sign up for leavin' St. Kevin's.

AARON: Still, I'm scared of what's goin on. It'd be more lonelier than ever if I thought Donna wasn't here no more. I imagine she comes up here to the graveyard betimes just to think on me, wishin' I was still alive, wishin' we was still to get married. It's bad enough being dead but it'd be far worse if she wasn't here to visit my grave no more.

MAGGIE: I wonder if my Tom ever comes. Or have he forgot me already, now that Edna Leonard got her claws into him. No, he wouldn't forget me. He couldn't. I dare say he got so lonely without me that he lost he's senses and took up with the first thing handy to fill up the gap. I expect he comes here often as he can, my Tom, and stands up there lookin' down at my grave rememberin'. Rememberin' how proud he used to be, linked into me, goin' up the road of a Sunday evening, him in his blue serge suit and me in my red dress just like I was right out of the catalogue. I dare say he misses me something terrible. I dare say he do.

ROSE: It'd be awful, certainly, if they all moved away. But they couldn't all go. Some of the Callahans 'd have to stay. I put it in my last will and testament for them to keep my garden goin'. The flower garden, not the vegetable garden. What odds about that. But my last wish was that they'd look out to the flowers, and every Sunday, while they was bloomin', that they put some on my grave. That was my dyin' wish.

MAGGIE: I allow the poor Callahans gave up goin' accordin' to your wishes the minute you passed away, my dear. Can't say I blame 'em either.

RAY: If they all left, our graves would soon go to hay with no one to rake the gravel and cut the grass. The alders 'd take over pretty quick and soon enough you wouldn't even be able to make out a headstone from the road. You'd have to crawl through the woods to know there was anyone ever buried here at all.

BILL: Not very nice to think you might be forgot about altogether. We got three generations of family younger than us up there, me and Bride. That's one good thing about havin' a big family like we had and living to a good age like us. You don't expect to be forgot about for a long time.

BRIDE: It breaks my heart to think they mightn't be around at all. Rememberin' is one thing. Being close is another. I hope, whatever happens, that they don't move away from here. Not all of 'em. I don't want to be buried in the woods forever with no one ever comin' by to say a prayer or anything.
(Sheila is weeping.)
JACK: Now, don't you go frettin' over stuff like that. It's just talk, that's all. We don't know what's goin' on up above, but I allow it's the same as ever. Your mom and dad and brothers and sisters, they're all still there, still keepin' your grave nice and tidy. Still missin' you and prayin' for you, so you'll get to go to Heaven. You'll be the first to go from here. I got no doubt about that. You just wait. If we get this time back again next year, you'll already be gone up to Heaven. And maybe some of the rest of us'll be there with you. If not, then we'll all be along later. Don't pay no attention to all the talk around you. Just think on how nice you'll like it up in Heaven, 'cause that's where you're going to go. And soon, too.
ROSE: Mr. Leonard's right, Sheila. Why don't you help me with my Rosary. I'm just finishing off the first of the five Sorrowful Mysteries.
NISH: *(Suddenly.)* Hell ...
JACK: Listen!
NISH: Hell ...
JACK: Hear that?
NISH: Hell ... o!
RAY: Who's that?
BILL: The hell if I know.
NISH: Hello!
JACK: Who could that be?
NED: You got me.
NISH: Hello! Hello!
MAGGIE: The devil come callin' us all to Hell.
NISH: *(Haltingly.)* No, girl ... not the ... the devil. Just ... just me.
JACK: Me who? Who're you?
NISH: *(Slowly.)* Me. Nish Rogers. I know you, Jack Leonard. And the rest of ye, too. Don't you remember me?
ROSE: It can't be Nish Rogers.
JACK: The Nish Rogers we knew couldn't be talkin'.
MAGGIE: Deaf and dumb all he's life.
JACK: Nish wasn't never deaf and dumb. He could hear things just as good as you or me. He couldn't talk is all.
BILL: Is you dead, Nish?
NISH: *(With less difficulty.)* Dead more 'dn a month now.
BRIDE: I can't believe my own ears.
NISH: Me neither.
JACK: Everything is out of kilter here, Nish b'y. None of us got the

wherewithal to be talkin'. Some of us is nothin' but a pile of bones now, but here we are yakin' away like it was the most natural thing in the world.

ROSE: It only lasts for a while though, don't forget.

NISH: I gathered that much. But what's it all about? Do anyone know?

RAY: It got something to do with All Souls Night, Nish. Or something like that. Being it's always night time here, we can't keep track of the hours. But this while over the years we figured out, accordin' to when we died and so on, that it's this night every year that we get our voices back. God only knows why, but it seems that's the way it goes.

NED: We was always told that the souls of the dead would be up and about on All Souls Night. Nobody never went anywhere near the graveyard on All Souls Night. Some wouldn't hardly step out the door. That could of had something to do with this fitout here, where we're able to talk the way we're doin'. Somewhere in the first beginnin', that stuff about ghosts and things might have something to do with it.

ROSE: Ghosts, my foot! There isn't no such thing.

MAGGIE: Oh, yes there is.

ROSE: No doubt some people will believe whatever they want to.

JACK: Never mind about ghosts. It ain't every day we get a chance to talk to Nish.

RAY: Never did have the chance. Even when we was alive.

BRIDE: It isn't any wonder to us that you can talk now, Nish. Now that you're dead like the rest of us. Strange all the same.

JACK: How come you never spoke up sooner? If you been here all the while, and you could talk, how come you waited so long before you spoke up?

NISH: I was just lyin' here wonderin' and listenin'. It never even came into my head that I could talk until ye all started in on resettlement. I wanted to have a say in that so bad I just started talkin' almost without knowin' it. And all of a sudden there I was sayin' hello and hearin' myself sayin' it. It was strange to me first, like I'd never get the hang of it. But now here I am talkin' on natural, like I was doin' it all me life.

MAGGIE: There's no end to miracles here, is there!

JACK: How'd you come to die, Nish?

NISH: I died out of sorrow, sir.

BRIDE: A broken heart?

MAGGIE: Nonsense. Nobody ever died of no broken heart. Heart attack maybe! But a broken heart, that's nothin' but foolishness.

BILL: Christ woman! I suppose the man knows how he died, don't he!

NISH: Maggie might be right, for all I know. I don't know nothin' about broken hearts or heart attacks or things like that. I only

know that it was sorrow and sadness that made me do it.
JACK: Do what?
NISH: Hang myself.
BRIDE: No!
ROSE: Sacred Heart of Jesus!
JACK: You went and hung yourself?
NISH: Yes, Sir! Put a end to it!
BILL: I'll be goddamned!
NISH: Got a length of rope, tied one end to the rail of the choir loft and the other end around me neck, and jumped over the rail. And that was that.
BRIDE: Not in church!
NISH: That's where it come to me to do it, and that's where I did it.
RAY: What went so wrong to make you go and do the likes of that?
NISH: They'll say I took leave of me senses, went mental. That's what they must of thought anyway to bury me in here with the rest of ye that all died proper. But I wasn't so crazy as they might think.
ROSE: What was it then?
NISH: Resettlement. That's what drove me to it.
RAY: Sounds like it's gone worse than we could of thought.
NISH: A damn sight worse.
JACK: How? How's it gone?
NISH: A couple of years now there's been nothin' but talk about it. But no one seemed to pay too much attention to it until last winter. Up 'til then, it was like it had more to do with other places, and nothing much to do with us at all. Then the meetings started and that was it. First it was the people against the government, and then the priest got into it on the side of the government, and then it was the people up against the government and the priest, and then, more and more, it got to be the people against the people. It got pretty ugly betimes because lots couldn't see no sense in movin out of here. And I was one of 'em, certainly. What was the sense of me movin' out of here into a place full of strangers? Here, at least, everyone knew me. They never expected me to talk to them like anyone else. A crowd of strangers in some strange place, they'd come talkin' at me, and expect me to talk back to 'em. And everything'd be all out of kilter. Not like here where everything went along right most of the time, even for the likes of me. So what sense would it make for me to go movin' to some place else? None at all, as far as I could tell. And there was lots like me too. Not that they couldn't talk or nothin' like that, but still they had their place here. They belonged to it and they was used to it and comfortable in it. Lot's like me couldn't see no sense in movin', couldn't see no sense in givin' up their homes and gardens and boats and stages and stores and whatnot, and goin' off to try and find the same things

someplace else among a crowd of strangers.
JACK: It certainly wouldn't make no sense to me.
BILL: It'd only be the younger crowd that'd do the likes of that, give up on the place they was born and raised in, the place their fathers and grandfathers worked all their lifetime to build up. The young crowd don't care about nothin', so why should they care one way or the other about the place they belong to.
NISH: It wasn't only the young ones. Everyone got caught up in it in the end. All winter long, at them meetings and everywhere else, you would say that nobody was goin' to shift out of St. Kevin's come hell or high water. But come spring you could tell she was changin'. No one was sayin' it. But you could tell. It just kind of took hold and couldn't be shook off. And by 'n by you could see no one was turnin' the land or takin' care of things the way they used to. And then word got around that they couldn't get a teacher for the school, so there'd be no school for the youngsters come fall. And then Father McCormick announced that he was leavin', on account of he's health, and that there wouldn't be no one to take he's place. Well, I guess that was final then. As good as done. And the next thing even the ones most against it signed up for their allowance. They figured they'd be forced out in the end anyway and there wouldn't be no shiftin' money for them if they didn't sign. So by 'n by the boards started goin' up against the windows, and everyone went about the business of gettin' ready to move, just like it was the most natural thing in the world. But no one was laughin' while they was at it, I can tell you. There was a sadness in most everything all summer, a sadness like a darkness over everything that no one could see through.
JACK: So it's goin' that way? They're really shiftin' out up there?
NISH: They're already shifted, sir. Every last one of 'em.
ROSE: Oh, no!
NISH: Nobody left up there at all.
MAGGIE: That can't be true. It can't be.
RAY: All gone?
AARON: All?
BRIDE: Gone for good?
BILL: Well then! That's something, isn't it!
NED: I knew it. I knew it.
JACK: You sure, Nish?
NISH: I wouldn't tell it if it weren't true, Jack. I wouldn't go tellin' lies the first time I could talk.
SHEILA: Mom and them?
NISH: I'm afraid so. I'm afraid they are, child.
SHEILA: Where they gone to?
NISH: Don't know for sure. Some is gone to Placentia. More to Arnold's Cove. And some of 'em is gone over to the Southern

Shore, around Renews, Capahayden, places like that. I'm not sure where your family went to. But they're gone out of St. Kevin's. I know that much.
SHEILA: Is it a long ways away to them places?
RAY: Far enough, girl. Far enough.
NISH: The distance don't matter anyhow. The steamer won't be stoppin' in here no more. There'll be no more comin' and goin' out of here no more. There isn't nothing left for anyone to stop in for anyway.
AARON: But we're still here!
BILL: A lot of difference that makes.
AARON: What'll become of her, off among strangers?
NISH: Who?
AARON: We was goin' to be married.
NISH: Oh, her. She went away right after your funeral. Haven't heard tell of her since.
MAGGIE: Didn't I tell you? Didn't I? And you so sure she was up there pinin' away in misery.
AARON: I allow it was too much of a torment for her. Maybe she couldn't bear to stay here without me. I allow she's lonely still. No matter where.
MAGGIE: Lonely in someone else's arms, I allow.
JACK: Now, Maggie. Never mind startin' that again.
MAGGIE: Well, it's true all the same. They're all alike.
ROSE: You should know.
MAGGIE: That Edna Leonard. I bet she just couldn't wait. Had her sights set on my Tom all along and just couldn't wait for me to be dead. And poor Tom all upset on account of me dyin' so quick of a stroke, not knowin' what to do. And then she comes along all dolled off, to say she's sorry. I can see it now. Poor Tom.
NISH: They're gone too. Gone with the rest of 'em.
MAGGIE: I allow it broke he's heart to leave me behind. I suppose he's miserable married to the likes of that. Is he, Nish?
NISH: They seemed to get on the finest kind. Seemed like a good match.
MAGGIE: Puttin' on a good face, I allow. Tom was always a good hand at that, you know. Smiled he's way right through the hardest times. That was Tom. That was my Tom. Always puttin' on a good face, no matter what.
ROSE: And the Callahans all gone? No one to look after the garden. No one left to take care of my grave?
NISH: Not a soul, maid. Not a single soul left.
BRIDE: It's hard to believe they're all gone.
NED: I knew it was goin' that way. But still I couldn't see it. I thought it'd turn around in the end. I just couldn't see 'em all pullin' out. Not like that.
RAY: But they did? All of 'em?

NISH: The last Mass was said of a Sunday, and the last of 'em left on a Monday. Unless they put it off a day or two to put me down here with the rest of ye. It was either that or lug me across the bay with 'em, I guess.

RAY: It's a hard thing to picture. Nobody at all up there. No smoke from the chimbleys. Nobody stoppin' at the spring well for a yarn. No lights in the windows. Nobody walkin' in the road. No dogs barkin' in the night. Nobody goin' into the droke for firewood. Nobody laughin' or singin' or dancin'. Or dyin' even.

JACK: It is a hard thing to picture.

NISH: I'd be the last of the ones dyin' here. I'll be the last ever buried in this place.

BRIDE: Not a very nice thought.

ROSE: A sad thing it is. Too sad to think of.

JACK: I can't imagine the place all emptied out. I can't see Maud goin' at all. It must of broke her heart to leave.

NISH: She didn't leave easy, I can guarantee you that. But she couldn't very well stay all by herself.

JACK: What about Peter?

NISH: Oh, Peter's been gone several months now. He left right after Aaron died. They had a inquest after that. He was pretty shook up over it. Anyway, he left as soon as it was over. Went away somewhere. Don't know where to or what at.

JACK: I allow, whatever, he'll make out alright. He'd be a good hand at anything, Peter would. Still, it would of been a help to Maud to have him home when it come time to move.

NISH: I don't think anyone could of helped her through that racket, Jack. All hands pitched in. But that didn't make it any easier in the end. She would of found it hard to move, no matter what. She had no heart for it, no heart at all.

JACK: I imagine she wasn't the only one had it hard goin'.

NISH: A lot took it hard, b'y. Phonse Flynn was what broke my heart.

BILL: How come Phonse?

NISH: I was up in the garden tryin' to drive the horses out, and I seen Phonse up at he's pump. You know the pump he had up there behind the house. And you know the trouble he always had with it, gettin' it to work. Phonse had a fashion, you know, to curse that pump up and down every time he went to it. Sometimes it'd work right off, and sometimes it'd be cranky as anything. But Phonse never give up on 'er. Not that I seen anyway. He'd curse and prime and prime and curse until she took hold. Then he'd go away, down to the house, with he's turn of water, just as pleased as anything. But, by God, this day it was different. It was just days before Phonse was goin' to shift. He had everything packed up to go. Even had the upstairs windows all boarded up and everything. Anyway, this time the pump just wouldn't take hold no matter what. And after primin' and cursin' a bit, and then primin' and cursin' some more, and still she was as dry as a bone, he went and picked up this big rock. He didn't know I was there all the time, watchin' from among the horses in the garden, and he went and got this great big rock, damn near as big as a boulder, and he heaved it at the pump. Now, that pump was iron. And it weren't about to just tumble over. No sir. That rock just bounced off 'er and rolled away in the grass. So Phonse went and got it again, and again he fired it at the pump. Her old handle just bounced up and down a bit, and that was that. So he took a third turn at 'er. Walked right over against the pump and smashed the rock down on 'er as hard as he could. The rock just rolled away again, leavin the old pump standin' there as much in one piece as she ever was. Well, Phonse was hoppin' mad be this time and into a real fit, cursin' and swearin' and stompin' all about. And just when I figured he was goin' to give up on it and go get he's water at the spring well or something, he takes one of he's buckets and hangs it over the lip and starts workin' the handle again. And you know what? She started to pump. He pumped 'er as easy as anything 'til he's buckets was full. Then he put he's buckets aside on the ground and laid he's hoop across 'em. And you know what he done then? He went and sot down on the edge of the bank and looked at that damn pump and started to bawl like a baby. He sat there on the bank lookin' at that contrary old pump and cried enough to break he's heart. And you know Phonse Flynn. He certainly were not a man to cry about things. Not even at funerals. But he cried that day, he did, and it damn near broke my heart to see it.

BRIDE: It fair breaks mine just to hear it.

ROSE: And we're left here with no one to care if we lives or dies.

RAY: Too late for anyone to care about that.

ROSE: Left here with no one to care one way or the other. I suppose the foxes'll get us yet, what's left of us. I suppose they'll dig us up and cart us off bone by bone until we're scattered from here to the Redlands and back.

NED: It won't make much difference where we end up scattered to, Rose. Not now. I'd just as soon come to nothin' as stay laid out here like this with nothin' to remember. I can feel the memories slippin' away already on account of I got nothin' to hang 'em onto anymore. I could remember most everything thinkin' things was mostly the same up there as when I left it. But now, knowin' it ain't the same at all, knowin' how empty it is of everyone and everything, I got no place to fit them memories into, and they're all slippin' away. Slippin' fast away.

JACK: It's like me tryin' to picture Maud movin' about the house. I could always do that, no trouble. Could always see her clear as day in the kitchen bakin' bread, fryin' toutons, knittin' mitts or whatever. But now, now that she's nowhere near that same house, that same kitchen, I can't get a grip on it at all.

AARON: While I thought she was still up there, I could see her goin' and comin'. Could see every shade of her face, and that nice way she had of smilin' like her whole face was lit up with a lamp, and the shine of her hair, the way it come down in front over her shoulder. Oh, I could see her all the ways she was to me, as long as I thought she was still there. But now, when I try to think of the two of us anywhere, like lyin' in the grass on Cradle Hill and places like that, I can't make her out clear at all. One minute she's there just like she used to be, and the next minute she's fadin' away like a ghost until she's gone altogether.

ROSE: All I can think of now is my garden growin' over with weeds. Nobody to take care of the flowers, nobody to care. That was the best pride of my life, that garden was. It was planted and tended accordin' to my word. And it was the nicest flower garden around, maybe even the nicest in all the bay. People told me so much. Every Sunday in summertime one of the family brought me a vasefull for my room. It was kind of a rule, you know. As soon as they came back from Mass on a Sunday they'd bring me a bunch of flowers from the garden set in a vase. Oh, they were lovely flowers. I had them come from away, you know. And whenever they were in bloom, oh I could smell the perfume of 'em comin' in through the window. What a lovely smell they had. And now they'll all be let go, with no one to take care of 'em. They can't manage by theirselves you know, like common flowers can. They got to have a lot of care, the ones in my garden have. And now, with no one left to look out for 'em, they'll get overgrown with weeds, and then they'll die, and they'll never come to bloom again. That's what fills my mind up now. That and the grass growin' up through the blue gravel on my grave. And never a flower brought to it ever again. *(Trying not to cry.)* It's enough to make a person cry.

BILL: I never minded dyin', when my time come to die, 'cause I could always think that after I was gone, when youngsters born after my time was growin' up, they'd come strollin' past my grave and they'd ask their fathers maybe, or their uncles, or whoever was older than them, "Who was that Captain Sullivan?" And the older fellow could tell 'em that Bill Sullivan was a master mariner, skipper of nine different vessels in he's time, one of the most respected sailin' captains that ever sailed out of Placentia Bay, the only man anyone knows who rode out the August Gale, the man who carried more salt fish across the ocean than any other man in livin' memory. That's what they'd know. And that's what they'd say if anyone asked. And there wouldn't be no lies in it neither. But now I suppose no one will ever be askin' who I was when I was livin', 'cause there'll be no way now they'll even know that I was alive. A tombstone standin' in the middle of the woods don't serve to remind nobody of nothin'.

RAY: I don't suppose we're jumpin' the gun by any chance. After all they wasn't gone anywhere by the time Nish ... died. Maybe they changed their minds and stayed. Maybe they're still there like they always was.

NISH: It was too late for anyone to change their minds after I went. It was all gone too far be then to be turned around. It was only the last of 'em left to go anyway. More than half was already gone. And the houses was boarded up, some of 'em knocked down altogether, everything packed up. The school was closed up all fall. The hardwood took down off the ceilings, the floors tore up. The only thing left to be closed up was the church, and I did that myself. I suppose they might of used it one more time after that, for my funeral, but they never planned on that. No, they're gone, there's no mistake about that. If you could go up and take a look, you wouldn't believe your eyes. You'd never say you was in St. Kevin's, that's for sure.

RAY: How come you closed up the church? Was the priest already gone?

NISH: No, he was still there. Said the last Mass that Sunday. Made a fine sermon about changes being sometimes for the best even if they was hard changes to make. And about how it wasn't a end to anything, but a new beginnin'. And how everyone should be thankful for the opportunities that laid ahead. And how we should face up to the future with courage and hope and all that. It was right after Mass that I went and hung myself.

JACK: How come Nish?

NISH: Father McCormack asked a few fellows to stay behind after Mass that Sunday to pack up some stuff he wanted to take away with him. Mostly things from he's house. And after we was finished packin' up what he wanted to take, mostly books as far as I could tell, he told me to go and make sure the furnace was out in the church and to lock up all the doors. I went, thinkin' it'd somehow be different in there. But everything inside was the same as it always was. Just like after any other Mass of a Sunday morning. The light from outside was streamin' in through the windows. The altar looked the same as ever, the candles all in a row, all them plastic flowers lookin' as fresh as the first day they was put there, the altar cloths all nice and white, the tabernacle cross gleamin' like gold. And that ugly old pelican there on the front of the altar still doin' her best to feed them scrawny youngsters. And the Blessed Virgin, up there above the altar, still standin' on her tip-toes on that cloud with all them fat little baby angels flyin' around. And all along the seats in the pews everything left lyin' there, missals and rosary beads and a scattered cap here and there, all lyin' where they was left just like any old Sunday. And when I went in to the vestry, to get the keys out of the drawer, it was the same in there. I expected it to be half empty, at least, but all the vestments was still hangin' in the closet; purple, gold, white, green, black. And the altar boys' garb hangin' in the cupboard where they was put after Mass. And three or four bottles of wine in there too. When I seen the wine, I thought to meself how close that batch come to being turned into the blood of Christ, and how, now, it'd never turn into nothin but a waste. I don't think it would of been half so bad if the place was emptied out, if it weren't so much like just another Sunday. But I got so full up that it was everything I could do to keep a hold of myself. And when I went to go out, to lock up like I was told, it struck me that I might be the last one ever in there. And then I just couldn't leave without sayin' one last prayer. So I went up to the altar rail and kneeled down and tried to think a prayer of some kind. But neither prayer that I could think of seemed to be the right one. And that's when I broke down for the first time since I was a baby I s'pose. And it weren't for the church I felt so bad, but for all that was goin' on outside. All the stuff goin' on all fall and still goin' on that same minute. And nobody able to do a damn thing about it, to put a stop to it. That was the worst, the painfullest part. And when I got up to go, I seen that all the statues, all them inside the altar rail and over in the corner, they was all starin' at me. Starin' right at me with their blank eyes. I always used to think how much they looked to be blind as bats standin' up there seemin' to be bored to death with their own holiness. But they never looked bored that mornin'. St. Joseph, St. Theresa, The Sacred Heart, Our Lady standin' on that snake with her toe broke off. When I was a youngster I used to think it was that snake that bit her toe off, and everytime I'd go to church, I'd look to see if he got either other one, but he never did. So there she was that day, with just the one toe missin', starin' right at me along with the rest of 'em. Like they was putting the blame on me for everyone goin' off and leavin' 'em. And I knew right then that I wouldn't be goin' nowhere. It weren't like I made a choice about it or anything like that. It was more like someone else made up me mind to it. It might of been the devil for all I know. But there wasn't no way around it then. There was just no way I could bring myself to go out there and watch 'em all packin' their gear, gettin' ready for to leave the next day, and all hands expectin' me to go along with 'em. It mightn't of been a very good thing to do, but I couldn't see as I had any choice about it. So I went around and locked up all the doors from the inside. And then I went into the basement, made sure the fire was out in the furnace, and then I got a piece of rope, a couple of fathoms of it, nylon, that was lyin' in the basement, and I went straight up into the choir loft and tied one

end of the rope to the rail and the other end around me neck. Then I got up on top of the rail and jumped. With the keys still in me pocket.
SHEILA: *(Weeping.)* Mom! Mom!
BRIDE: Hush, child. Hush now. There's nothin' to be frightened of.
ROSE: Poor thing. It's nightmare enough for all of us. But what it must be for her!
MAGGIE: Well, what would you expect with some of the things she hears goin' on all around.
JACK: She got her own things to be afraid of, I allow, with or without the stuff she hears.
BRIDE: She's just a child and she misses her mother.
SHEILA: *(Weeping.)* Mom!
RAY: *(Singing haltingly.)*

>As I roved out one evening
>T'was in the month of June
>The birds were singing merrily
>All nature was in tune
>
>The ...
>The ...
>
>As I roved out one evening
>T'was in the month of June
>The birds were singing merrily
>All nature was in tune
>
>The ...

That's queer. I sung that song a thousand times and never forgot a word of it. Now I haven't got the words or the tune neither.
(Singing awkwardly.)

>It was on a summer's evening
>All in the month of ...

No Sir! Just can't get it. The first time in my life I ever started a song I couldn't finish.
JACK: I wonder if that's a sign that we're runnin' out of time, gettin' on to the end of it. Remember all the times before, how it was either our memories or our voices started to fade away, until we couldn't speak or remember nothin' at all.
RAY: It certainly isn't like me to forget a song I know so good as that.
BILL: We never did get much more time than this out of it. It

always come to a end too soon.
ROSE: It should of ended before we knew what was goin' on up there.
BILL: It's come to a bad end, that's for sure. When you think of people livin' up there for hundreds of years gone past, and now, all-of-a-sudden, not a soul there to draw a breath. It's a bad end we come to.
NISH: I should of kept me mouth shut, like I done all my life.
JACK: It's none of your fault, Nish.
MAGGIE: I allow it's a part of the devil's own plan. That's what I allow.
BILL: It would of made a difference to this spell to know someone was still up there goin' on with what life we left behind. It would of made a difference.
ROSE: It's hard to see how anything'll make any difference anymore, after this. I feel like I'm worth no more than a emmit that got squat to death and swept aside. We lived for a while with high hopes, thinkin' we was something precious just because we was human beings. Seems now we was never no better than the emmits crawlin' around on the ground.
MAGGIE: Well, I never thought I'd be dead long enough to hear you talkin' like that, Rose. You who was always such a religious soul. Always thinkin' a few prayers was enough to get us out of this, get us into Heaven.
ROSE: I'm not sayin' I've give up on that. I'm just sayin' how it don't seem anyone cares about us one way or the other.
BILL: It's gettin' to look pretty hopeless to me.
AARON: Me too. More and more like Hell.
JACK: Now, there's no reason, really, to be thinkin' like that. I don't know where we are any more than ye do. I know we're not in Heaven but apart from that I wouldn't be too quick to say what this is all about. All we know for sure is that we're dead and buried and that there's some power at work, some power higher than us, that gives us this time to think things over.
MAGGIE: So, what's the good of that?
JACK: Well, we don't know right now. But look at it this way. If this is All Souls Night like we figured out, then it fits in someway with the stuff we believed in before we died. Like Ned said, one way or another we all believed, when we was alive, that the souls of them that was dead, would all be up and about on All Souls Night. And it got to be our souls that's operatin' here. It isn't our bodies, that's for sure. Most of us haven't even got tongues to talk with or brains to think with, and we're talkin' and thinkin'. What else could it be but our souls? And if that much fits into what we used to believe in, the religion we had when we was alive, then maybe the rest of it will fit in too, when the time comes.

ROSE: Like Heaven? The way we always pictured it?
JACK: Yeah.
MAGGIE: Like Hell, too?
JACK: Well, yes! Heaven and Hell too. But the point is, this state we're in don't fit any more into what Hell is supposed to be any more that it do Heaven. That's all I'm saying. That we still don't know for sure what lies ahead of us. And it could still be Heaven.
BILL: I don't know, Jack, b'y. I thought much the same as that before I knew the crowd up there was all gone away. But now, being left here where we lies, to be forgot about forever, it's hard to imagine anything good up ahead.
NED: What bothers me is, if God was in charge of this racket, what's He doin' keepin' a little child here all this time. What have He got to gain out of that? The poor girl hardly lived long enough to do anyone any harm, so I can't see how God could be the blame for keepin' her here. And then to smack her in the face with this stuff about her mother and father movin' away! Never to come back to the place she lived in and died in and is buried in. That's the height of cruelness if you ask me. And it got to be the work of the devil. No one else I knows, would do the likes of that.
BRIDE: Perhaps it's just that we're not long enough dead yet. I know I'm not here near so long as you, Bill, or the most of ye, and perhaps I got to stay even longer than ye. Who knows! Still, I'd like to think that sometime, sometime soon, we'll all be together up in Heaven. And then, what difference will it make where our crowd is scattered to? Then we'd know where they was, what they was doin' with theirselves. And I don't doubt for a minute that they'd still remember us, and think about us, and talk about us, no matter where they was livin' to? I feels tired now, too tired to think, like I'm fallin' asleep, and it's gettin hard to think anything at all.
BILL: I allow you are tired, my dear, after all this. It's enough to make anyone worn out, this is.
RAY: Just like me not being able to think of any songs. That's the way it's went before. The kind of tiredness that comes on just before this spell comes to a end.
JACK: Do anyone else feel like that? Like a sleepiness overtakin' 'em?
NISH: I do. And ... all-of-a-sudden it ... it's gettin' hard ... harder to talk. It's like I was ... was goin' back to the way ... the way I was when ... when I was a ... alive.
RAY: Don't worry about that, Nish b'y. It got nothin' to do with that. We'll all be deaf and dumb soon. Like we were since this time last year.
MAGGIE: Maybe now it'll be all over and done with. None of this

no more. And it'd be better, really. What's the use of being able to talk and think when there's nothin' more to be thought about or said?

NISH: I wish now that ... that they buried me ... outside ... outside of the fence. Or didn't bury me ... at all. I'm not ... not sorry for what I done ... to myself. But I do feel bad for ... for what I went and said. I'm sorry for that. It would of been ... better ... if I hadn't of told ye ... told ye what went on. It'd be better ... better if ye never knew.

JACK: No need to feel like that, Nish. The truth do hurt. But we got to put up with that. What went on up there is no fault of yours.

BILL: And besides, it's no worse for us than it is for yourself. You're here too, isn't you?

(Silence.)

JACK: Nish!

(Silence.)

You still there, Nish?

(Silence.)

Is he gone?

RAY: Nish!

(Silence.)

BILL: I allow he's gone.

JACK: Looks like it, don't it?

RAY: Poor bugger!

NED: Is he the first?

JACK: I suppose he is.

RAY: What about Aaron?

JACK: Aaron! You still here? Aaron?

AARON: Still here. Tryin' to remember ... something. Something to do with a girl and a ... a ...

JACK: Hard to remember, hey!

AARON: Like a dream I might of had. There's bits and pieces out of it. There's a cradle into it. A baby's cradle and a ring . ... and a girl. And there is a awful explosion, like thunder, and a bird, a bird goin' to wing, a bird with a woman's face flyin' out to sea. And I callin' out to 'er, callin' 'er to come back. But I can't remember her name.

(Silence.)

JACK: Aaron!

(Silence.)

RAY: Gone?

JACK: Gone!

NED: Gone and better off.

JACK: Aaron!

(Silence.)

He was a fine young fellow, you know. Him and Peter, the finest kind of fellows. I was always proud of 'em. Proud of the both of 'em.

ROSE: I'm sure you had cause to be, Jack Leonard. What father isn't proud of he's own sons? But what father don't turn a blind eye to their faults, too?

JACK: What is it you're gettin' at now?

ROSE: Well, I hate to say it, but the more I think of it the more this is gettin' to look like Hell to me too. It's the only thing that makes it all fit together.

JACK: I'd rather you kept on prayin' for something better, than to be talkin' like that, Rose.

ROSE: You take Aaron, now. I mean he come right out and said he committed sins with that girl, didn't he. And I dare say he did, the way they gets on these days. And that's a mortal sin, as you all know. And isn't Hell the place for them that dies with mortal sins on their souls, dies without repentance?

JACK: How do you know he died without repentin'? He might of gone to Confession a dozen times since then.

ROSE: There wasn't much repentance there as far as I could tell. And he certainly never said he was sorry for none of it. He was sorry he died so soon, but he never said he was sorry for what sins he committed while he was alive. And take Maggie. I don't mind sayin' it for you to hear either, Maggie. You never gave any hint of ever being sorry for the sins you committed. And they was the same kind of sins, sins of the flesh, mortal sins. And God knows Hell 'd be the proper place for the likes of you.

MAGGIE: It was no fault of mine that men found me good lookin'. Maybe you'd of had a few turns at it too, if you hadn't of been such a crippled up old witch all your life.

ROSE: That's what I mean, see. Do you call that repentence? Sure the tongue on that woman would be enough to send her to Hell, not even countin' all the other stuff.

MAGGIE: My, it's nice to be buried alongside of a saint!

ROSE: And that's not all either. Nish is another good case of it. Everyone knows suicide is just about the worst thing a person could ever do. I mean that is a terrible sin, no mistake. And where is Nish, now that he's dead? Right here is where. Right here in the same place with Aaron and Maggie. Now you put all that together. Where would you expect people like that to go when they died? Wouldn't you expect they'd go to Hell? And if that's where they went, and it's the same place we're all into, then don't that mean that we're all in Hell? God knows why we should be, but isn't that the way it looks? I mean don't it all seem to add up to that?

JACK: No, Rose. It don't. Because whatever about the rest of us, there's still Sheila. And whatever it is we're into here, she's here with us. And that's good enough for me to know that it can't be

Hell we're into. Like Ray says, maybe it's Purgat'ry. It could be that, I s'pose. But as long as she's here, then as bad as it is, it can't be Hell.

ROSE: I know it'd be a mistake on somebody's part if I ended up in Hell.

MAGGIE: Accordin' to all the Catechism I ever learned, Pride is one of the seven deadly sins. And if that's so, Rose Hepditch, my dear, you got enough of it in you to keep you in Hell forever.

BRIDE: *(Weakly.)* Mr. Bill! I feels like I'm gettin' weak. Like I'm fadin' away from ye. All that talk is all cloudy to me, like a fog. Words comin' and goin' all around with no sense to 'em at all. Too tired to keep up with it anymore. It's like I was dyin' all over again.

BILL: Don't go frettin', Bride. We'll all be goin' that way now. Into nothin'. It's the most we can hope for now, girl. And there's no harm in it. No harm at all.

BRIDE: *(Fading.)* I wish ... I could ... come over and ... and tuck you in.

BILL: I'm tucked in tight enough, Bride. It's nice to know you're here, though, not gone off on your own with the crowd up there. We lived a long spell together, me and you, and it's only fittin' that we're together here, wherever we is. I hope you haves a good sleep now, Bride, a good rest with nothin' or no one to bother you.

RAY: I think she's gone, Skipper Bill.

BILL: Is you, Bride? Is you gone, girl?

(Silence.)

Rest in peace, my dear. Rest in peace.

NED: You might as well wish me ... the same thing ... Skipper ... if you got a mind to ... because I'm on the way out too. Everything is closin' in on me.

JACK: There's nothin' to be done for it, Ned, b'y. Just let go easy is all.

NED: I wouldn't mind so much if ... if I could keep a good picture of the shop ... in my mind. I spent over half of my life in ... in that shop and ... I can't even picture it ... the way ... the way it used to be. Can't picture where things was ... where I kept things ... the biscuits ... or the kerosene ... or the cheese. I wish I could have ... one more look at 'er ... the way she used to be ... with the shelfs full of provisions ... right up to the ceiling ... and people comin' in and goin' out ... on their way up and down the road. It'd be a good memory ... like a snap ... to take with me. But mostly ... in my mind ... now ... it's a picture of 'er all beat up ... smashed to pieces. Everything beat to ... beat to ... pieces.

RAY: It's hard to keep anything good in mind anymore. It's a hard old racket we're into now, Ned, b'y.

NED: Well, it'll be ... goodnight to you now. Time ... time to close 'er

up ... for the night. Time ... to close ... 'er up for good.
RAY: Goodnight to you, too, Ned.
JACK: Goodnight, Ned.
BILL: Goodnight, Ned.
MAGGIE: *(Mimicking.)* Goodnight, Ned! What a lot of foolishness. Like that's all it was, just another night, with another mornin' comin' on.
JACK: Now, Maggie, don't go makin' it any worse than it is. It's just as well to be civilized about it.
MAGGIE: Yes, I suppose it is. Seein' as how we're into such a civilized place.
(Thunder.)
BILL: Ah, there it is, b'ys. Time for all of us to say goodnight.
JACK: Just like all the times before. The thunder on the first of it and the thunder at the end.
RAY: I wonder is it real thunder. Up above, I mean. Is it the night up there we're hearin', or is it just a thunder in the ground?
(Thunder.)
SHEILA: *(Screaming.)* Mom! Mommy!
JACK: It's only thunder, child. Just a bit of weather. Nothin' to be frightened about.
SHEILA: *(Shivering.)* It ain't that, Mr. Leonard, it ain't the thunder.
JACK: What then?
SHEILA: I'm frightened I won't get to sleep. Scared I'll be here wide awake all by me ownself, after ye're all gone.
JACK: No. No. I'll stay here with you, here by your side, until you falls sound asleep. I won't leave you here alone. I promise. Don't you go worryin' about that, now.
SHEILA: I don't want to be left all alone in Hell.
JACK: Now, see! That's just Rose puttin' things in your mind. Don't you pay any attention to stuff like that. It's only talk, that's all, and no truth to it at all. You're nowhere near Hell here, believe me. And you're not goin' to go to Hell either. It's Heaven you're goin' to. And soon, too. Sooner than you think. The best thing is to go to sleep now.
SHEILA: I don't feel sleepy.
RAY: Remember when I used to sing you to sleep? You was just a infant then. I'd come to have a spell with your father in the evenings after supper, and your mother would put you in my arms where I'd be sittin' on the daybed by the stove, and I'd sing you a little song I made just for you.
SHEILA: *(Singing.)* Sleepy-time child the sandman is
RAY: here.
SHEILA: He's sprinkling sand in your eyes.
(Pause.)
RAY: Your Guardian Angel will stay very near

SHEILA: *(Joining in.)* 'Til you wake with the morning sunrise
RAY: Sleepy-time child it's time to let go
Let go of your wide awake day
It's time to close your sleepy blue eyes
And let your dreams drift you away.

Sleepy-time child the stars are aglow.

JACK: *(Joining in.)* The moon is a silvery bright
Your Mommy and Daddy want you to know
They love you and wish you Good-night.

RAY: *(Alone.)* They love you and wish you Good-night.

SHEILA: *(Slowly.)* Now I lay me down to sleep
I pray the Lord my soul to keep.
If I should die before I wake
I pray the Lord ... my soul ... to take.
(Thunder.)
(Silence.)
JACK: Is she gone?
RAY: I think she is. And none too soon either.
JACK: It's a shame youngsters got to die.
BILL: It's a shame anyone got to die, if this is what it's all about.
MAGGIE: It's a shame I had to die. A shame for poor Tom, I mean. I wish I could talk to him. I feel like my voice is just about to leave me. I wish I could talk to Tom once more before it goes altogether. I'd tell him to save he's money, not to go wastin' it havin' all them High Masses said for me. I'd tell him to get on with he's own life, make the best of it, not to go wastin' he's time thinkin' about me all the time. But I suppose it'd be no good to tell him that. That's my Tom all over, you know. Even while he was married to the woman in he's bed, he'd be lyin' there in misery, keepin' it all secret to he's self, but wishin' all along that it was me, he's Maggie, lyin' there next to him.
ROSE: Do you really believe that, Maggie?
MAGGIE: Of course I don't. Rose Hepditch, you are the most insultin' person I ever run into. You think I'm so stunned as that, to be believin' such foolishness.
ROSE: Well, why would you be gettin' on like that, if you didn't believe it?
MAGGIE: What else would you have me do? Lie here thinkin' on nothin' but the truth? That he's up there now without ever so much as a thought about me in he's head? That he's probably happy as a lark being married up to Edna Leonard instead of me? He could of married me anytime he had a mind to, but he never did. Had he's sights set on her all along, I allow. No, girl,

I'm not near so foolish to believe the stuff I makes up. It's only that I wish he did miss me a bit. *(Weeping.)* I wish there was someone up there who might of been sorry to see me lyin' in a coffin. Someone who might of cried a tear to see me lowered in the ground. That's not too much to ask, is it? Just that somebody, anybody at all, would remember me enough to miss me, now that I'm gone.

ROSE: Well, bless my bones, if you don't beat all, Maggie Green! How could anyone ever make head or tail out of the likes of you? Sayin' one thing and meanin' another? No wonder they thought you was too contrary to live with, maid.

(Thunder.)

RAY: No good talkin' to Maggie no more, Aunt Rose. Them was her last words.

BILL: Yeah, it's one by one, and quick, we're goin' now.

ROSE: Time for me to go too. No sense hangin' on here any longer. I hope I got enough strength left to say one last Act of Contrition, that's all. So if ye'll excuse me, I'll be at my prayers, and leave ye to say your own. *(Praying.)* Oh, my God, I am heartily sorry for having offended thee. I detest all my sins ... *(Angrily.)* What's that I'm sayin'? I never offended You in my whole life, that I know of. And apart from Original Sin, which was certainly no fault of mine, I don't know that I got any sins to detest. The devil can take me, for all I care. But I'm done apologizin' for stuff I never did. I spent the best part of ninety years alive lyin' in bed tryin' to make up for sins I never even had the chance to commit. I'm sick and tired of it. And I'm not goin' to do it no more. So there! Like Maggie Green, might say, "You can take the Act of Contrition and ... and ... stick it!"

BILL: Good God, Rose, what's got into you?

RAY: It's a wonder He don't strike you dead, Aunt Rose.

ROSE: He already did, didn't He?

RAY: I mean it's a wonder He don't ... well, I don't know what he could do to you that's any worse than this, but, by God, Aunt Rose, I don't expect He'd take too kindly to that, girl.

JACK: Ah, that's just one of Rose's fits, sure. No harm in it. Just Rose into a temper, that's all. I'm sure God is not goin' to pay too much attention to that. Why don't you try some other prayer, Rose, besides the Act of Contrition, something harmless like a Hail Mary or something. It'll make you feel better.

ROSE: I feel better right now than I ever felt before in my life, or in my death either, for that matter. I should have give Him a piece of my mind the first time I woke up here and seen all the good all my prayin' did me. I wasted enough time on that. All my prayin' is over, and done with. Thank God! I spent so much of a century sayin' prayers, now that there's none left to say' I don't know what to be sayin'. So I'll just say good-night and be done of

it. Good-night and God bless.
JACK: That's the best, girl. That's the best.
BILL: So long, Rose, old girl. You was a independent creature, I'll say that much for you. Stubborn as a old barnacle right to the end. I allow you didn't have it no easier than anyone else, all them years in bed, no matter how much gab went on about it. But whatever it was or wasn't worth, it's over now. Over for you, and for me, and for the works of us.
(Thunder.)
JACK: Not much time left now.
BILL: None at all left for me, b'ys. Time for me to pass on.
JACK: Well, Skipper, havin' Bride here alongside must be a bit of comfort to you.
BILL: Yeah! No more I'll be leavin' she to go to Golden Bay. No more her havin' to wait and wonder, with the wind enough to knock the house down, and us out on the water with nothin' but a bit of canvas to get us home. No more of that misery for Bride, now. No more cryin' out of relief to see me comin' in with neither spar left upright, and every man-jack of the crew still aboard of 'er. No, sir, no more August Gales for Bride to ride out.
RAY: One in a lifetime is enough, old man.
BILL: Still, I could stand one more, myself, Ray, b'y. One more storm to be out in. One more load o' salt to carry back from Spain. One more trip to the West Indies. One more summer on the Labrador. Or just one more day out in a dory with a little gaff sail. That'd be enough. As long as it was on the water, it'd be enough. But them times is gone. No more of that for me. So it's just as well I knocked off rememberin' it. Just as well I knocked off everything all together. So I'll see ya b'ys. See ya.
JACK: Be seein' ya, Skipper.
RAY: So long, Bill. So long, old man.
BILL: So long, b'ys. See ya ... come ... come summer ... in Golden Bay.
(Thunder.)
(Silence.)
RAY: I guess we're all that's left then, Jack. You and me.
JACK: Looks like it, Ray b'y.
RAY: Our turn now, then.
JACK: Yeah, our turn now.
RAY: I wish I knew what to say to ya, Jack. But there's nothin' to say now that'd make any difference, is there?
JACK: You can tell me one thing, Ray, before the both of us is gone. I hadn't the nerve to ask you while the child and the women was still here. But you're a sensible fellow, always had a good head on your shoulders and I know I'll get a honest answer out of you. I been thinkin' more all the time that we might very well be cast off in Hell. Know what I mean? I'm not altogether certain about

it. But I must say, it looks that way to me. What do you think, Ray? Makin' no bones about it, do you think we're all stuck in Hell?
(Silence.)
Or do you think there's either shred of hope left yet? What do you think, Ray? Are we stuck in Hell or what?
(Thunder.)
Ray!
(Silence.)
You gone too, Ray? So quick as that?
(Silence.)
I guess you are then. And that means it's time for me to turn in too. It's a long night ahead, and no one to say goodnight to. *(Louder.)* Except you Maud, maid. *(Shouting.)* I don't hold it against you for goin', Maud. I want you to know that. I know you had no choice in it. And even if you did, I know it couldn't of been a easy thing to do. I hope you're not down-hearted on account of it. What with me and Aaron passed away and Peter gone off, there wasn't that much left here for you to stay on for, even if you could of. So I don't blame you none, Maud. The main thing is for you to be content. No sense grievin' over what's gone past. Just be glad you're alive, girl. *(Quietly.)* Wherever you are now, wherever you're gone to, just be glad that you're still alive.
(Thunder.)

A VOICE: The sleeping dead lie silent now in the soil of their discontent, their souls embalmed with their bones. The insects resume their remedy for rot and the echoless earth again fills up the mouths of the dear departed.

The darkness the dead inhabit inhabits the world above them, and even the animals move from minute to minute with unfamiliar fear. The pitch-black oval of water that is Chapel Pond slips slowly into Middle Brook and whispers its way down the dark land to its eternal communion with the darker sea.

The debris in the landwash flows in and out with the rise and fall of the ocean's endless edge. Here the relics of lives once lived glow in the phosphorescent dark. White plastic bleach bottles, red plastic motor-oil bottles, tin cans, bits and pieces of nylon rope (red, yellow, white, and blue.), an enamelled oven door, an iron damper, a rocking chair rocker, a broken cradle, a picture frame framing what might have been a picture of The Scared Heart, the keel and stern-post of an old skiff, pieces of longers and ochre-coloured boards, a rusty awl, a tobacco tin, a baby's bottle with nipple erect, pleading for a mouth. These are the artifacts, the left-overs of human lives, seeking their consummation in the sea or the sand.

In the graveyard below the waterfall of Ladore, where once the meagre rituals of the living sustained them in their fervent hope of everlasting life, the dead, lying alone in desolate death, their eyeless sockets blind to the geography of the sky, are unaware that the first snow of winter is just now beginning to fall on the vacant village of St. Kevin's.

The End

Young Triffie Been Made Away With

1985

Written by
Ray Guy

Young Triffie Been Made Away With was first produced by the Resource Centre for the Arts at the LSPU Hall, April 10-14 and April 16-21, 1985.

Director	Mary Walsh
Set Director	Gerald Squires
Doctor Melrose	Rick Boland
Grace Melrose	Janis Spence
Pastor Pottle	Andy Jones
Millie Bishop	Jane Dingle
Billy Head	Greg Thomey
Andrew Hepditch	Brian Hennessey
Washbourne	Charlie Tomlinson

YOUNG TRIFFIE BEEN MADE AWAY WITH

Act I
Scene 1 - November 1947, 7:30 pm

(The Melrose dining/living room. MRS. MELROSE is reading a magazine. She goes to the window, looks out, then returns to her original position. Enter DR. MELROSE. He has left his overcoat and doctor's bag in the porch. He removes jacket and throws it on a chair. He walks to liquor supply on the buffet by the dining table. He pours a drink.)

DR. MELROSE: Cheers.
MRS. MELROSE: I didn't expect you to be late, Percy. Not just for one of those.
DR. MELROSE: Well, Mrs. Bishop went into hysterics. She took some calming down. Or, rather, knocking out. Thought I was going to have to hit her with a chair. Of course, she was the one who found the ... er, is there any, um ...
(He gestures at dining table.)
MRS. MELROSE: *(Rising, laying aside book, starts toward kitchen.)* Of course there is. I'd say it's well past it's gourmet peak by now but ... What's that they say about a doctor's dinner? "A lukewarm dish after a hot dash toward cold ingratitude?"
DR. MELROSE: *(Pouring another drink.)* That's pretty good. Sounds original.
MRS. MELROSE: No. *Reader's Digest*, I think.
(MRS. MELROSE returns with a plate covered by another. Sets it on the table.)
DR. MELROSE: *(Seating himself.)* And there was a rumour that Pastor "Damnation" Pottle was arousing his little band of brethren to march off and do damage to Old Man Washbourne. So I had to stay and see that cleared up.
MRS. MELROSE: Washbourne. What could he have to do with anything?
DR. MELROSE: Nothing, I suppose. It's just that the good folk of Swyers Harbour think that the Pastor and his little flock would go for someone like Washbourne after this latest outrage against

God and man. He lives apart and alone. He's eccentric. This makes five now, you know. Anyhow, it was only a rumour. But to pacify the lot of them I had to take four men in the car and we drove in to the Pastor's little tarpaper tabernacle. The lights were all out in there but, by God, what they lacked in light they made up for in sound. Most appalling roars and screeches. Sounded more like the boiler room in hell than ... than anything else. But after some urging, the chairman of our little citizen's vigilante committee got out and went to the door. He tried his knuckles, then both fists, and then he literally had to pound on the door with a rock. I think the sudden silence was even more startling than the racket. By and by, out comes the Pastor. The Chairman stated the good burghers' suspicions and, by God, he went off like Mount Vesuvius: "Hellfire and eternal damnation to ye who bear false witness. The bottomless pit and sulphur and brimstone to ye what slandereth thy neighbour." A whole string of these mild endearments. Charlie came back to the car ... Charlie Piercy, it was ... looking like he'd just tangled with the devil himself. We could still hear him quarter mile down the road. It was something, I can tell you.

MRS. MELROSE: When did he come here?

DR. MELROSE: Who, dear?

MRS. MELROSE: The Parson. How long's he been in Swyers Harbour.

DR. MELROSE: Oh, I don't know. Must be seventeen, eighteen years ago. It was shortly after we came, anyway. You remember. His wife died in childbirth. She was one of my first, um, losses.

MRS. MELROSE: Of course, I remember, too, dear. Of course.

DR. MELROSE: Ha. Remember how he started off? He tried to proselytize out front of the Post Office. Mrs. Bishop ... Aunt Millie, she soon put the run on him. Poor Aunt Millie, she had her own little corner in hell permanently reserved from then on.

MRS. MELROSE: Yes, and then he rented the school. The school board was glad to take his couple of dollars until ... until he began hooking in a few Methodists and even the occasional Church of Englander. He got his walking papers once more.

DR. MELROSE: Right. But by then he was far enough ahead to set up shop in by the road ... in by the Twillick Pond, convenient for his total immersions. All he's gotta do is kick 'em out the back door. But I must say, the Pastor's got quite the grip on his little flock. Right by the short hairs. I've told you this before but I've had the scattered escapee, or bolter, you know, backslider, come in here claiming to be suffering from double pneumonia or something ... from being dipped, immersed, six months or a year before. Oh, he's got 'em copperfastened, all right.

MRS. MELROSE: (*Bitterly*.) But the fools. The idiots. They throw away their insulin. They practically let their appendixes

burst. Do you think it's because of his ... his wife, or something?
DR. MELROSE: Oh, I don't know, dear. With a mind like that who does? I mean, he let me take out her tonsils ... his daughter, what's her name, Triffie? And when she had that broken rib ...
MRS. MELROSE: Perce, you've *got* to do something. Accident, my foot. It's probably going on still. You *must* do something.
DR. MELROSE: Oh, come on, dear, I've told you how it is. I decided on that. It's the lesser of two evils. You know, I often wonder.
MRS. MELROSE: What?
DR. MELROSE: Pottle and his happy band. What do they get out of it? What keeps them ticking? What sort of kick do they get out of it?
MRS. MELROSE: They gloat. Gloating is a form of happiness. They know that when the rest of Swyers Harbour are suffering in hell's flames for eternity they'll be floating around on Cloud Nine. Oh, yes. Well, see for yourself. They're the bottom of the barrel right now, right. They come from the low end of the social scale. And the economic scale. They're more or less despised ... or at least ... mocked by their neighbours. But, by God, one day, the great Judgement Day, won't the tables be turned. Then they'll be the ones ... while the others are howling forever over a slow fire ... they'll be the ones who'll be enjoying the new chesterfield suites, the Aladdin lamps, the gas washing machines ... whatever goodies they suppose are waiting for them up there.
DR. MELROSE: That's why they're so hot to trot for the end of the world, I guess.
MRS. MELROSE: Ah, yes. Revenge is what they want. And they know it's coming sure and soon. So they gloat. And that makes them happy. What a comfort religion is, to be sure, in more ways than one.
DR. MELROSE: Guess you're right my dear, but it has not made the practice of medicine any easier for yours truly. It's like trying to outflank the witch doctor to inoculate some Hottentots or something. By the way, the Ranger's been sent for. Expected tomorrow. New chap named Hepditch, I think it is.
MRS. MELROSE: The Ranger? But they're only ...
DR. MELROSE: But this is the fifth, you see. There's something hellish going on here and that little bit of trouble we had this evening ... I mean, things could get out of hand.
MRS. MELROSE: Was she ... was she mutilated, too?
DR. MELROSE: Oh, yes. Her sexual organs were cut out completely. Really neat job of it, too, I must say. So were the other four.
MRS. MELROSE: And her legs were broken?
DR. MELROSE: Well, that's the odd thing. That's the only little difference from the others. Her legs were broken, alright, but only three of them. The other sheep had all four legs broken.

MRS. MELROSE: Why do they only pick on ewes, I wonder? Could that be some sort of clue?

DR. MELROSE: Oh, I don't know, my dear. It's a male world, I guess. Anyway, lordy, but Aunt Millie Bishop was a sight to behold. Couldn't blame her, I suppose. She'd gone out around her henhouse to look for one of her pullets and this ... this thing hit her square in the face. It was hanging by the neck with it's one unbroken leg pointing straight up at the sky like the finger of doom or something. "The Stranger," shrieks Aunt Millie. "It was the Stranger done it. I knowed it. I knowed it. I seen him."

MRS. MELROSE: The Stranger?

DR. MELROSE: Yeah. The Stranger. Every place like this comes equipped with a stranger. Surely you've heard of him. I'll bet the Stranger was around ever since Swyers Harbour was founded. Maybe before. Anyway, he's a lively old bird, the Stranger is ... especially during a war or just after. Lots of people have seen his foot prints in the sand or the snow or the mud. But few claim to have ever seen him.

MRS. MELROSE: Aw. It's just more of their idiotic hogwash.

DR. MELROSE: Maybe so, my dear. But, you know, the Stranger always leaves his calling card. If a horse is snorting and terrified in its stall in the morning, why, the Stranger has been sleeping on the hay all night. If the stage door is found open and a knife or a hatchet is missing ... the Stranger has been sleeping on a pile of nets. It's the Stranger, you see, who steals turnips from the cellar or hens from the roost. It's he who's spotted skulking through the woods on the other side of the harbour. And if, some pitch black night, someone is coming toward you and you hail him and he doesn't answer but picks up speed and hurries past ... well, you've just had a brush with the Stranger.

MRS. MELROSE: Oh, stop it, Percy. Surely you don't believe that nonsense. Good Lord, you're as soft in the head as these ... these people, themselves.

DR. MELROSE: Ok. Ok. But I think there's a reason they believe in the Stranger. Imagine it. Suppose you were stuck in an isolated place like this, hemmed in, little communication with the outside. Your imagination goes sort of funny. You get a little bit paranoid. After all, when these communities were first founded they were founded where they are for two reasons, fish and fear. Fish and fear of the Stranger ... the Pirate, the Navy, the Law, the Pillagers, the French. So you can imagine, my dear ...

MRS. MELROSE: Imagine. Imagine. Why the hell should I have to imagine what living in a suffocating, cretinous bastard of a place like this is like? Why? Answer me. Answer me.

DR. MELROSE: Now, Grace. Now, now. I'm just trying to say, darling, that to these people right now the Stranger could be an escaped murderer, a stranded German spy, a shell-shocked veteran, an army deserter, an escaped lunatic. And, yes, I suppose, even one of the walking dead. Anyway, I wish you could have seen Aunt Millie's hysterics. *She's* a true believer, no mistake about it. Ah, we mustn't make mock. She's got her troubles, too, Aunt Millie Bishop has.

MRS. MELROSE: What?

DR. MELROSE: Her son, what's his name? Vincent. You remember, you had him in your Sunday School class. Said he was the shyest kid you'd ever met. Blushed if you even spoke to him. Well, it seems the war has changed young Vincent. Yes, indeed. I hear that Aunt Millie's been hearing ... Good Lord, the secrets of the surgery—I'm getting to be a worse gossip than *she* is ... anyway, Aunt Millie's been hearing strange rumors about her concrete hero.

MRS. MELROSE: What?

DR. MELROSE: Her concrete hero. That's what she calls him. You know, conquering, concrete. Conquering. He's come back skirt crazy. And in a rather nasty way, too. Knocks 'em about. The good mothers of Swyers Harbour had better keep a shorter leash on their fair maidens, I'd say, with the concrete hero on the rampage.

MRS. MELROSE: Oh, Percy, who's doing this? It's loathsome. It's bestial. I know what these people are like. They're simple minded, they're retarded, they're ... they're ... but surely, not even the Pastor's crowd would be so low as to do something as ... as sickening as this.

DR. MELROSE: Well, while we're on a general condemnation of the natives, my dear, we shouldn't let our friends, the Yanks off the hook. I mean, they've got some small reason to be frustrated and bitter, haven't they? There are no ticker tape parades for them, yet. No hero's welcome. Their buddies have all long gone and they're stuck here. Stuck here until Stateside decides what to do with that anti-submarine camp out on the point. I don't know. Maybe even a sheep would start to look good after ...

MRS. MELROSE: Shut up. Shut up. Shut up. God, I can't stand it. When are we going to go? When? When? You promised. You promised. You said something might come up. You *always* say something might come up. You say it so often, but the only thing that comes up is my dinner. Look at you. Look at you. What are you now? A veterinarian. Dissecting sheep. Who'd have you? Where *can* we go? We're trapped. We'll never leave here. That's right, take another drink. Look at you, for God's sake. Look at your hands. Shaking like two butterflies. Sweet Jesu, I wouldn't trust you to slice bologna. Let me tell you something, Mister Doctor. Even these ... these ignorant wretches around here, they don't trust you any more. Oh, no. Rather than face having the wrong bits snipped off, they're going all the way to St. John's, some of them. Did you know that? Did you know that? Sure, we're going to go. Sure, sure, sure, sure, sure. Where? Let me ask you that. Where? The great whiskey doctor. Mayo Clinic, eh, doctor? Mount Sinai? A teaching position, perhaps? Yeah, teaching. Maybe you could still teach the little bastards to skin a cat, whiskey doctor. Whiskey doctor. Whiskey doctor.

DR. MELROSE: Oh, for Christ's sake, Grace, give it over. Can't we have just one day without your damned screeching solo. Just one. Look, girl, there have been some good bits, haven't there? Some good bits after all. Remember ... remember when we first came here. Remember that. We called it "Newfunlund" for the first three years. Lord and Lady Grenfell, we were. And the people. Then you thought they were quaint. Simple. Honest. Charming. A little averse to bathwater, perhaps ... but charming. Remember that dictionary you were going to make. All the funny old words and phrases. And your hooked mats. Lordy. We must have enough hooked mats to carpet the Kremlin. Nooo, it wasn't all bad. And didn't I get me a piece in *Maclean's Magazine*. "Doctor Pioneers Among the Icebergs." And my papers on malnutrition, and incest ... I don't know. I don't know what happened. Maybe it was that offer from the Royal Vic. What was that, ten years ago? Maybe if I'd, if we'd gone then. Yes, maybe that was it. I think, you know, that was our peak. That was our peak here. After that the bloom was off the rose. After that the long slide began. We should have known. We should have recognized it. That it was time to go I mean. That this quaint little place was turning into some kind of a hell hole for us. A hell hole that's driven me into this shit and you ...

MRS. MELROSE: (*She has begun to sob during her husband's tirade.*) Percy. Perce. Percy. For the love of God, give them to me, will you. Give them to me. Please. Please. I can't stand it. I feel like I'm going mad. Please, Perce. Please. Give me the pills. I'm begging you. Please.

DR. MELROSE: Oh, Lord. I can't Gracie. I can't. They'll kill you if you keep them up. Kill you in one of the ugliest ways possible. Can't you ... can't you just try, darling. Try to help yourself out of this somehow. Back out of it, somehow. I can give you the fifty milligrams again. Maybe that would ...

MRS. MELROSE: (*Screams, starts pounding the walls, ripping the tablecloth and stuff.*) Nooo. I want *them*. I want *them*. Give me them. I'll kill myself, Perce. I swear I'll kill myself. I swear ...
(*DR. MELROSE takes pills from his pocket and tosses them at her. She makes gurgling noises and scuttles off for the kitchen.*)

DR. MELROSE: Damn. Damn. Damn it all. Damn it *all*.
(*He smashes his half filled glass to the floor. He takes a new glass and pours himself another.*)

Curtain

Scene 2:

(A beach on a grey day in April. At the edge of the stage, the water line, the grey weathered corpse of a tree rocks back and forth to the sound of the surf. At front and right there is a boulder four feet in circumference. At front and left there's a smaller rock. There's the occasional screech of a gull. From behind the larger boulder, a .12 gauge shotgun is slowly raised. Then its owner, BILLY HEAD, slowly rises. He is trying to get a good aim on a seabird. Just when he appears to have it in his sights, there's the frantic yapping of a mid-sized dog from behind the rock at stage left).

BILLY HEAD: *(In a furious whisper.)* —Brandy. Brandy. Shut up, will you. Shut that, you. You bloody fool, you're going to make him dive on me. Be quiet, sir. Shut up.

(BILLY attempts another aim. He fires. But in the second before he does, Brandy erupts in another flurry of barking.)

BILLY HEAD: *(Shouts disgustedly.)* Damn. Damn your guts, Bran. You made me loose 'en. I have a mind to put a load right into you.

(He rises from behind the boulder and collects his baggage. He wears a cap with the ear flaps tied up, a denim jacket, dark felt pants, logans and woolen shooting gloves. He's got a canvas lunch bag with a blackened "piper" attached to one of its straps. Besides the gun, he carries an axe, a brace of rabbits.)

BILLY HEAD: Here. Here. Come here. What's gone wrong with you, anyway? What have you got there, now? A damn old tick-leach or something? *(He starts to walk across. After a few steps he stops, stares.)* Ah ... ? *(He flings down gun and axe and runs.)* Oh, God, no. Oh, God, God, no. No. No. Jesus, no.

(From behind the rock, he drags the dripping corpse of young Triffie into view, face up. Her coat is half off and her clothing ripped.)

BILLY HEAD: Oh, God, Triff, what ... What ... What did you want ... what did you want to go and do that for? Oh, you poor little jeezler. Jesus, Triff. My God, my God. Foolish, foolish ... Foolish, foolish, foolish. What did you want to go to work and do that for, Triffie? What did you want to ... What did you want to go to work and make away with yourself for?

(He flops the corpse face down trying to get a better grip under the armpits. Half its back is bare. There are wounds on it. He drops it in fresh astonishment.)

BILLY HEAD: You didn't ... Triff, you didn't ... You never made away with yourself. You ... you ... been made away *with*.

(Brandy whines.)

Curtain

Scene 3:

(The dining/living room at the Melrose house. DR. MELROSE and MRS. MELROSE and the visiting RANGER, Sgt. Andrew Hepditch, have just finished lunch. DR. MELROSE is helping himself from a bottle of scotch on the dresser behind him. MRS. MELROSE passes a plate of cookies.)

RANGER: Thanks, Mrs. Melrose. No, thanks. I had one of these great big train breakfasts on the way out. They're certainly getting back up to par, the dining car is, since the war ended.

DR. MELROSE: When did we last see you, Sergeant? Just before Christmas, wasn't it.

RANGER: Umm. The end of November. That sheep ... business.

MRS. MELROSE: *(Shudders audibly.)* Ohhh. Filthy. Bestial. Poor animals. Hideous mutilation. What sort of ... of sub-humans must they be.

RANGER: Umm. Bad business. But, you know, there was a similar thing at Whitbourne just the other ... just back in March. So, ah, I don't know. Doctor, you looked at the girl, of course.

DR. MELROSE: Yes. Oh, yes. They brought her straight here. *(Offers scotch.)* Help yourself, Ranger.

RANGER: Thanks. No.

DR. MELROSE: Yes, the young fella, Billy Head, I understand, found her in the beach somewhere around three o'clock yesterday. She'd been missing two days. There was some attempt at a search party ... dragging the harbour with cod jiggers, pitching out loaves of bread, that sort of thing.

RANGER: Bread?

DR. MELROSE: Oh. You haven't come across that one. Oh, it's some sort of religious thing, something in the Scriptures about, "Cast thy bread upon the waters ..."

MRS. MELROSE: Ha. " ... and it shall return to thee after many days." They actually believe that, you know, Sgt. Hepditch. They actually believe that, now, in 1947. That a loaf of bread will float until it comes to a standstill over a drowned body. It's almost medieval, isn't it? It's like a little piece of the Dark Ages trapped here for all time among these rocks. Trapped here and ... and ...

(DR. MELROSE glances at her sharply.)

MRS. MELROSE: Ah, yes. Would you excuse me a moment. I've got to, ah ... *(She clears off some dishes for the kitchen. Mutters.)* Quaint practices. Quaint.

DR. MELROSE: *(Pours more scotch.)* Anyway, the bread and the jiggers got 'em nowhere. It almost had to be young Head who found her.

RANGER: Ha. And how is that?

DR. MELROSE: Well, that's about all the young bugger does ...

prowl along the beaches, skulk through the woods with that dog and axe and gun of his. If it grows, he chops it down; if it moves, he slaughters it. I can't see how there's a trout or a partridge left.
RANGER: So this Billy Head found her. Who saw her last? Any talk around about that?
DR. MELROSE: Well, now, Ranger, I would venture to guess that I was one of the last persons to see the late Tryphenia Maude Pottle in a vital state ... if you could ever call the poor young creature that.
RANGER: I see. (*He makes a token rise as MRS. MELROSE returns and seats herself.*)
DR. MELROSE: Yeah. It was, um, three days ago. Her dear old dad sent her along to me. She had an ulcerated sore on her hip the size of a saucer. But, of course, the Christian gentleman, Pastor William Henry Pottle, holds that the motor car is Satan's chariot. He made her walk. Walk the, what, four or five miles from Swyers Harbour down along the railway track ... which is a little shorter than the road.
MRS. MELROSE: Charming specimen of humanity.
DR. MELROSE: Well, sir, I patched her up ... it wasn't too bad ... and off she went again. That was about, oh, two fifteen, two thirty. I didn't bother offering her a ride. I think she would have died first. She did, anyway.
RANGER: And she was found somewhere along the route?
DR. MELROSE: Yes, she was found about three parts of the way between Evans Quay, here, and Swyers Harbour. The railway comes pretty close to the shore there.
RANGER: And, doctor, you're pretty sure she didn't drown.
DR. MELROSE: No, no, no, no. She didn't drown. Oh, she was in the water, alright, perhaps a day or two. But the thing is, there was no water in her. But there was four deep stab wounds in her back. She was well and truly deceased before she ever hit the water.
RANGER: And, Doctor, the girl was retarded?
DR. MELROSE: Ah, yes. She had the mental gear of about a four year old. She was about, what, seventeen. Her mother died, you see, when she was born. There were ... complications. That's what left young Triffie dealing from a partial deck. That and ...
MRS. MELROSE: That and that certifiable monster of a father of hers. Go on, Percy, you might as well say it. Everybody knows ...
DR. MELROSE: Including the Sergeant, I guess, my dear. (*Offers bottle.*) Sure you won't have a touch, Sergeant. (*RANGER declines.*) Yep. The good Pastor Pottle. The Lord God Jehovah's self-appointed vicar. Hellfire and damnation, wholesale, retail and C.O.D. The thundering foe of idolatry, fornicating, card-playing, wine-bibbing (*Hoists glass*), nose-picking, pig-sticking, penicillin, combination underwear and the internal combusion

engine.

MRS. MELROSE: And chewing gum. (*An enquiring glance from the RANGER.*) Chewing gum. The poor little cretin found out the hard way about chewing gum. Two ribs ...

DR. MELROSE: (*Rather sharply.*) Grace. Sergeant, there are some things ... some confidences ... I mean, I'm still a doctor. I suppose I am. Ah, what the hell. It can't help and it can't harm the poor little brute now. Yes, the bastard fractured two of her ribs. Far as I can piece it together, he found out that she'd taken a stick of gum from a G.I. There are still what ... five or six of them out there at the anti-submarine camp. Caretakers or watchmen, until the Pentagon or whatever decides what to do with it. Anyway, the Pastor found out. And he put the boots to the girl. To him, you see, gum is a step on the road to tobacco. And tobacco is the stench of hell in a pack marked "Chesterfield." Oh, yeah. He gave it to her, alright. She had lots of bruises. So I went along and I strapped up her ribs and, Ok, Ok, she'd tripped and fallen against the woodhorse. Whatever.

RANGER: Well, now. In cases like that ...

DR. MELROSE: Inform our so-called welfare system? Contact that farce of an orphanage at St. John's? Pardon me, Sergeant, but lodge a complaint with you? Fine. In six months, perhaps a year's time, something *might* be done. Might. Might. What do you think would have happened to the poor girl, meanwhile, when the ... the man of God found out? If he suspected she'd babbled it out. Broken arms? Legs? Neck?

RANGER: Umm. Ah, the Americans, Doctor. Before my time, was there ever any ... ah ... trouble or ...

DR. MELROSE: Huh? Trouble? No, no trouble. Pretty well the same as all over Newfoundland. The locals took to the Yanks like ... like ...

MRS. MELROSE: Flies to a honey bucket. (*DR. MELROSE shoots MRS. MELROSE a quick glance.*)

DR. MELROSE: They got along just swell. At first, now, there might have been some hesitancy, some holding back. Our people were a little awed, I think. After all, these fellows had teeth, for God's sake. And they'd obviously seen the sun shine a few times in their lives. No, it was a pretty good interaction.

MRS. MELROSE: (*Sotto vocce.*) Like rape.

DR. MELROSE: Oh, God, Grace. Can't you ... Ah, that was silly, really. I don't think there was much to it. It was in '44, I think. Late in '44. A girl from here, in fact, claimed one of the G.I.'s had raped her. Ha. Anyway, the camp commander, whatever he was, put around an apology and assured everyone that the culprit had been shipped off to France immediately, stuck right up in the front lines and, by now, probably had his head shot off ... or worse. Well, a few weeks later someone saw the mad rapist

walking down Water Street. There was a stink, but no big thing. It soon blew over. The Yanks stepped up their distribution of ...
MRS. MELROSE: Spam. Comic books. Hershey bars. Trifles to pacify these childlike-people. They really are, you know, Sergeant. Do you know that ... One of my little women's groups ... Mrs. Head ... Mrs. Oral Head, she was the president ... She stood right up in a meeting and she proposed ... this was how she put it ... she proposed a vote of thanks to "them lovely Americans," she said, "for lending us that great big nigger man to do a stepdance at our little Christmas concert and sale of works." Well. Really.
RANGER: Ah, yes. Well. (*Noticing the time.*) Oh. Well, thanks for lunch, Mrs. Melrose, and thanks for putting me up, yet again. I dare say the bedbugs over at Miller's Boarding House are as ravenous as ever. (*They all rise.* MRS. MELROSE *carries off dirty dishes and returns for more.*)
DR. MELROSE: Will you see the body now, Ranger? It's just down there in the ...
RANGER: No. Ah, no. I'll ... I'll get to that later. Tell the truth, I never did have much stomach for that kind of thing. No, I have to take a dart up to Swyers Harbour ... if the old motorcycle has survived the tender mercies of the Newfoundland Railway. I'm expecting a telegram at the Post Office there.
DR. MELROSE: Ha. Well, Sergeant, I hope you're ready for Aunt Millie Bishop, because she is ready for you, for damnsure. Sees all, hears all, knows all, tells all ... or, at least ninety per cent of it. That's good old Aunt Millie, for you. That Post Office of hers is like the center of a spider web.
MRS. MELROSE: Dreadful creature.
RANGER: See you later, Doctor. Ma'am.
(*Exit RANGER. Exit MRS. MELROSE to kitchen with some dishes while DR. MELROSE turns to the scotch bottle on the sideboard. His back to the audience, he pours more scotch. There is the crash of a plate to the kitchen floor. He glances. He sighs. He drains the half tumbler of booze. He remains bent over, hands on sideboard as ...*)

Curtain

Scene 4:

(*The Swyers Harbour Post Office. There's a counter with a lift up flap, a set of weights, an old war bonds poster, sealing wax, some rubber stamps and pads, a small round stove with a kettle on it. Postmistress MILLIE BISHOP is sorting mail at the rear and does not look up as ... Enter the RANGER.*)
AUNT MILLIE: Be right with you. Won't be a minute. My, what a wonderful dose of mail is on the go. You'd never say the war

was over. I think there's more, if anything, since our boys come back from overseas. Ah, yes. That'll be old Washbourne's cheque. Three days late this month. A queer thing he haven't been around looking for it before now. I never knowed him to miss. Queer thing, that is. Oh, well, that old coot is queer in more ways than one, I'd say. Yes, sir, in more ways than one.
(Turns to RANGER at counter.)
AUNT MILLIE: Now, then, sir. What can I ... My God, the *Ranger.* My *God*, the Ranger. Oh, I *am* wonderful sorry, sir, to keep you waiting. I had no notion ... No, I tell a lie. I suppose I did have a notion you'd be here. Certainly, I had some notion. A person'd be pretty stunned *not* to have some notion the Ranger'd be sent for after that terrible, terrible tragedy what have afflicted our once-peaceful little community. Terrible altogether. Terrible, terrible. What's gone wrong with the world, at all, at all, at all. 'Tis the war, I puts it to. The war and them old atom bombs they do be bustin' off in the air. So many strangers on the go, too. You don't know who is who or what is what.
RANGER: Mrs.. ah ... Bishop, is it? I wonder if there's a ...
AUNT MILLIE: That is right, sir. Mildred Bishop, yes. And like I say, me a poor widow woman living alone by myself, b'y, in these terrible circumstances ... *(Has a few sobs into her apron.)* Excuse me, sir, I fills right up whenever I thinks about poor Mr. Bishop what was took from me. Aw, well. As Mrs. Eleanor Roosevelt once said, "'Tis better to have loved and lost than never to have loved at all." Truer words, I don't s'pose, was ever spoken. No, if I never had my dear son livin' here with me, now ... and he overseas three year puttin' the boots to Mister Hitler ... if I never had he under me roof these days I, I don't say I'd be able to strike a wink of sleep, not after what's goin' on here in Swyers Harbour, these days. His picture, sir, on the wall in his uniform. "Hail the concrete hero comes." Some sweet, sir, isn't he? ... although you don't want to be all the time praisin' up your own. No, that was never my way, that wasn't. But Vincent was spared, I says, the good Lord spared 'en from the bow'n arrer what flieth by day to be a comfort to his poor widow woman mother in these shocking times. Shocking times, sir, when there's vicious murderers runnin' around loose strikin' fear into this once-tranquil little community. Shocking times, Mr. Ranger, sir, when certain persons ...
RANGER: Ah, excuse me, Mrs. Bishop. I was expecting a telegram. Hepditch? Sgt. Hepditch?
AUNT MILLIE: My glory, sir. You must think I'm awful iggnernt. But things like this, you know, is hard on the nerves. Things like this is enough to rattle the patience of a saint.
(Picks up bundle of five or six telegrams and begins to sort through them.)

AUNT MILLIE: Hepditch. Hepditch. Hepditch. Ah. Pottle. From Whitbourne, I see. That'll be a message of condolences from Whitbourne. That crowd got a orphanage, something or another, over to Whitbourne, you know. Yes, and that ... that ... that *ting* of a Pottle goes over there once a month, god help the poor little fatherless and motherless innersents. And you mightn't believe this but 'tis true. He'd be gone a whole day and perhaps a night. And do you know what? All that time, he'd lock that poor young silly person up alone in that house. As God is me witness and me redeemer, sir. Lord knows what mighta happened to her. I meana say, the house coulda cotch fire, mightn't it? Easy enough done. Or she mighta been broke in on. And she mighta been interfered with. Easy enough done with some of the characters we got on the go here today. Sweet little thing she was, you know, although she wasn't all there. Sweet little thing. Always the one way. You'd always see her, any time the night or day, she'd always have this kind of a half of a smile on her face. No, she never caused no one no trouble, young Triffie didn't. Sorry. *Poor* young Triffie as she now is. Course you knowed right away she was half-simple. I meana say, anyone goin' around a place like Swyers Harbour all the time with a smile on their face, there *got* to be something wrong with their heads now, haven't it? It only stands to reason. Oh, now, sir, don't get me wrong, now. Don't get me wrong. There's nothing wrong with the place. A nice little place. A perfect little place. I always said that and I always will. 'Tis the people what's *in* the place what spoils it. If it wasn't for the people, this'd be the nicest little place you ever wish to see. Sorry, sir. Nothing for Hepditch.

RANGER: Thanks, ma'am. Ah, Mrs. Bishop, I'm staying down at Evans Quay with Dr. and Mrs. Melrose. I wonder ... if anything does come for me, would you give me a ring down there, please.

AUNT MILLIE: Indeed I will so, Ranger Hepditch. Indeed I will so. The very second your message comes I'll give you a ring. Er, sir, bold question but was she ... I mean to say ... was anything ... I mean to say, was the poor creature all there? Ha, ha. How silly is I, at all. We know she wasn't all there, don't we. What I'm tryin' to put through me is, there wasn't nothing missing, was there. Because me mind harps back to them ... them poor sheep last fall.

RANGER: I haven't seen the body yet, madam. I must be going. If there is a telegram you'll ...

AUNT MILLIE: Oh, you might be sure I will, sir. Oh, what's gettin' wrong with me at all. Manners, manners, manners. Ranger Hepditch, can I give you a nice cup of tea in your lap? I always got the kettle goin'. Generally always, anyway. That was always my way and I dare say I won't change me habits now, not at my late age, ha ha.

(Tea is poured, RANGER sits on a bench by the stove,
AUNT MILLIE sits on a chair.)
AUNT MILLIE: And how *is* Dr. Melrose these days, and Mrs. Melrose? My, I haven't seen them two people for a dog's age. Sweet little woman, Mrs. Melrose is. Sweet little woman. My what that woman haven't-a done for this place, there's no one knows. Wonderful little organizer, she is. Got all the women knitting socks for the soldiers. Head of the women's church league. All that kind of stuff you could mention. Certainly, the poor woman was always subject to wonderful bad nerves. Especially here lately. Only the other week, Mrs. Head, I think it was, was tellin' me she seen Mrs. Melrose take I don't know wether 'twas four or wether 'twas five different kind of pills out of her purse and take 'em. And some of they the biggest kind, she said. But she's in good hands, that's one good thing. If there's anything medical sinus can do, I'm sure Dr. Melrose'll do it for her.
RANGER: How long have they been here, Mrs. Bishop? Do you remember?
AUNT MILLIE: Oh, indeed I do, my dear man. Indeed I do. And I'll tell you the reason for why. Dr. Melrose is the one who borned my Vincent and Vincy will be, what, twenty-two year old this summer coming. That was the year they come to Evans Quay. They're from away, you know. Oh, yes. Some place up there to Ontario. Peter something, I think it is. Peterburrle, some such name as that. They most generally goes back there for a cruise in the summer. It seem to do Mrs. Melrose a world of good, that do. You can see the difference in her, oh, a month before they goes. Perks right up, she do. Oh course, when she comes back...Wonderful jolly man, Dr. Melrose, isn't he? Always had his little joke. Course, now, he likes his scattered drop, too, you know. And nothing at all wrong with that. My poor Mr. Bishop he ... he ... he *(Has a few sniffs into apron)* ... he liked his scattered drop, too, you know. Indeed, he did. Certainly, doctors is in a different categlory, isn't they? When you got that knife in your hand, you got to be so steady as the rock. Otherwise, you'd go to work and chop out the wrong bits. Quick as a wink. Wouldn't be very nice to have the wrong bits chopped out, now would it? I knows I wouldn't like to have no wrong bits chopped out of ...
(She spots door opening. Somebody's head pops in
and in haste attempts a retreat.)
AUNT MILLIE: *(Sharply.)* Here. Stop. Stop. You come right back here, sir. Ha. The very chap. You come right here and talk to the nice policeman. He's not goin' to hurt you. You're not goin' to be hove in jail and the bight of rope put around your neck *if* you never done nothing wrong.
(BILLY HEAD enters slowly, eyes down cast.)

AUNT MILLIE: Ranger Hepditch, this is the very lad what found her. Yer *Family Herald* and *Weekly Star* never come this week, Billy. Billy lives with Uncle Henry Alfred and Aunt Martha Head, Mr. Ranger. 'Dopted, of course, isn't you, Billy? Now you come here and tell the man how it was you come to find poor young Triffie 'cause he'll have it out of you first or last, mind. Indeed, he will.

RANGER: Have a seat, Billy. Mrs. Bishop, I wonder if we might have a little ... a little privacy, if you don't mind.

AUNT MILLY: Hmph. Well, I s'pose if ... Yes, certainly. Although the regulations do say, the post and telegraph regulations do say I'm not supposed to leave the office unattempted at any time. But, I s'pose the way things is going these days ...

(She reluctantly gets up to leave.)

RANGER: Now, then, Billy. You are the one who found Tryphenia Pottle, aren't you? Found her body.

BILLY: Eyup.

AUNT MILLIE: *(Sticks head back in door.)* Say, "Yes sir," and, "No sir."

BILLY: Yes, sir.

RANGER: And, Billy, about what time was it when you ...

AUNT MILLIE: And "please" and "thank you."

(She finally closes the door.)

RANGER: ... when you found the body?

BILLY: I don't know. 'Bout quarter past, half past two.

RANGER: And what were you doing? What brought you there to the beach?

BILLY: Birdin', sir. And lookin' at me rabbit slips.

RANGER: And you were walking along and you saw the body. Was it in the water or out? Half in, half out?

BILLY: No, sir. I had a gun on a shellbird. Bloody old dog was barkin at she. He dove. I lost 'en. It was he found she.

RANGER: Eh?

BILLY: Brandy. Me dog. He found she.

RANGER: Oh, I see. Your dog was barking at the body. And you went over. And what did you see.

BILLY: She, sir. Young Triffie.

RANGER: And she was dead. You could see right away that she was dead?

BILLY: Eyup. Dead as a nit. Sir.

RANGER: And, Billy, what did you think? What flashed to your mind? What was the first thing you thought must have happened?

BILLY: Dunno.

RANGER: Oh, come on now. Here was a girl dead on the beach. Didn't you wonder what happened? Didn't you wonder if she'd fallen in the water? Or jumped? Or was thrown in?

BILLY: Jumped. Made away with herself.
RANGER: Oh, and why is that?
BILLY: She ... she isn't ... she wasn't all there, sir. She never had the best of sense, at all. And her old man ...
RANGER: Yes. Her father. What about her father?
BILLY: He was ... he was wonderful hard to her.
RANGER: Oh, did she tell you? How do you know?
BILLY: That's what they all says.
RANGER: Yeah. Now, how did you discover she might not have made away with herself, that she didn't commit suicide?
BILLY: She was face up in the landwash, sir. Turned her over, drag her up above highwater mark. Coat half off. Dress was tore. Four stabs in her ... in her back.
RANGER: Right. Now let's get on with this. You dragged the body up the beach. Then what did you do?
BILLY: Went to old man Washbourne's.
RANGER: And who, pray tell, is old man Washbourne? Why did you go there?
BILLY: He only lives 'bout two, three gun shots from where ... she was. Told he to keep a eye on her. Foxes might get her. Crows have the eyes out of her.
RANGER: I see. Then what did you do.
BILLY: Home.
RANGER: Home, and then you spread the news. And so on and so on. Well, William, that's about it for now. You can go. (*BILLY rises to go.*) Oh, Billy. How well did you know young Triffie? I mean, did you talk to her very often. Things like that.
BILLY: Nope. She never talked much.
RANGER: Neither do you, my lad. Neither do you. Ok, then.
 (*Exit BILLY through front door. AUNT MILLIE
 immediately pops out the other door.*)
AUNT MILLIE: Ah, yes. Deep, deep, deep is young Billy Head. Very deep, indeed. Just so deep, sir, as one of them artisian wells. I often wonders to meself what do be goin' through his mind. Even as a child, you know, he never knocked around with the other youngsters. Never. Now, my Vincy, he was ... he was a bit on the shy side growin' up. Yes, a bit on the shy side. But never like *that*, thank God. Never like that.
RANGER: Well, thanks very much, Mrs. Bishop, for your help. And your tea. By the way, who is this Mr. Washbourne? Billy called him "Old Man Washbourne."
AUNT MILLIE: Ha. A good question, that is. A very good question, indeed. Who is he? All I can do is s'pose. I can s'pose he's this and I can s'pose he's that. And you bein' a man of the law, sir, knows you can't go around s'posin' about people ... especially when what you're dealin' with is a murder, and that the most gruesome and tragic kind. Everyone calls him Old Man Wash-

bourne because nobody knows what his first name is. Although he got three of 'em. Oh, yes. The initials is on his cheque. J.D.W. Washbourne. And he's one of them "esks." He got a "esk" to the end of his name. Ee, ess, Q, full stop. He gets a big bundle of newspapers and magazines from all parts, and the end of the month he gets a cheque, regular. My God, sir, he gets a cheque for five hun ... and they says 'tis a big check, too. No, he lives to hisself way over there around the point. Never married. He generally comes along here once a month for his mail and then he goes down to the shop and buys a bit of stuff. He's friendly enough, you know, in his way. He'll say good morning if 'tis in the morning and if 'tis in the evening he'll say good evening. Or he might say "Fine day," or "Wet day" as the case may be. Course, if 'tis in the winter he'll say "Blustery day" or ...

RANGER: Yes, yes, yes, yes. But, Mrs. Bishop, would you do me a little favor here and ... and "s'pose" a bit. I will keep that in mind, you know. That you're only supposing.

AUNT MILLIE: Yes. Well. What we always heard when we were growin' up is that his people was English and was quite the upper crust. They come over, that's what we were always told, now, they come over years and years and years ago to start up one of them pulp and paper mills down the shore. Anyhow, the whole thing was a failure. And on top of that, their house burned down. The father and mother was burned but Old Man Washbourne, as he is now, got clear. Oh, I s'pose he would have been fifteenish around then. I'm only s'posin', now. He hauled out his mother's corpse and some of the stuff from the house she used to prize. And he hid it away. Hid it away. What happened to him then, I don't know. Someone took 'en. I s'pose, or the orphanage or something. I do know that when he come back here he was a grown man. He put up his little house way over there around the point ... and that's the history of Old Man Washbourne, "esk" and I challenge anyone in Swyers Harbour to tell you more.

RANGER: I think you're on safe ground there, Mrs. Bishop. Thank you, again. You'll remember about that telegram, now.

AUNT MILLIE: *(Agitated.)* Ranger. Ranger Hepditch. I got to tell you something. I got to. It ... it been eatin' a hole right through me stomach. It been burnin' the bosom right off me. There's days ... there's days, so help me God, I thinks me head is goin' to blow right up and bus'. I been postmistress here for nigh on sixteen year. Never a minute's trouble. The inspectors is welcome to look at *my* books any day of the week, any hour of the night nor day. There never been a ting went astray from this Post Office, not in my time, there haven't.

(She has gone behind the counter and has lifted out a large cashbox from behind it. She lifts the lid but seems

reluctant to produce the goods.)
AUNT MILLIE: I minds me own business. Oh, I know there's tings. There's tings a postmistress learns in her line of duties. Tings she got to keep to herself. Like a doctor. Like a Ranger. But upon my soul to God, sir. I can't keep the like of this to meself no more. Not after what have happened. Last fall, it was. I got the shock of me life. I tipped out the mailbag on the floor as usual ... and this ...
(She takes magazine from cash box, flings it on the counter, and turns from it in disgust, arms folded.)
AUNT MILLIE: ... this fell out at me very feet. I nearly cast me stomach on the spot. The filth, sir. The dirt. I never knowed there was such things in the world before. The shockin' things they're doin' in them pictures. With the young girls ... and the young boys. The envelope was ripped, sir, as you can see. As anyone in the world can see. The envelope got ripped in passage ...
(Here she moves quickly to remove whistling kettle from the stove. It has, by coincidence, begun to whistle at this point.)
AUNT MILLIE: ... ripped in passage and that ... that ... *ting* fell out. Bold as brass. There's one been comin' every month like that, you know. I mean to say, an envelope like that. Same size. Same color. Same postmark ... Montreal. There's one come again today. You take notice of the name on it, sir? The name and address on that ... that ... shockin' dirt?
RANGER: W.H. Pottle. Swyers Harbour. G.D. Bay.
(Blood curdling howls from offstage.)
AUNT MILLIE: *(Shouts in that direction.)* It's alright, Vincy, baby. Mommie's here. Settle down, lambie. Settle down. Mommie won't let the dirty old boo-beggars touch her Vincy. Indeed, she won't, then. *(To RANGER.)* Ah, my, oh, my. The war changes people something wonderful, Mr. Ranger. 'Deed and 'deed and double-'deed it do. Shockin' nightmares my Vincy do be havin' since he come back. The old hag rides him night and day. She got more mileage put on poor Vincy than the doctor got on his motor car. When the bitter roars comes out of him in the middle part of the night I lifts three foot off the mattress, that's the God's truth.
RANGER: Too bad, ma'am. But I'm sure he'll get over it, eventually. They generally do. Thanks again for your help. I'm sure I'll be seeing you again.
(After RANGER leaves AUNT MILLIE bustles about. Looks out window to see if RANGER is truly gone. Then she takes another envelope like the one she'd shown the RANGER out of her cash box. She goes toward stove, puts on kettle ... Then she thinks better of it. Puts the envelope back in box and box back under the counter. She wipes her hands in her apron. There are several mailbags in a corner. She drags one behind counter.

The next is especially heavy.)
AUNT MILLIE: *(Calls to offstage.)* Vincy, honey. Vincy, sugar. Would you come down, please? Would you get up and come down and give your poor old mommie a hand, here? Will you come down and give mommie a lift with this old mail bag? Vincy, sweetheart. Vincy, baby.
VINCENT: *(Muffled roar from offstage.)* Fuck off.
AUNT MILLIE: My, my, my. Tut, tut, tut, tut. Poor little Vincy. What that boy been through there's no one knows. 'Tis only them what been through it knows anything at all about it. Yeah. He over there in foreign parts, strugglin' with the foal. Bustin' his poor young arse for King and Country. All the time under shot and shell and the battle's noisy dim. My God, sure, he must be bet, bet, bet to a streel. Far forth as his poor mother is concerned that poor boy can stay in his bed for the next three years and I won't say the one word about it. Not the one word. Changed a lot, though, Vincy is, poor baby. He used to be just so meek as a lamb. Wouldn't say boo to a goose. And now, oh, I don't know. He neither cares nor fears where night overtakes him. *(Sigh.)* The heart of a mother. The heart of a ...
(Here she picks a magazine out of the mail she's sorting.)
AUNT MILLIE: Ah, ha. Ah, ha. What's this, what's this. Yes, she might so well. She might so friggin' well. What's going wrong with Aunt Ducky Piercies head, at all, at all. Change of life, er what. Yes, she might so well, now, she might so well go sendin' off and havin' the *War Cry* come to her. Yes, that's all we needs, that is. That's all we needs here in this once tranquil little community ... the Salvation Army settin' up shop. Because if you wants my candid opinion about it, we got enough old cram here now. We got that ragin' monster of a ... a ... I don't know what, in there benighst the Twillick Pond. That harem scarem of a bilge-faced slackjacket ...
(Enter PASTOR POTTLE.)
AUNT MILLIE: *(Gasp. Sotto voce.)* Speak of the devil and his horns will appear. Day, P...Pastor Pottle. Sorry for your trouble, sir. Sorry for your trouble. A terrible, terrible trudgedy. Something shockin', altogether. That sweet little angel took from you. It took the heart right out of my body, that's the truth, when I heard about it. Indeed, it did. And she always so pleasant, always the half of a little smile on her face. Wonderful sorry for your trouble, sir.
PASTOR: Trouble, madam. Trouble? Tryphenia is, this day, safe in the arms of Jesus. She rests now in Abraham's bosom. Trouble? Oh, no. I rejoice in the Lord and am glad. Sin cannot harm her there. She has long been delivered from the pit of hell. Trouble? Fools and idolators may think so, perhaps, but never the truly born-again.

AUNT MILLIE: Well, yes, you're perfectly right there, Pastor Pottle. That's one way of lookin' at tings, I s'pose. If you're happy and you knows it, clap your hands. Still, 'twas a terrible way to go. Shocking, all together. The poor little thing was half-simple, we know, but God's own, that's what I calls them sort. God's own.
PASTOR: My mail, madam, if you please.
AUNT MILLIE: Eh? Oh, mail. Yes, yes, mail. Here we go. And here we go. And here we go. There you go, sir.
PASTOR: Is this all?
AUNT MILLIE: All? Yes, I think so. Yes, sir, that's the works. Er, was you expecting something else, Pastor Pottle? Was you expecting a parcel or anything ... or something else? (*He doesn't respond.*) My, 'tis something fierce, that's what it is, the way the mail is served these days. Them train hands, they slings it about. I thinks meself they jumps up and down on it for a bit of sport. Things goes astray, things gets broke open ... ah, when is the services, Pastor Pottle? When is the poor little thing goin' to be put in the ground?
PASTOR: That is small concern of mine, madam, or perhaps of yours, either. Tryphenia's soul has fled to mansions fair. Her earthly husk is of little concern to those who truly believe in the revealed word of God. She has been washed in the precious blood of the Lamb, in the soul-cleansing blood of the Lamb. She is now safe from the gainsayers and the naysayers, safe from the idle and blasphemous tongues of the ungodly and the unsaved of this satan-ridden place, safe from the whoredoms of Babylon and Swyer's Harbour, safe from the Christ-hating gossips and scolds, safe from the mockers and idolators, safe from the whoremongers and the fornicators, like that boy of yours ...
(*Oh, oh. Oh, oh. He has said that which he ought not to have said to one with a mother's heart. AUNT MILLIE skips out from behind the counter, blazing.*)
AUNT MILLIE: Wass that you just said? Wass that just come out of your mouth? Wass that you just said about my Vincy? No, I'm not afraid of you. I'm not afraid of the likes of you. Wass that you said about my Vincy, you ... you ... sanctimonious, God-bothering frigger? And he over there in foreign parts, into them trenchers givin' up his life's blood for Kinguncountry. He over there, with them bullets whizzin' around his poor head like the handfuls of gravel. He over there not knowin' from one day to another what breath was going to be his last. He over there, bustin' his guts to make the world safe for democracy. And for a specimen the likes of you to go to work and say ...
PASTOR: Back. Get back, you ... you Witch of Endor. Back, you scurrilous harridan, you arse-licker of Satan.
AUNT MILLIE: You can't daunt me, not the one little bit. My God is my God, sir. After what you said ... After what filth and dirt

you just said about my Vincy, my concrete hero ... I could ... could ram your blasted tambourine right down your throat. Yes, and jump right down after 'en. For the likes of you to go to work and say ...

PASTOR: Cease, you soul-sickened Jezebel, you fornicator with the anti-Christ, you devil-ridden bitch, you ...

AUNT MILLIE: Ha. Frighten *me*, would you? Fat, blasted chance. 'Cause I got the heart and the stomach of a Mother, sir, yes, and a Placentia Bay Mother on the top of that. Do you think there's no one knows. Do you think there's no one knows what happened the time that poor little creature got her rib broke. You thinks there's everyone around here is deaf and dumb, you thinks ...

PASTOR: I curse you in the name of the Lord God Jehovah. I curse your lying mouth. I consign your filthy soul to the pangs of everlasting hell. Cursed be she who revileth the pastor of the Lord Almighty. Cursed be she who blasphemeth against ...

AUNT MILLIE: Paugh. Stick your curses up your norstril. I slung you off these premises once before, sir, as you might remember, and I'm just the one to do it again, too. Now you get on out of it. Git. Git.

PASTOR: (*Flings Bible up in front of him with both hands.*) Stop. Stop, in the name of Jesus.

AUNT MILLIE: And you skitter to Jesus out of here, excuse my French, you skitter on out of here or else I'll ... I'll ...

(*She skips to the corner and grabs a broom. She jabs at his navel or thereabouts.*)

AUNT MILLIE: ... I'll reeve this broom handle right through your flamin' guts. Now git, git.

(*PASTOR backs away toward the door, trips on mailbag and almost falls. He gropes behind him for door knob, finds it and steps out. He hurls a final ...)*

PASTOR: The curse of eternal damnation be upon ...

(*AUNT MILLIE slams the door with a vengeance. She turns to walk away, panting heavily ... Hand to bosom. On second thought, she turns quickly, makes a little run, and kicks the door as hard as she can. Then, panting still, hand to bosom and limping slightly, she makes for the nearest seat.*)

AUNT MILLIE: (*To self.*) Not bad. Not bad for a ... for a Church of Englander. (*She flops down into a seat.*) Phew. My God, I think I'm havin' a ... (*Calls to offstage.*) Vi ... ahem ... Vincy. Vincy, sugar. Vincy, get up and come down, will ya. Vincy, baby. Vincy, I think your poor mommie is goin' to have a heart attack. Come down, will you, honey, and get your mommie a glass of cold water.

(*Pause.*)

VINCENT: (*Muffled roar from off stage.*) Fuck off.

AUNT MILLIE: (*Shakes head wistfully, sighs.*) Poor sweetheart.

Curtain

Act II
Scene 1:

(*Interior. Washbourne's house. It's small, rather cramped, modest in layout, ordinary in decoration, wallpaper, etc. But some of the furnishings—candelabra, paintings, etc., are far too grand for the place. There are books, newspapers, magazines everywhere. WASHBOURNE is in an easy chair, smoking a pipe. B. B. C. News is playing on a shortwave radio. There's a knock at the door. WASHBOURNE goes to it.*)

MR. WASHBOURNE: Ah. The long arm of His Majesty's justice. Sergeant, I see. Good day to you, sir.

RANGER: Sgt. Hepditch ... Mr. Washbourne.

MR. WASHBOURNE: Indeed, I am, sir. I am, indeed. Come in, come in. I'm not one, as I'm sure you are aware, by now, who's normally awash with company. Nor do I court it. But I'm sure that business gives me the pleasure of your company. Nasty business. Pray be seated, Ranger. If you can find a spot. Bachelors are supposed to be neat and tidy fellows. Prim and proper, even. Well, I suppose I'm the exception to that rule, too. Old Man Washbourn, the hermit ... that's me, to the good folk of Swyers Harbour. Recluse. Eccentric. But, you know, I rather think of myself as an anchorite. Yes, Washbourne, the anchorite. Has a better ring to it somehow. Do you indulge, Sergeant?

(*He offers an elaborate and expensive drinks tray.*)

RANGER: Thanks, very much. Yes, I will. Mr. Washbourne, you were one of the first to hear the news, I believe.

MR. WASHBOURNE: I was, indeed, yes. Water? The young Head chappie came to my door in a frightful state. He blurted out the thing and asked me to go watch by her. The beach is just a little way down there, you know. Yes, poor Billy was afraid the foxes and the crows might do her mischief. So I went. And there she was. He had the body laid out quite neatly on the moss, actually. He'd closed her eyes. And, do you know, he'd folded her hands over a watch. A pocket watch. His prized possession, I dare say. Rather touching, really.

RANGER: Hmmm. I see. And you waited, sir.

MR. WASHBOURNE: Yes, I waited, oh, possibly three parts of an hour when a motor boat came round the point. Gang of men in it. Head had brought the news, you see.

RANGER: Mr. Washbourne, do you know this Head fellow at all?

I mean, had you had any contact with him before now?
MR. WASHBOURNE: "Know" him, Sergeant? "Know" him? Good God, sir. I hope you don't mean in the Biblical sense. (*With levity.*) No, no, no, no, Sergeant Hepditch. I am sure that by now you know the story of "Old Man" Washbourne. It's the standard yarn in this parish and it's basically true. I've overheard it myself. And knowing *that*, you must know that I don't "know" anybody in this blessed vale of sunshine and shadow. Not personally, anyway. I don't know any of them. But I do know of them. It's astonishing what volumes and volumes of gossip you can accumulate by occasional visits to the Post Office and General Store. I've never gone out of my way to talk to the gentle folk of Swyers Harbour. Why should I? What do they talk *about*? The weather. The Fishery. And each other. A crucifying bore, don't you think? But, oh, yes, I know a good bit *of* them, I think. A good bit *of* them.
RANGER: Very well then, sir. What do you know of, for instance, this Billy Head?
MR. WASHBOURNE: He's a loner. That strikes a chord with me, as you might appreciate. He's no genius but he's not as stupid as he may appear. Oh, we've passed a few words here and there of late years. He'd be passing here, I'd have a brace of rabbits off him. Partridge. Trout. A regular Daniel Boone is young William.
RANGER: And that's the extent of your ... um ... aquaintance. You haven't talked to him or seen him more than that?
MR. WASHBOURNE: Oh, indeed I have, Sergeant Hepditch. Indeed I have. Once before, the young lad came to my door. And, once before, he was pretty much terrified. I had him in.
RANGER: Yes. And when was this, sir?
MR. WASHBOURNE: Last summer, sir. July. Toward the end of it.
RANGER: And what was the matter with him? Did he say? Did you talk to him then?
MR. WASHBOURNE: He came to me, I believe, because he had to talk to someone and there wasn't a single person in his blessed natal seat down there he could go to.
RANGER: Well, what was it? What was it? What got his pee hot, man? What?
MR. WASHBOURNE: Ah, you're closer than you know, Ranger. Closer than you know. Pee hot, indeed. Yes. It was the good Doctor Melrose's lady wife, sir. She'd cornered our Billy. And she'd threatened to have him castrated.
RANGER: Castrated, Sir?
MR. WASHBOURNE: Castrated. Denatured. Desexed. Deballed. He'd gone down to the clinic, apparently, to have a tooth pulled. And as he was leaving, the charming Mrs. Melrose more

or less sprang upon him, the old froth foaming at the corners. She put it to him, that the doctor would whip out his cruel little scalpel and ... snickerty snick ... off would come poor Billy's manhood. If, that is ... and here's the curious proviso, Sergeant ... if Billy so much as thought of, shall we say, getting a leg over the late lamented Pottle damsel.

RANGER: Good Lord. Why in the devil would she do that? The girl was retarded, I know, but ... was there ever any indication that Head was tomcatting after her. Anything like that?

MR. WASHBOURNE: I wouldn't know, sir. I wouldn't know. Although, God knows what the rising generation are up to these days. Our American friends have given them new standards, new goals, new aspirations. It is, after all, the era of the nylon stocking and the Hershey bar.

RANGER: But surely, sir, that's pretty savage stuff. Mrs. Melrose didn't strike me as that kind of a ... Mr. Washbourne, do you believe that yarn, yourself?

MR. WASHBOURNE: Oh, indeed I do, sir. Every blessed word of it. I believe it because Mrs. Melrose is probably capable of whatever you might imagine. That woman, sir, is a flaming drug addict.

RANGER: Now, look here, Mr. Washbourne. I'd better caution you. I've heard, yes, that Mrs. Melrose may take medicine for her nerves but ... Look here, sir, what makes you an authority on drug addiction?

MR. WASHBOURNE: Sergeant Hepditch, you've heard the saga of "Old Man" Washbourne. You know there was a ... there was a fire. And you know that ... I was there. I was rather badly burned, myself. They took me away. For month after month, they pumped me full of God knows what. It took me years, Sergeant, years to unhook myself from that blessed curse. Or is it curse-ed blessing, do you think? At first the pain made me scream out for it. And later, *it* made me scream out for it. Ah, yes, my dear man, I do know a little of the subject and from what few glimpses I've had of the lady Melrose there's no doubt about it. I shouldn't be very much surprised if the good doctor has brought her along by now to the jolly old morphine itself. He's a bottle-a-day man—common knowledge, sir, common knowledge ... and she's a pin cushion for a syringe. Ah, the poor damned pair of them. Ah, might I refresh your glass, sergeant?

RANGER: Yes. Yes, please. God, yes. But how in the name of ... How did they get themselves in such a stew? How did it come about?

MR. WASHBOURNE: Slowly. Very slowly. So slowly that by the time they realized what was happening, it was too late. They came here, you know, oh, twenty years or so ago. Some place in Ontario. He was fresh out of medical school. And she was hot to trot ... you know, eager to play the lady bountiful. Oh, I expect it was the great adventure for both of them. The Wilfred Grenfell thing, you see. The whole Schwitzer business. Off to a terribly remote area to do good works among the natives. And they did. They did. She was known as "a sweet little woman." I think some of them still call her that. Ha. She's about as sweet, now, as an unripe lemon. She organized women's groups and God knows what. You know, slowly but surely bringing the natives along. And he, well, he threw himself into it, boots and all. The classic rural doctor thing. Dashing off on missions of mercy, in dark of night. In blizzards. Small boats. Horse and slide. For perhaps ten years or so it was a jolly good show. But, you know, I think that slowly, very slowly, the place began to get to them. It started to close in. It dawned on them that they were trapped. And we both know what it was like in the Dirty Thirties. The health boys in St. John's didn't have a cent to bless themselves with. They had Melrose here and they were determined to keep him here. In later years, I'm sure they must have known that his scalpel got shakier as his hootch consumption rose. But you know *their* kind of logic ... better a perpetually pissed sawbones than none at all. It sometimes seems, doesn't it, Ranger, that St. John's looks on its outport brethren as second class citizens, indeed. Madam Melrose certainly does. As the place closed about her head, she developed a loathing for her parishioners. After all, you can't hate rocks and trees and water. I'm sure she sees them as sub-intelligent, incestuous, sub-human. I wouldn't be surprised if she thought Mr. Hitler had the right idea. Oh, she still trots along to play mother hen at her women's group. But she flings out the most bitter sarcasm at them ... in a form she believes to be well above their wooden heads. And as for the good doctor, well, things have changed, haven't they, now that the world has been made safe for democracy. Even St. John's is smartening up. I wouldn't be surprised if, sooner or later, Dr. Melrose got the bounce. And there'd be nothing more for him, then. He'd never doctor again ... not even cutting cats in Saskatchewan.

RANGER: (*Sighs, shakes his head as he gets up to go.*) Mr. Washbourne. For an, um, anchorite, you certainly don't miss many tricks. Not many at all, sir.

MR. WASHBOURNE: Why, thank you, dear fellow. I take that as something of a compliment. Um, Sergeant. May I tell you something. I wish you to understand ... I don't know why, but I do ... I wish you to understand that it took more than a ... more than a fire to make me what I am. There's one little bit that nobody knows about the story of "Old Man Washbourne". After my father set fire to my mother's bedroom, he shot himself dead.

Curtain

Scene 2:

The dining/living room at the Melrose house. The RANGER sits at the dining table. DR. MELROSE enters with a plate of beans which he puts in front of him. DR. MELROSE seats himself at the table but does not eat. He has his glass of scotch.)

DR. MELROSE: Hope you don't mind rewarmed beans, Sergeant. That's about the scope of my cooking talents. Mrs. ... Grace was feeling a little under the weather. So she's gone up to have a lie down.

RANGER: Oh, that's too bad. Nothing too serious, I hope.

DR. MELROSE: Oh, no. No, no. Just a bit of tension, I think. A spot of nerves. You know, Ranger, April, in a place like this, is the cruelest month in more ways than one. Well, now, you've had a busy day, I expect. I was thinking that Aunt Millie Bishop must have talked you up the wall. That woman comes up for air only half as often as the great white whale.

RANGER: Yes. Talking is no burden to her at all. Is there any reason ... I mean, she seemed determined to nail down the lid of Pastor Chummyjig's coffin. Have those two got a running battle going or something?

DR. MELROSE: Nooo. That's just her way. I mean, pick any one in Swyers Harbour or Evans Quay and good old Aunt Millie'll do the job on them, good and proper. She was just born like it. I think the Pastor might get under her skin a little more than usual because before he came, you see, Aunt Millie had it all in the palm of her hand. She was the ... well, if she wasn't cock of the walk she was queen of the roost, at least as far as churchy auxilliaries go. It's her hobby. Has been ever since the late, lamented Mr. Bishop went to his grave with a hobnail liver. She's got her concrete hero now, of course, and ... Oh, Cripes. By the way. Look, Andrew, old man, I don't want to complicate your hectic life but ... Mrs. Piercy was in this afternoon. Aunt Ducky Piercy, not a day over fifty-six and still able to read her Bible without the aid of glasses. Dorothy, actually. Dorothy Piercy. She was in to see me with her great lubberly daughter, Brenda, in tow. She wants to see you. Aunt Ducky, I mean. More beans, Sergeant? Anyway, Brenda, the fair damsel Brenda, had been interfered with. Good old Brit term that, "interfered with." Well, she wasn't really. Not in the technical medical sense that is. But, by God, the poor girl did have one hell of a black eye and there were some nasty finger marks around her throat. Ah, yes, the concrete hero strikes again. The beauteous Brenda and her concerned Ma have put the assault to the charge of Vincent

Bishop, late of the foreign wars, and I think they're determined to drag him before the bar of the King's Justice ... now that he's quit of the King's service. Frankly, he did come back one nasty little bastard. Between you and me and the gate post, Aunt Ducky Piercy isn't the first anxious ma to confide to me their fears for their vestal virgins. I don't doubt them. I mean, a young chap who uses *that* much Wildroot hairdressing must have a lubricious libido, don't you think? Have a drink, Sergeant? Good. More for us. Oh, I don't know. I suppose the poor fella got a sniff of gas, a bit of the old shell shock, whatever. But to put you in the picture, if he keeps on the way he's going, we'll have the pleasure of your company again, Ranger, before too many months are over. Either that or these talented digits will be called on once more to ... to abort, abort, abort. Ha. Hard to Port and hard to Starboard. Tea, Sergeant? No? Ok. Well, I can offer you that famous Yankee delicacy ... the potage that won the war ... I can offer you a Coca Cola if you want one? No? No bloody style, these Yanks. No bloody style. Can you imashiin ... can you imashing ... their ... their great General Eisenhower ... their great General Eishenower ... *Him*, saying like ... like the Lord Amiral Nelson ... Ike, saying like the Lord Aml Nelsom ... "May the great God whom I worship..." "May the great God whom I worship..." Difference, see. Difference between the good old US of A and the Dominion of Canada, Dominion of Newfoundland. Great God whom I worship. Great god whom I woship. Jesus H ... Johnny. Johnny. Sergeant Hepditch. Jesus H. Johnnie Walker Christ. And his wife. Nan ... Nancy, Nancy whiskey. Johnnie Walker and Nancy Whiskey, Christ. (*Sings*.) "Nancy got me by the knees." Care for a drink, Sergeant? May the great got womb I sershps. Scuse me, Sergeant Hepditch. End of a long day. (*Sings*.) "When you come to the end of your day, day, and you sit alone with your gawdd..."
(Pats RANGER on the back.)
DR. MELROSE: Sor...Sor ... sorry, Andrew. I *am* subject to the bottle, old man. Subject to the bolle. Johnnie Walker. (*Pours self another*.) Look at it, Ranger Hepditch. Looked. The ... ah ... the ... ah ... The great god whom I worship. Oh, cheese. Just remember. Just remember. Telegram. Aunt Millie. Aunt Millie Bishop. Tongue hung in the middle and flaps both ways? A'Millie sent a boy long. Telegram. Telegram for you, Mister Ranger, Sir. An ... And ... Andrew.
(RANGER tears open and reads telegram.)
RANGER: Perce. Percy. Doctor? Doctor? This is headquarters. They say ... they say ... that Pottle ... that Pottle ... has been buggerin' the bejesus out of that orphanage they've got in Whitbourne ... buggerin the bejesus out of that orphanage they've got in ... Years. He's been at those children for years. The matron

saw in the newspaper what had happened to his daughter. She couldn't take it any more. She went to the Ranger Station in Whitbourne and spilled her guts. Well, well. This puts a new complexion on things. Percy, would you do me a favor? Would you phone down the line to Harmonville and ask the Ranger there ... Bill O'Mara, it is ... ask him to hop the train tonight and stop here. I'll have Pottle at the station and he can take him on in to St. John's.

DR. MELROSE: Sure.

RANGER: And, could I borrow your car? It's high time I clapped the cuffs on the Pastor. I could kick myself for not having seen him before. Funny, isn't it, how we always try to put the nastier business off 'til last.

DR. MELROSE: Will you need any help? Can I give you a hand. Right now he's probably in at his church.

RANGER: No. No, thanks. I'm sure I can handle it. What time is the train due?

DR. MELROSE: Ah, about 11:30 if she's on time ... not a likely prospect. You take care of yourself now.

(Exit RANGER.)

(After a moment of so, enter MRS. MELROSE in her dressing gown. She is shaking visibly.)

MRS. MELROSE: Perce, what's that? What was that?

DR. MELROSE: The Pastor. Hepditch has gone off to arrest him.

MRS. MELROSE: What? What for? Does he think Pottle killed the girl? Did he say? Did he say?

DR. MELROSE: Well, after this, he very well may. No, he's found out that the Pastor has been, um, molesting children in that orphanage they run at Whitbourne. He had a telegram.

MRS. MELROSE: Oh, Perce. *(Puts arms around his neck, sobs.)* Oh. Perce. What a relief. What a blessed relief.

DR. MELROSE: Yes. I suppose you *could* call it that.

Curtain

Scene 3:

(Interior of Pastor Pottle's church. There's only one person around, the PASTOR. He's nailing up black crepe. There's a white, mid-sized coffin in the middle of the aisle near the front of the church. Its lid is a bit askew.)

(Enter RANGER.)

RANGER: Are you William Henry Pottle?

PASTOR: *(Not looking around.)* I am not, sir. Our Pastor is at home with his private thoughts and his God at this time.

RANGER: Is he expected here?

PASTOR: He will be here. Shortly.

RANGER: I'll wait, then.
PASTOR: You may wait if you wish, Mister Ranger. All are welcome in this house of God. But the mannerly thing to have done would be to have asked.
RANGER: Yes, you're right. You're right. I should have asked.
PASTOR: We have our dignity, too, you know. It's too often forgotten. Too often forgotten. The bitter sneers and the mockers who think themselves better than we are. Ah, yes. Lots of them in Swyers Harbour. They ignore the word of God. Their parroted prayers, their lip service to the Scriptures. They taunt us for our convictions and our manner of prayer. They jeer us for our ways and our beliefs.
RANGER: Well, that's hardly right.
PASTOR: Even in the school yard. Many's the time my little girl would come home, tears streaming down her cheeks, her heart breaking. She'd be just passing by the playground and the children inside would shout, Holy Roller. Gabble Guts. Jesus Jiggerjogger. They would pelt her with mud and filth. They'd try to snatch her little Bible away. Well, they'll all suffer for their sins soon enough. For what they did to my little lamb. The sins of the fathers upon the children unto the third and forth generation. Offend my little one, will they? Better a milestone were hanged about their necks and they were drowned in the depth of the sea. They will cry out in their anguish and god will hear them not.
(By this time he's down behind the RANGER with the hammer in his hand. We see it is the PASTOR, but the RANGER, while he might suspect it to be him, doesn't know for sure. He has never met POTTLE.)
PASTOR: We'll have our own school, one day, glory be to God. A place where the pomps and vanities of this wicked world may not enter. Where our children will learn nothing but respect for their elders and their betters. Where the rod of chastisement will not be spared, nor the sins of blasphemy and idolatry and fornication encouraged.
RANGER: Excuse me, at about what time are you expecting the Pastor?
PASTOR: He'll be here, Mister Ranger. He'll be here. The abominations of this cursed placed weigh heavily upon him. There's evil here. The evil of Sodom and Gomorrah. The evil of Babylon and the worshipers of Baal. Ah, yes, God has turned his face from them. Satan hath dominion. Their hearts are as black as the raven's wing. The slaughter of the innocents, the degradation of God's creatures, Revelations, 22, 15: "For without are dogs, and sorcerers, and whoremongers, and murderers and idolaters and whosoever loveth and maketh a lie." "Whosoever loveth and maketh a lie." The postmistress, Mister Ranger. You

have talked to the postmistress, I dare say. Her business is to love and make a lie and her pleasure is to bear falsewitness. That son of hers. A raging whoremonger. Oh, yes. I know. He sought to bend an innocent little girl of this congregation to his vile lusts. Praise God, he was not successful. How many more, I wonder. How many more. All have sinned. All have sinned and have fallen short of the glory of God. The doctor, a wine-bibber and raging, sunk into the demon rum, the devil's brew, not worthy to bear the same title, not fit to be called by a name of the Great Physician. Murderer, Mister Ranger? Who is to say. I once had a dear one ... And the woman, his wife. Crazed by the potions of hell. Defiler of the temple of her body. Consumed by dark and bitter hatred, trembling on the brink of self-destruction. The merchant, stiffnecked and prideful, bloated with avarice, snatching the mite from the widow and the orphan. Those Americans, like a swarm of locusts, ravishing, pawing, seducing. Debauching the innocent, beguiling serpents, Satan-sworn fornicators. That old man in the woods. What guilty secrets there? What darkness has set him apart from the custom and hearts of his fellow man. Ah yes, Mister Ranger. The evil one is alive and kicking in Swyers Harbour today. Looks like he's winning. Yessiree, bob, looks like the great serpent is winning. But is he? Is he? No. And again, no. And again, no. And again, no. "For the same shall drink of the wine of the wrath of God, which is poured out without mixture into the cup of his indignation." "And they shall be tormented with fire and brimstone in the presence of the holy angels and in the presence of the Lamb." "And the smoke of their torment ascendeth up forever and ever." "Praise the blood of the Lamb." (*Sings.*) "There is a fountain filled with blood, drawn from Emmanuel's veins. And sinners plunged beneath that flood loose all their guilty stains. Loose all their guilty stains. Loose all their guilty stains. And sinners plunged beneath that flood, loose all their guilty stains."

(He whistles the tune. RANGER, quietly moves to the rear, observing. The PASTOR appears not to notice him.)

PASTOR: (*Sings.*) "Have you been to Jesus for the cleansing power, are you washed in the blood of the lamb..." "Are you fully trusting in His grace this hour, are you washed in the blood of the lamb." "Are you washed, are you washed, in the soul-cleansing blood of the lamb." "Are you washed, are you washed, in the precious blood of the lamb." Are *you* washed in the blood, Mister Ranger?

(Sings. He slips in and out of one song to the other. As indicated by the words, he works up toward his final outburst.)

PASTOR: "Lay aside those garments that are stained with sin, and be washed in the blood of the lamb..." "There is a fountain

filled with blood, drawn from Emmanuel's veins..." "Are you washed in the blood of the laaamb." (*Bleats like sheep, louder and louder.*) Baaaa. BAAAAA. *BAAAAA.*
(*At this last, he suddenly grabs the end of the coffin and gives it a heave, sort of end over end. It crashes to the floor. The lid has flown off and it is empty. PASTOR stands there with the hammer held above his head. Motionless. The RANGER walks quickly forward, places hand on shoulder. Slowly, he lowers the hammer, then drops it.*)

Curtain

Scene 4:

(*The Melrose dining / living room. Present are DR. MELROSE, MRS. MELROSE, BILLY HEAD, AUNT MILLIE BISHOP and MR. WASHBOURNE. The door to the outside porch is slightly ajar. They just sit around for awhile. MRS. MELROSE taps the table with her fingernails. DR. MELROSE has got his customary glass. AUNT MILLIE is heaving mighty sighs. BILLY is tapping chair or table leg with his foot. They all keep glancing at the clock. The atmosphere is tense. Finally...*)

AUNT MILLY: (*Sighs.*) Oh, my, where's he got to, at all, at all, at all. (*She gets no response.*) (*Sighs.*) ... at all, at all, at all, at all. Last time I sot eyes on him, he was where he most generally is, poor baby. He was in bed the last time I seen him. I couldn't tell the man no more than that. For the reason why, I didn't *know* no more than that. I told yez all that comin' down here in your motor car, didn't I, Doctor Melrose?

DR. MELROSE: You did, Aunt Millie. Four times, I think.

AUNT MILLIE: Because, I mean to say, I know the Ranger is only doin' his job but it hardly seem fair, somehow. No, it don't. Because he suffered a lot, you know, in them long war years. He been hardened in the crucible of battle.

MRS. MELROSE: Was he the second or merely the third person to cross the Rhine, Mrs. Bishop?

AUNT MILLIE: Oh, I couldn't tell you that, my dear. I couldn't tell you that, Mrs. Melrose, ma'am. My Vincy never talks about his war ventures, poor honey. He was never one to go around boastin' about his part in bringin' down Mister Hitler, my Vincy wasn't. Not like some. Not like some I could mention. Make you sick. My God, they goes on and on and on and on and *on* about it. And on and on and on and on. (*Sighs.*) Turn ya guts.

MR. WASHBOURNE: Could it be possible, madam, that he is abiding in the fields?

AUNT MILLIE: Wass that, sir? Wass that you said, Mr. Washbourne, sir?

MR. WASHBOURNE: Could it be possible that he is abiding in the fields, ma'am, keeping watch over other people's sheep by night?

DR. MELROSE: Good Lord, is the moon full again?

AUNT MILLIE: Oh, *don't* say that, Mr. Washbourne, sir. Please don't mention that word. Goes right through me like a knife, the word "sheep" do. It do so. But that's a thought, though, isn't it. That's a thought. Perhaps the poor young creature took fright when he heard the Ranger was comin'. Took fright and runned away and hid his self down into Uncle Oral Head's and their's stable. That's the closest one to we, anyway.

DR. MELROSE: Billy. Did you happen to take notice of ...

BILLY: Nope. Not there. I looked. P'raps ... p'raps he took to the country, Ma'am.

AUNT MILLIE: Oh, my God. The thoughts of it. The thoughts of it. The Ranger out hooftin' it through the tuckamores after my Vincy like, like, like he was a mad dog or something. There's no justice. There's no justice left in this world whatsoever. That Ranger Hepditch ... that Ranger Hepditch'd be a lot better off if he was out tryin to catch that ... that ... that *ting* of a Parson Pottle.

(Rest are all startled at the news.)

DR. MELROSE: How did *you* know ... Ah. The party line. The good old party line, eh, Aunt Millie?

AUNT MILLIE: Yes, and I'm not one bit ashamed of it, Dr. Melrose. Not one bit ashamed. Because we got nearly exactly the same two rings, hasn't we? Nearly exactly the same. Yours is three longs and a short and mine is three shorts and a long. So. The world is come to a pretty pickle if a person can't make a honest mistake, that's what I says.

MR. WASHBOURNE: Doctor, what's all this then? What's that old bugger, Pottle, up to now?

DR. MELROSE: Sergeant Hepditch got a telegram from headquarters. Seems the matron of that orphanage—Pottle's orphanage, I guess we call it—the one at Whitbourne, well, she read about Triffie in a newspaper and her conscience got the better of her. The little old Bible-thumper had been roundly stuffing the girls and the boys for, lo, these many years. Matron, too, apparently.

AUNT MILLIE: Oh, my God. *Stuffin'* em. You mean he been killin' them precious little orphans and stuffin' 'em like you would a ... a ... a old rooster or something? Oh, my God, my God, my God, my God.

MR. WASHBOURNE: No, dear lady. Stuffing them as an old rooster does a hen. Rodgering them. Behaving in a fashion which some would say is seemly only to the matrimonial couch ...

and then only if both participants can at least ... as our quaint local phrase would have it ... can at least look down into a flour barrel.
AUNT MILLIE: Ooooooooh. And didn't I know it. And didn't I know it. You should see what old dirt, what old filth that ... that ... that *ting* been getting through the mail. You wouldn't believe ... Is you all right, Miz Melrose, my dear? Is you ok?
(MRS. MELROSE has been bending over slightly, clutching her stomach with her arms.)
MRS. MELROSE: *(Snappish like.)* Yes. Yes.
AUNT MILLIE: Anyway, ...
MR. WASHBOURNE: Anyway, doctor?
DR. MELROSE: Well, Hepditch collared him this evening, put him on the eight-thirty eastbound ... he'd phoned down the line for another Ranger to take charge of Pottle. But no more than five miles out, Pastor Pedophile got clear somehow, jumped from the train, and there you go. They phoned here for the Ranger. They phoned here and gave me the message for the Ranger.
MR. WASHBOURNE: The Ranger is unaware, then, that Pottle is loose.
DR. MELROSE: Yes, he is. He phoned the Post Office and when Aunt Millie told him Vincent wasn't around, he went off to try to find him, himself ... asked me to collect you people in the car.
AUNT MILLIE: He's the one done it. Got to be. He made away with that poor maid. That .. that ... that *ting* is so far sunk into degradation there's nothing he wouldn't do. Wouldn't you say so, Mrs. Melrose, ma'am?
MRS. MELROSE: Ha. Degradation. How do you recognize it in a place like this. It's like a black cat in a coal pound at midnight. Better to be in hell with a broken back. A merciful God invented the Black Death for places like this.
DR. MELROSE: I don't know. I guess Sergeant Hepditch has got his own ideas by now. Maybe he has. He's said nothing to me.
MR. WASHBOURNE: Billy. Daniel Boone. Would you mind terribly, lad, if we told these people our little secret.
(BILLY looks startled.)
MR. WASHBOURNE: Yes, I think we'd better. Can't wait all night for the jolly old Ranger. Now then, Will, my son, you came down here last summer to have a tooth drawn. Did you see Mrs. Melrose, then?
(BILLY doesn't respond.)
MR. WASHBOURNE: Cat got your tongue, boy. It wasn't your tongue that Mrs. Melrose threatened you with the loss of, was it? But you never know, Billy, if you don't use it. What did Mrs. Melrose say the doctor might do to you? Come on, come on. Get it out, sir. Get it out.

BILLY: (*Mumbling.*) Chop the gear out of me, sir.

MR. WASHBOURNE: Eh? Chop the ... chop the what out of you, William, m'lad?

BILLY: (*Loudly.*) Me gear.

MR. WASHBOURNE: Merciful heaven. Dock your dangling participles, eh. Tch, tch, tch. Sounds a bit uncivil, don't you think. Why in the world would the good doctor's lady wife threaten to disconnect the old cods, Will, me worthy Nimrod. Did she say? What, what, what?

BILLY: If...if I ever fu...fooled around with young Triffie.

MR. WASHBOURNE: Ah, ha. Madam?

MRS. MELROSE: (*To Will.*) You little bastard. Yes, I did. Yes, I did. He's her brother. He's her brother, I tell you. Can you imagine what the issue of those two might look like? What a pretty stew ... incest on top of retardation. Two heads, perhaps. Eyes in the middle of its stomach? Maybe two extra of everything. A lump of abomination, a twisted, ugly thing ...

DR. MELROSE: Grace. Grace, please. That isn't strictly true, medically. But, yes, it's true, Billy. It's true, alright. You are Triffie's brother. I'm sorry it had to come out like this.

(*BILLY commences to sniffle quietly.*)

DR. MELROSE: Yeah. Well, you see, when first ... when we first came here ... the Heads, Billy's adopted parents, they were getting up in years, even then. Well, they had a standing order with me then, sort of. They wanted to adopt a baby. A boy. Soo, I spread the word around and a month or so later I got a letter. A letter from a classmate of mine, Jim Kennedy. He's still practicing up in Twillingate. Jim told me he had the goods. An unmarried mother was prepared to give up her baby. So that was it. A few weeks later Jim's nurse arrived, a few papers were signed, and the Head's had their wee bairn. Billy.

AUNT MILLIE: Well, this is a wonderful strange thing to me, this is. It is so. How come I never heard nothing at all about it before. Never the one word about it.

MR. WASHBOURNE: Ah, you're good, dear lady, but not perfect.

DR. MELROSE: Anyway, a couple of years after that, the Pottle's moved here. They had Triffie. Missus died.

AUNT MILLIE: Yes, but Dr. Melrose, sir, how did you ...

DR. MELROSE: How did I make the connection. I didn't. Not until last summer. I got a letter from Jim Kennedy. He'd seen a picture of Pottle in a newspaper. A religious congress or something. He'd recognized the Pastor. To top it all off, he offered a description of the late Missus Pottle, Billy's mother ... tall, skinny girl, red hair and a slight limp.

MR. WASHBOURNE: The Pottles didn't know. Nobody knew who Billy's parents were except you, your doctor friend and possibly your spouses. Er, Dr. Melrose, hadn't you better, ah ...

(He indicates MRS. MELROSE who has been declining into the DTs throughout. She is now clearly in hard shape.)
DR. MELROSE: Yes. Yes, I'd better do it now.
(All watch as he picks up bag, takes out needle and dose and sticks it into MRS. MELROSE.)
DR. MELROSE: I love you, Grace. I love you.
MR. WASHBOURNE: (To BILLY.) Ah, don't take it so hard, lad. It's all right, now. You are who you are right now. That's what you'd do well to remember. I'm sure the Heads, your parents, are extremely proud of you, sir. It'll all come out in the wash.
AUNT MILLIE: Yes, that's right, Billy, sweetheart. I s'pose there's neither 'nother two people in the world tinks so much about their boy as they do. Look what our Bible tells us, now, Billy. Look what our Bible tells us: "As the tree is bent so the twig will grow." There you are then. You'd be a wonderful sight more bent than you is now if *he* had'a reared you up.
(MRS. MELROSE moans.)
AUNT MILLIE: My Lord, sir, is she goin' to be all right. Sweet little woman.
MRS. MELROSE: *(Babbling.)* Pregnant. Pregnant. Sister pregnant. He made his sister pregnant.
DR. MELROSE: Grace. Stop it. Stop it.
MR. WASHBOURNE: Billy? What do you say, sir?
BILLY: I s'pose so, sir.
MR. WASHBOURNE: Good Lord, William. What possessed you. Why did you do a thing like that?
BILLY: Dunno. Because she ... she threatened me not to.
MR. WASHBOURNE: Ah, yes. I see, I see, I see. Forbidden fruits, eh, lad. You'd been warned not to. Threatened with rather unpleasant usage if you did. That must have inflamed any strange attraction you had to Triffie in the first place. Forbidden fruits. I once had an erotic dream about a nun. Carmelite order I think she was. Absolutely top drawer, as I somewhat dimly recall. Yes, indeed.
AUNT MILLIE: Tch, tch, tch, tch. tch. Mr. Washbourne, Esk, sir!
MR. WASHBOURNE: Did you notice ... did you know this, doctor.
MRS. MELROSE: He killed her. Didn't you, doctor? *(She holds out shaking hands, mockingly.)* Doctor. Doctor. Whiskey doctor.
DR. MELROSE: Oh, Grace, Grace. My poor, poor dear. Oh, what the hell. We've come to the end now, anyway. I think the Ranger has his suspicions. He mentions a second autopsy, a second opinion. Yes, yes, I suppose you could say I killed young Triffie. She came down here, as you know, the other day, with an ulcerated leg. As I was examining her, I discovered she was pregnant. She told me ... I finally got it out of her that, yes, the only possible candidate was Billy. The Pastor himself never did go that far. Perhaps that's what's driving him mad. Mrs ... Grace overheard.

She forced ... she persuaded me to abort the girl. Grace wasn't herself. God knows, neither was I. She was screaming. Rip it out. Rip it out. Just as I was about to ... Grace grabbed my arm. I couldn't save the poor girl. It all went terribly wrong. No one could save her after that. And, yes, later I put stab wounds in her back. And I dropped her from the boat where I was pretty sure she'd wash ashore where she did. I knew they'd bring the body here, that I would be the only examiner. I thought I'd be able to cover over ... to keep quiet .. the ... the ... other. My God, what wretchedness. What wretchedness, eh, Mr. Washbourne. Why do these things ...

BILLY: (*The door is opening, slowly.*) The Ranger.

(*But it is PASTOR who surges into the room. He has a knife and a broken leg. He is one desperate looking piece of business.*)

AUNT MILLIE: Oh, my Blessed Saviour.

MR. WASHBOURNE: I think not, dear lady. I think not.

POTTLE: The all-seeing eye of the Lord God Jehovah. The all-hearing ear of the Lord. Oh, ye generation of vipers. Who hath warned thee to flee the wrath to come. Mine ears have heard. I should have been told (*He points at BILLY.*) I had a right to know. I had a right. "Woe unto him who offendeth one of these, my little ones." "Better ... better for him that a milestone be hanged about his neck and he were drowned in the depth of the sea." Ah, yes. You butcher. You unbeliever. You Jezebel. And the Lord God commanded Abraham ... And the Lord God commanded Abraham to slay Isaac, his only son for a sacrifice unto the Lord. For a sacrifice unto the Lord ...

(*He advances on BILLY to do him damage. DR. MELROSE springs between the two.*)

DR. MELROSE: Oh, no you don't, you crazy bastard. Oh, no you do ... aaaarrrgh.

(*POTTLE gives him four or five underhand stabs to the guts, etc., savage and snake quick. POTTLE turns back to BILLY. WASHBOURNE has brought up his silver headed cane and fetches POTTLE a good one on the back of the head. He goes to the floor.*)

MR. WASHBOURNE: See to the doctor. See to the doctor. (*He kneels down. Shakes head.*) Not a chance for the poor man, now.

AUNT MILLIE: (*Shaken but still in control.*) Mrs. Melrose. What's wrong with Mrs. Melrose? She fainted away ... er what.

MR. WASHBOURNE: (*Goes to her.*). She's ... she's dead. (*Picks up syringe, container. Reads label on latter.*) Good Lord, he's killed her. The doctor's killed her. There was enough morphine in here to drop a Clydesdale.

AUNT MILLIE: Oh, Mr. Washbourne, sir. What are we goin' to do? What are we goin' to do? I don't think I can take no more of this. Me poor heart. Me poor heart. I wonder where she keeps

her tea pot.
MR. WASHBOURNE: There, there, dear lady. Not much we can do, is there? The Ranger might be here in ten minutes. He may be hours. I suggest we could do worse than go home.
AUNT MILLIE: But how, sir? How? He's the only one around here who can drive a motor car. Or was.
MR. WASHBOURNE: Well, we'll just have to leg it.
BILLY: What about he?
MR. WASHBOURNE: Umm? Oh, yes.
AUNT MILLIE: He'll come to. He'll come to.
BILLY: (*Picking up knife.*) Cut his throat, sir.
MR. WASHBOURNE: No, no, no, Billy. No, no, no. We've had enough for a day. We've had enough for a life time. Hmmm. Billy, I saw a hammer in the porch. Fetch it. Quickly. And a stout nail. Quickly, now.
(*BILLY returns. They both hunker in front of POTTLE, concealing him from audience. Sound of hammering. Are they putting the nail through his skull? They stand up and aside revealing POTTLE nailed to the Dining Room table by one hand.*)
MR. WASHBOURNE: All secure, I think.
BILLY: Where they got her, sir?
MR. WASHBOURNE: Who, Lad?
BILLY: Young Triffie, sir.
MR. WASHBOURNE: Oh, out there in the surgery, I expect. Why?
BILLY: I wants me watch back, sir.
MR. WASHBOURNE: Oh, no, Billy. No,no,no,no. Mustn't be an Indian giver, lad. What's given is given, Billy. What's given is given. Ready, dear lady. Got your torch? Well, good people, what do we do about this little business? Do we know what happened? Were we here at all? Do we help Mr. Ranger with his inquiries? Or are some things better left alone? Ah, well, let's sleep on it, shall we. Come, lad. Away we go, dear lady.
AUNT MILLIE: Oh, Mr. Washbourne, sir, what a going on. What a goin' on. And that's the God's truth. Do you think, sir, when them American's goes ... do you think when them American's goes back home where they come from that ... that our little community will be the once-tranquil place it used to be?
(*MR. WASHBOURNE chuckles at such an astonishing remark. Then laughs. Then laughs harder as they exit, not bothering to shut the door. AUNT MILLIE and BILLY HEAD, not comprehending, but chuckling along with MR. WASHBOURNE as they exit.*)

Curtain

Hanlon House
A Comedy

1988, 1991

Written by
Greg Thomey and Bryan Hennessey

Production History

Hanlon House was first produced and performed (and co-directed by the authors) in August 1988 as part of RCA Theatre Company's Second Space Programme. An expanded version (directed by Greg Thomey) was subsequently produced as a Main Stage production by RCA Theatre Company in May 1991. For both stage productions, the set was designed and dressed by the authors, and Harold Hiscock served as both Lighting Director and a sympathetic artistic advisor.

This expanded version of the script was later produced for CBC Radio by Chris Brookes in the Fall of 1991.

An abridged version (directed by Derek Norman) was subsequently produced for television by Red Ochre Productions as one-third of *The Hall Trilogy* in November 1991, for release in 1992. This version won an award as "Best Drama Under 60 Minutes" at the 1992 Atlantic Film Festival.

In all four versions, Greg Thomey and Bryan Hennessey played the roles of "Gary" and "Dad" respectively.

Notes on *Hanlon House*
by
Bryan Hennessey

This deceptively simple One Act Play is a modest and unassuming look at a moment in the lives of two very ordinary people, Gary Hanlon and his crabby father, Gus. They spend the entire play dancing around each other, avoiding conflict, trying and failing to communicate with each other. Nothing much happens: there is no great crisis, no resolution. Nonetheless, it seemed to strike a responsive chord with audiences: after all, who hasn't had a parent with whom they can't hold a sensible conversation? The characters and the situation, mundane as they are, are immediately recognizable to anyone who's had either parents or children.

It should be noted, of course, that this *is* a comedy—a human comedy about humans. There is no great point being made, other than that people are funny and sad and even the most tedious lives can be funny and sad as well. What particularly interested Greg and myself was how what is *not* said is as important, if not *more* important, than what is actually said between the characters. There are long pauses and uncomfortable silences interrupting Gary's and Dad's desultory conversation, and these pauses and silences tell us as much about their relationship as any amount of dialogue would do.

Gary and his Dad exist in a kind of emotional limbo, neither of them able to express what they might actually feel about each other. What *do* they feel? Hard to say. Dad would like Gary to settle down, get a decent job, get married, have kids ... all the normal things parents expect from their children. Gary just wants to be able to live his life in his own way. Is Dad disappointed in Gary's apparently aimless life? Yes, but what can he do about it? Exactly nothing. Can Gary ever live up to Dad's expectations? Probably not. They live in different worlds. Dad is a product of his times: in his day (as he is fond of saying, *ad nauseam*), a man went to Church, worked hard for a living, and supported his family. Those are the parameters of Dad's world and nothing can get past them.

Gary simply wants to enjoy himself a bit, although his boring job in a wiener factory in Toronto doesn't satisfy him in the least. But it is *his* life and his world, for better or worse. Gary would rather be doing something interesting, something he could enjoy (to quote from the script), but he has also accepted his situation and doesn't mind it too much, because the money is so good. Dad, for whom work is strictly a utilitarian means to an end, will never understand the concept of wanting to work at something you *enjoy*. That is simply not a part of his life equation.

In the end, there is some evidence of mutual affection. How could there not be? Even if your parents drive you nuts, you can't help but love them anyway, simply because they are your parents. And the opposite is also true: no matter how annoying your children may be, you still love them because they're *yours*.

As is often the case, our intentions have been rather misunderstood by some critics. The most common complaint is that there is no tension, no growth in the characters, no satisfying resolution of conflict. Greg and I both feel that such criticisms miss the point by a mile. It is precisely because there *is* no conflict/resolution that we were attracted to the characters and their stultifying relationship. Gary and Dad are who they are, and they will most likely always be that way. If there was a confrontational Second Act, the play would severely stray from its purpose and the characters would cease to interest us. They would then be "characters" in a "play". and not the slightly annoying, slightly lovable, slightly foolish but always recognizable real people that we wanted to write about.

Some people have said that there should be a Second Act because the piece raises too many unanswered questions. Again, they're missing the point. We felt that a tidy, wrap-up-the-loose-ends plot resolution would only result in our kow-towing to other people's preconceptions. We seriously considered writing a Second Act, but it became clear to us that the piece worked best as a One Act. That's how it was carefully designed in the first place and we didn't want to tamper with it to the point where it lost its thematic/theatrical integrity. In actual fact, there's nowhere for a Second Act to go without imposing some arbitrary or inappropriate theatrical mechanics on the largely plotless "plot".

[One final note: for this play to work properly, it is almost essential that the actors have some genuine affection for each other. There is a "sweetness", for want of a better word, inherent in the play that is best realized by two actors who really like each other. That may be asking a lot, but it certainly helps the performances. Greg and I truly enjoyed working together, and in every performance of the play our mutual enjoyment was evident across the footlights. Such things can be sensed by an audience and can only make for a better show for everyone.]

The "HANLON HOUSE" Set

A lower-middle-class living room somewhere in St. John's, Nfld.

Stage Right
Downstage against the wall: a telephone table with chair. Telephone and telephone book. A small crucifix and some family photos on the wall. Possibly a flight of ceramic geese or ducks. A wall thermostat near Stage Right Exit.
Parallel to Stage Right Wall: a couch, covered with a "throw" and some comfy cushions. In front of the couch, a small rug and a coffee table.
On the coffee table: an assortment of magazines (*National Geographic, Decks Awash, The Columbian*), an ashtray, a package of cigarettes and a lighter, a Viewmaster and some slides.

Stage Centre
Against the back wall: an upright piano. On top of the piano, assortment of knick-knacks, a plant, several books between bookends (*Ben-Hur, Moby Dick*, several books about John F. Kennedy, *Dominic Savio: Boy Saint, the Shroud of Turin*), a lamp.
On the wall above the piano: a framed photograph of John F. Kennedy. Downstage: Dad's chair, a recliner, covered with a "throw".

Stage Left
Downstage, near the wall: a futuristic lamp and revolving chair (Sylvia's "space chair", à la *The Jetsons*), a record player and several albums (*The Harmonicats, Ravi Shankar, Bing Crosby, John F. Kennedy Memorial album*, etc.). The record player is positioned in front of a bricked-up fireplace.
On the mantlepiece: assorted family knick-knacks, photos, a "Best Cadet" trophy, a fish bowl with one goldfish, a small tin of fish food.
On the wall: more pictures, a holy water font near the Stage Left Exit.

HANLON HOUSE

Lights Up

We see DAD cross from Stage Right to Stage Left in the hallway behind the piano. After a moment, we see GARY, with a towel on his head, cross in the opposite direction.

Enter DAD, Stage Left, with a folded newspaper, which he tosses onto his chair. He glances briefly at the messy living room, then goes to the record player, flips a record over and blows dust off it. He cleans it with a chamois cloth, puts it back on the turntable and places the stylus arm on the record. It is Peg O' My Heart by The Harmonicats. A kettle whistles to a boil Off Stage. DAD notices it with some annoyance. Luckily, it stops whistling just as the first notes of Peg O' My Heart begin.

DAD crosses to Stage Right, picks up the open telephone book from the couch and replaces it on the telephone table. He picks up the telephone and wipes it clean with his handkerchief before placing it on the table. He straightens a "throw" and the pillows on the couch. He goes to the piano, closes the open lid and puts the piano bench back in place. He straightens the "throw" on his chair, notices the ashtray on the coffee table (there is one cigarette butt in it). He picks up the ashtray and, holding it slightly away from him, takes it out of the room, Stage Left.

Enter GARY, in singlet and jeans, from the bathroom, Stage Right, with a towel still around his head. He is carrying a cup of tea and a dish containing a couple of huge, misshapen cookies. He turns up the wall thermostat, sits down on the couch and puts the tea cup and dish on the coffee table.

GARY becomes aware of the music playing and stealthily tip-toes to the record player, where he slowly fades the volume down and removes the stylus arm. He takes a record out of a shopping bag and places it on top of the first disc. He fades up the volume—it is Speakers Swinging (it sounds like pulsing white noise). He studies the album cover, listens to a couple of brief excerpts from the record, each sounding more unpleasant than the last. He decides to put on a Ravi Shankar record instead. He returns to the couch, picks up the newspaper on the way and flips through it until he comes to the

Horoscopes, which he examines before abandoning the paper. He picks up a Canadian Tire catalogue instead.

DAD enters Stage Right with the clean ashtray. He turns the thermostat down, places the ashtray on the coffee table and sits in his chair. Noticing the Ravi Shankar music, he looks at the record player, then at GARY. He looks away, then at GARY again. GARY laughs at something in the catalogue. He 'feels' DAD's look, puts down the catalogue and takes the towel off his head. GARY tries to eat a cookie. It is too hard and he taps it on the table. DAD looks at him. GARY munches on the cookie, dropping crumbs on himself, then brushing them off onto the rug.

DAD gets up and leaves the room, Stage Left. He comes back with the vacuum cleaner. He unplugs the record player, making the record wind down with a groan. He plugs in the vacuum cleaner, turns it on and pulls it over to the couch. He begins to vacuum the rug. GARY lifts his feet and puts them on the coffee table. DAD stares at the feet. GARY swings his feet up. DAD finishes vacuuming, then unplugs the vacuum cleaner and takes it out of the room, Stage Left. GARY stretches, makes a stretching noise (a cross between a moan and a yawn) and rolls over on the couch.

DAD comes back with a plant sprayer and sprays a plant on the mantelpiece. He then sprays a plant on top of the piano. He sprays over GARY. GARY doesn't react. DAD puts the sprayer on the piano and checks his watch. He goes to the mantelpiece, picks up a small tin of fish food and taps some of its contents into the fish bowl. He taps on the bowl several times.

DAD: Come on ... come on ... that's a good little fella ...
  (*DAD continues to tap on the fish bowl.*)
GARY: (*Slightly annoyed.*) Dad ... what are you doing?
DAD: (*Turns to look at GARY*) Oh, Gary ... the Kraken wakes. (*Pause.*) Gary, pick me up some Tetra-Mint Fish Food on your way back, will you?
GARY: (*Bemused.*) But I'm not going anywhere.
DAD: (*Stops tapping at last.*) Well, go somewhere, and on your way back from wherever it is you're going, pick up some Tetra-Mint Fish Food. Get the large one this time.
GARY: The large one!? My God, there's only one fish in the tank. How much food can one fish eat? (*Pause.*) What happened to the rest of 'em?
DAD: They all had *ick*, so I gave 'em the flush. I think I'll get the snails next, keep the tank nice and clean. (*Pause.*) Where are you going, anyway?
GARY: I wasn't going anywhere.
DAD: I thought you were going to get some Fish Food for me. You got a mind a minute, Gary. Like your Mother.
  (*DAD sits down in his chair. Pause.*)

DAD: So you're not going to go to Trades School, are you Gary?
GARY: (*Sighs.*) Dad ... we've been over that, now, a million times.
(He picks up the Viewmaster from the coffee table and starts looking at some slides.)
DAD: Well, I wish you would have told me that when you were sixteen. I wouldn't have spent a fortune on that Junior Welder's Kit. Money down the drain. But that's nothing new. Like Sylvia for the world. (*Pause.*) Hurry up, now, and get ready. You'll be running around mad at the last minute, as usual. You should be the first one at the gate, feet on the canvas, first thing.
GARY: But I don't have to be anywhere.
DAD: Sure, you got to be downtown to the Royal Trust to get your ride out to Mount Pearl.
GARY: Yes, at five o'clock.
DAD: Well ... you should be outside, walking around. Getting some air into your lungs. Go out and get some sun on your back. Look at you, you're white as a ghost, you're like a sheet. You're not getting your proper rest, Gary. When you should be home resting up, you got to be going out ... you're turning into a regular night owl ... you'll be sprouting little wings soon ... I s'pose you'll be out swooping over the barrens, catching mice next ... and that room in there ... what do you want to have it so dark in there for? You could grow mushrooms in there. (*Pause.*) Gary!
GARY: What?
DAD: What do you want to have the blanket tacked up to the window for? You're like Elvis Presley or someone.
GARY: It's too bright.
DAD: It's supposed to be bright. It's the daylight. You should be up, getting things done. Sun comes up ... that's your cue. (*Pause.*) And you never got in touch with the U.I.?
GARY: Well, the phones are either busy or there's no answer.
DAD: You'd think now with 37% unemployment they could find someone to man the phones ... crowd of 'em ... (*Pause.*) So they never found your file?
(GARY puts down the Viewmaster and sits up.)
GARY: Well, the last one I talked to kept saying things like, "Well, if it's not here, it's not here", and, "You'll just have to wait and see". See, missus transferred it back here because she thought I was moving back.
DAD: That's what you told her?
GARY: No.
DAD: Well, what did you tell her?
GARY: I told you.
DAD: What?
GARY: I told her that I was coming down here but I didn't know for how long but not to change the address on the claim or to move it down here.

DAD: So what did she do?
GARY: She changed the address on the claim and moved it down here.
DAD: Did she have the double-digit I.Q. or did she have the full three digits?
GARY: I believe it was the double-digit.
DAD: A lot like yourself. Sure I need a code-book to figure out what you're talking about half the time. You'd confuse Einstein. (*Pause.*) Are you finished in the bathroom?
GARY: Not yet.
DAD: You spend some time in there.
GARY: Well, where else am I supposed to go? I can't very well go over next door to Archibald's every time ...
DAD: But my God, Gary, you get the place some steamed up in there. It's like The Narrows. It's like being down there on Chain Rock. What do you got to be washing all the time for?
GARY: I don't know, I just wash once a day.
DAD: But my God, Gary, it's not like you're down a coal mine.
   (*GARY takes a cigarette out of its package. He flicks the cigarette lighter several times before it lights. He takes a puff.*)
DAD: You shouldn't be smoking, Gary.
   (*GARY exhales and extinguishes the cigarette.*)
DAD: It's all right for an old man like me ... not much time left. But there's no sense talking to you. You'll change your mind now when you're up in St. Clare's with a tube down your nose ...
   (*GARY picks up a magazine and stands up.*)
DAD: Where are you going with that?
GARY: I got to go in the bathroom for a second.
DAD: Well, don't be in there all day. You'll be in there now, reading that from cover to cover.
   (*GARY exits.*)
DAD: And Gary ... ?
   (*GARY enters the room backwards.*)
GARY: (*Slightly pained.*) Yes?
DAD: Don't go dropping that and getting it all wet, like you did with my Knights of Columbus.
   (*GARY exits again. The telephone rings. DAD gets up to answer it.*)
DAD: Phone hasn't stopped ringing since you've been back, Gary.
   (*He lets it ring one last time before he picks it up.*)
DAD: Hello? (*Pause.*) No, he's in on the toilet. (*Pause.*) Oh, hello, Wanda. How are you doing? (*Pause.*) Oh, I'm very good, I suppose. How are you doing at College? (*Pause.*) Oh, I see. Well, how are you doing at Compu-College then? (*Pause.*) Yes, I'll tell him. Bye.
   (*DAD hangs up the phone. He calls out to GARY.*)
DAD: That was Wanda, Gary. She told me to tell you to call her.

So I told you, now. So call. (*Pause.*) Are you going to have something to eat before you leave?
GARY: (*Calls from bathroom.*) Maybe.
DAD: (*Sitting down on the couch.*) Well, it's out there in the cupboard. You can make yourself a breakfast or a lunch or a brunch or whatever it is you call it. I guess that's why we fought the two World Wars, so everyone could lie around staring at the ceiling all day and then get up to make brunch.
(He begins to tidy up the newspaper. GARY enters, carrying the magazine and a suitcase.)
DAD: You wash your hands?
(GARY gives a slightly pained nod. He places the suitcase in the middle of the room and carefully replaces the magazine on the coffee table so DAD notices it. GARY opens the suitcase, pulls out a shirt and a pair of sneakers and begins to put them on. DAD, folding the newspaper, notices an ad.)
DAD: Meeting of the Head Injury Society tonight. (*Pause.*) You should take a run in. Join up.
(He puts the paper on the coffee table.)
GARY: Who was that on the phone?
DAD: That was Wanda. She wants you to call her before you leave.
GARY: I will.
(He combs his hair, using the nameplate of a "Best Cadet" trophy on the mantelpiece as a mirror.)
DAD: Wanda's a nice girl, Gary.
(*Pause.*)
GARY: Yeah?
DAD: You know, you should think about settling down.
GARY: With Wanda? I don't think Karen would be too impressed.
DAD: I didn't say with Wanda. I was just saying you can't bounce around like a pin-ball all your life. You're flying around like a gull. Why don't you pitch somewhere?
GARY: I don't know.
DAD: And who's this Karen, anyway? Who's that, your new ball-and-chain?
GARY: Yeah.
DAD: I don't guess you ever think about getting married?
GARY: No ... not really.
DAD: Well, you should. You're a grown man. Twenty years ago, now, you'd be married with four or five kids. You wouldn't be out running around like a young fella.
GARY: But I don't want four or five kids.
DAD: (*Exasperated.*) I'm not saying to go out and have four or five kids. I'm just saying you should think about some kind of ... stability. (*Pause.*) I saw Gerry Adams over at Mass. He just had the new baby.
GARY: Oh, yeah. Gerry had a baby. Must have been a miracle

birth.
(GARY smiles. DAD gives him a look.)
DAD: His wife was there ... Drensalla, or Droolsalla, something like that. Anyway, he's doing very good. He was asking how you were. I told him you were home ... that you were leaving Friday ... you were going to Moncton to see your Mom ... vague as ever ... back and forth, up and down, can't make up your mind, floundering around like a fish out of water.
GARY: Oh, good. *(He sighs.)* What does *he* do now?
DAD: I don't know, he said he was doing Security Maintenance or something electronic to do with it.
GARY: That's right, he's a night watchman.
DAD: There's worse things, Gary, there's worse things. *(Pause.)* I don't guess you ever think about going to Church?
GARY: No.
DAD: Next time you're going by, go in. Do the Stations. Kneel down, say a prayer. Light a candle. Sure, you'd be out of there in 25 minutes.
(No response from GARY.)
DAD: You should endeavour to do that.
GARY: I'll think about it.
DAD: Yes, well ... don't strain yourself. *(Pause.)* You should seriously consider doing that. *(Pause.)* I guess you're too busy streeling up and down Yonge Street day and night. *(Pause.)* I don't suppose you believe in God. *(Pause.)* Gary?
GARY: Well ... I don't know.
DAD: That's a good answer. That'll come in handy when you're up at the Gates of Heaven. "I don't know". That's almost as good as "I'm an agnostic". Fourteen years old, calling yourself an agnostic. Heathen is more like it. *(Pause.)* What are you going to say to St. Peter when you're up at the Gates of Heaven? What are you going to say to him?
GARY: *(Smiling.)* I'm with the band.
DAD: Very funny, Gary. I suppose if they had a bar over at Church you'd be the first one in line.
(GARY sits down in Sylvia's revolving space-chair.)
GARY: Well ... I'd like to believe there is a God ... sort of like ... most people. *(Pause.)* I mean, I'd like to believe there's some point to existence ... but ... I think the belief most people have ... in organized religion ... is a very shallow one.
DAD: You're not exactly a deep-water fish yourself.
GARY: I mean ... people hoard all their lives and then they expect some reward for leaving ... like a loot bag or something. It's like a loot-bag approach to life.
DAD: A loot bag?
GARY: Yeah, you know, when you leave a birthday party ...
DAD: I know what a loot bag is, Gary. But we're talking about

God. I mean, it's a Yes or No answer. And you're talking about loot bags. I don't know where you get it. It's definitely Sylvia's side of the family.

GARY: *(Giving up.)* Why do we always have to talk about this?

(He gets up, idly spins the space-chair around. DAD gets up and moves to the record player.)

DAD: Sorry, Gary. I'm just trying to have a simple conversation with you. Excuse me for trying.

GARY: It's hardly a simple conversation ... the meaning of life.

DAD: I guess the mysteries of the universe were a lot simpler when I was a young fella.

GARY: I guess.

(DAD plugs the record player back in. GARY makes a bee-line for the couch. GARY's Ravi Shankar record picks up speed and volume. DAD takes it off. He sorts through the albums until he finds the JFK record.)

DAD: I suppose when I get up to heaven I could put in a word for you.

GARY: Thanks.

DAD: Once a Catholic, always a Catholic, Gary.

GARY: Apparently.

(DAD puts on the JFK record. It is the Inaugural Address.)

GARY: Oh, Dad, don't go playing that now ... please.

DAD: *(Holding up the album cover.)* First and only Catholic President, Gary.

GARY: Yes, I know.

(DAD takes off the record.)

DAD: Tsk, tsk. You got no sense of history, no interest in current events.

GARY: It's hardly current.

DAD: Well, it's not solved yet. *(Pause.)* You never watch the news or read a paper. I don't suppose you even remember where you were when Kennedy was shot "that day in Dallas".

GARY: Well, I imagine I was either ... in the playpen or tied on to the cherry tree.

(DAD moves to the piano, looks at the photo of JFK on the wall above it.)

DAD: The book's not closed on that one yet. It's always interesting to speculate ... Say you're sitting where you're sitting now ... and you're shot in the throat ... your head goes back *(He demonstrates.)*. That's simple physics. Laws of motion. *(Pause.)* And the part that preys on my mind is ... how could he hit a moving target at that distance? It don't add up, Gary, it don't add up.

(DAD sits in his chair.)

GARY: You're still going on about that. When I was little, you had books and albums about it. You had the JFK album, the Pope Paul VI album, Spanish in 12 Easy Lessons ... it was like I was in training for the FBI.

DAD: Sure, you're always going on about the CIA ... and the Canadian Food Guide is a government conspiracy to keep Maple Leaf Meats in power ... and the Contras ... Contra this and Contra that ... Contragate, Contra, Contra, Contra ... who were the bloody Contras anyway?

GARY: (*Slowly.*) Well ... the Contras were basically ... a bunch of mercenaries who were hired to overthrow the Nicaraguan government.

(Blank stare from DAD.)

DAD: I see.

GARY: It's like ... if a bunch of Newfoundlanders with bullet belts were hired to go down and overthrow St. Pierre and Miquelon ... that'd be a mercenary action ... and that's basically what the Contras were.

DAD: A bunch of Newfoundlanders with bullet belts?

GARY: Well ... it's just economics. If the U.S. can control Latin American countries, the American companies can get a better return on their dollar. United Fruit can set up shop down there and not have to worry about unions or paying minimum wage ... they can pay people a couple of dollars a week ... the country's probably going to be run by a military dictatorship that's friendly to the U.S ... Unions won't exist ... less overhead ...

(Long pause.)

DAD: Oh, yeah ... (*Pause.*) And Gary, you never think about going back to Trades School?

(GARY just stares at DAD, who stares right back.)

DAD: It's always nice to have a trade to fall back on. Well, I guess you could always get a job bagging groceries over at Dominion. Sure, your old buddy Mike O'Leary is Head Bag Boy over there now. You should look into that. You could probably land a job. Get your foot in the door. Work your way up.

GARY: (*Patiently.*) Dad, I got a job.

DAD: Oh, yeah, the one Bhagwan got you?

GARY: Dad, his name is David Rasheen Pim.

DAD: Whatever. So, where you working? A dog food factory?

GARY: A wiener-stuffing plant.

DAD: Same thing. (*Pause.*) Isn't that against his religion? Stuffing wieners?

GARY: Not that I know of.

DAD: It's against some religion, I know that. I was just reading about it in the *Geographic*. (*Pause.*) So you started that as soon as you got there?

GARY: Well ... I didn't start right away because there was only part-time available, and part-time would just screw up my U.I.

DAD: Oh, yes. The Great God U.I.

(DAD muses for a moment, then looks at GARY.)

DAD: My God, Gary, you're after getting to be some size. You're as big as your Uncle Ted.
(GARY grasps at the chance to change the subject.)
GARY: Oh, yes, what's Ted up to now? How's it going with him?
DAD: Oh, you know ... one day at a time. He's still out in Kelligrews.
GARY: Oh, yeah. What's he doing now?
DAD: As little as possible. I think he gets up off the couch and he lies right back down again ... worn out. He's like some kind of missing link. The place out there smells like a camel tent. That's Ted, though ... the original Ringling Brother. He got to be smoking up dope now, day and night. Why do people got to be drugged up? I'm breaking the law now, as I speak. Legally, I'm supposed to call the cops. Technically, I'm Ted's accomplice. I could be behind bars now, chained on to Ted. He can't go to the mail box without smoking a "bong of weed". He showed me his greenhouse out there. You'd think, now, that he'd give that up, at his age. I don't understand it, Gary.
GARY: Well ... some people smoke dope when they're home ... or when they socialize, just to make things easier. It's like ... when you go to a cocktail party, you have a drink ...
DAD: Cocktail party!?
GARY: It's a normal, acceptable thing to do.
DAD: Yes, but, Gary, I'd have a Rye & 7 ... I wouldn't go on a ... a ... a drug trip!
GARY: But liquor is a drug ... people get high on it ,,, *(Pause.)* When you smoke dope ... uh ... it changes the way you look at things.
(Blank stare from DAD. GARY tries again.)
GARY: It's like ... it's like a ...
(He has a flash of inspiration.)
GARY: ... a Viewmaster! You see things differently ... more detail ...
(Long pause. DAD is nodding and staring at GARY.)
DAD: And, Gary, you never think about going back to MUN?
(GARY just looks at DAD.)
DAD: You should think of buckling down and doing some hard work for a change. Get an education. You can't just hang around with that crowd of yamyucks for the rest of your life. You got to admit, Gary, they're a rum lot. *(Pause.)* And why do they got to dress up like that for? Surely to God they could afford a new pair of decent pants between them. I got a closetful of cords in there. I got a full wardrobe for under sixty bucks. When the backside goes out of your pants, you buy a new pair or you sew a patch on. Why do they got to walk around with the arse out of their pants or their knees out or holes in their undershirt?
GARY: It's just fashion.
DAD: Fashion? Fashion! Don't talk to me about Fashion. Sure I

was voted Best-Dressed Man on Bulley Street two years in a row. (*Pause.*) I suppose it'd be too confusing to have a button-up shirt. Or a neck-tie. My God, I suppose that'd stump 'em altogether. Crowd of dope addicts ... the world's gone drug mad. (*Pause.*) And now I'll have to be having the mandatory urine check. I'm just heaving boards around down there, I don't see why I got to have a urine check. In my day now, you'd be the first one at the gate. You'd do a day's work, the whistle'd blow and you'd go home out of it. They wouldn't want to be all the time sampling your urine. (*Pause.*) So ... what do *you* do at work?

GARY: Stuff wieners.

DAD: I see.

GARY: Well ... I sit on an assembly line and make sure all the wieners are the same size.

DAD: (*Genuinely interested.*) Oh, yeah ... and you like that?

GARY: (*Attempting sarcasm.*) Oh, yes, I love it. (*Pause.*) No, I hate it. It's ridiculous. It's mesmerizing. The noise is deafening. It's endless. Wiener after wiener after wiener. I just sit there in this chair and watch the little dogs go by. It's maddening. But the money's great, so I can handle it. I just wish I could be doing something that was halfways interesting, something I enjoy.

DAD: Something you enjoy?

GARY: Yes.

DAD: Something interesting?

GARY: Yeah.

DAD: Take up a hobby! Finish your model Deusenberg up there ...

GARY: Dad, I'm not twelve ...

DAD: I don't understand, Gary, I can't understand you ... you got the full-time job, all the overtime you want, double-shifts, triple-shifts ... you got it knocked.

GARY: I'm going mad ...

DAD: That's the workaday world, Gary. Don't tell me, ask me. That's the real world now, that's not Walt Disney Presents.

GARY: It's sickening, though. You wouldn't believe what they put in the wieners. It's not fit to eat.

DAD: Yes, I know, Gary, but nothing's fit to eat, now that you're gone Vegetarian. (*Pause.*) Vegetarian ... you're not a Vegetarian. What are you ... a macro-Vegetarian? A lacto-Vegetarian? Vegetarian ... (*Pause.*) Boom or bust. Everything in spurts. Like your jogging phase. Tsk, tsk. If you're going to go at something, go at it the right way. There's a right way and a wrong way to do everything. It's like the garbage. How many times do I have to tell you? Separate the wet from the dry, wet from the dry ... (*Pause.*) Wet from the dry. (*He motions with his hands—"wet from the dry".*) Oh, by the way, I found your Snack-Pack out there in the garbage. What kind of a vegetable is a Snack-Pack made from?

GARY: What are you out rooting around in the garbage for?
DAD: Vegetarian ... you should take a page out of Terge's book. *He's* a vegetarian.
GARY: Who?
(DAD motions towards the floor.)
DAD: Terge ... downstairs.
GARY: Oh, right. Where's he from?
DAD: Oh, he's from the University.
GARY: No, I mean, what country is he from?
DAD: I don't know ... Sri Lanka or Ceylon or somewhere. Some sticky place, anyway.
GARY: Dad, don't you think $385 a month is a bit steep to charge him for the crawl-space down there?
DAD: Sure that's reasonable, Gary. He's got the use of the bedroom, use of the rumpus room, use of the ping-pong table, the cold water tap ... full use of the furnace.
GARY: Use of the furnace? What are you talking about?
DAD: Well, there's no lack of heat down there. He can't get enough heat. I believe he'd curl up on the radiator like a cat if he could. He's probably down there now lying around half-naked, stupefied by the heat. Reminds me of you. *(Pause.)* He don't mind doing a chore, though. Raking the lawn, or out at the mulch ... cleaning the drains. Never a word out of him. He's like the son I never had.
GARY: Thanks.
DAD: They're a very polite race, though. Very polite. That's probably why they lost their country. I suppose Toronto is glutted with them up there.
GARY: Yes, well, that's one way of putting it.
(GARY sits on the piano bench and opens the piano lid.)
DAD: Now, where are you living, exactly? You're in Toronto?
GARY: I was just outside it.
(DAD moves to the couch, picks up a map on the coffee table and unfolds it.)
DAD: Yes, but where exactly? I got the map of the Greater Metropolitan Area ... put a circle around where it is.
GARY: I don't know exactly where it is because Karen and Bhagwan ... *(He corrects himself.)* ... Karen and *David* are after moving since I left. But it's outside Toronto, and we got a house.
DAD: Oh, you actually got a roof and everything. You've come a long way, Gary ... roof to roof. *(Pause.)* So what does this Karen do? What is she ... a student?
GARY: No, she's an Iridologist.
(DAD thinks about it for a second.)
DAD: Oh, yeah ...
(GARY plays the opening bars of Fur Elyse. *Then he plays the* Fist Song, *followed by* Chopsticks. *Finally he does a* glissando

up and a glissando *down the keyboard. Pause.)*
DAD: You ever get your ears checked?
GARY: No.
DAD: You should. You don't want that infection to come back. *(Pause.)* Your little violin is still in there in the closet, you know. You should take that when you're going.
GARY: It's safe in there, though.
DAD: I guess. *(Pause.)* You could probably get a hundred dollars for that.
GARY: Yes ... I wouldn't really want to sell it, though.
(GARY sits in DAD's recliner and uses the lever to sit back.)
DAD: Careful with that, now. *(Pause.)* Your report cards are in there. Had 'em out the other day. "Could do better" ... *(Pause.)* And your trunk is still down in the basement. I'd like to clear all that out of it down there. It's all gone musty. *(Pause.)* Do you want a package of ham to take with you?
GARY: No, thanks. *(Pause.)* What's that out in the pot?
DAD: Halibut.
GARY: What, soup?
DAD: No ... just boiled.
GARY: Oh. Poached halibut.
DAD: Help yourself.
GARY: No ... no, thanks.
(Pause.)
DAD: *(Sighs.)* I don't know, Gary, you're going around like a gypsy. One minute you're going to Trades, next minute you're going to MUN, then you're off to T.O ... I guess it could be worse. You could be a Communist. *(Pause.)* You're not a Communist, are you?
GARY: No. Too much bookwork.
(GARY gets up, takes another record out of his shopping bag and puts it on. It is Music of the Upper Amazon. *It sounds like a cacophony of monotonous chanting voices.)*
DAD: Leave that off for a while.
(GARY takes the record off.)
DAD: What was that ... a City Council meeting?
(Pause.)
GARY: I got to use the phone.
DAD: Local call?
GARY: Moncton.
DAD: I'll put on the egg-timer.
(DAD gets up and goes out to the kitchen, Stage Right. GARY sits at the telephone table and dials a long-distance number.)
GARY: Hi! Yeah ... yeah ... uh huh ... yeah ... tomorrow morning ... yeah ... uh huh ... tomorrow evening ... yeah ... uh huh ... yes ... yes, yeah, sneakers ... yeah, hold on a minute.
(GARY leaves the room, Stage Left. DAD comes in and notices

the phone off the hook. He picks it up gingerly.)
DAD: Hello? Oh, hello, Sylvia ... yeah ... yeah ... yeah ... tomorrow morning ... yeah ... uh huh ... tomorrow evening ... yeah ... uh huh ... yes ... yes, yeah, sneakers ... yeah ...
(GARY comes back with the Ferry Schedule and his windbreaker. He stops and watches DAD talking to Mom, not wanting to interrupt. DAD notices him.)
DAD: Yeah ... here's Gary.
(DAD extends the phone to GARY. GARY motions "keep talking", DAD insists. GARY takes the phone and DAD goes back to the kitchen.)
GARY: Hi ... yeah ... yeah ... that's good, then ... ten to seven ...
(The egg-timer goes off.)
DAD: *(Calls from kitchen.)* Three minutes, Gary! Write a letter!
GARY: I'm gonna go now ... see you when I see you. Bye bye. Yeah ... bye ... uh huh ... bye now. Hello?
(GARY hangs up the phone. DAD comes back into the room and sits in his chair.)
DAD: Call Poppy now.
GARY: Aw Dad, I don't want to call Poppy now ... I wrote him that letter, that's good enough. He can't hear on the phone anyway. He always thinks I'm you and starts swearing at me.
DAD: Years ago, now, you couldn't wait to see Poppy Hanlon. You were like a cat in a car window. Remember ... you used to be fascinated by his friend with the two stumps. But now, you haven't got time for an old man. Better things to do. Everyone got a full schedule.
GARY: What did he do? Poppy?
DAD: He worked.
GARY: No, but I mean what did he *do*? What did Poppy do ... as a job?
DAD: Oh ... everything. *(Pause.)* He used to work in the lumber woods. He was a logger ... and then he worked in a tannery. He was out West for a while ... out in the Dakotas, panning for gold ... and then he worked in the mines here ... he ran a store ...
GARY: And what did *his* father do? My great-grandfather? Poppy Senior.
DAD: *(Deadpan.)* He was a movie star.
(GARY looks at DAD.)
DAD: He worked. He ran a stable.
GARY: A stable?
DAD: Yeah. He supplied horses for the taxis.
GARY: Poppy was in the Great War when he was really young, wasn't he?
DAD: Oh yes. Poppy *caused* the War. I believe he defeated the Hun single-handed ... from all accounts. *(Pause.)* There's pictures of him there in the photo album.

GARY: Yes, I know ... I was going to ask if I could have one.
(DAD thinks about it for a second.)
DAD: Yes, boy ... take 'em all.
GARY: I don't want them *all* ... there's one there I'd like to have where he's standing outside a barn. He's got really big hands.
(GARY gets the photo album out of the piano bench. He flips through the pages, takes out a photo.)
GARY: What's the medal for?
DAD: For marrying Nanny Hanlon.
(GARY puts the photo in a folder and puts it in his suitcase.)
GARY: You never went overseas, did you, Dad?
DAD: No, no. The Quartermaster's Store was my H.Q. *(Pause.)* That's "Headquarters", Gary. Someone had to keep the troops clothed and shod.
GARY: Shod?
(DAD gestures impatiently at his shoes.)
DAD: Shod! Shod! You got no education, Gary. I don't know why I paid the School Tax for the last eon. *(Pause.)* Well, it's either you got a major World War with full employment or peacetime with everyone on their backs. I guess it's the lesser of two evils. *(Pause.)* I was thinking, if the Super Powers wanted peace they should get Sylvia involved. They should send Sylvia over. Just let her nag at them for a week or so and they'd be worn down to a nub. They'd agree to anything. *(Pause.)* What's she doing now?
GARY: Mom? As opposed to last week? *(Pause.)* She's still working for the NFB, I imagine ... they just moved into a new house.
DAD: *(Mildly amused.)* She can't be satisfied ... the two door wasn't good enough for her, she had to have the hatchback ...
(DAD cocks his ear suddenly. He hears something, somewhere.)
DAD: Do you hear that?
GARY: What?
DAD: Do you hear that?
GARY: *What?*
DAD: He's hammering.
(He gets up and goes out Stage Left to investigate.)
DAD: *(Off-stage.)* He's up on the ladder now, measuring the height of the house ... oh, no ... he's building a scaffold!
(DAD comes back in.)
DAD: This could mean weeks ... months ... He'll be up there hammering away ... night falls and he'll still be up there hammering away. It's like a disease, some kind of horrible, wasting disease. He's always got a second-hand car out there, racing the engine ... He's the nicest kind of fella, nice as pie ... always says Hello ... nice as pie ... he goes inside ... the hammering never stops. What's he building over there? An Ark? *(Pause.)* Go over, now,

Gary ... wait till he's up on the roof ... get the ladder ... bring it home and we'll take the rungs out of it.
(They both smile.)
GARY: I got to go now.
DAD: Oh, yeah ...
(GARY gets up and goes to his suitcase. He zips it open, takes out a cloth cap and lays it on the floor. DAD looks at the hat. GARY notices the Speakers Swinging album and quickly stuffs it into the suitcase, which he then zips shut. He places the suitcase by the door.)
DAD: You got your ticket?
GARY: Yeah.
(GARY goes to the telephone table and picks up his windbreaker.)
DAD: You're all packed?
GARY: Oh, yeah. Oh, I left those cookies Wanda made in there in the tin.
DAD: I'll use 'em for doorstops.
(GARY goes off Stage Right and comes back with a badly-gift-wrapped box. He places it on the coffee table.)
GARY: There's a present for you.
DAD: Oh ... good. I'll open it later.
GARY: Well ... you might as well open it now.
(DAD sits down on the couch and looks at the gift.)
DAD: Fine job with the wrapping.
(He carefully and tediously unwraps the box and opens it. He takes out a Dustbuster and examines it.)
DAD: Oh ... very good. (Pause.) What is it?
GARY: It's a Dustbuster.
(DAD nods.)
GARY: It's for dust.
DAD: You should save your money.
GARY: I got it on sale, There's a Warranty. And there's batteries already in it. It's all charged up. Took me sixteen hours. *(Pause.)* Enjoy.
DAD: Very good. Thank you.
(GARY prepares to say goodbye.)
GARY: Okay then ...
(DAD stands up and pulls a twenty dollar bill out of his pocket.)
DAD: Here's twenty dollars now, in case of an emergency.
GARY: No, that's okay, Dad, I got money.
(DAD continues to offer the money.)
DAD: No, no, go on now, you take that.
(GARY finally accepts the money.)
GARY: Thank you.
DAD: Be careful with that, now.
GARY: *(Looks at the bill.)* What's it going to do? Blow up?

DAD: You should save that. You should have that when you come back.
GARY: Then what are you giving it to me for? Put it in the bank, collect interest ...
DAD: That's right ... 9 and 3/4 per cent ...
GARY: That'll be about ... 48 cents.
DAD: Yes, you'll be 48 cents ahead of it.
(GARY puts the money in his wallet.)
GARY: Oh ... say goodbye to Rose for me.
DAD: I will.
GARY: How's her hip?
DAD: Good. Right as rain. *(Pause.)* Now listen. Don't be staying up all night with your barbecue buddies. Get your eight hours. You want to be bright-eyed and bushy-tailed. You don't want to be the last man on the bus. You should be out at the ferry a full two hours before she leaves.
GARY: At six o'clock in the morning?
DAD: Be first in line. And when you get on, stay put. Don't go wandering around, you're liable to lose your seat. And take your Gravol, 'cause you don't want to be seasick, throwing up all over total strangers again.
GARY: That was twenty years ago, Dad ...
(GARY picks up the cloth hat from the floor and puts it on.)
DAD: I don't think those ferries are safe, Gary ... you should be careful. Get a bunk next to a lifeboat. I don't want to be reading about you when she goes down. *(Pause.)* Why don't you stay put, Gary? You're like the Littlest Hobo. *(Pause.)* And you never called Wanda.
GARY: I'll call her later from Heber's.
DAD: I bet you will.
(He looks at GARY's windbreaker and hat.)
DAD: That's all you're wearing? It's not that warm out, Gary ... wind's after changing. What happened to that hat I gave you? You're after losing that, aren't you?
GARY: No, I still have it.
DAD: Well, why don't you wear it?
GARY: I got a hat.
DAD: That's not a hat, that old cloth thing. You need a good wool one on your head. You're going out on the North Atlantic, Gary, you're not going to Gilligan's Island.
(GARY digs through his suitcase, finds the woolen hat and puts it on. DAD looks on as GARY rolls up the sides of the hat and tilts it forward at a rakish angle, again using the "Best Cadet" trophy as a mirror.)
DAD: That's more like it. 'Cause you know how much body heat you lose out of the top of your head ...
GARY: 90 per cent.

DAD: (*A little surprised that GARY actually remembered something he'd told him.*) That's right.
(*GARY takes a camera out of his suitcase.*)
GARY: Just stand still for a minute.
(*He takes a picture. The flashbulb blinds DAD momentarily. GARY puts the camera away.*)
DAD: Well ... look after yourself now ... take 'er easy ...
GARY: I will ... see you at Christmas ... look after yourself ... don't burn the place to the ground.
(*GARY puts out his hand. They shake awkwardly.*)
DAD: And if you need anything ... (*Pause—DAD almost laughs.*) Call Sylvia.
(*GARY almost laughs as well. They break the handshake.*)
DAD: Go on now, you'll miss your ride.
(*GARY picks up his suitcase and goes to the door. He turns to say a final goodbye.*)
GARY: God bless ...
(*DAD nods. He has finally run out of words. GARY leaves. DAD follows him off Stage Left. Pause.*)
DAD (*Off-stage, calls after him.*) Put that hat back on!
(*DAD comes back into the living room. He pauses for a moment. He looks at the Dustbuster on the coffee table. He begins to tidy up. The phone rings and he goes to answer it.*)
DAD: Hello? (*Pause.*) Oh, hello, Wanda. (*Pause.*) Oh, I'm very good, I suppose. (*Pause.*) No, you just missed him ... he's gone out to Heber's. (*Pause.*) Yeah ... yeah, I told him ... he said he'd call you later. (*Pause.*) All right then. Bye bye, Wanda.
(*DAD sits down at the telephone table and carefully dials a number.*)
DAD: Hello, Rose ... it's me, Gus. (*Pause.*) How're you doing? (*Pause.*) What are you doing? (*Pause.*) Yes, he's gone. He said to say goodbye. (*Pause.*) No ... sneakers. (*Pause.*) Well, why don't you come on over? (*Pause.*) All right. See you then. Bye bye, Rose.
(*DAD hangs up the phone. He goes to the record player and puts on, once again, Peg O' My Heart by The Harmonicats. He straightens the "throw" on his chair, puts the photo album back in the piano bench. He folds up the "throw" on the couch and sits down. He picks up the Dustbuster and switches it on. It makes a "vroom" noise. He tries it out on a speck of dust on the couch, on the floor, on the mantelpiece. HE LIKES IT! He picks up GARY's cup and dish and takes them out to the kitchen, "vrooming" the Dustbuster from time to time as he goes. The Harmonicats play on as the LIGHTS FADE DOWN.*)

The End

Flux

1993

Written by
Pete Soucy

Flux was first produced in a one-act version by the Resource Centre for Arts, March 22 – 24, 1989, at the LSPU Hall, St. John's, Newfoundland.

Director	Pete Soucy
Jill	Mary Lewis
Claude	Clarke Hancock
Joey	Randy Follett
Music	Eric West
Set and Props	Pete Soucy

Subsequently *Flux* was rewritten and remounted as a full-lengh production by the Resource Centre for Arts, Nov. 14 - 18, 1990, at the LSPU Hall, St. John's, Newfoundland.

Director	Pete Soucy
Jill	Jennifer Scurlock
Claude	Clarke Hancock
Joey	Randy Follett
Music	Paul Steffler
Set	Don Short
Props	Tish Holland

The first production of *this* full-length version of *Flux* was a co-production by Live Bait Theatre '93 and the Eastern Front Theatre Company. The premiere performance was staged at the Windsor Theatre, Mount Allison University, in Sackville, New Brunswick on August 25, 1993.

Director	Mary Vingoe
Jill	Kiersten Tough
Claude	Lorne Pardy
Joey	Randy Follett
Set Design	Stephen Osler
Lighting Design	Bruce MacLennan
Costumes	Gary Markle

Original music written and performed by Paul Cram

Scripts for both the one-act and two-act versions of *Flux* can be ordered in copy-script – format through the
Playwrights Union of Canada
54 Wolseley St., 2nd Floor
Toronto, Ontario M5T 1A5
fax (416)947-0159

Character Descriptions

CLAUDE (Rhymes with "ode"): Recent art school graduate, early 20's, alternative-fashion conscious. He is genuine despite his verbosity.
JILLIAN: Student and social hyper-activist, a little younger than Claude.
JOEY: Pipefitter, late twenties.

Music

The music referred to throughout the script was conceived to reflect each of the characters. When played individually, each piece speaks of an individual. However, the melodies blend together in the "Combined Music" to suggest how the relationships have become resolved. There exist two sets of scores; the original music composed by Paul Steffler for the 1990 RCA production and the Paul Cram set for the Live Bait/Eastern Front production. The former is available through the playwright, the latter through Mary Vingoe at Eastern Front, Dartmouth, Nova Scotia.

Setting

A cluttered living room/art studio of a cheap apartment. The main entrance is UC, the entrance to the kitchen is UL, and the hallway exit that leads to the unseen bedrooms and bathroom is UR. There is a small table with two chairs DR, a well worn sofa RC, with a small TV. There is also a low support DCL on which sits an unfinished sculpture*, around which is scattered a variety of art materials. This is CLAUDE's work area. JILLIAN's desk, piled high with the paraphernalia of a social activist, is L, although several boxes of her stuff are everywhere. Long dead plants sit here and there. The room speaks of considerable visual experimentation (CLAUDE) and general disorganization (JILL).

*The sculpture is an important metaphor for CLAUDE's inhibition. It can be constructed out of a variety of materials—coloured wire, styrofoam, sticks, etc., but he must be able to work on it during the course of the play. Most importantly, an adjustment or addition to the sculpture at the designated point in the script should allow the piece to suddenly reflect what it represents— "flight". This has been accomplished differently in each of the productions of *Flux* to date, and is a special challenge for the designer. The audience should almost experience the same frustration as CLAUDE as he tries desperately to work out just what's "wrong" with the piece.

FLUX

Act One

Scene 1:

(In the darkness we hear JILLIAN'S MUSIC, an experimental, disjointed collection of sounds. Lights up to reveal Jillian sitting on the sofa. She is reading from notes and energetically scribbling more. She sips an odd-coloured substance from a glass, grimacing slightly at the taste. Her attention is caught by the sculpture. After some thought, she gets up to add a substantial piece to it. She returns to the sofa to evaluate her addition.

CLAUDE enters from the hallway, shirt unbuttoned. He looks fatigued—the music obviously annoys him. He shuts it off.)

JILL: 'Bout time. (*Beat.*)
CLAUDE: Mmmmm.
JILL: What kept you up so late?
CLAUDE: Just reading. Watching TV.
JILL: What was on?
CLAUDE: (*Takes the cassette out of the deck.*) Info-mercials. Steak knives. Cut a car in half, still slice tomatoes paper thin.
JILL: (*Back to her work.*) Why do you keep doing that?
CLAUDE: Can't sleep. My clock is mixed up.
JILL: I noticed you didn't get any work done. Again.
CLAUDE: No. (*A look, then.*) What's this? (*The tape.*)
JILL: Peffler Stall.
CLAUDE: Never heard of 'em.
JILL: You met one of them at the film society party.
CLAUDE: Yeah? What's he look like?
JILL: Green crew cut. Yellow frames.
CLAUDE: (*Beat.*) Oh, that guy. He cornered me for a half an hour.
JILL: That's the guy.
CLAUDE: When's his CAT scan?
JILL: You don't like his stuff?
CLAUDE: I didn't say that. *He's* pretty burnt.
JILL: But *it* isn't.

CLAUDE: I dunno. "Artwork is not responsible for its creator", you know.
JILL: Right.
CLAUDE: I hate it.
JILL: What's wrong with it?
CLAUDE: You want it back on?
JILL: No, not if you can't bear it.
CLAUDE: I'll turn it back on.
JILL: No, don't.
CLAUDE: You don't want it back on?
JILL: Just tell me why you don't like it.
CLAUDE: (*Beat.*) Well, "ethereal innovation" does leave one a little "content-malnourished."
JILL: You got that from some class.
CLAUDE: So what? It's true.
JILL: Well Melissa finds it "hauntingly evocative." She's using it in the festival.
CLAUDE: She is?
JILL: So does Jacqueline.
CLAUDE: Oh, I see.
JILL: I guess it requires an intuitive response rather than an acquired one.
CLAUDE: Hey, why so nasty?
JILL: You always have to try and intellectualize it. Why can't you be a little spontaneous, for God's sake.
CLAUDE: I was. I spontaneously didn't like it. (*Beat.*) I could be wrong, I suppose.
JILL: No, don't start that. You said what you think. Leave it. (*Beat.*) What do you think? (*The sculpture.*)
CLAUDE: About what? Oh. I didn't notice.
JILL: I think it works, somehow. Gives it direction or something.
CLAUDE: (*Beat.*) Uh huh. I suppose so.
JILL: You don't have to agree.
CLAUDE: I haven't.
JILL: Maybe it's your point of view. Move over here.
CLAUDE: (*Moves, looks—beat.*) Oh, yeah.
JILL: Oh yeah what?
CLAUDE: It looks different from over here.
JILL: Meaning?
CLAUDE: (*Beat.*) It doesn't look the same as it does from over there.
JILL: Oh, stop.
CLAUDE: I don't know the answer you want.
JILL: I don't want *an* answer, I want *your* answer. Something to do with an honest opinion.
CLAUDE: Oh. (*Beat.*) I don't know. Honestly. Jill, it's too early, I can't concentrate.

JILL: If it's not right, it's not right. (*Gets up to remove it.*)
CLAUDE: Just leave it for a bit.
JILL: I was only experimenting to see if I could spark something.
CLAUDE: So leave it.
JILL: (*Removes the piece.*) Stop accommodating.
CLAUDE: I'm not.
JILL: You are!
CLAUDE: (*Beat.*) Okay, maybe a bit...
JILL: Ha! See? You know, this funk of yours is really starting to be a drag. (*Going through piles of paper, collating.*)
CLAUDE: I'm just a little lost on things. I'll snap out of it. (*Starts to rub JILL's back as she works.*)
JILL: I've got a million things to do. You know I haven't got time to deal with a terminal introspection thing.
CLAUDE: Okay, I'm trying.
JILL: Just get on with it.
CLAUDE: I told you. I just don't feel in control right now.
JILL: You've hit the big world and it doesn't work like the art college.
CLAUDE: Actually, it does. That's probably what I'm having trouble adjusting to.
JILL: Well, you don't necessarily have to adjust yourself to death, you know. You are allowed to find fault, work against things.
CLAUDE: Please, Jill.
JILL: Like the group show. (*Beat.*) That's it, really, isn't it?
CLAUDE: No, that's not it.
JILL: It is. You've been agonizing about it for weeks.
CLAUDE: Partially, I guess. The group show and ... I don't know.
JILL: When do you talk to Robert again?
CLAUDE: This afternoon.
JILL: And is he going to give you an answer?
CLAUDE: Who knows? I don't know if I even want one. My stomach is killing me.
JILL: Y'know, maybe it's your mood that's turning *them* off, too.
CLAUDE: I just have to "Emanate Affirmative Ambience," right?
JILL: Exactly. It works.
CLAUDE: Does it?
JILL: (*Beat.*) What's your game plan?
CLAUDE: What game plan?
JILL: For the meeting. I know you've gone over and over it.
CLAUDE: No I haven't. It's just a meeting.
JILL: Look, I'll be Robert. (*Sits on the sofa.*) You come in and sit down.
CLAUDE: Not now.
JILL: Come on, Claude. It might clarify things.
CLAUDE: I'm not up to it, really.
JILL: Try it. What can it hurt?

CLAUDE: It won't help. It'll just make me more anxious.
JILL: It will not. It's good preparation. Come on.
CLAUDE: (*Beat.*) Oh, alright. Let's just say I'm already here.
JILL: No, over there and come back again so we know it's started.
CLAUDE: But...
JILL: Just ... Claude!
CLAUDE: Okay, alright. (*Walks away, turns, and heads back.*) Robert. How you doin'?
JILL: (*Stands to shake CLAUDE's hand.*) Claude, you old sonovabitch.
CLAUDE: He won't say that.
JILL: It'll be some standard good ol' boy greeting. Just go with it. Now, come in again.
CLAUDE: Jill...
JILL: Again.
CLAUDE: (*Re-enters, grudgingly.*) Robert, you old sonovabitch.
JILL: (*Hand shake.*) Claude, great to see ya. Have a seat.
CLAUDE: Thanks. (*Sits—beat.*) So. Am I in or out?
JILL: Gee, that's ... sure straight to the heart of things, there, Claude. Well, it's like this. We met, we reviewed your work—it's a strong portfolio, we all know that—and we just have a few questions.
CLAUDE: Okay.
JILL: First of all, how is it that you see your work appearing in this particular show?
CLAUDE: Well ... I know that, each year, the exhibition takes on a couple of new artists, people that have worked hard, and displayed some expertise ...
JILL: Yeah, yeah, true. But what I really want to know is what your work would contribute above that of other artists we might consider.
CLAUDE: Above? I don't know that it would contribute *above* ...
JILL: What do you see as your strengths?
CLAUDE: That's ... that's a difficult question ...
JILL: Come on, Claude, spit it out. Why the hell should we let you in?
CLAUDE: (*Beat.*) I don't know. Why the hell not?
JILL: Why not? Let's see. Your technique is a bit too strong, your stuff is terribly accessible, and you don't drink with us.
CLAUDE: Jesus, I knew it!
JILL: (*Breaking.*) Look, you know there's some of that there, Claude. Deal with it!
CLAUDE: I can't! It's all smoke-screens. Just excuses.
JILL: So expose that.
CLAUDE: It's no good.
JILL: You're wasting all your energy on this childish anxiety.
CLAUDE: Well, this has been a terrific help.

JILL: (*Beat.*) You look terrible. Not like yourself at all.
CLAUDE: I feel worse.
JILL: Here, try some of this. (*The drink.*)
CLAUDE: Why?
JILL: It's good for what ails you. Just try it.
CLAUDE: (*Drinks.*) Aghh! God! What is it?
JILL: (*Packing her knapsack.*) I got it from Jacqueline. Great for energy, and organ purification. That kind of thing. She knows all about herbal medicine and stuff.
CLAUDE: That too, huh? Pooo-ey, what's in it?
JILL: Root fibre, mineral muds. Who knows?
CLAUDE: Tastes like shit.
JILL: I don't find it so bad. (*CLAUDE tries to hand it back.*) Naah, I'm full.
CLAUDE: I thought so. (*Pours it into a plant.*)
JILL: No, I could have put it back in the bottle!
CLAUDE: Sorry.
JILL: It costs a fortune!
CLAUDE: Really? How much?
JILL: I can't tell you, it's embarrassing. Oh, can you pick up my cheque at the clinic?
CLAUDE: Sure.
JILL: I'll be lucky to get half of this done as it is.
CLAUDE: Why, what's on your agenda?
JILL: Oh, God ... a class ... the refugee benefit, Amnesty meeting, food shelter ... then the sub demonstration.
CLAUDE: Boy, you're really spreading it thin.
JILL: And I have to help my cousin Joey look for an apartment.
CLAUDE: He can't find an apartment on his own?
JILL: He doesn't know his way around yet.
CLAUDE: Oh. (*Beat.*) I'm starting to miss you.
JILL: Claude, I don't need the guilt trip. I'm not the one that dropped out altogether.
CLAUDE: I know, but ...
JILL: "Claude Young, the sinewy, hyperactive, dynamo." Remember that?
CLAUDE: Yeah.
JILL: (*Beat.*) I promise this will be the last benefit for awhile. The last petition, the last demo ...
CLAUDE: What petition?
JILL: (*Beat.*) Goddess Magazine. (*Pause.*) Boy, I am really scattered, aren't I?
CLAUDE: I'm not saying a thing.
JILL: I have to drop some things and focus on exams. I have to. I'll never finish otherwise.
CLAUDE: Be a shame to lose your term. I'm on your side, you know?

JILL: You always are. I'm late, what time is it?
CLAUDE: No idea.
JILL: (*Gathering up more stuff.*) Listen, don't forget my cheque.
CLAUDE: I won't.
JILL: And good luck.
CLAUDE: Yeah. Thanks.
JILL: And get some work done.
CLAUDE: Uh huh. (*Beat.*) Jill?
JILL: (*Almost out the door.*) What?
CLAUDE: I admire your energy, you know. I really do. I don't want you to think ...
JILL: I don't. It's true. All this stuff is competing for our time. And it's alright for you to fight back. (*Beat.*) It's reassuring.
CLAUDE: Good. Well. See you later.
JILL: Bye. Think action.
(*JILL exits. CLAUDE looks around, sees the sculpture, lies on the sofa, looks at the ceiling, sighs. CLAUDE'S MUSIC is heard—transition.*)

Scene 2:

(*The music fades. Evening. CLAUDE sits on the back of the sofa. He holds an abstract portrait of JILL, wondering where to hang it. He considers a spot, but decides against it. JILL enters carrying a knapsack and thick folder of notes.*)
CLAUDE: Hi.
JILL: Hiiii!
CLAUDE: How'd it all go?
JILL: (*Unloading her stuff.*) Great! God, what a *great* day.
CLAUDE: Uh huh.
JILL: You won't believe what happened.
CLAUDE: What?
JILL: You really should have been there. It was amazing.
CLAUDE: Well, tell me.
JILL: Okay. We were ... (*Sees the back of the portrait.*) What's that?
CLAUDE: Oh, I'll show you after.
JILL: You finished something?
CLAUDE: Yeah, it's not much.
JILL: But that's great, Claude. Let me see.
CLAUDE: Naw, I'll show you after. C'mon, I want to hear all about it.
JILL: Oh, well, it was Jacqueline again. She is just amazing.
CLAUDE: She sure is. What'd she do?
JILL: You had to see her. She is so precise. Right up front.
CLAUDE: Uh huh.
JILL: Beautiful. I was in *awe*. Everybody was.

CLAUDE: What, at the submarine protest?

JILL: No. We never actually made it to the harbour. This AIDS rally that we didn't even know about came by, and they were taking this massive petition to City Hall. We figured we could fit it in since the sub wasn't leaving 'til five.

CLAUDE: Of course.

JILL: So when we get there, there's media galore! I guess that's why we couldn't get much coverage at the harbour. That's what it was.

CLAUDE: Anyway.

JILL: Anyway, "your worship" is too gutless to show, naturally, so finally his assistant squirms out to accept it. And he says, you know, "they're working on a program", it's "foremost in their minds", blah, blah, blah. "Any day now, homos".

CLAUDE: He's taken the course.

JILL: I'd say. But that's when Jacqueline stepped in. It was unreal. The crowd just seemed to part, like in the movies. And there she came, glowing through. The air went dead. I swear to God, it was one of those cosmic pauses where everybody takes a breath at the same time or something. Perfectly on cue. And she started to speak. She spoke very quietly. And with such control. There wasn't a sound.

CLAUDE: What did she say?

JILL: Everything. She talked about family ... and frailty. (*Getting emotional*.) She talked about innocence, and tenderness ... about hope ...

CLAUDE: Emotional stuff.

JILL: It was so powerful. Even the reporters applauded. Can you believe that?

CLAUDE: And cameras got it all.

JILL: No, you know, I don't think they did.

CLAUDE: Why not?

JILL: I guess they were so wrapped up.

CLAUDE: What? That's crazy.

JILL: I thought so too, but ... like I said, you had to be there. And anyway, Mr. Man just mumbles something about it being a real priority, and backs through the door as though nothing happened.

CLAUDE: Ah, so. (*Beat*.) Sort of a waste of time, then.

JILL: What do you mean a waste of time? We were all very deeply moved.

CLAUDE: I mean in terms of impact. Getting your message through.

JILL: There's more to acts of conscience than impact, I hope.

CLAUDE: Sure. Of course there is. I didn't ...

JILL: I mean, there is still the sublime experience.

CLAUDE: Yes, I'm just saying that ... sure, it was a rewarding

catharsis, but I guess it fell short of being effective, that's all.
JILL: It was the kind of thing that solidifies commitment, launches a new phase.
CLAUDE: (*Beat.*) Yeah. You're right. I'm just being dismissive again.
JILL: No, I know what you're saying. And it's true, I suppose. I just hate to think of such a passionate, life-affirming moment not making a difference.
CLAUDE: Well, it has. Like you say, you're rejuvenated. That's important.
JILL: Why are you arguing my side again all of a sudden?
CLAUDE: Um ... I dunno.
JILL: Stop it, will you? You used to argue black and blue, even when you were dead wrong.
CLAUDE: But you hated that.
JILL: So what? Now you're on my side no matter what?
CLAUDE: No. I just, well, I'm trying to avoid unnecessary friction.
JILL: Maybe there's no such thing, Claude. Maybe it's absolutely necessary. Maybe it's part of a healthy balance.
CLAUDE: Alright, okay.
JILL: ...driving me nuts.
CLAUDE: Look, let's forget it. (*Beat.*) You wanna see this? (*The portrait.*)
JILL: What is it.
CLAUDE: A gift.
JILL: For me?
CLAUDE: Yeah, of course.
JILL: What for?
CLAUDE: Nothing. Putting up with my whining.
JILL: (*He passes it to her—beat.*) Oh, Claude.
CLAUDE: You like it?
JILL: It's ... it's fabulous.
CLAUDE: It's a bit crude.
JILL: No, I love it. There's the melted-record hat you made out of my ABBA's Greatest Hits album. You used the Christmas shot?
CLAUDE: Yeah. I love that one.
JILL: I think I was a little pissed off about it all.
CLAUDE: A *little*?
JILL: (*Sings.*) "Knowing me, knowing you ..."
CLAUDE: (*Spoken—flat.*) Aaaaaaaaaa ...
JILL: "There's nothing more that we can do, knowing me, knowing you ...
CLAUDE: Aaaaaaaaaa ...
JILL: I loved that album.
CLAUDE: I won't tell anyone if you won't. Scary to think that was only a couple of years ago.

JILL: I look so menacing. Thank you.
CLAUDE: You're welcome. It just turned out that way.
JILL: There's a nail here somewhere. (*Hangs the picture where Claude decided not to.*) God, I look so confident.
CLAUDE: Glad you like it. (*A hug.*)
JILL: Well. You did it. You got past the block.
CLAUDE: Do portraits count?
JILL: Sure. Congratulations, you're back on track.
CLAUDE: Well ...
JILL: This calls for a celebration.
CLAUDE: I don't think Robert would agree.
JILL: (*Beat.*) Uh oh.
CLAUDE: Yup.
JILL: No.
CLAUDE: Doesn't look good.
JILL: What did he say?
CLAUDE: Oh, he can't confirm anything right now, you know. "In a week, maybe."
JILL: Did he say why?
CLAUDE: He didn't have to. They're just not interested.
JILL: What, he didn't like the show?
CLAUDE: He didn't see it. None of them showed at the opening, remember?
JILL: He didn't catch it at all?
CLAUDE: Apparently not.
JILL: What about the review?
CLAUDE: Doesn't matter. It was written all over him.
JILL: They're just running the club thing, Claude. You don't sit at their table.
CLAUDE: I guess I got caught up in theoretics and lost the whole point.
JILL: Bullshit. Listen to you. You were on fire and certain about that work, and now you're ready to throw it all out just because Robert has a problem. Have a spine, Claude. The majority is always wrong.
CLAUDE: Oh, right. I forgot.
JILL: God, you guys are so full of self-pity.
CLAUDE: Hey.
JILL: It's true. Look at Jacqueline, for Christ's sake. *She* has a reason to *complain*, but you don't hear her whining, and drowning in self doubt.
CLAUDE: Alright. You win.
JILL: She worked five years to get that job.
CLAUDE: I know.
JILL: Forgetting that a *man* might apply.
CLAUDE: White flag is flying, Jill.
JILL: It's criminal.

CLAUDE: If we're going to argue we should take opposite sides.
JILL: And now she has nothing.
CLAUDE: Why are we talking about Jacqueline?
JILL: Because there's more going on than this stupid exhibition that apparently has become the end of the world to you.
CLAUDE: It's not just the exhibition.
JILL: Well, what then?
CLAUDE: (*Beat.*) If I knew I'd be getting somewhere. I just ... I don't know where I fit anymore. I've lost my point of reference. I can't even communicate with you these days. You're so invested in all these other things.
JILL: Well, I can't stop everything just like that. Couldn't you have given me some notice that you were heading for a crisis?
CLAUDE: Sure. "Jill, my confidence is waning, by tomorrow I'll be questioning just about everything, and I'll be a real mess a week from Tuesday. Please cancel Somalia."
JILL: Well, I don't know what to do! You're not an issue!
CLAUDE: What?
JILL: No, you know what I mean. You're not a toxic dump-site, or a neo-fascist race-supremacy league I can march against. Those are easy. I know what they are, where they are. (*Beat.*) Where are you, Claude?
CLAUDE: (*Shrugs.*) I've never been here before.
JILL: Oh, Claude. (*Beat.*) Listen, I've got to go.
CLAUDE: What? Where to?
JILL: Jacqueline's.
CLAUDE: You just got home.
JILL: (*Picks up her coat.*) I'm sorry, I promised. It might be on the news.
CLAUDE: But ... but they didn't get visuals.
JILL: (*Gathering stuff.*) Yeah, but pictures aren't everything.
CLAUDE: On TV they are. (*Beat.*) We can watch here.
JILL: I told her I'd be over.
CLAUDE: Please, Jill. I've been waiting for you.
JILL: I'm sorry, Claude, I really am.
CLAUDE: Well ... what about supper?
JILL: (*A look.*) Order out.
CLAUDE: That's not what I meant.
JILL: And I might as well tell you, I may stay the night.
CLAUDE: What? Why?
JILL: We've got work to do on the newsletter.
CLAUDE: C'mon ...
JILL: You wouldn't want me to screw up on the newsletter.
CLAUDE: Of course not, but what am I going to do?
JILL: Work on your sculpture. You don't want to lose your momentum.
CLAUDE: Awwwww ...

JILL: And I'll see you tomorrow. (*Beat.*) I am sorry, Claude.
CLAUDE: For how long? (*She's gone. He shouts out the door.*) Well call me!
(His eyes find the sculpture—freeze. Lights fade—CLAUDE's Uptempo music.)

Scene 3:

(Lights reveal CLAUDE working on the sculpture. He wears a work apron and is animated in sync with CLAUDE'S music. He is tentative, but seems determined to make something work. JILL enters quietly—CLAUDE doesn't hear her. She watches him for a moment until her eye is caught by the portrait. CLAUDE notices her.)
CLAUDE: Hey, when did you get here?
JILL: Just now. (*CLAUDE stops the tape.*) You're working.
CLAUDE: Yeah. (*Beat.*) You didn't call last night.
JILL: No. You knew where I was.
CLAUDE: It was busy. Was the phone off the hook?
JILL: Of course not. It must be broken.
CLAUDE: (*Beat.*) Yeah, I guess so.
JILL: I think it's coming along fine.
CLAUDE: Mmmm. (*Looks at her, she turns away.*) How'd the newsletter go?
JILL: Fine. We got a lot done. It should be ready on time.
CLAUDE: Good. That's a load off your plate.
JILL: Yeah, really.
CLAUDE: One down, twenty-five to go?
JILL: Don't even mention it. I'm so tired.
CLAUDE: Look, you know I never meant anything ...
JILL: Oh, I know, Claude. It was me.
CLAUDE: No, I know it's hard. I can't stand being around me either lately, but it's harder to leave. I keep tagging along.
JILL: I have too much on my mind.
CLAUDE: Yeah. It's a busy time. I hope people appreciate everything you're doing.
JILL: That's not why I'm doing it.
CLAUDE: No, but a little recognition never hurts.
JILL: I suppose so.
CLAUDE: Then again, how would I know?
JILL: (*Beat.*) You're really low, aren't you?
CLAUDE: Nope. I refuse to succumb. I'm seeking new horizons, setting new goals.
JILL: Really? What are you on?
CLAUDE: Another day. I refuse to die.
JILL: That sounds better.
CLAUDE: Onward and upward, inside and out, reach for the sky.

JILL: Don't use it up all at once.
CLAUDE: That's all I had anyway. (*Beat.*) When did you finish?
JILL: Finish what?
CLAUDE: The newsletter.
JILL: Oh, we were up all night.
CLAUDE: Well, listen—go for a nap. I'll keep it quiet, make some lunch and bring it in.
JILL: Love to, but I can't.
CLAUDE: What's on?
JILL: Lots and lots and lots.
CLAUDE: Oh. (*Beat.*) So four o'clock is off?
JILL: Four o'clock?
CLAUDE: Tanzig Kasgowski at the Wall to Wall, remember? The Cranial Scrape lecture.
JILL: Oh, no! Is that today? Damn.
CLAUDE: Why, what are you doing?
JILL: I told Joey we'd get together for supper. I really wanted to hear Kasgowski.
CLAUDE: Call him, tell him to come later.
JILL: I've already cancelled once.
CLAUDE: So what, he'll live.
JILL: He's on his way.
CLAUDE: It's a bit early.
JILL: He volunteered to make some bread first.
CLAUDE: Oh, yeah? Wow, he's a pipefitter isn't he? I can't wait to meet this guy.
JILL: Yeah. He's alright. A bit narrow, but you have to allow for him being from home.
CLAUDE: Uh oh, fresh from the bay. Did he have the butterflies all over the house, too?
JILL: Oh stop, they were my mother's. Did you get my cheque?
CLAUDE: Yeah, I did. (*Digs it out of his back pocket and hands it to her.*) But Sara said it's only half?
JILL: What? Oh, shit.
CLAUDE: What?
JILL: Nothing.
CLAUDE: Come on. The food bank or the shelter?
JILL: Neither.
CLAUDE: What, then?
JILL: (*Beat.*) Damian's legal fee fund.
CLAUDE: Oh, I can't believe it. You can't afford to support Damian!
JILL: Well, he's desperate, Claude. Put yourself in his place.
CLAUDE: Now, *that* I can't do.
JILL: Why not?
CLAUDE: I don't know. I just can't picture myself burning my shorts at City Hall.

JILL: Well, what was he supposed to do?
CLAUDE: Write a letter.
JILL: Pretty conventional, don't you think?
CLAUDE: Logical!
JILL: Damian can't follow their rules.
CLAUDE: No, he can't! I'm impressed he can manage to dress himself in the first place.
JILL: Now that's a nasty thing to say.
CLAUDE: Seriously, how can you do it?
JILL: I don't know. But I just have.
CLAUDE: Jillian, Jiii-lii-an ...
JILL: I can't very well take it back now.
CLAUDE: Just explain that you can't afford it.
JILL: I won't do it anymore.
CLAUDE: Yeah, right.
JILL: I won't, okay?
CLAUDE: God, half your pay cheque because dick-head Damian insists on sunning his buns in a public park.
JILL: Claude, Joey will be here any minute. I don't want a fight.
CLAUDE: Alright, alright. I'll tape the lecture and I'll see you suppertime.
JILL: Well, ... we aren't staying here for supper.
CLAUDE: Where are you going?
JILL: Over to ...
CLAUDE: Jacqueline's.
JILL: She offered, and I couldn't ...
CLAUDE: Okay. It's alright. I'll see you over there, then.
JILL: (*Beat*.) She's only expecting two.
CLAUDE: I'm not even invited?
JILL: It's not like that. It's just that it's her place and she doesn't have a lot of room ...
CLAUDE: I'm not that big, Jill. How about if I stand?
JILL: Don't be sarcastic. She was good enough to let Joey come.
CLAUDE: What's the big deal?
JILL: It's .. it's hard to explain.
CLAUDE: Please try.
JILL: She's ... she's got this feasting ritual that has certain restrictions.
CLAUDE: What?
JILL: It's awkward and complicated, but I have to respect it.
CLAUDE: And what, I fall into the "shun zone?"
JILL: No. You just don't qualify, I guess.
CLAUDE: Why not?
JILL: How do I know? It's got something to do with her pottery or something.
CLAUDE: (*Beat*.) Oh, well. Why didn't you say so. The pottery conflict. Of course, no problem.

JILL: Look, it's not my fault. She sees her plates as sort of spiritually charged and ... oh, wait, I've got something terrific to show you. This is absolutely fantastic! (*She takes a cracked bowl out of her knapsack.*) You won't believe this. It happened last night. (*Holding up the two halves.*) What do you think?
CLAUDE: Holy war, is it?
JILL: Forget that. Just look at it.
CLAUDE: (*Takes the pieces.*) Let's see.
JILL: Yin and Yang.
CLAUDE: Uh huh.
JILL: Isn't it great? A piece of contemporary high tech cookware microwaved into an ancient spiritual symbol!
CLAUDE: Pretty heavy.
JILL: It really works, doesn't it? Think about it, the primary metaphysical balance manifesting itself in such a mundane vessel!
CLAUDE: Yeah.
JILL: I mean, I really think there's something sublimely profound here. It speaks to me so strongly.
CLAUDE: Well, it's kinda neat ...
JILL: Don't you find it profound?
CLAUDE: (*Beat.*) Well ...
JILL: What? Just look at it. It's so powerful.
CLAUDE: Yes, I see it, Jill.
JILL: (*Taking the pieces back.*) Oh, God. You of all people, Claude. Come on. We were in awe. It was like a revelation. We ... it was like we experienced a miracle!
CLAUDE: She's really having an affect on you, isn't she?
JILL: Jesus. Jacqueline and I connected so well on this. We didn't have to say a word. It was pure communication—we knew exactly where we both were. And it was the same place. We really connected.
CLAUDE: That's great.
JILL: And you know what else? She *thought* you'd probably miss it.
CLAUDE: What? Look, ...
JILL: Or rather that, very likely, you'd *dis*miss it.
CLAUDE: Wow, she has me all figured out. I only met her once.
JILL: Well, her perception is uncanny, I must say.
CLAUDE: And this is why I can't go to supper?
JILL: Perhaps it's just your general attitude.
CLAUDE: What attitude?
JILL: Your attitude.
CLAUDE: *What* attitude?
JILL: You know!
CLAUDE: No, tell me.
JILL: Your plastic pro-everything policy.

CLAUDE: Heeey!
JILL: And now you're just sulking over not being invited to supper!
CLAUDE: Jillian! (*Beat.*) What's going on with you? You're like someone else all of a sudden. The last couple of days, when I do get to see you, you're so hostile. (*A knock at the door.*)
JILL: That's Joey.
CLAUDE: Jillian!
JILL: We'll talk about it later.
CLAUDE: But ...
JILL: Later! (*Opens the door.*) Hi, Joey.
JOEY: Howyadoin?
JILL: Come on in. I just have to change. (*JOEY enters.*)
JOEY: No sweat.
JILL: Ah, this is ...
JOEY: Clod! Right?
CLAUDE: Claude.
JOEY: Oh.
JILL: Claude, this is my cousin Joey.
CLAUDE: Pleased to meet you.
JOEY: (*Shaking CLAUDE's hand.*) How ya gettin' on?
CLAUDE: Good.
JOEY: Sorry about your name, there. Jillian showed me your write up in the paper. I guess they had it spelled wrong.
CLAUDE: No, the spellings are the same.
JOEY: Oh. (*Beat.*) That must be a bitch, huh?
CLAUDE: Uh ... yeah.
JILL: Have a seat, Joey. I'll only be a minute.
JOEY: Right on. (*Sits on the couch, looks around.*)
CLAUDE: (*As JILL moves to exit.*) Jill ... (*JILL stops him with a look and an open hand, points to Joey. CLAUDE obeys. JILL exits. Silence. Then, finally.*) So. (*JOEY looks at him—beat.*) Soooooo ... you're working on some construction in town.
JOEY: Yeah.
CLAUDE: Where about?
JOEY: City Annex.
CLAUDE: Oh, yeah. Bit of controversy there, huh? (*JOEY shrugs.*) You know, about it blocking the view of the harbour.
JOEY: Don't know, boy.
CLAUDE: Oh. (*Beat.*) How long you around for?
JOEY: Eight, nine months. Unless we go on strike.
CLAUDE: (*Beat.*) Right.
JOEY: (*Spotting the sculpture.*) Hey, what's this for?
CLAUDE: That's ... a sculpture I'm working on.
JOEY: Yeah? What's it do?
CLAUDE: Well, nothing really. (*JOEY looks at him.*) Well, when it's finished I hope it will say something.

JOEY: Yeah? Why, you got a tape deck in it?
CLAUDE: (*Smiles but realizes that JOEY is serious.*) No. I don't mean it will actually talk. I hope it will communicate something. To the viewer.
JOEY: Like what?
CLAUDE: Well, what it means to me may not be the same thing it will mean to anyone else. I hope there'll be many interpretations.
JOEY: Why?
CLAUDE: Well, so each individual can bring and take away something personally valuable.
JOEY: Oooh. So you mean you want everyone to figure out the riddle on their own.
CLAUDE: Sort of.
JOEY: And they might come up with their own answer that might be completely different than yours.
CLAUDE: Right.
JOEY: But how do I know you got an answer in the first place?
CLAUDE: Well, it doesn't matter, does it?
JOEY: I dunno. Seems to me a lot of people might get upset to go figuring something out for a long time and then find out that you didn't have an answer in the first place.
CLAUDE: No, look. You're way off the point here. There's no *answer*, although I assure you I do have a clear intention in mind.
JOEY: Alright. Just wondering. It's kinda neat, whatever it is.
CLAUDE: Thank you. I appreciate your interest.
JOEY: Pas de sweat.
CLAUDE: (*Beat.*) Uh, one thing, Joey. I wouldn't use the word "bitch" over at Jacqueline's.
JOEY: No?
CLAUDE: (*Beat.*) Naw, go ahead and use it.
JOEY: Bit touchy is she?
CLAUDE: I wouldn't worry about it.
JOEY: Whatever you say. Wild spot you got here.
CLAUDE: Yeah. I guess it's a little different.
JOEY: You get to hang around in the house a bit, do you?
CLAUDE: I work here.
JOEY: Yeah? So this is all you do?
CLAUDE: (*Beat.*) Yup. This is all I do.
JOEY: Right on! (*CLAUDE rolls his eyes.*) Man, you guys got it knocked.
CLAUDE: You bet.
JOEY: I suppose you get all kinds of those big grants you hear about, wha?
CLAUDE: Tons of 'em.
JOEY: Wicked! I could go for this for awhile.

CLAUDE: Why don't you?
JOEY: What? Write away for a grant?
CLAUDE: Why not?
JOEY: Don't you have to have some kind of papers, or drawings or anything?
CLAUDE: Nah. Just pick up the phone and let them know what you want.
JOEY: Really?
CLAUDE: Pas de sweat.
JOEY: Would I have to dress up funny?
CLAUDE: Only a little bit.
JOEY: Hey, maybe we could trade off. You take my job.
CLAUDE: Well, I don't know about that. I don't know much about pipefitting.
JOEY: Don't need to.
CLAUDE: I don't?
JOEY: Nah. Just pick up the phone and let them know you're coming. (*CLAUDE does a double take—JOEY smiles.*)
CLAUDE: (*Beat.*) Excuse me for a minute.
JOEY: Sure, boy.
   (*CLAUDE exits for the bedroom. We hear the following mumbled argument. Meanwhile JOEY studies the sculpture a moment and then, as he looks around, switches on the music. He listens for a moment and finds it funny. He boogies a bit.*)
CLAUDE: Jillian, what's going on?
JILL: I don't want to discuss it now.
CLAUDE: But you're so angry.
JILL: I'm not angry.
CLAUDE: You're thoroughly pissed off.
JILL: I'm just frustrated.
CLAUDE: What, about the bowl?
JILL: No. Not about the damn bowl.
CLAUDE: Well what then?
JILL: Your inconsideration.
CLAUDE: Of what?
JILL: Of things I care about.
CLAUDE: Like the bowl.
JILL: No.
CLAUDE: Jill, I don't know what you're talking about.
JILL: Well, you should.
CLAUDE: I've never seen you like this.
JILL: And I don't have time to talk about it.
CLAUDE: If this is serious, I think we ...
JILL: Not now, okay? Ready, Joey?
   (*JILL enters with CLAUDE following. JOEY switches off the music.*)
JILL: Ready, Joey?

JOEY: All set.
CLAUDE: Jillian?
JILL: When I get home, Claude. If anyone calls, take a message. Let's go, Joey.
(JILL exits.)
CLAUDE: Call me!
JOEY: Catch ya later, Clod.
(JOEY exits.)
CLAUDE: *(Beat.)* Claude.

Scene 4:

(It is late. CLAUDE sits on the sofa. The TV is on, but he appears to be in a trance. A sudden knock at the door startles him.)

CLAUDE: Who is it?
JOEY: *(Poking his head in.)* Just me, boy. Joey.
CLAUDE: You gave me a bit of a start.
JOEY: Wake you up?
CLAUDE: No. Come in.
JOEY: Jillian asked me to pick up some stuff.
CLAUDE: How come?
JOEY: I think she's plannin' on stayin' over.
CLAUDE: Again? Wow, what is this?
JOEY: Got me, boy. Want me tell her to come home?
CLAUDE: What?
JOEY: You know, "No way. Get back here, now."
CLAUDE: Oh sure, that would really go over well.
JOEY: Suit yourself.
CLAUDE: What does she want?
JOEY: Pair of jeans, toothbrush, and a box of stuff for some kinda news bulletin. She said you'd know where it was. Listen, you haven't got any beer, have you?
CLAUDE: No, I don't think so.
JOEY: Mind if I check it out?
CLAUDE: *(Beat.)* Not at all. *(JOEY exits to the kitchen.)* Why did she say she was staying over?
JOEY: She didn't. Hey, you got a whole dozen in here. *(Returns with a beer—drinks.)* Boy, that's good. They only got wine over there.
CLAUDE: I tried to call, but I guess the phone is still out.
JOEY: They got it hauled out of the wall.
CLAUDE: Are you sure?
JOEY: Yup. I guess they don't want nobody buggin 'em.
CLAUDE: I guess not.
JOEY: That Jacqui missus is pretty weird, if you ask me.
CLAUDE: Why's that?

JOEY: She's got all this smelly stuff burnin', all kindsa ooga-booga-boo pictures up everywhere, big black cat. Spooky.
CLAUDE: Yeah?
JOEY: Oh, yeah. (*Sits on the sofa.*) Man, you think this place is freaky.
CLAUDE: What's the conversation about?
JOEY: What, this one?
CLAUDE: No, over there.
JOEY: Oh, I dunno. A lot of weird stuff I never heard of. I got a feeling Jacqui didn't take to me too good. Maybe I said something.
CLAUDE: Why, what did she say?
JOEY: She just sorta pretended I wasn't there. Fine by me.
CLAUDE: Uh huh. I know what you mean.
JOEY: You too?
CLAUDE: In a way.
JOEY: Jill's really different. Nuthin' like she was back home. I think she mighta been sucked up by a UFO and got brainwashed. Man.
CLAUDE: Well, she's certainly come a long way.
JOEY: (*Beat.*) I s'pose. Guess you had something to do with that, did ya?
CLAUDE: I've had an influence.
JOEY: Uh huh. Pretty heavy duty.
CLAUDE: I guess, if you haven't seen her since she left home.
JOEY: Nope. Don't suppose I ever will, now.
CLAUDE: What?
JOEY: See her. Like she was, I mean.
CLAUDE: I think you're exaggerating.
JOEY: Gone off with the aliens, she is.
CLAUDE: Okay, okay, whatever. What else were they up to?
JOEY: Nuthin' at all. Mumbo jumbo. That supper they cooked up was pretty wild, too. Buncha soggy greens and gook. I kept waitin' for something to eat. Sure, I had to hit Kentucky Fried on the way over here.
CLAUDE: Did Jill say anything about me?
JOEY: Mmmm, oh, yeah. She was tellin' Jacqui about how you didn't like her cracked bowl and stuff. I remember that 'cause they went on about it forever.
CLAUDE: Shit.
JOEY: (*Beat.*) Not gettin' along too good, huh?
CLAUDE: Mmm, no. Not the best.
JOEY: That's rough, boy. Who needs it, right?
CLAUDE: Not I. Not now.
JOEY: I used to get all torn up by the women. I stays away from 'em now. Don't bother me a bit.
CLAUDE: That's ... good for you. Look, I umm ...

JOEY: Not that I don't like women, y'know. Gave up the butts too. Cinch. It's all mind power, is what it is. Gotta get a brain lock on it and stick at it.
CLAUDE: I know what you mean. Listen ...
JOEY: Course, being broke all the time helps a bit.
CLAUDE: What time is it?
JOEY: Got me. One? Two?
CLAUDE: Well ...
JOEY: Whatcha watchin?
CLAUDE: I wasn't really. It's just a nature program. Small Speckled Warblers. (*Exits to bedroom.*)
JOEY: Yeah? What's goin' on?
CLAUDE: (*From off.*) Um ... they're trying to get this one back in the air.
JOEY: Looks like it's workin'. He's goin' pretty good there now.
CLAUDE: Yeah, but he keeps coming back, smacking into the tree.
JOEY: Yeah? Why doesn't he take off?
CLAUDE: (*Entering.*) There are several theories.
JOEY: You mean, they're tryin' to help him out, but he won't go?
CLAUDE: That's right. I really wasn't going to watch it all.
JOEY: That's a bit stunned.
CLAUDE: (*Beat.*) Well ... anyway (*Moves to turn off set.*).
JOEY: Don't turn it off on account of me, boy. I love stuff like this.
CLAUDE: Oh.
JOEY: I wonder if they just lose their map or something? You know, they're all frigged up, like.
CLAUDE: I dunno. (*Exits for toothbrush and newsletter material.*)
JOEY: Like, say you're in, say, Montreal, and you're followin' a guy who knows his way around. If he gets lost, then you're really screwed, aren't you, boy?
CLAUDE: (*Entering.*) You ask for directions.
JOEY: Aha! As long as you can speak French.
CLAUDE: I get your point.
JOEY: See, that's why I picked Montreal. People could be givin' you all kindsa directions, and you haven't got a clue what they're sayin', so you're screwed, right?
CLAUDE: (*Beat.*) That you are.
JOEY: Not that you'd keep walkin' into the side of a building or anything, just because you were lost.
CLAUDE: No. Maybe he's simply giving up.
JOEY: What, packin' it in? A warbler?
CLAUDE: They're intelligent creatures.
JOEY: That's what I mean.
CLAUDE: (*Moves to the main exit with stuff.*) Anyway, here are Jill's things.
JOEY: Not going to watch it?
CLAUDE: No, I think I'd better hit the sack.

JOEY: Oh. Yeah, I guess it's kinda late.
CLAUDE: You don't mind, do you?
JOEY: No, boy, no sweat (*Drains his beer, moves to door.*).
CLAUDE: Listen, tell Jill ... just say good night for me.
JOEY: (*Shrugs.*) You got it. (*CLAUDE watches the TV, sips his beer, shakes his head.*) Bad mess in the big city. (*JOEY exits.*)
(*Fade to black as CLAUDE's Downtempo music is heard.*)

Scene 5:

(*Lights rise and music fades on CLAUDE asleep on the sofa, fetal position, and wearing a melted-record hat. It is midmorning and a plate is on the floor next to his shoes—we hear the music theme of 'Early One Morning' from The Friendly Giant, a children's show. JILL enters. She is uneasy. She notices CLAUDE, studies him for a moment, then turns off the TV.*)

JILL: (*She sits next to him. After a moment she gently removes the hat and studies it.*) Claude? (*She touches him.*) Claude?
CLAUDE: Mmmm?
JILL: Time to get up.
CLAUDE: Oh. What time is it?
JILL: About quarter to eleven.
CLAUDE: Wow. I was really out. You just getting home?
JILL: Uh huh. You were up late again.
CLAUDE: (*Yawns.*) Yeah.
JILL: You should stop that. It's wearing you out.
CLAUDE: Hmmm, I know. I couldn't sleep. Hey ... wait. Deja vu.
JILL: This?
CLAUDE: Yeah. You waking me up. Everything. Even what I'm saying right now. It's still going.
JILL: (*Beat.*) Um, what am I supposed to say next.
CLAUDE: Exactly that. I remember all of this.
JILL: Gee, remember when this used to happen all the time?
CLAUDE: Yeah ... oh, I think it's over. Yeah, we used to connect on these regularly there for awhile.
JILL: Yeah, it was uncanny.
CLAUDE: When did that stop?
JILL: I'm not sure. Quite awhile ago. It used to come and go.
CLAUDE: Yeah. I'd forgotten all about that.
JILL: Me too. It was almost scary.
CLAUDE: It was amazing. We were almost metaphysically siamese.
JILL: Yeah. (*Beat.*) You got the hat out.
CLAUDE: (*Beat.*) Oh, yeah. I just saw it and just picked it up I guess.
JILL: These were all the rage after you made this one. Everybody

had them.
CLAUDE: I guess it struck a chord. There was a lot of spare vinyl around. (*Beat.*) That was a great Christmas, y'know. The best one ever.
JILL: Yeah.
CLAUDE: Your first one away. I didn't think you were really going to do it.
JILL: My father had a fit.
CLAUDE: He never liked me.
JILL: He never likes anyone.
CLAUDE: (*Beat.*) We had the geodesic tree, the prophylactic decorations ...
JILL: Your electric, real-cool-jewel, far-out, formidable, freakness, plutonic, super-hydraulic, spasmatic bummer, flip-me-out-and-check-my-oil, "Like Wow, Man", punch.
CLAUDE: Ouch, don't remind me.
JILL: And ... the fire on the beach ... in the falling snow.
CLAUDE: (*Beat.*) I'll never forget that. Big flakes. Bigger than I've ever seen them. We watched them melt on your stomach, afterwards ...
JILL: Yes. I remember that.
CLAUDE: It wasn't even cold. The fire painted ... what's wrong?
JILL: Oh ... you know ... I just ...
CLAUDE: What?
JILL: Those were ... Let's, um ... let's change the subject. Okay?
CLAUDE: (*Beat.*) You alright?
JILL: Yes. I'm fine.
CLAUDE: (*Beat.*) Wood-smoke in your hair ...
JILL: Claude, please.
CLAUDE: Okay, alright.
JILL: Did you tape Kasgowski?
CLAUDE: Yes. Yes, I did.
JILL: Thanks. Was it good?
CLAUDE: Uh, yeah. Yeah, it was great.
JILL: What was he saying?
CLAUDE: Oh, it was, y'know ... he went into ... I can't remember.
JILL: No? Didn't you hear it?
CLAUDE: Yes, I ... I tried to concentrate, but ... I can't remember a word. I guess I was distracted.
JILL: Claude.
CLAUDE: But I do have it on tape, so ... Uh, how come you're just getting home, anyway.
JILL: We were up late. Working.
CLAUDE: I see. How did supper go?
JILL: Fine.
CLAUDE: Not according to Joey.
JILL: Why, what did he say?

CLAUDE: I think he felt out of place.
JILL: Did he? I don't know why.
CLAUDE: He found Jacqueline pretty cool.
JOEY: He said that?
CLAUDE: He did. And it bothers me that she's taken such a disliking to me, too.
JILL: She doesn't dislike you.
CLAUDE: No?
JILL: She doesn't quite trust you, maybe.
CLAUDE: Why not?
JILL: She doesn't think that you speak your mind.
CLAUDE: Whose do I speak?
JILL: You know. She feels that you only say what you feel you're supposed to.
CLAUDE: And you agree. (*Beat.*) Jesus, now I'm a conformist. This is turning into a nightmare.
JILL: Don't take it like that. You're just not rocking the boat much lately.
CLAUDE: So? I'm not even in the boat, Jill. Joey said the phone was unplugged.
JILL: (*Beat.*) Yes. It was.
CLAUDE: Why did you say it was broken?
JILL: (*Getting up.*) I don't know, Claude. I didn't want to spend all night on the phone rehashing everything.
CLAUDE: That's not what I asked. Why did you lie to me?
JILL: I didn't want to hurt you.
CLAUDE: Well, now I'm hurt.
JILL: (*Beat.*) I'm sorry.
CLAUDE: What's going on, Jill? (*Beat.*) Jill?
JILL: (*Beat.*) Oh, Claude. The last thing I want to do is ...
CLAUDE: What is it, Jill? Tell me.
JILL: (*Beat.*) Okay. Here it comes. (*Beat.*) I feel we're at an impasse.
CLAUDE: An impasse?
JILL: (*Beat.*) Yes. I'm sorry. But I have to get out.
CLAUDE: Jillian ...
JILL: That's it. I have to leave.
CLAUDE: (*Beat.*) It's that bad?
JILL: That's not quite all of it.
CLAUDE: What more can there be?
JILL: (*Beat.*) Oh, Claude. I don't know how to put this.
CLAUDE: (*Pause.*) There's someone else.
JILL: (*Nods—CLAUDE sits.*) It took me by surprise, Claude, it's the last thing I thought would happen. You know I'd never hurt you on purpose.
CLAUDE: It crossed my mind, but...
JILL: I'm so sorry.

CLAUDE: I can't believe it.
JILL: I had to tell you.
CLAUDE: Oh, my God. Someone else?
JILL: It's true.
CLAUDE: (*Pause.*) So you haven't been sleeping at Jacqueline's?
JILL: Yes, I have.
CLAUDE: And he's been coming over there!?
JILL: No.
CLAUDE: Well, so where have you been seeing him?
JILL: (*Beat.*) Her.
CLAUDE: (*Beat.*) Her? (*Beat.*) Jacqueline!? (*JILL nods.*) Hoooooly shit!
JILL: Claude, it's the last thing I expected ...
CLAUDE: No!
JILL: ... but all of a sudden there it was.
CLAUDE: Oh, my God!
JILL: We just seem to have this uncanny ability to understand each other. And there's no denying it. What can I say?
CLAUDE: This is unbelievable!
JILL: It is.
CLAUDE: Jacqueline!?
JILL: And I can't blame you for not accepting it.
CLAUDE: Not accepting it! (*Beat.*) Did I say I can't accept it?
JILL: No, but. You don't have to.
CLAUDE: I think I'll decide if I can accept it.
JILL: I just meant ... you're entitled to a period of denial, at least.
CLAUDE: (*Beat.*) Well, it's not like it's the first time it's ever happened to anyone. Right?
JILL: No, I suppose not.
CLAUDE: It's a big world. These things happen.
JILL: Probably, but ...
CLAUDE: Jesus, are you sure, Jill?
JILL: Yes, Claude. I've never felt like this. (*Beat.*) There's magic.
CLAUDE: Oh, wow. Thanks.
JILL: It's not a reflection on you.
CLAUDE: Ha!
JILL: It's just different with Jacqueline.
CLAUDE: Well, I should hope so.
JILL: I can't explain it. I am sorry.
CLAUDE: (*Beat.*) This is really what you want?
JILL: It is.
CLAUDE: What *you* want?
JILL: Yes.
CLAUDE: There's nothing I can say? Wow.
JILL: (*Beat.*) I think it's best if I clear out quick and clean. I'll just take some clothes and come back for the rest on the weekend. (*CLAUDE stares.*) Do ... do you want to keep some of the plants?

CLAUDE: No. They're dead, Jill.
JILL: (*Beat.*) Yeah. This is best for both of us, Claude. You'll see.
CLAUDE: Will I?
JILL: Yes, I truly believe you will. (*Beat.*) Well. I'll get my clothes then. (*Exits, then, from off.*) Uh, look, this is a bit awkward, too ... well, more than a bit, but I figured it would take you some time to find someone to cover my rent. So I thought I should get you a temporary roommate. I hope that's okay. I mean, it's the least I should do. I'm leaving what I owe here on the dresser, okay? I'll get him to call and talk to you first. Don't worry, you'll like him. He's not particular.
CLAUDE: Who?
JILL: Your roommate.
CLAUDE: What roommate?
JILL: I just told you.
CLAUDE: This is going a bit fast for me. You mean you got someone already?
JILL: I thought I should.
CLAUDE: Jill, the last thing I need now is company.
JILL: This'll work out. Trust me.
CLAUDE: What? Wait a second. Who is it? (*A knock on the door. CLAUDE freezes for a moment, then answers it. JOEY stands in the doorway with a suitcase and a six-pack of beer.*)
JOEY: (*Entering.*) How's she goin', Clod buddy? Where do I park it?

(*JOEY's uptempo music, fade to black.*)

Act Two
Scene 6:

(*"JOEY's Music" plays as house lights fade. Music fades as the lights reveal JOEY sitting and studying the sculpture. It appears he has been doing so for some time. He finishes a can of Vienna sausages without losing his concentration. After a few moments of tilting his head this way and that, he stands to gain a higher point of view. Slowly, he circles the table, retrieving his can of beer from the armrest of the chair on his way around, and finally stands on the chair. With great care, he, almost as if being drawn by an unseen force, places the beer can precariously on the highest point of the sculpture. Elation. CLAUDE enters carrying a knapsack, portfolio, and large bag of materials. Neither is aware of the other for a moment as CLAUDE dumps his cargo, and JOEY continues to appreciate his addition. CLAUDE notices JOEY first.*)
CLAUDE: Joey. Home early?

JOEY: Nope.
CLAUDE: (*Beat.*) No?
JOEY: Bad back.
CLAUDE: Oh. See a doctor?
JOEY: What for?
CLAUDE: Your back.
JOEY: Not a real one. (*Jumps down.*) Mental health day.
CLAUDE: Oh. Of course. Did it work?
JOEY: Huh?
CLAUDE: Nothing. (*Brings his materials to the sculpture.*) So what did you do all day?
JOEY: Watched TV. Made some bread.
CLAUDE: More bread. Great. (*Exits to the kitchen.*)
JOEY: Jillian called. She's coming over to get her stuff.
CLAUDE: When?
JOEY: In the middle of Oprah.
CLAUDE: What?
JOEY: About an hour ago, I s'pose.
CLAUDE: What was?
JOEY: Jillian.
CLAUDE: (*Returning with a buttered slice of bread.*) No. When is she coming over?
JOEY: Ooooh. I dunno. Soon, I guess. How's the bread?
CLAUDE: (*Calling back as he exits to his room SR.*) It's okay. We have quite a stockpile there, you know.
JOEY: Yup. Great smell, eh?
CLAUDE: You should try whole wheat sometime.
JOEY: (*To himself.*) Never turns out the right colour.
CLAUDE: Can't hear you.
JOEY: (*Louder.*) Maybe next time. (*CLAUDE enters putting on a pastel coloured shirt.*) Hey, nice blouse. Your sister's?
CLAUDE: (*Beat.*) No.
JOEY: Ooops! Almost hooked you! Huh? Wah?
CLAUDE: What else did she say?
JOEY: Who, Jillian?
CLAUDE: Yes, who else?
JOEY: Oh. Nuthin' really.
CLAUDE: Did she want to speak to me?
JOEY: You weren't here.
CLAUDE: Yes, but did she ask. Before she found out I wasn't home.
JOEY: She asked if you were around.
CLAUDE: But not to speak to me?
JOEY: No, just to see if you were around.
CLAUDE: How do you know it wasn't to speak to me?
JOEY: 'Cause I asked her.
CLAUDE: And she said no?

JOEY: She said she just wanted to pick up her stuff.
CLAUDE: Oh.
JOEY: And I said, "Good, 'cause he's not home."
CLAUDE: *(Beat.)* Right. *(CLAUDE sits at the sculpture and thinks.)*
JOEY: Guess you're still pretty pissed off about all that, huh?
CLAUDE: Sorry?
JOEY: About ... you know. All that kinky stuff.
CLAUDE: What "kinky stuff?"
JOEY: You know, Jill and ... Jacqui.
CLAUDE: It's a perfectly legitimate relationship.
JOEY: Weeeeell, whatever you say. Gotta steam you up a bit, I bet.
CLAUDE: No, Joey. If you must know, I'm not in the least upset. I'm somewhat confused, and more than a little bruised, but I'm not angry. I understand these things.
JOEY: Ooooooooh.
CLAUDE: Not from first hand experience!
JOEY: Alright. Only kidding you, boy. No odds to me, anyway.
CLAUDE: Well, good. I'm glad to hear it.
JOEY: 'Cause *I* definitely don't, right?
CLAUDE: Right. Fine. *(Starts taking out materials.)*
JOEY: Just lettin' you know. I only been here a week, and it takes a little time to cover some of the big topics.
CLAUDE: Well, let's consider it covered.
JOEY: Perfect. *(Beat.)* Think she'll be back?
CLAUDE: How should I know?
JOEY: You understand these things.
CLAUDE: Well, not that part.
JOEY: That would be really touchy, wouldn't it?
CLAUDE: Why?
JOEY: You know *(Grimaces.).*
CLAUDE: Joey, please.
JOEY: Sorry. 'Nuff said. You work away, I won't bug you a bit. *(He watches silently as CLAUDE prepares his materials. CLAUDE is unnerved, but determined to continue.)* Clod?
CLAUDE: Claude.
JOEY: Right, sorry. Y'know, I was looking at that thing a lot today. It's a weird thing, y'know?
CLAUDE: Yes, Joey. *(Having just seen the beer can, he removes it from atop the sculpture.)* It's a weird thing.
JOEY: I dunno. I keep asking myself, "Self, what the hell is that thing?" I say ... "That must be the second weirdest statue ..."
CLAUDE: " ... I've ever seen!" Now look, it's a sculpture, not a statue, and not only do I not feel like talking right now, Joey, but somehow I sense that a discourse on the aesthetics of the non-representational art form would be a fairly pointless exercise in any case. So, unless you have some objection, I'd rather work

without the benefit of conversation. Alright?
JOEY: (*Beat.*) Oh. (*He picks up the weekend comics and lies on the chesterfield.*)
CLAUDE: (*Works for a bit, calms.*) Sorry. I had a shitty day.
JOEY: Oh. (*Beat.*) No go, huh? How come?
CLAUDE: I dunno. Doesn't matter.
JOEY: Musta been a reason.
CLAUDE: They said something about "incompatible conventions", and "admission of paradigmatical shift", or something. I couldn't concentrate.
JOEY: Uh huh.
CLAUDE: I wouldn't mind, I mean it'd be fine if I believed that's all there was to it.
JOEY: Sounds pretty serious.
CLAUDE: It's crap. They just don't want me. I don't get it. It's as though they consider the work naive. *Naive.* I mean, I'm aware. I'm on top of what's happening. I follow the literature closer than most of them. Maybe that's the problem. Rampant insecurity. (*Beat.*) Maybe they just hate me.
JOEY: Could be.
CLAUDE: Why would they hate me?
JOEY: I dunno. Why do you figure they might?
CLAUDE: They don't hate me. It's just an overwhelming indifference. To me and everything I produce. Something's wrong.
JOEY: Maybe they don't like how it's always weird and hard to figure out.
CLAUDE: Uh, forget it. I appreciate the counselling.
JOEY: What counselling?
CLAUDE: Just ... I forgot where I was for a second.
JOEY: I was only thinking that they might like it if they knew what it was. You know, if it's a castle you could put a little flag on top, or if it's a lion a few whiskers and a tail wouldn't go astray.
CLAUDE: I'm not getting into this, Joey!
JOEY: Is it one of those?
CLAUDE: You said you weren't going to bug me!
JOEY: I know, I know. (*Beat.*) So the castle and lion are out, huh?
CLAUDE: Yes!
JOEY: Oh. (*Beat.*) See, that's the problem, as far as I'm concerned. That's all I'm saying.
CLAUDE: You're sure?
JOEY: That's my opinion.
CLAUDE: No, are you sure that's all you're saying?
JOEY: Oh. I got you. Right you are. (*Returns to his comics.*)
CLAUDE: (*Burns a bit, but finally.*) Joey, say it was a *castle*.
JOEY: Aha!
CLAUDE: No, it's not. But let's just say it was a perfect replica of ... the Friendly Giant's castle, alright? Little flags, little draw-

bridge ... everything.
JOEY: The little cow that jumps up over the moon?
CLAUDE: Yes, yes, the cow and everything.
JOEY: And the little chair for two to curl up in?
CLAUDE: Let's just stick with the outside.
JOEY: Alright.
CLAUDE: So the castle is in the gallery, it's obvious what it is. You come in, walk up to it, look at it ... and then what?
JOEY: I say, "Pretty good castle."
CLAUDE: Right, and then what?
JOEY: Well, I'd probably check out the detail and everything, you know.
CLAUDE: Fine. But that's about it then, isn't it? There's not much left to stimulate further inquiry is there?
JOEY: I dunno. I might see if I could figure out which window Rusty and Jerome and those little raccoons, or whatever they were, used to play the music in.
CLAUDE: Yeah, yeah. But you see my point?
JOEY: I didn't like those little guys much. What do you figure they were, anyway? They never said nuthin', just played them little flutes.
CLAUDE: You can see how limiting simple duplication can be, though.
JOEY: That rooster, on the other hand, he never shut up. Downright saucy he was.
CLAUDE: Oh, Jesus, what have I done?
JOEY: Anyway, then I'd check out what else was around, I suppose.
CLAUDE: There, yes! Of course you would! You're finished with the little castle because it's just a little castle. All you have to do is identify it and you're done. That's why I'm trying to make something that requires some investment, some ... some inner discourse.
JOEY: Oh. Inner discourse.
CLAUDE: That's the goal.
JOEY: Ummm. I guess you know what you're doing, then.
CLAUDE: I'm trying.
JOEY: But do *they*?
CLAUDE: Do they know ... of course they do. They're artists. Professionals. They're not *laymen* like ... a lot of people.
JOEY: Oh. Well, that kills my hunch then, doesn't it?
CLAUDE: Yes, I hope it does.
JOEY: Yeah. There it is. (*Pause.*) I guess Jerome and Rusty and the two rats must be giants, too, huh? (*CLAUDE stares silently at JOEY.*) You know, I never thought about that before. (*A knock at the door. CLAUDE gets up, stops.*)
CLAUDE: You want to get that?

JOEY: Sure. (*Answers the door.*) Hello, Jillian.
JILL: (*Her clothes and hair style now reflect Jacqueline's severe fashion sense.*) Hi, Joey, how you doin'?
JOEY: Perfect. Wow, you're lookin' pretty freaky.
JILL: Uh, yeah, a little different. Sorry, I took longer than I thought.
JOEY: Yeah, look who showed up in the meantime.
JILL: (*Sees CLAUDE—beat.*) Hello, Claude.
CLAUDE: Hi.
JILL: I ... just came to get my stuff.
CLAUDE: Yeah. Joey said. (*Beat.*) Um ... cuppa tea?
JILL: I don't ...
CLAUDE: Only take a minute.
JILL: (*Beat.*) Sure, okay.
CLAUDE: Joey ... would you get the tea?
JOEY: No thanks, I'll have a beer.
CLAUDE: Uh ... (*Signals to JOEY.*)
JOEY: Hey! Hey, I'll make the tea. You guys just sit and talk. How's that?
CLAUDE: Thank you, Joey. (*JOEY exits.*)
JILL: (*Beat—CLAUDE stares questioningly.*) What?
CLAUDE: You knocked.
JILL: Oh. Yes. I stood there wondering about that, myself. I guess I felt I should, somehow.
CLAUDE: (*Beat.*) I understand. (*Silence.*) How's ... Jacqueline?
JILL: She's fine.
CLAUDE: (*Indicating a pin JILL is wearing.*) Her's?
JILL: A gift.
CLAUDE: Oh. So you're getting along okay?
JILL: Yup. Pretty good.
CLAUDE: Not "great?"
JILL: (*Beat.*) What can I say? She's ... brutally sincere. Stimulating, insightful, frank,...
CLAUDE: Good, good. That's good. That's how she struck me at the library that day. Frank. Insightful. (*Beat.*)
JILL: That's ... how she is.
CLAUDE: The, uh, apartment's big enough? And ... no major problems? With the plumbing, or anything.
JILL: Enough room for us. Everything seems okay.
CLAUDE: Good. Good. (*Silence.*)
JILL: Claude, I know this is difficult.
CLAUDE: What?
JILL: I have moments myself ...
CLAUDE: Jill, I told you, it's fine. I can empathize with the emotional transition that you're going through. And I accept it, fully. I do, honestly. I'm not confined to the oppressive male psyche. I appreciate your needs and I support you in your ...

endeavour to fulfil them. Really. And I think Jacqueline understands that as well.
JILL: Yes, she does.
CLAUDE: Good.
JILL: We've talked about it.
CLAUDE: (*Beat.*) You have?
JILL: Yes.
CLAUDE: What ... why? What did she say?
JILL: Oh, nothing really.
CLAUDE: Tell me.
JILL: I shouldn't have said anything.
CLAUDE: Brutal sincerity?
JILL: (*Beat, breath.*) She says you're full of shit.
CLAUDE: What?
JILL: She says, "he doth protest too much", and that you're just over compensating for the real psychological trauma caused by this rupture in your fragile, sexist mind-set.
CLAUDE: What?
JILL: She says that you're feeling socially and emotionally castrated, and figures you'll probably want to get laid silly in order to reaffirm your "cromagnon manhood."
CLAUDE: No!
JILL: And she feels that your energetic support of the women's movement is just a political prerequisite for survival within the artistic community.
CLAUDE: Aw, God! Political prerequisite ... that's old stuff! C'mon, Jill, that's a speech we've both heard before.
JILL: Well ...
CLAUDE: Oh, come on! I don't believe this!
JILL: It's just what she thinks.
CLAUDE: Oh, yeah? Give me a break! That bitch would say that anyway!
JILL: That what?
CLAUDE: She can't even grant me the slightest potential for empathy? What, do none of us care?
JILL: I'm not sure.
CLAUDE: Jesus, Jill. Where the hell are you? You believe that?
JILL: I don't know.
CLAUDE: Oh, man! She's actually convinced you?
JILL: I make my own statements!
CLAUDE: She's ... awww nnnoooo ...
JILL: Stop it, Claude. You asked me, I told you.
JOEY: (*From the doorway.*) Tea's ready. (*Enters, delivers the two cups.*)
JILL: Thank you, Joey.
CLAUDE: (*Beat.*) Wait a second. You couldn't have boiled the kettle that fast.

JOEY: Boil the kettle?
CLAUDE: You've got to boil the kettle, Joey.
JOEY: (*To JILL.*) Not hot enough?
JILL: It's fine, thanks.
JOEY: (*To CLAUDE.*) I could pour your's back and boil it up a bit.
CLAUDE: No, it's alright.
JOEY: Suit yourself. (*To JILL.*) Nuked it in the microwave.
JILL: (*Smiles.*) How do you find it here, Joey?
JOEY: Oh, just like home. A little quiet. But I get a charge out of Clod's statues. Pretty weird, eh?
JILL: Yes. I guess they are.
JOEY: How's your new spot?
JILL: Great. I've even lost a little weight with the natural foods.
JOEY: Yes, I don't doubt that a bit.
JILL: It's really good if you give it a chance.
JOEY: I dunno. Think I'd rather eat the lawn. Same thing.
JILL: Don't be silly. It's so nutritious. I could never go back to the food at home. All that meat.
JOEY: Sure, you're the one that used to be face and eyes into the meatloaf.
JILL: Well, that was a long time ago.
JOEY: She used to love my meatloaf.
JILL: It's full of toxins, you know. The antibiotics really weaken your immune system.
JOEY: Some good though.
JILL: Joey, you've got to try new things.
JOEY: Me? Sure, I couldn't even get you to go for a green pea.
JILL: That's different.
JOEY: I used to have to dig a hole in her mashed potato, and fill it full of green peas so she had them in her mouth before she knew what was happening.
JILL: You used to throw them in my milk when I wasn't looking.
JOEY: Yup, and she used to drink it back until ... gump, mouth fulla peas.
JILL: Yuck.
JOEY: That wasn't the best. The best was when I used to pick her hot dog up, put a roll of 'em down the middle of the bun, and when she'd take a bite, she'd be lookin' at half a mushy pea hangin' out the end.
JILL: Stop, it's making me nauseous.
CLAUDE: She still hates them.
JOEY: Yeah?
JILL: It's one thing I haven't quite managed to get past.
JOEY: Oh. Glass of milk?
JILL: Stop.
JOEY: Wiener?
JILL: Joey!

JOEY: I s'pose I'll have to scrounge up a bowl of dandelion soup or something. Oh, I made some bread. Want some?
JILL: No, that's alright. Thanks anyway, I've gotta go.
JOEY: (*Exiting to kitchen.*) Take a loaf with you, we got loads.
CLAUDE: He loves to make bread.
JOEY: I love to make bread.
JILL: We've still got six loaves from last week.
CLAUDE: You should see what's inside.
JOEY: (*Entering.*) Here we go. Fresh from the counter.
JILL: Thank you, Joey.
CLAUDE: Doesn't Jacqueline make bread?
JILL: No.
CLAUDE: Dough boys?
JILL: Not that I know of.
CLAUDE: Not that she couldn't, of course.
JOEY: I got a great recipe. Works every time.
JILL: Maybe next time. I really have to go. (*She fetches her box, leaving the bread on the chair.*) Thanks for the tea, Joey.
JOEY: No prob.
CLAUDE: Hey, don't forget your bread. (*Puts it on the box.*)
JILL: Right. Thanks.
CLAUDE: (*Beat.*) Listen ... let's grab a coffee somewhere.
JILL: I'm really busy.
CLAUDE: C'mon. Squeeze me in, Jill. Please.
JILL: I don't think it's a good idea.
JOEY: Half an hour, Jill. I need to talk to you.
JILL: I can't Claude, not now.
CLAUDE: I'll call.
JILL: No. Don't. I'll call you, but I can't say when.
CLAUDE: I'll be here.
JILL: Bye, Joey.
JOEY: Catch you later.
CLAUDE: Jillian, I ...
JILL: Please, Claude. Don't start apologizing 'til I'm gone, will you? (*She exits.*)
CLAUDE: (*Beat.*) Sorry, Jill. (*Makes brief eye contact with JOEY, then moves away.*)
JOEY: Doesn't seem very happy, does she? (*Beat.*) Of course, it is a strange thing she's into. (*Beat.*) Confuses the hell out of me, anyway.
CLAUDE: Well, of course it does, Joey.
JOEY: Yeah, of course.
CLAUDE: I mean, it would, wouldn't it? Nothing would throw me for a loop more than if it didn't. Actually, you know, I'd be impressed if you were to grasp anything outside the realm of pipe gauges and slow motion replays.
JOEY: Are you mad at me, Clod?

CLAUDE: Claude. No, I just don't know how to deal with you, Joey. You baffle me. Forget it.
JOEY: Really?
CLAUDE: Really.
JOEY: I sort of had it the other way 'round. I mean, I don't use no fancy words or nuthin'. You, now, you got more school in you than I got in my whole family. And you're even smart besides. Sure, when you let loose with a stream of humdingers, like you can, it all sorta ... mushes together 'til it sounds like music to me.
CLAUDE: It's not that I think you're stupid.
JOEY: It's not like you have a hard time figuring out what I'm tryin' to say, either.
CLAUDE: It's not what you say. It's the way you think. It's so ... so simplistic.
JOEY: (*Beat.*) Yeah.
CLAUDE: But there's more to things, Joey. You can't just accept the standard viewpoint on everything. (*Beat.*) No, of course not. If you just stop like that, you ... travel in reverse. You get left in the past.
JOEY: See, this is where I get baffled. Now, how can you be stopped and be going in reverse at the same time? Gary, at work, he screwed up his transmission once and used to back up while he was in park, but ...
CLAUDE: No, Joey, no! I just mean that if you don't at least stay open-minded, you chance being ... invalidated by contemporary ... new ways of thinking.
JOEY: Didn't know there were old ones.
CLAUDE: And it's not a question of evaluation. It's simply one of being aware and taking risks. You always take the safe perspective on things.
JOEY: I take the only one I know.
CLAUDE: Exactly. And I'm saying you need more than one.
JOEY: (*Beat.*) Sheesh, at work they call me the radical.
CLAUDE: What?
JOEY: Sure. They figure me living with a fruity artist type is pretty wild stuff.
CLAUDE: I'm not ... "Joey the Radical."
JOEY: I know what you're like, but these guys figure that anyone who wants to sit around and make pretty pictures has gotta be. Me living with one flips them out. So, you see, I'm pretty hip.
CLAUDE: Yes, please forgive me. I've misunderstood you all along. You're really very hip, very hip indeed.
JOEY: Sure. I even get a charge out of this crazy stuff you're always making.
CLAUDE: Look, just what is it about this "crazy stuff" that gives you such a charge?
JOEY: It's just weird. I dunno. Sort of funny.

CLAUDE: Sort of funny. See, Joey? I don't understand.
JOEY: I don't mean "HA HA" funny. I mean it's kinda neat, in a way. Y'know, how it don't look like anything I ever seen before.
CLAUDE: That's because it's non-representational. (*Blank from JOEY.*) It's a concrete, abstract expression of a concept. (*Blank.*) It's supposed to be a shape that expresses a feeling instead of a thing that you can see or touch.
JOEY: (*Slowly.*) Ooooh. I see.
CLAUDE: Good.
JOEY: Like a hiccup or a fart.
CLAUDE: No! Like an emotion or an idea!
JOEY: Oh.
CLAUDE: ...like a hiccup ...
JOEY: So?
CLAUDE: What!?
JOEY: So what is it?
CLAUDE: Nothing!
JOEY: C'mon, what does ... what does it ...
CLAUDE: Symbolize?
JOEY: Yeah.
CLAUDE: (*Beat.*) Forget it. You wouldn't be interested.
JOEY: Sure I would.
CLAUDE: Alright then, you wouldn't understand!
JOEY: So?
CLAUDE: So there wouldn't be much point then, would there!?
JOEY: You are mad at me aren't you?
CLAUDE: Joey, ... your turn to cook.
JOEY: Not going to tell me?
CLAUDE: Pleeease!
JOEY: Alright, alright. (*Beat.*) I'd really like to know, that's all. (*Exits to kitchen. CLAUDE looks at the sculpture, sighs, fade to black.*)

Scene 7:

(*Lights up, CLAUDE is still working on the sculpture. JOEY enters from the kitchen carrying two plates of hamburgers and french fries.*)

JOEY: All set.
CLAUDE: Great, I'm starved. (*He sits at the table.*) Ooooo, hamburgers.
JOEY: Yup. Looooove hamburgers.
CLAUDE: (*Chewing first bite.*) Hmmm. I must admit, although you embody the definitive meat and potatoes approach to things, you do alright with a pound of medium ground.
JOEY: Thanks, Clod.
CLAUDE: (*Beat.*) You're welcome.

JOEY: Pretty good, coming from a veggie.
CLAUDE: How did you know that?
JOEY: Dunno. Maybe I guessed.
CLAUDE: How does one guess something like that?
JOEY: Maybe it was your eyes.
CLAUDE: My eyes?
JOEY: Yeah. All veggies have this guppy look, like they're in shock all the time. You know ... (*Makes bug eyes.*)
CLAUDE: (*Smiles.*) Hah. Yeah, that rings a bell.
JOEY: When did you start again?
CLAUDE: Eating meat? Couple of years ago or so. Most of us did, I guess.
JOEY: How come?
CLAUDE: I don't know. It was a statement of some kind at the time. I forget exactly what about. Glad I gave it up, though.
JOEY: You mean "took" it up.
CLAUDE: No. I'm glad I gave up my vegetarianism.
JOEY: That's sort of like giving up "giving up."
CLAUDE: Eh?
JOEY: Giving up vegetarianism. Same as ... swearing off going on the wagon, right?
CLAUDE: (*Beat.*) Sort of.
JOEY: Yeah.
CLAUDE: So?
JOEY: Nothing.
CLAUDE: Why'd you bring it up?
JOEY: I dunno. I just didn't never hear anyone put it like that before.
CLAUDE: Double negative. Pass the salt?
JOEY: What?
CLAUDE: The salt.
JOEY: (*Passing it.*) No, before that.
CLAUDE: Double negative. You said " Didn't never." That's a double negative.
JOEY: Going to make me look that up, aren't you?
CLAUDE: It's simple. You said that you " Didn't never hear of it." "Didn't" negates "never", reversing your intended meaning. (*Beat.*) Look, if I want to say, for example, that the food is lousy, I'd say "The food is not good." If I said that the food "isn't not good", then I'd actually be saying that the food was fine, wouldn't I?
JOEY: And you wouldn't mean that.
CLAUDE: Not in this example, no.
JOEY: Well, if I wanted to say, for instance, that the statue was lousy, I'd make it short and simple and say, "The statue sucks."
CLAUDE: Listen, I was only trying to illustrate a point.
JOEY: I know. So was I.

CLAUDE: No. You don't understand me, Joey. I picked the food as my example arbitrarily.
JOEY: Okay.
CLAUDE: All I was trying to say was that two negatives make a positive. I was not making a personal evaluation of your cooking.
JOEY: I got you.
CLAUDE: You did.
JOEY: Sure.
CLAUDE: You understand my method.
JOEY: Uh huh.
CLAUDE: And you understand the double negative.
JOEY: I think so.
CLAUDE: Prove it.
JOEY: How?
CLAUDE: Give me an example.
JOEY: Of a double negative?
CLAUDE: Yeah.
JOEY: (*Beat.*) Giving up vegetarianism really means you've taken up eating meat.
CLAUDE: Forget it, this is hopeless. (*Gets up.*)
JOEY: What?
CLAUDE: Just forget it! (*Exits to his room.*)
JOEY: Alright.
(*JOEY picks up what is left of CLAUDE's fries. As he eats, the sculpture catches his eye. He wanders over to it and, after some thought, offers it a fry. It declines. He eats it. Fade to black—"CLAUDE's Music."*)

Scene 8:

(*Music fades as the lights reveal CLAUDE as he is rearranging the furniture. The sculpture has been moved SR, the dining table C. The portrait of Jillian has been taken down and leans, backwards, against the wall SL. CLAUDE is positioning the sofa downstage from the kitchen doorway as JOEY enters with a large bag of flour.*)
JOEY: Hiyo, Clod. (*Hangs up his coat.*)
CLAUDE: Joey. Where you been?
JOEY: Working on something. Got some flour.
CLAUDE: More flour?
JOEY: Yeah. Whatcha doing?
CLAUDE: Oh, just a little rearranging. Don't we have enough ...
JOEY: How come?
CLAUDE: Well, mostly for a change, but also to improve our space.
JOEY: Yeah?
CLAUDE: Yeah, the way we were arranged before really didn't make much sense. The work table cut off the major traffic route

that runs from the dining table to the kitchen. Now that distance is both reduced and unobstructed. See?
JOEY: Uh huh. (*Moves in front of the sofa.*)
CLAUDE: Space is something we often fail to consider, Joey. We tend not to think of it as the malleable element it is. The concrete objects that occupy space should be regarded as containers and definers of the more important three dimensional areas that exist between and around them.
JOEY: Uh huh. (*Beat.*) Want a beer?
CLAUDE: No. Thanks.

(*JOEY turns to go into the kitchen but finds himself obstructed by the sofa. He steps on and over it, and disappears into the kitchen. CLAUDE is frozen for a moment, then moves behind the sofa to study the problem. JOEY returns with his beer, steps over the back of the couch and sits on it. He looks straight ahead for a moment.*)

JOEY: Was that wallpaper always here or did you put it up yourself?
CLAUDE: Put it up myself.
JOEY: Is it me, or does it look a bit squish?
CLAUDE: It's intentionally deviated from the norm.
JOEY: You put it up squish on purpose?
CLAUDE: I ... yes. (*JOEY laughs.*) Fine, Joey, as long as I don't have to explain it.
JOEY: I'm not laughing at it. I think it's a neat idea. I'd never think of doing that.
CLAUDE: Well, it's not as though it was a decision made on a whim, you know. (*Beat.*) I hardly went through the trouble just for a lark. (*Another blank stare.*) I meant something by it.
JOEY: It's okay, you don't have to explain it to me.
CLAUDE: Look. (*Beat.*) We're surrounded by a cold, sterile, regulated, man-made environment. So much so that we lose touch with the natural irregularity of the real world. This all sounds incredibly naive, I know. Anyway, our attitudes and values have become as practical and predictable as our architecture. By hanging the wallpaper ever so subtly askew, and thereby frustrating the perpendicular conformity, I make a statement. Think about it. What could it be that I'm trying to say?
JOEY: Uh ...
CLAUDE: Take your time.
JOEY: Mmmm ... Maybe that ... there's more than one way to put on wallpaper?
CLAUDE: Obviously. And?
JOEY: That ... that it doesn't always have to go on straight?
CLAUDE: Keep going.
JOEY: And that a man's wallpaper is his own business!
CLAUDE: No! Go back a step.

JOEY: Oh, um ... how about ... that the instructions don't always show the only way to do something?
CLAUDE: Yes!
JOEY: That we can do it our own way if we want to?
CLAUDE: Yes!!
JOEY: That we can sort of make ... new ways?
CLAUDE: YES!!
JOEY: Better ways?
CLAUDE: That's it! That's it!
JOEY: It is?
CLAUDE: Absolutely!
JOEY: Wow. And all this time I just thought the floor was off.
CLAUDE: You hit it, Joey! The value of the individual, the complacency of the public, the importance of taking risks ...
JOEY: Yeah?
CLAUDE: "The majority is always wrong" ... as Jillian used to say ...
JOEY: All that, huh? Jesus, you blow me away, Clod.
CLAUDE: Well, ...
JOEY: Shit, you've got philosophy hidden in your wallpaper. That takes a special kind of mind, buddy.
CLAUDE: Now, now.
JOEY: I never met no one thinks like you do.
CLAUDE: Double negative.
JOEY: What?
CLAUDE: Nothing. Sorry. Thanks, Joey.
JOEY: Ohhh, yeah. One of those. See? I can't even get that far, and you talk through your walls. You make statues that mean something that I can't even guess.
CLAUDE: It's no big deal.
JOEY: Sure it is. You know, if you'd just take a minute to size up what you got, I bet you'd be a whole lot happier.
CLAUDE: What do you mean? Don't give me that look, Joey.
JOEY: I just think you should give yourself a break, that's all.
CLAUDE: Oh, yeah?
JOEY: Yeah, let up. You always expect a lot from yourself, and then turn around and shit all over everything you come up with just because someone else has.
CLAUDE: That's not true.
JOEY: Seems to me.
CLAUDE: I practice objective self-criticism. It's healthy.
JOEY: Dumpin' on yourself?
CLAUDE: Objective—criticism. Impartial. The same I get from others.
JOEY: Right. What about that guy in the paper that dumped on your display ...
CLAUDE: Exhibition.

JOEY: ... or what's-his-face who raked you at the party?
CLAUDE: Opening! And critical feedback from one's peers is generally considered valuable.
JOEY: By who?
CLAUDE: By everyone. Artists. By me.
JOEY: Even when the peers are pricks?
CLAUDE: Joey, these people are not interested in petty, gratuitous, ... malicious, mud-slinging.
JOEY: They're above all that.
CLAUDE: Yes, they are.
JOEY: They're right and you're wrong.
CLAUDE: Not necessarily ... that's not what I said.
JOEY: Well, which is it?
CLAUDE: They ... it depends.
JOEY: On what?
CLAUDE: On what the situation.
JOEY: Clod?
CLAUDE: Claude!
JOEY: If you could just make up your mind, maybe you wouldn't be so paranoid.
CLAUDE: Paranoid! I'm not ... listen ... Jesus, you too! I can't believe this. Christ, why do I even bother? I let myself get all worked up by assholes who don't even know what they're talking about!
JOEY: Well, this is my point...
CLAUDE: Oh, fuck you, Joey! Fuck you and your advice! I've had it with your Goddamn questions, your fucked up commentary! I get that crap from everybody and I don't need yours, so go to hell. Yeah, you, Robert Shithead, and his Merry Band of Arsewipes, you can all go to hell. And take Dr. Jacqueline fucking Hyde with you! The whole lousy lot of you piss me off, and I wish you'd all just pack up and die.
JOEY: *(Pause.)* That's the spirit.
CLAUDE: AAAAAAAAAAAAAAAAAAAAAGH! *(Paces mechanically. Silence, big breath, then finally.)* Sorry.
JOEY: What for? You're right, what the hell do I know?
CLAUDE: Still.
JOEY: No, boy. That was a good one.
(Beat).
Feel any better?
(CLAUDE shakes his head.)
JOEY: Worse?
CLAUDE: Numb. I just feel numb.
JOEY: *(Beat.)* Uh huh. So what are you gonna do now?
CLAUDE: I think I'll do this for a year or so.
JOEY: Oh. Do me a favour, will ya?
CLAUDE: Not now, Joey.

JOEY: I wouldn't ask but ... it's buggin' the hell out of me.
CLAUDE: What.
JOEY: Your thing there (*The sculpture.*). Tell me what it's all about, will you?
CLAUDE: Why? It's not going to work out, anyway.
JOEY: No?
CLAUDE: I don't think so.
JOEY: How can you tell?
CLAUDE: Something's wrong. Or missing or something. It's hard to explain.
JOEY: I know what you mean.
CLAUDE: You do?
JOEY: Sure. I made some bread like that once.
CLAUDE: Oh.
JOEY: Knew before I put it in the oven that it was going to die on me. Weird, isn't it?
CLAUDE: Confuses the hell out of me, Joey.
JOEY: See, bread is something you can't really fix once it's in the oven. What's done is done. But this here, this has something about it. Something that gets at me.
CLAUDE: Yeah?
JOEY: The more I look at it. It's ... it's like when you're at a movie, and the picture is all fuzzy, because the guy running the machine ain't paying attention? You're dying for him to turn that knob, y'know, and it's taking forever and forever. And just when you're sure he's never going to do it, and you're about to explode ... whoosh! The picture clears. And everything is more perfect than ever before. It's like a warm rush that drops the knots out of your knees and lets your shoulders down half a foot.
CLAUDE: Uh huh.
JOEY: Well that's sort of what this does to me.
CLAUDE: It amazes me that you're so caught up on it.
JOEY: Amazes *you*? Just focus it, will you?
CLAUDE: (*Smiles.*) I'll try.
JOEY: You got to put a little ... (*JOEY starts to talk with his body, gyrating this way and that.*) ... like, sorta ... or maybe ... kinda, and ... so that it...
    (*CLAUDE has started to twist a little too, when JILLIAN enters quietly. She watches the dance for a moment.*)
JOEY: ... does a ... like...
CLAUDE: What?
JILL: Hi, guys.
CLAUDE: Jillian.
JOEY: How you doin'?
CLAUDE: I didn't hear you knock.
JILL: I ... I didn't. Sorry.
CLAUDE: It's okay.

JILL: What's going on?
JOEY: We were talking about the sculpture.
JILL: Yeah?
JOEY: Yeah, we get into it pretty heavy sometimes.
CLAUDE: Well...
JILL: You've changed things around a little.
JOEY: Clod did it. It clears up all the traffic flows and spaces everywhere, right?
CLAUDE: Right.
JOEY: Helps you get some exercise when you want a beer too.
CLAUDE: Right, so ... what brings you over?
JILL: I just ... thought I'd pay a visit.
JOEY: Uh, I gotta run to the shop to pick something up. I'll just ... go ... and come back in a little while.
JILL: It's okay, Joey.
JOEY: No, really, I do have to pick something up. Should be just about ready by now. We'll see you in a bit.
CLAUDE: Thanks, Joey.
JILL: Bye. (*JOEY exits. CLAUDE waits for JILL to begin. She sees her portrait, facing toward the wall, and picks it up. She turns it over to look at it.*) Don't know how I could have forgotten this.
CLAUDE: It's the last thing.
JILL: Yes, I guess it is.
CLAUDE: Is that why you came?
JILL: No. No, it isn't.
CLAUDE: (*Beat.*) So what's on your mind?
JILL: I guess I really came to...
CLAUDE: Yeah?
JILL: You know. (*Beat.*) It's kind of awkward...
CLAUDE: What happened?
JILL: (*Beat.*) Oh, God, we just ... nothing went right. I ... I couldn't keep up with her demands.
CLAUDE: Ah.
JILL: It was constantly "Do this", and "We've got to do that". Her commitments piling on top of mine, and always taking priority. And always a major guilt trip. I couldn't even see friends without her consent. Not that I had the time, anyway. I mean, I was accommodating my ass off, but it was never good enough.
CLAUDE: I see. So it didn't work out.
JILL: No, it didn't. She's an amazing woman, incredibly talented. And it destroys you, to just get smudged out like that. She'd dangle the affection in front of me like a carrot, and I'd be hopping around, all for the sake of a little approval. It was a nightmare.
CLAUDE: That's how she struck me at the library that day.
JILL: I don't remember you saying that.

CLAUDE: I didn't want to rain on your parade. You were in awe.
JILL: Yes. I suppose I was. Anyway, I came up against it when she all but told me to skip my exams.
CLAUDE: Oh, wow.
JILL: She said it was selfish of me when there was so much work to do for an able-bodied activist. I actually considered it. But in the end I just told her that you helped me pay for the term, and that it was important to me.
CLAUDE: And she said?
JILL: It was like I killed the cat. She said I was more or less personally accountable for untold suffering and injustice, just because I had the nerve to want my credits.
CLAUDE: The ultimate crime.
JILL: So we had a real nasty thing, and ... it was pretty awful. She almost "decreed" that I was to stay and behave.
CLAUDE: Hmmm.
JILL: (*Beat.*) I'm so sorry Claude.
CLAUDE: (*Beat.*) Thank you.
JILL: What's the matter with me?
CLAUDE: Nothing's the matter.
JILL: Why am I so stupid?
CLAUDE: Come on, Jill.
JILL: No, really.
CLAUDE: You just found something out, that's all.
JILL: Like how stupid I am.
CLAUDE: Just chalk it up. At least you're willing to take risks.
JILL: A lot of good that's done me.
CLAUDE: That's the process. Consider yourself a step ahead.
JILL: A step ahead? I'm right back where I started!
CLAUDE: No, you're not.
JILL: I am! Look at me!
CLAUDE: Now you're all the wiser...
JILL: Jesus, is there any end to your understanding!? Why can't you just get pissed off at me for once?
CLAUDE: Jill...
JILL: Come on, Claude, admit it! You're livid over this. You are, and you're fighting it because you're terrified of compromising your damn "openness!" It's pathetic! You know, if you could get past this insufferable support trip you're into, you might start responding like a normal human being!
CLAUDE: That's not fair.
JILL: I mean it! It's like you've got some self-inflicted, new-age, plastic inner-child, mental disease, that kicks your own balls every time you need them!
CLAUDE: Hey!
JILL: How come Jacqueline fought harder to have me stay than you did? Huh? Was that because she cares more? Or just

because she has the guts to fight for what's important to her? What the hell would you object to? Huh? What could I do? I walked away, and rejected you outright, and now I can just waltz on back and all's fine? Where's your self-preservation!?
CLAUDE: Who said you could come back?
JILL: (*Beat.*) What?
CLAUDE: You can't come back, Jill. Not now. I know I could have said no long ago. I should have about a lot of things.
JILL: I can't come back?
CLAUDE: No, this has been painful for me, Jill. I haven't started to sort it out.
JILL: But ... I'm sorry. It was a mistake.
CLAUDE: That doesn't change it.
JILL: Claude...
CLAUDE: And you're right, I should have fought harder, but it's too late for that, too. I guess I just don't like setting restrictions.
JILL: You are now.
CLAUDE: Yeah, I am. My timing's not the best.
JILL: (*Beat.*) I ... I wasn't thinking. (*Beat.*) Are you sure?
CLAUDE: (*Nods.*) You've got to take care of yourself at some point, Jill. If you're not solid, how can you support anything else?
JILL: I just didn't take time to weigh it all out, Claude.
CLAUDE: No, you didn't. I think this is for the best.
JILL: (*Beat.*) So ... I should go, then.
CLAUDE: When you're ready. Unless you have a meeting waiting on you.
JILL: Of course I do. (*Beat.*) They'll survive without me.
CLAUDE: That's the spirit. (*Pause.*) Where you gonna stay?
JILL: I don't know. I didn't ... Erica's three-floor experiment in open living?
CLAUDE: You could do worse.
JILL: There's no doubt about that. (*Beat.*) Well. That's it then.
CLAUDE: That's ... it.
JILL: (*Beat.*) Goodbye, Claude. (*Silence. JILL finally gets up to leave with the portrait, but stops before reaching the door.*) Would you do me a favour? Could you hold onto this for awhile?
CLAUDE: Sure. Long as you want.
JILL: Thanks. (*She smiles, an embrace, she leaves. CLAUDE hangs the portrait. JOEY enters carrying his sculpture, wrapped in a garbage bag.*)
JOEY: Hey, that was quick.
CLAUDE: Yeah.
JOEY: She looked a little upset. Bad news?
CLAUDE: Not too bad.
JOEY: Good, good. Is she comin' back?
CLAUDE: I don't think so.

JOEY: Oh. That's too bad. I figured she might be fed up with what's-her-face by now.
CLAUDE: It appears she is.
JOEY: Oh. (*A look from CLAUDE.*) None of my business?
CLAUDE: Afraid not.
JOEY: Right on.
CLAUDE: Good.
JOEY: Hey, I've got a surprise. Something I put together at the shop. It's not quite dry yet, but I wanted to get your opinion.
CLAUDE: What is it?
JOEY: Just hang on a minute. Are you ready?
CLAUDE: Sure.
(*JOEY unveils the sculpture with a flourish. It is a crudely constructed man, made with drainage pipes. It is painted to match CLAUDE's current attire. CLAUDE is hesitant. JOEY beams.*)
JOEY: Well?
CLAUDE: Uh...
JOEY: What do you think? (*CLAUDE cautiously takes it from JOEY.*) Watch it, it's a little tacky.
CLAUDE: Uh huh.
JOEY: Well? Feedback from one's peers and all that, you know.
CLAUDE: What is it, Joey?
JOEY: It's a man! I made it out of scraps from around the shop.
CLAUDE: Yes, I see.
JOEY: Notice anything about it?
CLAUDE: Not in particular.
JOEY: Look at the colours.
CLAUDE: The colours? Oh, yeah ... this is me.
JOEY: Yeah! You got it! It was the weirdest thing, y'know? I went down to clean out the rest of my tools, and I saw all these bits of stuff in the corner. I said, "I bet I can put that together and make something!" I've been working with this stuff for years and I never ever thought of making nothing out of it. Anyway, so I started to weld this piece to that piece, and then I found this big three-way that looked just like a head, and POW! I knew exactly what to do! It was so easy. And the more I added, the more it reminded me of you!
CLAUDE: Great.
JOEY: I only had to paint it, and voila, statue of toi!
CLAUDE: Amazing.
JOEY: So, what do you think?
CLAUDE: It's ... interesting. Very direct.
JOEY: Uh huh...
CLAUDE: (*Beat.*) And I would say that it has a certain ... unity.
JOEY: Okay...
CLAUDE: And I definitely think that you've captured a likeness.

JOEY: You think so?
CLAUDE: No question about it.
JOEY: You're not just saying that?
CLAUDE: No, I really think you have.
JOEY: Well, guess what?
CLAUDE: What?
JOEY: It's yours!
CLAUDE: Really.
JOEY: Yup.
CLAUDE: I don't know what I can say, Joey, I'm sure. (*Leans it against the sculpture.*)
JOEY: Don't mention it. But listen, I would like something from you.
CLAUDE: What?
JOEY: (*Beat.*) What yours is all about.
CLAUDE: Oh, Joey...
JOEY: Come on.
CLAUDE: Why?
JOEY: I just gotta know. What's it, top secret or something?
CLAUDE: No, it's just...
JOEY: You're afraid, aren't ya?
CLAUDE: Of what?
JOEY: That you haven't done it.
CLAUDE: No, that's not it.
JOEY: So tell me.
CLAUDE: Oh, alright! If you really want to know.
JOEY: I do.
CLAUDE: (*Beat.*) Well, I'll tell you. It's ... it's supposed to...
JOEY: Yeah?
CLAUDE: I was trying...
JOEY: Come on...
CLAUDE: I wanted to reflect the ... I can't, Joey.
JOEY: Oh man! It's got something to do with ... (*Arms back, flight-like.*) ... with ... flying. Right?
CLAUDE: (*Beat.*) How did you know?
JOEY: I knew it! You can just feel it!
CLAUDE: Yeah?
JOEY: I knew it!
CLAUDE: Really.
JOEY: Right on!
CLAUDE: Flight.
JOEY: Flight! That's exactly it!
CLAUDE: Wow.
JOEY: Flight!
CLAUDE: Yeah.
JOEY: I been dreamin' about this for days.
CLAUDE: Unbelievable. Really?

JOEY: Really!
CLAUDE: (*Beat.*) Now I don't know what to say for sure, Joey.
JOEY: I think it's been said, Clod buddy.
CLAUDE: Maybe so. Thanks, Joey.
JOEY: Thank you. And you're right, you know. The castle don't quite cut it. Whew! That's a load off.
CLAUDE: I feel a little lighter myself.
JOEY: Look up. Look waaaay up...
CLAUDE: And I'll call Rusty.
JOEY: Wicked!
CLAUDE: Well, well, well.
JOEY: Man. I guess I nailed it down just in time, too.
CLAUDE: What do you mean?
JOEY: Well, I sorta got another surprise.
CLAUDE: Oh, yeah?
JOEY: Yeah. Now I know this might leave you in a bit of a spot, but it looks like I'll be movin' out.
CLAUDE: How come?
JOEY: It's a long story.
CLAUDE: What's going on?
JOEY: I sorta lost the ol' job.
CLAUDE: What happened?
JOEY: I guess the foreman likes his pipes nothing but perpendicular. (*Beat.*) Ever so subtly askew, you know.
CLAUDE: Uh oh...
JOEY: Yup.
CLAUDE: "Joey The Radical."
JOEY: That's me.
CLAUDE: Jesus, I thought you just took another day off.
JOEY: Ah, it's no big deal. I was pretty tired of it anyway. The boys are pretty narrow-minded.
CLAUDE: I see. Christ, and I thought I had a bad day.
JOEY: You did.
CLAUDE: So. You're going home?
JOEY: I guess so.
CLAUDE: That's too bad. What do you think you'll do?
JOEY: Pogy, get another job.
CLAUDE: Uh huh.
JOEY: Maybe open a bakery or something.
CLAUDE: That's not a bad idea.
JOEY: You think?
CLAUDE: Why not?
JOEY: Sure, I'm hooked now, I might even make up the odd sculpture.
CLAUDE: Go for it. I think you may have the knack.
JOEY: Me too.
CLAUDE: So this one is sort of a ... going-away present.

JOEY: Yeah. I mean, I don't know you real good or nothin', but I thought you might like it.
CLAUDE: I do. I really appreciate it, Joey. Thanks.
JOEY: You're welcome. Claude. (*Beat.*) Anyway, I guess you have work to do, so I'll just bug off and leave you alone.
CLAUDE: Uh, where you going?
JOEY: I dunno. For a beer or something, I guess.
CLAUDE: Maybe I'll join you.
JOEY: Want to? Sure! We might even have a good time if we're not careful.
CLAUDE: S'pose I'll risk it.
JOEY: I s'pose you will.
CLAUDE: I hope we can find a bar we can both agree on.
JOEY: Geez, I hope we can find a bar that will let the both of us in!
(*JOEY exits first. CLAUDE grabs his jacket is about to exit when JOEY's "man", leaning against the sculpture, catches his eye. He moves to it and balances the beer can on top. He exits. Fade to black—"Combined" music.*)

Catlover
A Play for Stage

1990

Written by
Janis Spence

CAST OF CHARACTERS

in order of appearance

HESTER POLGLAZE is between 45 and 50 years old, and works at "Yard Dreams", a garden furniture store.

ARCHIE POLGLAZE is in his mid-seventies and has Alzheimers disease. He is HESTER's father-in-law.

RODDIE POLGLAZE is between 25 and 30 years old and is HESTER's son. He is an architect.

TERRY WILLARD is any age and is the host of a hit T.V. show.

TADJEK is her cameraman and **DAN** is her sound man.

EDWIN POLGLAZE is HESTER's estranged husband, RODDIE's father and ARCHIE's son. He is between 45 and 50 years old.

This play was first performed at the LSPU Hall Theatre in St. John's, Newfoundland in June of 1990.

Produced by the Resource Centre for the Arts, Directed by Janis Spence and Starring:
  Maisie Rillie .... Hester
  Bryan Hennessey .... Archie
  Greg Thomey .... Roddie
  Frankie O'Flaherty .... Terry Willard
  Sebastian Spence .... Tadjek
  Jody Richardson .... Dan

It was subsequently performed at The Ship's Company Theatre in Parrsboro, Nova Scotia, in 1992, the Tarragon Theatre in Toronto, Ontario in 1992 and The Stephenville Festival Theatre, Stephenville, Newfoundland, 1993.

CATLOVER

Act I
Scene 1:

Lights up on a sprawling, sparse living room, functional but not necessarily comfortable. Upstage centre or somewhere in a prominent position, is the front door. A downstage left or right entrance, possibly a hallway, leads to the rest of the house which is never seen—the kitchen, bathroom and bedrooms. There are no knick-knacks, objets d'art or scatter rugs to soften the austerity of this room. This is the home of a person with a debilitating brain condition; a person descending into confusion and the startling fearlessness of infancy. Watch out for sharp corners, slippery rugs, breakable objects that could cut elderly curious fingers.

There is a stereo and a T.V. but neither has been switched on in a few years.

We find HESTER POLGLAZE on the phone to her sister-in-law BERNICE BELBIN. HESTER is attractive in a hasty, thrown together kind of way. She has a slightly messy perm, wears lipstick and smart heels (because BECKY DIRDLE of "Yard Dreams" likes her staff to look nice) and she is a chain smoker.

HESTER, holding the telephone, paces up and down and around the living room, sometimes lighting on a chair for a few seconds, then getting up and going to the window.

HESTER: Yes ... yes I know that, Bernice, ... umhum ... uhhuh ... Yes I know, I did all that, but sometimes ... uh huh ... yeah ... uh huh ... but sometimes ... hum hum ... uh huh ... that's true ... but sometimes ... yeah ... I realize that ... uh huh but sometimes ... Oh God, Bernice, do you think I don't think of that, when this happens it's all I *do* think about, but sometimes—BUT SOMETIMES, NOT ALL THE FACTORS AND CIRCUMSTANCES GOVERNING ONE MISERABLE LIFE FALL INTO PERFECT ... line ... Yes, Bernice, I'm upset, and I'm tired, too—I don't really get as much sleep as I need ... of course that's all it is ... Look I've got to go now, Roddie will be bringing him home any minute ...

No, no, not in the mall, they found him in the parking lot ... well they found most of his clothes but the security guard gave him a sweater and that knitting shop, the "Woolgatherers", the woman in there gave him a pair of hand-knitted socks, twenty-five bucks ... Oh no, I didn't mean *gave*, I meant ... oh what difference does it make, he's safe and Roddie's bringing him home, and I'm really tired, I'm going to try and get a cup of coffee and a bite to eat before they get here ... Yes, I'm eating ... that's what I just said, but I can't get something to eat while I'm on the phone to you ... I'm eating all sorts of things, Bernice, food ... carrots, bread, bananas, I don't know, food!!! ... vitamin B12 ... Yes I'll remember that ... Bernice, I have to have a cup of coffee ... yeah, ok ... well come by and visit him ... he doesn't mean that stuff, you know that ... Really? He said that to you? ... I never heard him say that ... (*Slight guilty grin.*) ... well, obviously only a brain impaired person would say such a thing to his own daughter ... uh huh ... yeah I know he looks like he's doing it on purpose ... well, maybe you and Gardner could come over while he's asleep and maybe I could go to a movie or something ... I'm not implying anything, Bernice ... well there's less and less chance every day of spending *quality* time ... hang on a second.

(*We hear a commotion outside the front door. HESTER covers the mouthpiece with one hand and listens to the following scene in quiet resignation.*)

ARCHIE: No ... no ... my mother's coming to get me—my mother's coming to get me ...

RODDIE: Granddad, for God's sake cut it out! Your mother's *not* coming to get you, we're going in the house.

ARCHIE: No, no, no!!! Help me! He's taking all my money! Help me!! My mother's coming to pick me up, my mother's coming to get me, he's taking all my money!!! Help ...

RODDIE: (*Obviously trying to put his hand over Archie's mouth.*) Jesus God, Granddad, SHUT UP!! Shut up will you ...

ARCHIE: (*Beginning to cry.*) She won't see me, she won't see me, she won't see me ...

(*The front door opens and RODDIE half drags, half pushes the sobbing ARCHIE into the room.*)

HESTER: (*To Bernice.*) Here they are now, I've got to go, Bernice ... yes, I'll tell Roddie to call you. (*She hangs up.*) Archie, Arch. Everything's ok, you're home now.

ARCHIE: My mother's coming to get me, I have to go.

RODDIE: Granddad, your mother's long gone ...

(*ARCHIE bursts into fresh tears.*)

ARCHIE: I have to go home, I have to go home ...

HESTER: Don't tell him things like that, it just makes everything worse—Arch, it's all right—you *are* home and you can calm down now.

(ARCHIE *turns to the front door and tries the knob.* RODDIE *immediately blocks him and makes sure that the door is securely locked, but* ARCHIE *just keeps crying and rattling and turning the door knob.)*
HESTER: (*To* RODDIE.) Why do you say things like that to him—you know it upsets him—Arch, Arch, come and sit down—Arch, do you want some juice—I know, some applesauce—would you like some applesauce? —come on, come away from the door ...
RODDIE: Where was his identity tag? It was practically welded on —how did he get it off? What did you do with your identity tag, Granddad? How did you get it off? Have you got a chainsaw hidden somewhere ... huh?
HESTER: Roddie! Now you just calm down—you speak quietly to him—do you hear me—he can't help it ...
RODDIE: I'm sorry. I've only been up since four o'clock this morning, searching for him ...
ARCHIE: Annabel, Annabel, OPEN THE DOOR, OPEN THE DOOR!
HESTER: Archie, let's go in the kitchen and get some juice, and you can help me put things away in the cupboard, would you like that ...?
ARCHIE: (*Still crying.*) Annabel's coming to get me, ANNABEL, ANNABEL ...
HESTER: Archie, Archie ... (*She begins to rub his back with a soothing motion.*) ... come away from the door. (*She manages to lead* ARCHIE *away from the front door.*) That's it, come and sit down.
ARCHIE: No, no—she won't see me—she's coming to get me—I have to get in the truck.
(*He turns and makes for the door where he resumes the turning and rattling.*)
HESTER: You should have a rest before the truck comes.
ARCHIE: My mother said she'd pick me up—I'm going to be late—I have to get in the truck.
RODDIE: Oh, my God, mother, how do you stand it?
HESTER: Roddie, you're just making things a lot worse. If you relax it might help him out ...
RODDIE: I don't see the point in pretending his delusions are real—I don't see how that can help matters.
HESTER: Archie, you've been walking around for hours and hours—you've got to have a rest—we all need a rest—now come on, come away from the door and sit down.
ARCHIE: I don't know you! —get away from me! —what are you doing here?
RODDIE: (*His voice rising.*) Listen you crazy old coot, she's a goddamn saint, that's who she is ...
HESTER: Roddie—I'm begging you please ...

ARCHIE: Annabel! Annabel! Open up this door—open up this door right now!

HESTER: Archie—everything is all right—you are home, and you are safe—there is no need to open the door because we are all going to sit down and rest, ok? Ok, Arch? Come on, Hon, we'll just do it real slow, and real easy—that's it—here we go.
(She rubs his back again. ARCH looks a little blank but he calms down. Physically he's quite exhausted, his brain is simply neglecting to let him know. She leads him over to a chair but he won't sit down.)

ARCHIE: Get the dog off there ...

HESTER: *(To imaginary dog.)* Here, pup, here, pup—that's it—there, Arch, look he's gone ...

ARCHIE: No, he's still there ... *(He starts to whimper.)* ... He wants to bite me.

HESTER: *(In exasperation lifts the chair cushion and tips the chair.)* There! That's definitely it! He's gone now, look, he's going out into the kitchen—see ...

ARCHIE: *(He has forgotten the dog completely.)* There's the truck—the truck is here to get me.
(He starts for the front door again but both HESTER and RODDIE grab him and force him down into a chair or on the couch. RODDIE practically sits on him.)

RODDIE: Did you see that stuff with the dog? He didn't mean it—he's just having us on half the time—son-of-a-bitch, he's just having us on ...
(ARCHIE starts to sob hysterically.)

ARCHIE: Help! Help me! The dog is biting me—OW—help. The dog is biting me ...

HESTER: Roddie, go out in the kitchen and get a dish of applesauce out of the fridge, it's on the top shelf, a little blue Chinese dish.

RODDIE: Good God, Mother—you're as batty as he is—you can't combat degenerative brain disease with applesauce ...

HESTER: No, no! I put a few of his trancs in it before you brought him home just in case he was upset. Please, Roddie, just do as I ask.

RODDIE: Can you handle him?
(ARCHIE is grizzling now.)

HESTER: Yes. He'll be fine. Go on.
(HESTER sits next to ARCHIE and holds his hand. When RODDIE leaves the room he seems to relax and he seems more familiar with HESTER and the room.)

HESTER: Arch, no, no, look at me, look at me, do you know my name?
(ARCHIE looks fearful and as if he might cry again.)

HESTER: No, no! It's all right—I'm Hester. Say it. Say, Hester ...

ARCHIE: Hester.
HESTER: That's it. Hester.
ARCHIE: Hester.
HESTER: That's right. I'm Hester. I'm your daughter-in-law and we're at home. Your home and my home, and everything is ok ...
ARCHIE: (*Nodding his head.*) You're Edwin's wife.
HESTER: (*Pleased and surprised.*) That's right. I'm Edwin's wife.
ARCHIE: Where's Edwin gone now? I want all that hockey stuff out of the back porch—someone's going to kill themselves out there.
HESTER: (*Sadly.*) He's not home, Arch. He's gone out for a while. Just relax now ...
  (*RODDIE comes back in with the applesauce.*)
RODDIE: I was looking for a blue Chinese bowl. It was in a yellow bowl. This is it, isn't it? This is the applesauce.
HESTER: Oh, I thought it was in the little blue Chinese bowl—yes, that's it—here, Arch, here's your favourite.
  (*ARCHIE is becoming a little agitated again.*)
ARCHIE: That old dog, boy, he's got some bite, it hurts like hell ...
  (*He begins to cry quietly.*)
HESTER: Roddie, I think it would be better if you went out in the kitchen again—I think he's better when it's just me ...
RODDIE: Are you saying I'm bothering him?
HESTER: Well, after something like this, he's more confused than usual and he's better if he only has to deal with one person at a time—besides I think something's hurting him—Arch—did you fall and hurt yourself?
  (*HESTER offers him a spoonful of applesauce.*)
ARCHIE: I CAN DO IT BY MYSELF!
  (*He angrily grabs the bowl and the spoon and eats the applesauce as fast as he can. He then sits and glares at them.*)
RODDIE: (*Controlled and pretending to ignore ARCHIE's behaviour.*) Mother, I'm going to make a trip to the supermarket. I noticed that you hadn't had a chance to do any shopping ...
  (*ARCHIE begins to measure things; the air, the chair he is sitting on, the floor in front of him, etc., with an imaginary tape measure.*)
RODDIE: (*Very calm.*) What is he doing ...?
  (*Pause.*)
HESTER: He's measuring things.
  (*Pause.*)
RODDIE: Do you think you could make him stop doing that for just a few seconds ...
HESTER: Arch. Arch. Give me the tape ... give me the tape—we can start putting it all together tomorrow—now that we know the measurements, ok? ... ok?
  (*ARCHIE hands her the imaginary tape. HESTER takes it*

from him but is embarrassed to be seen accepting an imaginary prop by RODDIE. For a split second she doesn't know what to do with it—then with an obvious gesture of her hand the tape measure disappears. ARCHIE is now more subdued and appears to be getting a little sleepy.)
RODDIE: Anyway, as I was saying, I noticed that there was precious little in the fridge—I'm going to make a run to the supermarket for you—do you want to make a list?
(RODDIE takes a little notebook and pen out of his pocket. He carefully opens the notebook to the latest page then hands both book and pen to HESTER. HESTER looks as if she is accepting a school examination paper. She takes the note book and pen then seems to wait for further instructions.)
RODDIE: Well, make a list. What do you want me to get?
(Pause.)
HESTER: I usually do a bit of shopping every day—I just didn't get out today. I was waiting by the phone all day ...
RODDIE: Well, make a list. I'll go and get some groceries and maybe you could get Granddad into bed ... maybe, or do you need my help—he seems all right now though ...
HESTER: *(Suddenly galvanized.)* Right. Hmmm, Let me see. Ah ... Oats. Rolled oats. Get a few pounds ... and ... *(She looks very thoughtful.)* Oh ... get some ... fruit ... any kind ... er ... let me see ... juice ... and some applesauce—yes, three or four cans of applesauce ... and some catfood—not dry—wet.
(She hands him the notebook and pen.)
RODDIE: That's *it*? Oats and juice and applesauce and cat food? Mother, there's nothing out there. There's no milk or tea or bread—there's nothing in the fridge—there's one stick of shrivelled brown celery in the crisper and a yellow bowl of applesauce—that's it! That's all there is in the kitchen!
HESTER: Don't be silly! We get TV dinners—Bernice is always sending over hundreds of fishcakes and all sorts of ingenious things made with organic meats and soy grits—you'd be amazed at the amount of food that passes through here ...
(Pause.)
I am eating! I am! I promise you! My God, I had to tell Bernice the same thing! ...
(ARCHIE begins to moan quietly.)
RODDIE: Right. Well, I'll do that. I'll be back in a little while. You're sure you're ok?
HESTER: I'm fine. When I get him sorted out, I'll get something to eat ... I mean, when you get back I'll make something. You are staying for supper, aren't you?
RODDIE: I could do that, yes, if you want me to ...
(Pause.)
HESTER: Well, of course I want you to ...

ARCHIE: He bit me, he bit me, he bit me ...
HESTER: Where does it hurt, Arch? Show me where it hurts ...
RODDIE: I'm gone.
(RODDIE takes out his car keys and leaves by the front door.)
HESTER: Does your head hurt? *(She puts her hand on his forehead.)* Does it hurt?
ARCHIE: Yes. It hurts.
HESTER: Did you fall down?
ARCHIE: The dog bit me.
HESTER: Where did he bite you? On your hand?
(ARCHIE shakes his head.)
On your leg? Did he bite you on your leg?
(ARCHIE shakes 'no' again.)
Where? On your ankle?
(ARCHIE nods and leans forward to touch his ankles and then his feet—he begins to moan again.)
HESTER: Your feet? Your feet hurt?
ARCHIE: *(Nodding and crying.)* That old dog's got some bite ...
(HESTER kneels down to take ARCHIE's shoes off. She does it as gently as she can; he is in obvious pain. She then takes off one of his socks and sees that his foot is raw and blistered from continuous pacing and wandering.)
HESTER: Oh, Archie. You poor old thing. That's not a dog bite, Arch ...
(HESTER gets up and leaves the stage by the downstage entrance for just a moment, then returns with a tin of ointment. She kneels down again and begins to put ointment on ARCHIE's battered feet.)
HESTER: No dog did that. You did that with all your wandering about. Look at those blisters. Oh, Arch, your poor old feet ...
(ARCHIE grabs her hand and stops her ministering. He looks around to make sure he's not overheard. Then in a loud ccnspiratorial whisper ...)
ARCHIE: They won't let me out of here. Will you help me to get out?

Blackout and a few bars of music
End of Scene 1.

Scene 2:

(It is now an hour or so later in the day. ARCHIE's pills have taken effect and he is safely in bed. HESTER has her shoes off, her feet up and a drink in her hand. RODDIE is pacing up and down.)
RODDIE: Mother, you are forty-nine years old.
HESTER: I know exactly how old I am, thank you.

RODDIE: He's exhausting you. This house is exhausting you. That ... creature you keep in a box in the basement is sucking precious drops of life out of you. Why do you do it? I mean, I'd understand a little more if it was your own father ... but ... well, hell! It's *his* father and *his* cat ...

HESTER: (*Indignantly.*) And *he* was *my* husband and that old man you collected this afternoon from the K-Mart parking lot is your Grandfather and my Father-in-law, and that poor old rat bag in the basement is that same tiny stripy kitten that you used to whirl around your head like a boomerang when you were three ...

RODDIE: He's twenty-three years old—he has bald spots on his bum as big as loonies for Chrissake—Mother you are becoming a zoo keeper.

HESTER: You are talking about your Grandfather and the family pet!

RODDIE: Family pet! Diablo is an ancient, acutely hostile, semi-wild animal who is dying, and he could probably use a hand doing it—Mother, it's painless!

HESTER: I took him to the vet. She said he's fine. She said his quality of life is fine ...

RODDIE: His quality of life? His quality of life? For God's sake, Mother, look at him! It takes him an hour to get out of his box or lie down; he's bald, he's incontinent, he's going blind and deaf, not to mention he's got some sort of cancerous growth in his nose that secretes a hideous liquid that sprays all over the place when he decides to have a bit of a shake, *usually* in the kitchen—one could hardly call him the *family pet*—the family health hazard is more like ...

HESTER: He's quite happy down in his box by the furnace—it's warm, hardly anyone ever goes down there, only me—he's fine—he'll go when he wants to go! When he's good and ready! Who knows, maybe he'll outlive the Guiness Book of Records cat, he was twenty-six. Anyway I'm not having him put down, so stop nagging me. (*Pause.*) Besides. Your father loved that cat. He taught him tricks. It's very difficult, almost impossible, to teach cats to swim or do somersaults—but he taught him tricks. He even had a tiny motorcycle helmet made for him when he took him riding on the bike. Diablo would ride on his shoulder with a little cobalt blue crash helmet on his head. You probably don't remember, but people just used to stop dead in their tracks.

RODDIE: Yep. Great. That's just wonderful. Granddad is a nut case, and good old Dad, besides being a world class runner, had an unnatural relationship with a cat. What do you think my chances are? Hmmmm? I really don't know what to tell Lorraine! Maybe we just shouldn't have children!

HESTER: I don't think there was anything wrong with *Edwin's* brain. Baxter Dirdle thought he was a whiz! He gave him a big fat promotion—talked about getting him in the family business. Oh, yes, it was all Dirdle and Polglaze—Polglaze and Dirdle—he wouldn't have done that if he thought there was anything wrong with the man's brain! I'm sure your father *is* ... or *was* every bit as smart as—what's her Dad's name?

RODDIE: Bernardo.

HESTER: Bernardo Piccolo. What is he? Mafia?

RODDIE: He's a law professor, Mother. His wife, Didi, has just published a very exciting book on anthropology and both Lorraine and David are med students. I suppose one of them might be a bit concerned about the family Lorraine is marrying into. I know I would be.

HESTER: You are assuming that I find them totally acceptable, right off the bat, without even meeting them. Maybe I'd hate them. You can be just as smart as you want, you know, and still have secrets; things you want to cover up. In fact people like that very often have more ...

RODDIE: They are a very open, warm, loving family, mother. I consider it a privilege to be joining them. Anyway, they're expecting you to come up for the wedding, and of course you are not going to hate them. I'm sure you'll end up liking them every bit as much as I do.

(Pause.)

HESTER: I don't think I can come up, Roddie. I can't just leave Archie. He gets very agitated and upset. Sometimes it takes days to calm him down. Just give them my apologies. *(Pause.)* Besides, if *she's* just written a book on anthropology, she'll be able to understand why a middle-aged woman, who singlehandedly takes care of an aged, brain-impaired person, can't willy-nilly go flying off to Burlington, Ontario whenever she feels like it!

RODDIE: Mother, we're talking about my wedding. Hopefully, the one and only ...

HESTER: I know, dear, and I'm really sorry. I just can't leave your Granddad. New faces upset him. His routine, no matter how hard you try not to, is upset. He gets frightened. I'm used to him getting up in the middle of the night and packing his things; he's done it nearly every night for two years, and he's pretty quiet about it—but when there are other people in the house, he gets in a frenzy—then he's packing and shouting, throwing things around, getting dressed ... calling out to people passing by ...

RODDIE: Exactly! You are coming around to precisely my point! He is literally holding you prisoner here. You are trapped in this house!

HESTER: I am not trapped! It is my choice to stay! It is my duty to stay and take care of Archie! I would try to explain it all to you, but you'll come across it by yourself—I hope. You live and

learn, Roddie. Don't be so quick to think you have it all figured out. *(Pause.)* Besides, I don't see anyone else in the family volunteering to look after him. Do you?
(Pause.)
RODDIE: Duty is one thing, Mother, economics is another.
(Pause. HESTER is deflated. He's got her and she knows it.)
HESTER: Oh, well ... yes ... I suppose ...
RODDIE: Half your salary ... no, more than half your salary, goes to poor benighted babysitters who only stay once anyway! How many days did you take off work this year?
HESTER: Only a year ago I could leave him by himself—well, I asked Helen next door to look in on him at regular times in the day ...
RODDIE: Not to mention the new locks and the child-proofing, all the windows virtually barred up, and the heat ...
HESTER: Do you begrudge him staying warm?
RODDIE: I know why you keep it so hot in here—I, for one, will never forget Christmas '89 ... the first time I bring Lorraine home to meet "THE FAMILY" ... And now, Lorraine, I'd like you to meet Gramps—whoops, sorry, I forgot to mention he likes to come to the dinner table in the buff—she did her best to hide it, but she was really rattled ...
HESTER: Why? Didn't she ever see a man naked before?
RODDIE: I shall ignore that, Mother—Lorraine is a med student—she very kindly and graciously depersonalized the entire situation ...
HESTER: She what? She did what to the situation?
RODDIE: She said she was familiar with his particular type of behaviour—that she'd come across it when she'd done the psych wards ...
HESTER: Well, let's hope Bernardo or Didi don't wind up on one of her psych wards; she might find herself a whole lot less familiar with everything.
(Pause.)
RODDIE: She's going to be a fine doctor, Mother ... *(Pause.)* I think maybe you're just a tiny bit jealous ...
(Pause.)
HESTER: *(Genuinely bewildered.)* Jealous? Jealous of what?
RODDIE: Well, you know—when only sons get married—no girl is good enough, etc., etc.
HESTER: You're quite wrong. I like Lorraine. I think underneath it all she's got a very kind heart. Roddie, I want you to be happy—more than anything I want you to be happy—I want you to get married, have children—who you pick is not up to me—I'm the last person in the world to pass judgement on my son's choice—My God, look at my track record ...
RODDIE: I'm surprised you still have so much faith in marriage—

I would have thought that it would be one of the last things in the world you'd recommend to the next generation.

HESTER: I'm not exactly recommending it. I suppose I think that any brush with it makes you tougher, tests your mettle, gives you some kind of definition, even if that definition is the one thing that makes you leave it ...

RODDIE: Is that what happened with you and Dad?

HESTER: What?

RODDIE: The definition—is that what made him disappear—I mean your theory about it ...

HESTER: Oh, God, Roddie, why are you always asking me questions about it? I don't know. I have no theory about it. Anything might have happened. We'll never know. That's all there is to it. (*Pause.*) Did you tell Lorraine about it?

RODDIE: I didn't see any point. I told her my father was dead. Well, he is, legally, I mean.

HESTER: You should have told her.

RODDIE: Sometimes its nearly driven me crazy wondering where that no-good bastard is. When I was ten, I figured he might have joined the French Foreign Legion—but by the time I was fourteen, I knew he was probably skulking around down in Miami, drinking tequila sunrises, ogling broads on the beach ...

HESTER: Roddie!

RODDIE: Sorry, Mother. Sometimes I wish I knew him so I could just ... know who I don't respect. You know what I mean.

HESTER: I know it was a hard time in your life, Roddie.

RODDIE: That's alright, Mother, there's no need to apologize, it wasn't your fault.

HESTER: I wasn't going to apologize. I was going to say that at some point in your life you have to give up all that bitterness about who did what. It just serves no purpose—what happened, happened. It's happened to lots of people, the world over; people say they're going to the store and they're never heard from again. It's as simple as that. We will never know the answer to some things in this world.

RODDIE: Not if you don't ask the question!

HESTER: Well, ask away, for heaven's sake, I'm going to have another drink, do you want one?

RODDIE: Mother, I have been doing my level best to have a serious conversation with you for the past hour. I am trying to impress upon you the seriousness of this whole situation! I only have your interests at heart. You know that. I don't mind helping to subsidize this ... arrangement; but I don't think it's good for your health; I don't think it's good for Grandfather and I think it's only cruelty to animals to keep that fur covered stick insect alive in the cellar.

HESTER: You know I hate taking money off you ...

RODDIE: I already said I don't mind, but it's definitely going to be more difficult in the near future. When Lorraine and I get married, we'll certainly be able to use all our combined incomes.
HESTER: Roddie, if I didn't have to ask you ...
RODDIE: I know. I know. What I'm trying to say, Mother, is—well, I don't know how much longer I can go on helping out financially.
(HESTER finishes her vodka, gets up, exits to kitchen, returning with a fresh vodka in a tall glass.)
HESTER: All good things must come to an end. Or should I just say, all things must come to an end ...
RODDIE: I don't think this is an appropriate time to be facetious, Mother.
HESTER: Who's being facetious? It's true.
RODDIE: Let *me* take Diablo out to the clinic and then you and I can have a serious talk to Dr. Laracy ...
HESTER: And where are you going to park me?
RODDIE: I know you won't be sorry to leave here. Was there a day, when I was growing up, that we didn't live in hope of getting out of this place? ... Anyway, I want you to gather all your tax stuff together, I'd better get down to it, while we have a bit of peace and quiet.
HESTER: Do whatever you want, although I don't know why you just don't let things run their natural course. Diablo can't have that long to go, and Arch, well, Arch ...
RODDIE: Mother, you are running way from the inevitable! You really have to face up to things—because if you don't, whatever will become of you?

Blackout and a few bars of music
End of Scene 2.

Scene 3:

(We hear a fairly loud electronic click, then Terry Willard's VOICE OVER, in the black.)
TERRY WILLARD: Is this on? Did you switch it on?
DAN: Yeah, you're on ...
TERRY WILLARD: Are we rolling?
TADJEK: Any time you want. Just say the word.
TERRY WILLARD: Ok. I'm going to do the intro as we're going up to the door ... Edwin? Edwin, are you ok?
EDWIN: Er ... yeah ... yeah ... I'm ok.
TERRY WILLARD: Ok. Here we go! Roll 'em—no, wait a minute. Tadjek—is his name Tadjek?
DAN: Yeah. His name is Tadjek.
TERRY WILLARD: Tadjek—be sure to get in good and close as

soon as she opens the door—and stay with me or Edwin or Hattie ...
EDWIN: Hester.
TERRY WILLARD: Right. Hester. Ok? And forget Homes of the Rich and Famous, the place looks like a dump—*(This is more a comment on Terry's taste than the Polglaze residence.)*—sorry, Edwin—How're ya doin' big guy? Ok. Roll 'em!
(Lights snap on. We see RODDIE sitting at a desk or a table presumably going through HESTER's household accounts, invoices, tax gear and ARCHIE'S RRSPs and suchlike. HESTER is thinking and smoking. The doorbell rings. HESTER and RODDIE jump. They are not expecting anyone and the doorbell is loud and insistent. HESTER opens the door, then stands in total shock as she sees TERRY WILLARD with a microphone, speaking to a hand-held video camera.)
TERRY WILLARD: Nineteen years ago today, at 11:15 on a Saturday night, Edwin Polglaze said to his wife, "Do you want a Mars Bar, I'm going to the store". His wife, Hester, replied, "no, get me a Laura Secord French mint—the one in the green wrapper", and they were the last extraordinary words exchanged by this couple until today!
(TERRY WILLARD turns from the camera, and goes straight for HESTER.)
TERRY WILLARD: Hester Polglaze, this is probably *the* most exciting day of your life because the "Terry Willard Show" has brought your husband Edwin Polglaze home from the store. He's a few years late, but HERE HE IS!!
(By now the cameraman and the sound technician are in the living room recording the entire scene. As TERRY dramatically introduces EDWIN, he hesitantly edges in through the front door. He looks like he suddenly realizes that this whole thing might be a bad idea. HESTER is reeling and certainly feeling the effects of a few vodkas. She flings herself against the wall as if about to be shot. TERRY and the CREW stay with her.)
HESTER: *(In shock.)* Edwin.
EDWIN: Hi, Hester.
TERRY: *(To HESTER.)* So you do, indeed, know this man?
HESTER: *(Trembling and barely able to speak.)* He's my husband.
(RODDIE has been watching the proceedings as if in a dream. He now gets up slowly and walks toward his mother.)
RODDIE: Who is he? Just what in the name of God is going on here?
HESTER: Roddie ... darling ... this is your father.
EDWIN: Roddie ... my God ... little Roddie.
RODDIE: *(Gazing incredulously at EDWIN.)* My father! ... You're all nuts! What is this, a three ring circus? What are you all doing here? ... *(Points to TERRY WILLARD.)* Who's she?
HESTER: It's Terry Willard. It's that new T.V. show ...

TERRY: Great! You watch the show ...
RODDIE: *(Very calm.)* I want you all ... to get out ... of this house ... right now ... Do you all understand?
(The CAMERAMAN moves in closer to RODDIE, sensing an impending blow up.)
RODDIE: Get that fucking thing out of my face ... do you hear me?
(RODDIE gives the CAMERAMAN a poke in the shoulder.)
TADJEK: It's ok, man! Stop freaking out! We won't use hardly any of this, most of this will be edited out ... just calm down—we're only going to use 30 seconds, if that ...
(RODDIE springs on the CAMERAMAN and tries to wrestle the camera away from him.)
RODDIE: You son of a bitch!!
HESTER: Roddie —Oh, my God ...
EDWIN: Roddie ... please ... look, this is all my fault ...
RODDIE: *(To EDWIN.)* You get these assholes out of here! Do you hear me! Then you and I will have a chat.
(RODDIE goes back to pushing and shoving TADJEK. DAN—witness to dozens of scenes like this—slowly comes to the aid of his confrere.)
DAN: Hey, man, cut it out. No need to get so emotional ... stay cool.
TERRY: *(To HESTER and EDWIN.)* People have very different reactions to this sort of situation. Tadjek, get over here. Now, how are you feeling, Hester?
HESTER: I'm feeling very shaky. I'm trembling all over.
TERRY: And you, Edwin, how are you doing, how are you feeling?
EDWIN: *(Conscious of the camera.)* Well ... er ... a bit like Hester, I guess ... I'm shaky, and yes, maybe trembling a bit ...
RODDIE: This is madness! Do you realize that this is private property? If you don't get out of here, I'm going to call the cops—I'll sue you, every one of you.
TERRY: You're obviously very hostile—is this strictly a thing with your father or are you mad at the world, so to speak.
RODDIE: *(To TADJEK.)* Turn that off!!! I'm warning you ...
EDWIN: Maybe this wasn't such a good idea ...
(RODDIE grabs the camera and he and TADJEK wrestle again.)
HESTER: *(Still in a daze.)* Edwin, where were you? Where have you been?
EDWIN: Well ...
TERRY: No, no! Wait a second! Tadjek, Dan, could I have your attention.
RODDIE: This is invasion of privacy!
(By now both TADJEK and DAN have abandoned their equipment and have pinned RODDIE's arms behind his back.)
RODDIE: Son of a bitch!!!!

DAN: Jesus, relax, man! We got a job to do. Like Tadjek says, we probably won't use you—I mean there's a definite limit to people's interest. They don't want to know about *all* of this. They can only concentrate on one thing at a time ...
TADJEK: Yeah, man, face facts! Give us a break—calm down—you're not the star of this one, so chill out ...
TERRY: Guys, I need you! Roddie, be good, will you. If you shut up, we could wrap this up in just a few minutes—I mean this is only five minutes out of the whole show—why don't you give us a break?
(RODDIE stops struggling.)
RODDIE: I don't believe this! This is incredible! And you all love it—you're all crazy.
(TADJEK and DAN get their equipment together again and get in position to film HESTER, EDWIN and TERRY.)
TERRY: Thanks, guys. Now, Hester, you just asked Edwin a very important question—could you ask him again please.
TADJEK: Ok, go ahead—we're rolling.
HESTER: Edwin, where did you go?
TERRY: No, no. You said, "Edwin, where were you? Where have you been?"
HESTER: Oh, sorry. Er—Edwin. Edwin, where were you? Where have you been?
(Enter ARCHIE in his pyjamas, bathrobe and hat. He has heard the commotion and is very agitated. He sees the crowd and stops for a second.)
EDWIN: Dad! Dad? It's me, Edwin ...
(ARCHIE runs or shuffles at them, all the while making shooing motions with his hands.)
ARCHIE: You get away from her, you leave her alone ...
EDWIN: Dad, I'm sorry—I am! Just give me a chance to explain.
ARCHIE: *(Retreating to his long-past schooldays.)* Don't you take her lunch, don't you dare take her lunch ...
TERRY: *(To no one in particular.)* Is this Mr. Polglaze Senior? Mr. Polglaze, how do you feel, seeing your son, Edwin, for the first time in nineteen years?
HESTER: Arch, Arch ... now calm down—all right, everything's fine.
RODDIE: A fucking three ring circus ...
EDWIN: Lunch? Whose lunch? What is he talking about?
ARCHIE: *(Bellowing.)* I want to go home! I want to go home! Annabel! Annabel! Annabel! Annabel!
EDWIN: Hester, what's wrong with him? He's calling out for my mother! She died in 1964—nobody told me about this! What's wrong with him? Hester?
(ARCHIE begins to tear off his own clothes. HESTER tries to stop him.)

HESTER: No, Arch, no! Stop it! Come on, hon, you've got to calm down ... he's having a catastrophic reaction—it's anything out of the ordinary—a crowd of people—he picks up the vibes ...
(EDWIN is stunned.)
EDWIN: He's gone crazy! My father has gone crazy! Why didn't anyone tell me? Why was this kept from me?
TERRY: We figured you should only deal with one thing at a time.
EDWIN: I should have been prepared ...
(Meanwhile RODDIE has joined HESTER in an attempt to subdue ARCHIE. The following conversations (the beginning of each marked *) take place at the same time.)
*HESTER: Arch, we're going back into bed now, ok? *(To Roddie.)* We might have to use the Posey restraint ...
RODDIE: Where's Fellini when you really need him—I just can't believe all of this—it's just ridiculous, that's all—just plain idiotic—for Chrissake, Archie, stop bucking and kicking ...
(ARCHIE is completely panicked. He bellows like a bull and refuses to move an inch.)
HESTER: I think it's going to take more than just you or me—we need some help—Edwin, I think we need your help to get him back into bed ...

---

*EDWIN: *(To no one in particular.)* Oh, no! I can't handle this! This is too much! This was a big mistake! Roddie hates me, my father has gone crazy—he doesn't even recognize me ... Oh, God, why did I do this? Why did I let them talk me into doing this? I must have been out of my mind ... Oh God ... I wish I'd had something to eat today ...
(Then, in reply to HESTER'S plea for help.)
EDWIN: Oh, no. I don't think so, I wouldn't know what to do—it's probably best if you guys handle it—I mean, you two know what's what ...
HESTER: Please, Edwin—we've got to get him into his room.

---

*TERRY: Are you getting all this?
TADJEK: Man, this is wild—are you going to keep all of this?
TERRY: Probably not all of it. Some of it, though.
DAN: Sounds not too good.
TERRY: That's ok. We can use some of this under the credits and the theme. It'll look great. How did the rest of it look, did you get really good close-up shots of her?
TADJEK: Oh, yeah, I got her—real good close ups. It's funny, though, she seemed half in the bag to me.
TERRY: Oh, yeah? Is that so. Hm, I'd better make a note of that.

(ARCHIE is now fighting for his life. TERRY, TADJEK and DAN all join in the efforts to subdue him and move him back into the bedroom. With all of them holding a limb or a bit of

torso they manage to cart him out through the downstage entrance. TADJEK and DAN are the first to reappear. They go to pick up their equipment.
RODDIE is hot on their heels.)
RODDIE: Uh uh. No. Sorry, boys. You're definitely not taking a camera or recorder in there and that's it! That's the bottom line! Do you understand?
TADJEK: Ok. Ok. I understand where you're coming from—really, I do. Soon as Terry is ready, we'll be out of your hair—no sweat—that's all there is to it.
RODDIE: When is this show going to be aired?
DAN: Well, we never know for sure. We always have a couple of stories in the can—then again some things are topical ...
RODDIE: How do I get my face out of this entire scene? What's the procedure?
TADJEK: I don't know. Talk to Terry. Maybe she'll edit you out, although you're pretty interesting—I mean your reaction—so hostile and everything, man, they love that!
RODDIE: Who loves it? What are you talking about?
TADJEK: The home audience, man, I mean this is *real* shit—not some stupid T.V. sit-com. They really get off on this stuff—I mean, lookit. This is low budget, tacky shit, but it's a hit! We got the highest ratings in the country! That little broad is incredible! She's gonna change T.V. People want *real*!
(RE-ENTER TERRY a little bit mussed. She goes to her purse and takes out her makeup. She pats her hair and re-applies lipstick.)
TERRY: Now, there's a man who likes his own way!
RODDIE: Are you definitely going to run this ... this .. hideous invasion of privacy as a show?
TERRY: That's the story!
RODDIE: I shall do everything in my power to have it stopped.
TERRY: Look. This doesn't have a whole lot to do with you. This isn't your story. It's their story. Besides, out of twenty-seven shows we've only had two lawsuits, and we settled out of court—everybody was happy ...
(Pause.)
RODDIE: All right. If I can't stop you running the show, then I want my mug edited out of it ...
TERRY: Well, big guy, come by my office and we'll talk about it, ok? Or better yet, we could go out for a drink ...
RODDIE: Couldn't we settle this now, in an honourable way?
TERRY: Honourable way? What are you saying, honourable way? This show—my office—gave your father twenty grand for his story. Twenty grands-worth of sweetener to bring home to his loyal little mate, who, I gather, has been carrying the torch for nineteen years, and I'm with you on that score, pal—I can't see it

either—but there you go! We pay good money, all you have to do is give a completely honest and natural reaction to the camera. I mean, is that so hard? All people want to know is that they're like everyone else in the world—up to their necks in shit. This story is a happy ending, for heavens sakes! We've done stories that would make your squash racket curl. We had one old lady drop dead of a heart attack when she was re-united with her forty-seven year old son after thirty-five years. She only had time to say his *name*. We had a guy that was widowed *seven* times, he became a hermit—talk about depressed—and we actually went on a live kidnapping ...

RODDIE: Oh, God, spare me.

TERRY: No, no kidding! We interviewed the kidnappers and talked to the victim the whole time—I mean by the end of the week we were family—the crew, the kidnappers, the victim, the victim's family, the cops, the kidnap specialists ...

(EDWIN and HESTER reappear looking dazed and bedraggled.)

HESTER: I'd like you all to leave now ... it's been a very upsetting day ... I have a terrible headache ...

EDWIN: *(To HESTER.)* Come and sit down—I know this has been a terrible shock ... *(To TERRY.)* When will you be wanting me for the studio stuff?

TERRY: I'll be in touch. Well, folks, its been a slice. Thank you very much. Remember now, if any of you manage to get your lives straightened out, be sure to let me know how it's done. All the best! Tadjek, Dan, are you guys ready?

TADJEK: Yes, ma'am. See you folks—thanks.

DAN: Yeah, I'm ready to roll—goodbye.

(THE TERRY WILLARD SHOW leaves through the front door. The three family members are left stunned and silent. They do not look at one another. Then ...)

HESTER: So where the hell were you, Edwin, and did you get me a bar?

Blackout
End of Act I

Act II
Scene 1:

(Lights up and we find HESTER, EDWIN and RODDIE in exactly the same position as at the end of ACT I. HESTER and RODDIE are staring at EDWIN, and all three of them have tall drinks.)

(Silence.)

EDWIN: Well, I guess that just about covers it.

(Long pause.)
RODDIE: Do you consider that an explanation? *(Pause.)* "I was a travelling mendicant seeking some sort of truth." What does that mean? Frankly, I think we deserve a real explanation, don't you?
HESTER: What's a mendicant?
RODDIE: A beggar.
HESTER: You were a beggar?
EDWIN: Well ... in a sense ... yes ... I was a beggar, spiritually speaking, that is ... but listen, before we get into any of that—well, I was just wondering if either of you is ... er ... hungry? I'd be glad to take you both out for something to eat ... at my expense, of course ... it's just that I never ate today ... I was sort of nervous ...
RODDIE: I bet you were!
HESTER: Roddie went out a few hours ago and got an entire fridge-full of food, I'll get you a sandwich if you like ...
RODDIE: You can't get him a sandwich ...
HESTER: Don't be silly, Roddie! Of course I can get him a sandwich. I've made a tidy career out of making people sandwiches and I wouldn't want to miss a chance to display my expertise. What can I get you? Roddie, what did you get in the way of sandwich makings?
(Pause.)
RODDIE: *(Ungraciously.)* Tuna, flakes of ham and turkey roll. And there's cheese.
HESTER: Do you want tuna, flakes of ham or turkey roll? Or cheese?
EDWIN: I don't want to put you out, really ...
RODDIE: It's a little bit late for that, isn't it?
HESTER: You're not putting me out ...
(HESTER exits to kitchen then returns immediately carrying a pill container.)
HESTER: Anybody else?
(She calmly takes the top off the container)
(Pause.)
EDWIN: What are they?
HESTER: Ten Milligrams.
EDWIN: Er—thanks. Yes, I will.
HESTER: Roddie?
(Pause.)
RODDIE: *(Grudgingly.)* Oh, all right. I suppose this is what they're for ...
HESTER: Edwin, what would you like? Tuna, turkey roll, cheese ...
EDWIN: Do you have any fruit? Or vegetables maybe ... or a slice of bread, wholewheat bread ...

RODDIE: I got bananas, apples and oranges.
EDWIN: Oh, yeah, that's great! That would be fine!
HESTER: Do you want me to make them into a fruit salad, or do you just want them on a plate—or shall I slice them up?
EDWIN: Well, sliced up and together, maybe ...
HESTER: Shall I leave the peel on the apple?
EDWIN: Er—sure. Yes, that would be fine ...
HESTER: But not the core ...
EDWIN: No, not the core.
HESTER: Ok. One fruit salad.
RODDIE: Mother, you should eat something. You just picked at supper. You're looking peaked. You need to keep your strength up.
HESTER: Oh, I'll nibble on something.
EDWIN: Is ... er ... all that still a problem? I mean—well, you know what I mean, of course.
HESTER: You mean am I still anorexic? Well, yes, I'm anorexic. Or at least I have been, recently. I'm not anorexic now. Quite the opposite—in fact I'm getting huge! Anyway, here we go, fruit salad!

(HESTER exits to peel, chop and slice. EDWIN and RODDIE sit silently, not looking at each other. After an unbearable, tense pause ...)

RODDIE: After you left, I wouldn't sleep in my bed. I used to go downstairs every night, put on your old winter jacket and curl up on your workbench. Mother would try to make me go upstairs to bed, but I wouldn't go. I thought you might come home in the middle of the night. Grade two was a write-off for me! I didn't get enough sleep and I was allergic to the mould in the basement.

(Pause.)

EDWIN: Roddie, if I could reverse some of the things in my life ...
RODDIE: It was too bizarre for me to handle! I was the kid whose father vanished—without a trace—
EDWIN: I know how you must have felt ...
RODDIE: Without a trace, on his way to the store! I mean, according to historical accounts you never even made it as far as the store!
EDWIN: No kidding! Who said that?
RODDIE: What?
EDWIN: That I never made it to the store?
RODDIE: Well, everybody. Mrs. Ford and her son, Dennis, apparently they were both there—he was helping her lock up—they said you never appeared that night.
EDWIN: I did so. I didn't buy anything, but I went in and stood at the magazine rack for ten or fifteen minutes. I was reading a joke book. Then I put it back in the rack and left. How odd that they didn't see me.

RODDIE: There was an investigation after Mother finally broke down and called the police, and Mrs. Ford and Dennis both said they'd seen you the previous evening and that you'd seemed depressed. Lots of people thought you'd killed yourself.
EDWIN: I would have left a note.
RODDIE: I knew you hadn't killed yourself. I just didn't feel that you were dead!
EDWIN: Roddie, I know I'll never be able to make it up to you ... but do you think you might—just might—sometime in the future, maybe—find it in your heart to forgive me?
RODDIE: I mean, not even a phone call, or a postcard! You could have sent a postcard. Then when the other kids tormented me about "The Case of the Vanishing Dad", I could have said "lay off, he's a travelling mendicant ..."
EDWIN: I only said that before, about being a mendicant, because I don't know how else to describe my life, or the changes in my life, then, or now, for that matter ...
RODDIE: And now you not only come waltzing back into our lives, but you bring a bloody TV show with you! What are you trying to do, finish us off?
EDWIN: Roddie, all I can say to you is ...
RODDIE: You ran away! You create a big stir, everyone suffers horribly for years, and now you're back with a giant reverse fuss! What a guy! You're impossible to ignore! Here, or poof (*He flicks his fingers.*) there. You're a big presence, I'll give you that!
EDWIN: All right, I ran away, as you put it! Now I've sort of been run home. Roddie, it was fate or a cosmic accident, I don't know what to call it! I didn't have the courage to call you and your mother when I came back to town. I mean, for Gardner Belbin to have recognized me at that gas station store—I mean a gas station he never goes to—has never gone to in his life before, don't you see, I was brought home! After I ran into Gardner in the convenience store and he says "oh, by the way, I'm married to your sister Bernice", well, things just took off from there—Miss Willard, the TV show ...
RODDIE: The twenty grand!
EDWIN: Well, yes. That, too ...
RODDIE: The average TV show is 26 minutes long. What can we expect in the rest of the freak show?
(Pause.)
EDWIN: Well ... there's a re-enactment of me and Gardner meeting out at the gas station—the convenience store—well, the *men's* room in actual fact, and then there's a very small bit on ... well ... the homecoming—and of course some studio interviews, in fact, mostly that sort of thing ... Miss Willard said...
RODDIE: Have you no shame about running home? Being *run* home.

EDWIN: Why should I have any shame? I'm sorry the method upsets you so much but can't you see how appropriate it is? —Well, it may not be entirely appropriate, but it's what fate decreed, and I can't go against it or deflect it or actively fight against a force stronger than myself! This was meant to be ...

RODDIE: I want you to get that show cancelled! I want you to give the money back and I want you to disappear again in a normal, reasonable, fashion. How does that sound?

EDWIN: Roddie, things have to run their course. This seems to be the direction at this moment in time. This is, perhaps, the beginning of the healing time ...

RODDIE: What have you been doing for the last nineteen years, taking lots of pop psychology courses?

(Pause.)

EDWIN: Your mother tells me you're an architect. A good one.

(Pause.)

RODDIE: Mother has an untutored eye ...

(Enter HESTER carrying a bowl of fruit salad, a napkin and a spoon, all of which she hands to EDWIN.)

HESTER: I do not. All I said was, the last building you designed looked like a toaster. All skylights and funny narrow windows on the sides, but nothing on the front or the back! It looked like a four-slice toaster. But you did that very nice school board building, the one with the moat ... *(To EDWIN.)* Was he telling you about the buildings he designs?

RODDIE: Yes, we've just been having some very pleasant chit-chat out here, swapping amusing stories of the *LAST NINETEEN YEARS*!

EDWIN: I think it's wonderful that you've done so well.

RODDIE: No thanks to you ...

EDWIN: I knew from day one that you were a super smart kid.

RODDIE: Is that why you took off? Afraid of the competition?

EDWIN: I said to your mother, "he is going to be something special."

RODDIE: Uh huh!

HESTER: He did say that. I remember him saying that ...

RODDIE: You're not even mad at him, are you? You're treating this bizarre nightmare as if it's normal or rational; as if he is a normal, rational human being ... instead of a ... a ... family criminal!

HESTER: Well, I know for sure he's a human being and so am I! And I've had enough excitement and upset for one human being to bear in one day! So please calm down, Roddie. Get yourself a drink, take another pill or run around the block—anything! Just be still for a while!

(Pause.)

RODDIE: I'm going to go and call Lorraine. I could use a little

sanity.
HESTER: Roddie and Lorraine are engaged to be married ...
EDWIN: Congratulations.
(He offers his hand but RODDIE chooses to ignore the gesture.)
RODDIE: I told her my father was dead! You are you know, legally.
(RODDIE exits to kitchen to call Lorraine.)
(Pause.)
EDWIN: So, I'm dead.
HESTER: I knew you weren't, in my heart. But when you were declared legally dead the finality was a comfort. It felt a lot better to be a widow than just a hastily abandoned wife. *(Pause.)* Archie, Roddie, and I went out to the Ponderosa and had the "all you can eat surf and turf" by way of a little celebration. It was a funny day. I didn't know whether to laugh or cry ... so I did both ...
(Long pause.)
(Both EDWIN and HESTER are awkward and embarrassed. This is the first time they have really been alone together since EDWIN's return.)
HESTER: How was the fruit salad?
EDWIN: Oh, good. Very good. Really hit the spot. Natural carbohydrates give you energy, pick you up.
(Pause.)
HESTER: Are you sure you don't want a sandwich? There's lots of stuff—and you're not putting me out ...
EDWIN: No. No. That's just fine—best to eat light under stress ... Oh, I didn't mean ...
HESTER: No, no, I understand. *(Pause.)* But if you like carbohydrates, there's cookies out there—butter cookies—expensive, thin little jobs—I don't know what kind.
EDWIN: No, no. Thank you. Maybe later on.
HESTER: Tea? Coffee?
EDWIN: No, thanks ...
HESTER: Another drink?
EDWIN: No. Absolutely not. I really shouldn't have had that one. I've had a little trouble with the gut, so I've been cutting back a bit ...
HESTER: Ah. I see.
(Long pause.)
HESTER: *(Suddenly very animated.)* Well, for heaven's sake, Edwin, I didn't tell you—we all forgot to tell you!! How silly of me—it never occurred to me.
EDWIN: What?
HESTER: Diablo is still alive! He's down in the basement. Roddie made him a box and he's down there next to the furnace.
EDWIN: Diablo? Still alive? My God, Diablo?

HESTER: I'll go get him. He's twenty-three, you know.
EDWIN: I can't believe it. My God, that's really old ... I'll come down, don't disturb him ...
HESTER: I bring him up sometimes. He enjoys a bit of company. Besides, the bulb is out down there ... I'll get him, I'll be right back.
(HESTER exits to go down to the basement. EDWIN looks exhausted. He reaches into his jacket and takes out two small gift-wrapped boxes. He contemplates these presents for HESTER and RODDIE for a moment and then puts them back in his pocket. HESTER returns carrying a simple RODDIE-designed post-modern cat box with a vaguely Greek temple roof-line. She places the box on the sofa and gently removes the lid.)
HESTER: There he is. He didn't even wake up. Diablo, puss, puss, Diablo, wake up, look who's home.
EDWIN: *(Reaches into the box and strokes the cat.)* I can't believe it. You're still alive. Son of a gun—Diablo, hey, boy, how are you? *(To HESTER.)* His fur is falling out—he's got a lot of bald spots.
HESTER: He's very old. Roddie thinks we should have him put to sleep, but I don't think I could do that.
EDWIN: Oh, my God, Diablo ... Who's the best puss? Hey, Diablo—who's the champ? Well, son of a gun ... look! His eyes are open—he's awake—I think he recognizes me ...
(There is a nasty short-tempered yowl from the box and EDWIN hastily withdraws his hand.)
EDWIN: *(Shocked.)* He bit me! He's drawn blood!

**Blackout and a few bars of music
End of Scene 1.**

Scene 2:

(Lights up and we see EDWIN, an improvised bandage on his bitten finger, sitting with his head between his knees. The sight of blood makes him faint. HESTER is smoking and clutching a cold wet facecloth and RODDIE is pacing.)
RODDIE: Look, if you really think you need a tetanus shot, I'll give you a ride to the hospital.
EDWIN: I don't know—what would you do?
HESTER: How do you feel? Are you in pain?
EDWIN: No. My finger's stopped hurting—it's just that the sight of blood makes me faint.
RODDIE: Do you want to go to the hospital?
EDWIN: How long does it take for tetanus to set in?
(Pause.)
HESTER: *(To RODDIE.)* Do you want me to call first?

RODDIE: (*To HESTER.*) He's going to be fine. Diablo doesn't even go outside anymore.
HESTER: (*To EDWIN.*) That's true. And he certainly doesn't catch anything anymore. The last time he ate a mouse or a rat was ten or more years ago ... all in all he's pretty clean.
(*EDWIN moans and holds his head. Enter ARCHIE who has woken from his nap. He looks bewildered and quietly manic.*)
ARCHIE: When the moon is up, all the Americas will be red.
(*ARCHIE starts nodding and pointing at the front door.*)
RODDIE: Well, that's it! Now we've got the whole ward up!
(*HESTER puts the face cloth over her own face and is just too tired to deal with Archie. EDWIN forgets the cat bite and only has eyes for DAD.*)
EDWIN: Dad. (*Pause.*) Dad, do you know who I am? (*He gets up and slowly goes over to ARCHIE.*) Dad, I'm Edwin. (*Pause.*) I've come home.
(*ARCHIE looks vague and nervous.*)
ARCHIE: The boys are gone out. They're gone out to play.
EDWIN: You know I'm your son, don't you? I know that you know that ...
ARCHIE: You'd better go now—the boys are not here ...
EDWIN: (*To HESTER and RODDIE.*) He knows me. In his mind, he knows me. He's talking about the boys, he means me and Gilbert. Dad—tell me you recognize me—say my name.
ARCHIE: (*Looking scared.*) Annabel, Annabel ...
EDWIN: Yeah, that's right! That's Mom! Mom's name was Annabel; then there was us—Edwin, Gilbert, and Bernice.
HESTER: Stop it, Edwin! He's going to get upset. Don't badger him.
EDWIN: Just say Edwin, Dad. C'mon!
HESTER: Look, if you want to stay up with him round the clock ...
RODDIE: I'll do it. Come on, Granddad. Lets go in the kitchen and get some applesauce. Ok? (*Then to HESTER.*) It's all right. Sit down, relax.
HESTER: You should try him at the bathroom, too ...
EDWIN: No, I'll do it. I'll take him to the bathroom, and I'll get him something to eat ...
(*ARCHIE is now sandwiched between EDWIN and RODDIE, both of whom are openly vying to give nursing care.*)
RODDIE: Look! He doesn't know who the hell you are and being around new faces freaks him out!
(*ARCHIE begins to whimper. He is afraid and he doesn't know what is going on.*)
ARCHIE: I have to go home now ...
EDWIN: You are home, dad. This is your house. You built it ... Dad, say Edwin ...
RODDIE: He doesn't know you! Leave him alone!

ARCHIE: His face was blue when they brought him home—he was all blue ... poor little Edwin's dead ...
(ARCHIE begins to cry.)
EDWIN: That's not me! That was Gilbert! Gilbert shut himself in that old fridge ...
ARCHIE: Annabel cried forever ... All she does is cry ... poor Edwin, poor Edwin ...
EDWIN: That's not me! That was Gilbert! I'm alive!
RODDIE: Come on, Granddad, let's go! Do you need to use the bathroom? Come on, we'll have a go, anyway.
(RODDIE purposefully moves ARCHIE offstage.)
RODDIE: *(Continued.)* ... then we'll get some applesauce ... that's it ... then maybe a nap.
(EDWIN is sad and bewildered.)
EDWIN: He really doesn't know me. He thinks I'm Gilbert ...
HESTER: He doesn't think you're anybody. All his memories are scrambled up, and his brain can't make sense out of anything anymore ... he doesn't remember any of us.
EDWIN: I wanted to put things right with him. I wanted to talk to him. I wanted to talk to all of you over the years. I just didn't know how to go about it.
(Pause.)
HESTER: Why did you come back, Edwin?
EDWIN: I wasn't going to. I was just going to come back and look at you all, without you seeing me. But then I ran into Gardner, or Gardner ran into me, and ... well, that was that.
(Pause.)
HESTER: Was it so terrible between us that you had to go and never look back?
EDWIN: No, no! No. Of course not. It had less to do with you than the terrible confusion in my head—the helpless, hopeless way I felt about my life.
HESTER: You never said anything. I had no idea you were feeling helpless and hopeless. You'd just had a promotion—we'd put a down payment down on that house out in Marble Estates—our son was the best all-round grade one student of the year—and your cat won a "Wacky Pets Swim Meet" ... where does the confusion come in?
(Pause.)
EDWIN: Hester—I found selling prosthetic limbs and medical rubber supplies for "Dirdle and Dirdle Prosthetics" very depressing. Baxter was very good to me and the money—well, the money was as much as anyone like me could expect to make, I mean, then, at my age—but, goddamn it, Hester, my father got me that job—and working with Baxter honking in your face all day long ...
HESTER: I know. I work for Becky.
EDWIN: Really. Becky Dirdle. Well, well. You work for her?

HESTER: She was bored, so Baxter bought her a store. "Yard Dreams". She drives a white Jag, grows bonsai trees and sells cute and outrageous yard ornaments and furniture. I work in the store.
EDWIN: Baxter and Becky. Well, well ...
HESTER: She looks exactly the same as she did twenty years ago—from a hundred feet away, that is. She periodically brings me over boxes of used panty-hose and interesting things in jars that she finds at the back of her fridge ... anyway, sorry. So you hated your job—I can understand that.
EDWIN: I felt as if I was meant for something else. I felt that I had talent, or talents, but they were like crumbs in my pockets. Pockets of crumbly talents running out through holes. Like Hansel and Gretel in the woods. And they were being eaten by lizards and snakes and scruffy vultures. I started seeing Mamie in the office as a truffle pig. I actually wouldn't tell her the date one day. I withheld it from her. I felt as though it was classified information, along with all the other details of my life that she loved to snuffle down. And Baxter's brother-in-law, Harris Lovecomb—I started seeing him as a moth-eaten jackal—always looking for leftovers, "Don't forget now, if you decide to go to the movies ..." or "I was thinking of dropping around for a chat", or "Where are you going on Sunday". I hated him. He always had egg or canned gravy on his tie. And Mrs. Ford, at the corner store, she was a giant sea-lion barking at me ... "Well, and what's your crowd up to today?" It got so I didn't know whether she meant you and Roddie and Dad and Bernice, or the new emerging personalities that were forcing these awful animal hallucinations on me ...
(Pause.)
HESTER: I had no idea. You never said anything. But then again I suppose we were waiting to move out of Archie's house before we began to talk ... or live ... or ... or ... you know ...
(Pause.)
EDWIN: Hmmm. Yes. You mean ... you mean sex ... that sort of thing ...
HESTER: Uh huh. Yes. Yes, I do.
(Long pause.)
EDWIN: You feel cheated about the house as well. You wanted your own house.
HESTER: Edwin, you left on Saturday night. We were packed and ready to move into 124 Ladyslipper at eight o'clock on Monday morning. And after eight years of living with your sister, Bernice, and your Dad—well, as it turned out, Arch and I got along just fine—but Bernice and I didn't. I think it's a true fact when I say your sister has a hard time keeping slaves, she works them to death. From the time that I got pregnant and we got

married, Bernice didn't do a dish, cook a meal, make a bed or wash so much as a sock. Of course, you and Arch didn't either, but, back in those days, that seemed normal. We had no money, no privacy, and no fun. Then, literally *hours* before *release*, you take off into the wild blue yonder.

EDWIN: You must hate me.

(Pause.)

HESTER: No, I don't hate you. I don't love you any more, so I can't hate you. *(Pause.)* I used to go fifteen or sixteen rounds with you, in my mind, in the middle of the night. I certainly hated you then. A couple of times I toyed with the idea of putting a contract out on you ...

EDWIN: You weren't serious.

HESTER: As serious as you get at five o'clock in the morning when you haven't slept for a few months. But after a while I got used to it all—it's funny how you get used to anything—and now, now you're almost a stranger. Or a character in a book I once read or a movie I saw.

(Pause.)

EDWIN: You didn't ... remarry. You stayed here with Roddie, all these years.

HESTER: Just after you left, Bernice met Gardner and got married. I didn't have a job, Arch's business was giving up the ghost, so the three of us stayed here and made the best of it. Until Arch got sick. Until then it was just fine.

(Pause.)

EDWIN: Poor Archie. Poor old guy ...

(Pause.)

HESTER: And what about you? Did you remarry.

(Pause.)

EDWIN: No ... well, yes, sort of. For a while. We didn't go through a ceremony or anything ...

(Pause.)

HESTER: Did you have more children?

(Pause.)

EDWIN: Yes.

(Pause.)

HESTER: How many? What are they?

(Pause.)

EDWIN: Two girls. One is fourteen, the other is twelve. They're with their mother.

(Pause.)

HESTER: What are their names? The children ...

(Pause.)

EDWIN: Friedebourg and Lisette. Frieda is fourteen and Lisette is twelve.

HESTER: Very exotic names. Very different.

EDWIN: Their mother is German-Greek ... we weren't together long.
HESTER: Ah.
(Pause.)
EDWIN: It was when I was trying my hand at writing and I was travelling around.
HESTER: So you've travelled. A lot?
EDWIN: A fair bit. See, I always felt in my heart that I was an artist. I wasn't sure what sort of artist, but an artist, nonetheless. And routine, or staying still, can stifle any sort of creativity. I was definitely compelled to travel.
(Pause.)
HESTER: So what sort of an artist are you?
EDWIN: Well, that's an interesting question. You see, sometimes the medium is totally meaningless or unimportant. Whereas the level of spiritual involvement is paramount. I mean, I've written things, I've painted pictures, I've taken photographs, and one night I danced with this bunch of Watusi guys, and, I kid you not, it was more balletic than your Royal Winnipeg. So when you ask, what sort of an artist, well the question contains the answer. If you see what I mean?
HESTER: Not really.
EDWIN: Well, when I lived on Corfu, I wrote a little operetta-type thing called "Cat Snores in A Flat Minor", and then, later, a more serious, abstract piece for stage called "Dogess as Bitch"; but anyway, I talked this guy who was with the English Holiday Makers Drama Club into doing "Cat Snores"—but they missed chunks out—the male lead had half a bottle of ouzo before going on stage and nobody in the cast could play any of the musical instruments called for in the piece—it was a total disaster; but I realized that even though the audience hated it, and it sort of looked like a total shambles, it wasn't. In its own way it was perfect. The drunk guy, nobody able to play the music, missing out big bits, well, that was how it was meant to be, at the moment. It was natural art replying to the human wellspring of creativity *(Pause.)* Does that make it any clearer?
HESTER: No.
(Pause.)
EDWIN: Hester, I don't blame you for being hostile. It is an entirely natural reaction.
HESTER: I'm not hostile. I simply don't understand what you're talking about. Are you an artist or are you not an artist? I mean, what's your present status?
(Pause.)
EDWIN: You're angry. I can hear it in your voice.
HESTER: I used to be angry, I'm not any more. Now I'm just trying to be politely curious about your life, but I'm obviously not

grasping the point you're trying to make.
(Pause.)
EDWIN: This is difficult. You live on a ... more literal plane that tips and spins eternally; I just slide off. I have no foothold ...
HESTER: You mean a more boring plane ...
EDWIN: I never said that.
HESTER: Go right ahead. You're probably right. Well I'm glad you found fame and fortune. It's too bad you didn't take Diablo with you. The two of you would have made a great vaudeville team.
EDWIN: He's the most remarkable animal I've ever come across—yes, I missed him, too. *(Pause.)* Hester, I have something to give you. *(He reaches into his pocket and takes out a thick white envelope.)* I didn't exactly find fame and fortune, you can tell that by just looking at me—but the TV show—well, they paid me twenty thousand dollars—for the story and the rights to it—and ... well, I want you to have it.
(He hands her the envelope.)
(Pause.)
HESTER: I don't want it.
(Pause.)
EDWIN: But it's for you. I did this for you. I couldn't come back with ... nothing ... please take it—I want you to have it.
HESTER: I wish you hadn't come back at all. Everything's upset and changed ... and now you're offering me money.
EDWIN: I'm sorry I hurt you so badly. What I did was a terrible thing; I have never stopped thinking about it—I have never stopped thinking about you.
HESTER: You make it sound like I just hung around being hurt for the last nineteen years. I did have a life; not much of one, I'll grant you, but it was mine; and after the first rough year or two, I rarely thought of you. Except, of course, when I ran into people who said, "by the way, did you ever hear from ...?"
(Pause.)
EDWIN: You do hate me!
HESTER: I don't hate you!
EDWIN: And I don't want you to hate all men because of me ...
HESTER: How dare you take credit for how I feel about all men!
EDWIN: Hester. Please—I do understand—with all my being—I mean, I did live through this whole thing too ...
HESTER: And you can stop being so brutally sensitive ...
EDWIN: What I wanted, more than anything, was to come back and find you happily married or—you know, relating to some guy—whatever. As long as you were happy and ... loved. That would have made me happy.
HESTER: Edwin, you're full of shit!
EDWIN: I think you're a saint to have stayed here to take care of

my father and my son. Not many people would have stuck it out. Most people would have folded under the strain. But no. You denied yourself and did it! I always knew I loved you, I just didn't realize how strong you were ...

HESTER: Look! I haven't been on my own all these years. There were men—I went out with lots of men. I even went to bed with Baxter Dirdle for heaven's sake!

(Pause.)

EDWIN: You didn't! Not Baxter!

HESTER: Yes, Baxter! He was ghoulishly delighted that you'd vanished. He kept talking about dragging the harbour while he had his hand up my skirt. So, I finally gave in. I said, what the hey! He gave me the red Toyota which you probably saw out in the driveway.

EDWIN: Baxter? But Baxter was my friend—we were going to become partners.

HESTER: And Harris Lovecomb.

EDWIN: Oh, my God, you didn't. Not Harris Lovecomb—how could you—Harris is pathetic ...

HESTER: Depends upon how you look at him. He has natural talent and he always keeps his place well stocked with the best booze. And remember that garage you used to take the car to, the one on the hill.

EDWIN: Automotive Art?

HESTER: Right. Well, I didn't go out with Art, but his buddy that worked there, the mechanic ...

EDWIN: Oh, my God! Not Barney?

HESTER: No, not Barney, the other one—tall, long hair—poncho and huaraches ...

EDWIN: Dwayne.

HESTER: That's right, Dwayne. Then, when I used to go to Baxter and Becky's cottage ...

EDWIN: I don't want to hear any more. I get the point. You have just gone from one man to another ...

HESTER: No, that's not true. Ten years ago I fell in love—with one man—and he fell in love with me.

EDWIN: Anyone I know?

(Pause.)

HESTER: Yes, as a matter of fact. It was nine and a half years ago to be exact, right after the office Christmas party that pretty well closed the business. Arch and I got a bit loaded, back here at the house ...

EDWIN (*Shocked.*) No!

HESTER: Yes. Me and Arch. We fell in love and lived in this house as man and wife, until he got sick. And he was good to me, and I don't just mean generous with the housekeeping money! He was sixty-two when we got together and for a man of sixty-

two he was amazingly virile and agile. In fact, I had a hard time keeping up with him.
EDWIN: I don't know what to say ...
HESTER: I remember thinking at the time that Annabel died one happy lady ...
EDWIN: Don't you dare talk about my mother that way, don't you dare...!
HESTER: For four glorious years, I was very happy. Roddie was away at college, and Arch and I went through his savings—every penny that I imagine would have gone to you and Bernice. We went to New York and Niagara Falls and the Gaspe Peninsula—we went camping and actually had candle-light dinners next to the van on beaches and cliffs—we watched the sun go up and down—we went to a Nana Mouskouri concert in Quebec City—we did all the things that you and I were waiting to do once our lives were established. But most of all, we gave and received love.

(Pause.)

EDWIN: You slut!

Blackout and a few bars of music
End of Scene 2.

Scene 3:

(Lights up and we find HESTER and EDWIN sitting quietly with tall Vodkas and something. RODDIE has an overnight bag over his shoulder and is pushing an overstuffed duffel bag to the front door.)
RODDIE: I gave him a bowl of oats and some applesauce. He went to the bathroom; he did everything. He's asleep, but I didn't put the restraint on him.
HESTER: Thanks, Roddie. *(Pause.)* Have you got everything?
RODDIE: *(He kicks the duffel bag.)* Yeah, I got my laundry—oh, there were a couple of pairs of jeans that weren't quite dry—I left them in—I'll pick them up on my way to the airport tomorrow.
HESTER: Ok. Well, give my best to Lorraine and say hello to her parents.
RODDIE: Ok, I will—and don't forget, the movers will be at my place on the 24th at nine a.m.
HESTER: And I just give the key to Mrs. Finch.
RODDIE: If she's not home just leave it in the mailbox.
HESTER: Right then. Well, give me a kiss.
RODDIE: I'll see you tomorrow on my way out and I'll call you as soon as I get there.

(He gives her a big hug and a kiss on the cheek. The two of them are awkward in front of EDWIN. There is a long pause.)

EDWIN: (*Goes to RODDIE with his hand extended.*) Will you say goodbye and shake my hand?
RODDIE: (*Hesitates for a second.*) Goodbye.
(*He shakes hands with EDWIN.*)
(*Pause.*)
EDWIN: Roddie, do you remember the ruffle-ratty?
(*Pause.*)
RODDIE: No. (*He turns and opens the front door.*) Good luck.
(*He leaves and quietly closes the front door. There is a short silence.*)
EDWIN: You must be very proud of him.
HESTER: He can be a bit overbearing at times, but since Arch got sick he's terribly worried about me. He's had too much responsibility in his life ... but he is reliable ... completely reliable.
(*Pause.*)
EDWIN: Did he ... know about you and Arch ...?
HESTER: He must have done. We never talked about it. I wanted to several times, but no particular time ever seemed right. But he never said a word ... not one word.
(*Pause.*)
EDWIN: I'm sorry for what I said to you. It was just jealousy, I guess ...
HESTER: That's all right. There's no reason for me to take offence. I don't really mind how you see it—or anybody else for that matter.
(*Pause.*)
EDWIN: Hester, I want to come home.
(*Pause.*)
HESTER: Well, you are home, I guess.
EDWIN: No, I mean ... home.
HESTER: (*Pause.*) You mean ... you and me?
EDWIN: Why not? We could give it a try ... (*Pause.*) I could move into the spare room, no strings attached ... (*Pause.*) And I could help take care of Dad ... Archie. You need help, I know you need help.
HESTER: You mean like the "man"? The "hired man"?
EDWIN: Sort of. You say Roddie helped you out a lot. Well, I could do those things—of course, I mean, whatever it requires ... (*Pause.*) Hester, meet me half way. Come on! I know I'm a good man. I mean, I know it's in me—I just haven't given me a chance. I know I left you high and dry—I know I should have called, or written,—but I just didn't know how. I tried several times, but I couldn't. I just couldn't. And then it got to be so long—that it was impossible. Do you see? Do you know what I'm talking about.
(*Pause.*)
HESTER: I had a dream that I was ... cradling a badly injured

little foetus. It was loosely wrapped in a man's white pocket handkerchief and I held it in both hands. I knew I had to get it some sort of medical attention, but I couldn't move. The poor little thing in my hands bleated and I was in agony to do something; to relieve it's awful suffering—to stop that pitiful little "meep", "meep"—but I just couldn't move. The air around me was thick and heavy and I seemed to have too many clothes on. I was suffocating under woolly layers and belts and scarves, and something on my head that made it impossible to turn around; to look away ... I tried to close my eyes, but I couldn't, not even a blink—and then, in a flash, I was out of my body and sitting beside myself. But it didn't look like me, it wasn't really me—it was a huge old Russian grandmother in a babushka, rocking a shrivelled potato in her hands and crying. *(Pause.)* Well, I figured out that the little thing, that fully there, but unborn, creature, that pitiful little homunculus, is the embodiment of all my guilt—every miserable promise I've never kept, every irresponsible act, every petty, mean, cruel, unjust ...

EDWIN: Sounds like your own psyche to me ...

HESTER: That's what I just said ...

EDWIN: No, you said "the embodiment of guilt". You made it sound like a lump of guilt in your hands—I think it's *you*, your psyche, your inner being—*you* are calling out to *you* for help! *You* want *you* to do something! Something decisive. And I could be it! I could be the help you need ...

(Pause.)

HESTER: Every once in a while, when I can't sleep and I'm feeling especially low, I go and cuddle into Arch for a while, if he's asleep. It makes me feel better. *(Pause.)* What would happen the first night I crossed the hall, I wonder.

(Pause.)

EDWIN: I totally respect your feelings—not just your feelings—I will completely respect your privacy—the way you live your life. And who knows, maybe eventually ... well ... who knows.

HESTER: Not that it will be an issue for ever. I don't know how long I can keep Arch at home ... Do you really mean to help out? Do you know what it entails?

EDWIN: Not entirely. But I'll do it! I'll learn. I owe him ... I owe you ... *(Pause.)* Please give me a break, Hester. I don't really have any place else to go.

HESTER: You've got twenty grand.

EDWIN: I still want you to have it, and I would like to stay here for a while.

(Long Pause. HESTER is in deep thought. EDWIN gets up and goes over to the stereo and goes through the albums arranged beside or underneath the turntable. He selects, then puts on a record.)

EDWIN: It's the last song on this side. (*We hear "Midnight" by the "Shadows".*) Remember this? I dreamt about this last night. I heard this in my dream.
(He walks over to HESTER and offers his hand. She is awkward and embarrassed. She gestures no, but EDWIN is persistent. HESTER gets up slowly and they begin to waltz, at first hesitantly, then slowly getting into the dip and swing of it. When they loosen up they dance like the sexy high-school couple they once were, her with both arms around his neck, him surreptitiously feeling her up. The stage is bathed in a deep dreamy blue light, but we can still see ARCHIE emerge from the downstage entrance, only half dressed for the street. These days he can barely decide what article of clothing goes where. In stockinged feet, pyjamas and bathrobe just visible beneath a top coat or parka (buttons askew), hat on, and carrying a suitcase, he is following the secret call of his disease, to wander, to move on. He shuffles gently to the front door and quietly opens it. He stands for a moment, looking at HESTER and EDWIN. Does he remember them; one or both, or do they simply resemble someone he used to know? He pads softly over the threshold and leaves, closing the door as quietly as he opened it. Neither HESTER nor EDWIN see him enter the room or leave. The record ends, the lights slowly go back to normal. HESTER and EDWIN stay in each others arms.)
EDWIN: (*His face buried in her neck.*) You feel so good ... Oh, Hester ... you have no idea ...
(HESTER comes to. She gently pushes EDWIN away. She has had a very hard day, she is exhausted and maybe just a little drunk.)
HESTER: Edwin, this is all too much. This morning you were dead, and now ...
EDWIN: Now I'm alive and I'm home! You've got to believe me, Hester. You have to trust me. I'm not going to leave you in the lurch—I'm going to make up for everything—will you let me come back in?
(Pause.)
HESTER: Where are you staying now?
EDWIN: At Leggler's Bed and Breakfast. I could go over now and get my stuff! That's what I'll do—I'll go over and get my stuff—but I'm going to leave this. (*He takes the white envelope out of his pocket and one of the gift-wrapped boxes.*) The whole business will take me half an hour — no, less! I'll fly there and I'll fly back.
(EDWIN puts his coat on, kisses HESTER and then exits. HESTER stands there looking after him. She is suffering the shock of severe indecision and is suddenly terrified of the whole

prospect of Edwin's moving back home. She wanders around the room wondering what on earth to do. She tries to light a cigarette but finds that her hands are shaking so much the lighter flame dances. She consciously steadies herself. She lights the cigarette then picks up the phone, then decides not to dial. She stares at the phone, then decisively grabs it and dials a number. It rings several times before being answered.)

HESTER: Becky! God, I thought you were out! ... What? ... *(She looks at her watch.)* It is! I can't believe it! Becky, you can go back to sleep until noon ... I'm sorry, I didn't mean to wake Baxter, listen, I need a favour. Your place in Montreal—your apartment, is anybody staying there right now? Oh. *(Disappointed, then brightening.)* ... Do you think she'd mind if I stayed in the other room ... for a while ... I don't know ... oh, stuff; look I'll call you next week. I'll tell you every grisly detail ... Becky, I'm having one of my attacks, I can't eat anything—everything's just too much. I have to get away ... Why would I tell Baxter, for heaven's sake? Baxter's probably got an apartment, a better apartment, just around the corner from your apartment, and for exactly the same purposes ... I'm sorry, Becky ... Well, I told you I'm a little strung out ... all right ... thanks, thanks, Becky. Listen. Don't you tell anyone about this either, Ok? Uh huh ... I got it ... Marie Helene Thiboult ... how do I get a key? ... Ok, thanks again, Becky ... sorry about work ... I'll call you ... No, I'm alright for cash ... see you, hon, bye, talk to you soon.

(She hangs up.)

(HESTER exits briefly several times and comes back on carrying a suitcase, an armful of clothes, a pair of boots etc. She packs, puts on her coat then picks up the twenty grand. She stands thinking about it for a moment then she carefully divides it in half. One half she puts back in the envelope, the other half in her purse. All of a sudden she thinks of ARCHIE. Slowly she walks towards the downstage entrance, then cannot bring herself to go in and say goodbye. She turns around and heads for the front door, but remembers one final thing. She walks back to where she has left the envelope containing EDWIN's share of the money, and takes a pen out of her purse. She writes ...)

HESTER: Edwin. I'll call you. Me.

(On her way to the front door she stops by the cat box and strokes the furry bum just visible between the tiny porticoes of RODDIE's first architectural project.
EXIT HESTER. Seconds later we hear the doorbell. When it is not answered, the doorknob turns slowly and the door opens. EDWIN sticks his head around the door, then comes in. He is clutching a suitcase, a box of books and a suit bag. He stands looking around the room expectantly, then...)

EDWIN: Hi! It's me ...
(EDWIN listens intently ...)
(Long pause and a very slow fade to black as music, just as slowly, fades up.)

Please use some piece of music akin to "Echoes" by Pink Floyd.

The End

The Only Living Father

1991

Written by
Tom Cahill

THE ONLY LIVING FATHER

The Only Living Father was commissioned by Theatre Newfoundland and Labrador as part of the Company's 10th anniversary celebrations, and a workshop production directed by Edmund MacLean was first presented in Corner Brook in February 1991, with John Aylward as Joseph R. Smallwood.

Mr. MacLean gave the play its first professional production at the Corner Brook Arts and Culture Centre in June 1991 with Lorne Pardy in the role of the Charismatic Newfoundland political leader, setting by Don Short and original music by Jim Payne. This was followed by a tour of provincial Arts and Culture Centres in January 1992.

In the summer of 1992, THE ONLY LIVING FATHER, produced by Mulgrave Road Co-op Theatre, directed by Edmund MacLean and starring Lorne Pardy, completed an extensive tour of Nova Scotia, New Brunswick, Prince Edward Island and Ottawa, and in the summer of 1993 was featured at the Stephenville Festival. In January 1994, produced by George Zukerman for Overture Concerts Ltd. and sponsored by the Canada Council, the one-man show reached audiences in the Yukon and Northwest Territories, British Columbia, Alberta and Saskatchewan, completing its tour with a week long engagement at Toronto's Tarragon Theatre, and returning to Newfoundland in March for a month-long school tour sponsored by the Department of Cultural Affairs.

AUTHOR'S NOTE

"In the theatre all biography is fiction, and some fiction is autobiography, and what a play can achieve is to take time past and present and thread it through the needle of the years, providing the audience with a pictorial statement."

(British playwright MICHAEL HASTINGS)

This is essentially what myself and director Edmund MacLean aimed for when we discussed a one-man show on Joey Smallwood. We never asked the distinguished gentleman's permission, or contacted the family for advice or endorsement after his death. Instead, we relied on his own writings, Richard Gwynn's biography, interviews and remembered conversations and events. Thus our 'pictorial statement' has evolved into a memory play, with the leading part becoming not one of caricature, but hopefully a role any actor could interpret for all time.

TOM CAHILL

THE ONLY LIVING FATHER

Act 1
Scene 1

(As the theatre lights dim we hear on the soundtrack the Christmas carol "Angels We Have Heard on High" in the distance. Then it swells to fill the hall.)

SOUNDTRACK: Gloria, In excelsis Deo & etc.
Gloria, In excelsis Deo & etc.
(The last notes fade as a spotlight comes up on a solitary figure putting on a suit jacket he takes from a coat rack. He adds a white silk scarf, dark outer coat and a black homburg hat, and comes down to stand and stare at the audience through horn-rimmed glasses, and waits a long beat before he speaks.)
JRS: I was born!
(He waits for the audience to respond, looking back at them, like an owl.)
Born on December 24, 1900, in the little lumbering town of Gambo, Newfoundland ...
(He pauses to smile broadly, announcing with triumph.)
Canada!
I say I was "born", because years ago, in a Newfoundland outport, there were apparently other ways to arrive. I remember hearing my mother confide to a friend about a neighbour's baby that "he wasn't born, his aunt had he". That meant the village spinster had paid the ultimate price for committing an indiscretion with a visiting sea captain. Not being able to afford the usual trip to Halifax 'to have her tonsils out', a married sister took the baby to rear up and save her from embarrassment.
(He takes off his homburg hat and lays it on a table.)
Our Irish neighbours explained their sudden family additions by announcing "he wasn't born, he was come across". That meant someone else's infant had been stolen by the fairies and abandoned in the woods, and they did the only proper thing, and took it home.
I had one playmate who, they said, "wasn't born. He was left

on the grass and the sun brought him out". I was never quite sure what that meant, but I do recall he was always quite thin and miserable, and looked uncommonly like the Anglican Minister. Which might account for the erudite explanation.

Anyway, I was born.

Born on Christmas Eve, 1900. That accounts for the music.

Kind of a nice time to appear, don't you think? Christmas? And at the turn of a century, too?

(He gestures back over his shoulder with a thumb at the source of the celestial music.)

Of course, my mother didn't have those choirs of angels singing to her. And not one of the one hundred and seven souls living in Gambo, reported seeing a star over Charlie Smallwood's tiny frame house at the end of our one muddy, rocky road. And no wise men showed up for my nativity, either. Perhaps because it came at the end of a three-day blizzard.

But I did receive three great gifts at birth. The gift of absolute conviction that whatever I would do was right. The boundless energy to pursue my convictions. And the gift of gab, to persuade others to join me.

Some enemies later suggested that being born on the same day as another distinguished personage 1900 years earlier made me even think I was Him. Anyway, I ended up in the same business He did, trying to save the world. Or at least my part of it, Newfoundland.

It was only later I decided to throw in Canada for good measure.

(He wanders to a table to sit and open a battered family photo album.)

The Smallwoods, good English Methodist stock, came to Newfoundland via Prince Edward Island, when my grandfather David decided to start a saw mill in Gambo. It was he who chose the names for his first grandchild, deciding to call me after two prominent men of the time he admired; Sir Joseph Chamberlain, Britain's Secretary of State for the Colonies, and Field Marshall Lord Roberts, the Empire's most eminent soldier.

My mother was a Catholic named Minnie Devanna, and she had shocked her family by marrying Charlie Smallwood in the Gambo Methodist Church. Three of her sisters followed suit, and married Protestants too. But the Devannas exacted a savage revenge years later, when the sisters not only returned to the Roman fold, but persuaded their husbands to turn Catholic as well.

But not my mother!

As a matter of fact, a few days after I was born the leading Catholic layman in Gambo tapped on her door while the men were away in the woods cutting logs, to whisper that the priest was visiting from nearby Dark Cove, and it was her chance to have the new child baptized in the true faith. He was shattered when Minnie told him he could go to hell and take the priest with him.

I was the oldest of thirteen children, seven girls and six boys. I was a very tiny baby, and I had bow legs. (*He looks down at them.*) They had to be straightened out by strapping me into laced boots that reached to my knees. I wore them until I was five or six.

But that's not what worried my mother most about me. There was something else. I never spoke a word until I was three. For years she lived in mortal fear her firstborn would be deaf and dumb. Well, I certainly made up for that, didn't I?

When I was six months old my father, tired of the lumber woods, moved the family to St. John's to seek his fortune. But finding no work, he began to drink. He was a solitary drinker, the worst kind. He would bring home several bottles and for days he would be drunk. Then he would start to sober up.

I remember my mother was always able to tell when this miraculous moment arrived. She would rush out of the house to walk a mile and a half into town to buy him a flask at the nearest public house and bring it home to help him taper off. Then he would not take a drink for two to three months, before breaking out again. But it was a horrible co-existence, childhood and liquor, and it left me with such a hatred of alcohol that I was forty before I could touch a drop on social occasions without wanting to throw up.

And so our growing family spent most of its time moving from one wretched tenement to another. For a while we tried to make ends meet by keeping a small farm, with a pig and a few hens. I was especially fond of our pig, and would steal a wilted cabbage leaf from the kitchen to share with him privately and hear him grunt with satisfaction. The day he was slaughtered I stayed away from home. I've never eaten fresh pork since.

I guess it was inevitable that I'd end up in public life, because the three great heroes of my early years weren't musicians, hockey players or movie stars. They were politicians. But I had hard luck with all three of them.

I was a runny-nosed St. John's street urchin of nine when I saw my first one. He was Sir Robert Bond, Prime Minister of the Dominion of Newfoundland. As the son of a wealthy merchant, he'd made himself everybody's hero years before, saving the country by pledging his personal fortune as collateral for a loan when financial collapse threatened the local Savings Bank. Now when was the last time you heard of a politician doing that? Today they're using the country as collateral to fill their own bank accounts.

Every Friday afternoon in summer, it was Sir Robert's custom to walk from his hotel, greeting the peasantry on his way to the train station to board his private car for a weekend at his country estate at Whitbourne.

One Friday, as I was hanging around a vegetable stall trying to filch a fresh carrot, he suddenly appeared and stopped, resplendent in top hat, Prince Albert Coat and doe-skin gloves, to chat with the proprietor.

I quickly wiped my nose with a dank mitten and sniffed in the residue beneath, in case he might speak to me, also. Alas, I was only left to savour the scent of sumptuous cologne as he brushed past. But I remember thinking; that's what I want to be. A man with the power to save his people from disaster. A leader who could walk the streets forever after, honoured and respected by a grateful public.

Bond presided over our little country's golden age, giving Newfoundlander's, for the first time, the two things they needed to prosper: honesty in government and good prices for their fish.

After all, we'd been treated pretty shabbily by the British ever since they hired an Italian sailor to find a route to the wealth and jewels of the orient in 1497 and he bumped into us in a fog, instead. Oh, we'd had lots of visitors before Giovanni Caboto, of course. There were the Basques in the 1400's in their whaling boats. The Vikings in the 900's in their longboats. St. Brendan and his Irish monks in the 500's in their leather boats. And my friend, Geoff Stirling tells me, before that Newfoundland was a part of the lost continent of Atlantis.

(He heaves a sigh of frustration.)

And Quebec thinks its got a distinct society!!!

But when John Cabot went back and told the King his rowboat couldn't get through the codfish when he tried to come ashore, the English added Wednesday to Saturday as a mandatory fish day and forbade anyone to build a house with a chimney in it, or cut wood within five miles of the shore in the new territory. This did wonders for their West Country fish merchants, but it played merry hell with our chance to become a centre of culture and prosperity in the new world.

It was Robert Bond who tried to rescue us from being Britain's North American door mat by negotiating a free trade agreement with the United States. Our fish and minerals would be allowed into that lucrative market duty free, in return for landing and bait rights on Newfoundland shores.

God in heaven, how the Basilica bells rang out and people danced in the streets when the signing was announced. I remember asking my grandfather what it was all about and he said, "We've come into our own at last, my son. The Cinderella of the empire has met her handsome prince!"

But the jealous Canadian sister soon screamed to Mother England that our treaty was part of a devious scheme to cripple the Nova Scotia fishery, allow the rapacious Yankees to eventually annex Newfoundland, and, in time, all of Canada, ending forever the British presence in North America. London refused Royal Assent and the treaty died, and our hopes for adoption by rich Uncle Sam were replaced by an enduring mistrust of dog-in-the manger Canadians that would remain to haunt my own political career half a century later.

And then the local dog pack set upon the crippled stag. Bond was climbing a wharf at Western Bay in a subsequent election campaign when a man in the crowd kicked him in the stomach, knocking him back into the freezing water where he almost drowned.

"I have had my fill of Newfoundland politics," Sir Robert wrote a friend from retirement at Whitbourne, "and I turn from the filthy business with contempt and loathing." And so we mourned the loss of our only statesman, and my very first hero. But I learned from him one valuable lesson. No matter how prosperous or well-governed, our little country could never survive on its own.

Then, one day, shortly after my 10th birthday, the gloom was dispelled, the sky opened up, and a wondrous, beautiful new world was provided for me. My Uncle Fred, a successful businessman, pitying brother Charley, with his drinking problem and large family, offered to take the bright oldest boy, and put him through High School.

I was given new clothes, books and pocket money and enrolled as a boarding student at Bishop Feild College in St.John's, where all the rich merchants sent their sons. I might as well have died and gone to heaven.

The very first day at 'Feild' I got my nickname. Walter Lesman, the chief name-giver cornered me. "Who are you?", he demanded. When I told him he said "Smallwood? That means 'splits'", an old Newfoundland word for kindling used to light fires. Years later an old lady at a Corner Brook campaign rally took it a step further, when she shook her fist at me and yelled "Mister Joey, I'll beat you into sawdust, and that's goddam small wood". But for the time being at Bishop Feild, I was "Splits".

And, you know, I'm not bragging when I say I was a wonderful student! I literally ate the books. History, biography, fiction ... there was nothing I couldn't or wouldn't read! But I hated Algebra. In class the headmaster would say, "Alright, everyone, get out your Algebras. Joe, go read your novel."

I was a natural rebel from the start and led two successful strikes at Bishop Feild, one for better food in the dining room and one against being kept in for not attending compulsory church service.

Then, around grade Nine I got bored with it all, and ran away from school.

I decided I would learn the printing trade, and then become a journalist and writer. I got myself hired at a newspaper called the *Plaindealer* as a printer's apprentice for $1.50 a week. I gave my mother a dollar for board and kept 50 cents for pocket money. I was fifteen years old.

And, politically, I resolved to be a Socialist. I had no idea what a Socialist was, but it sounded rebellious and anti-establishment, and besides, I had a new hero. His name was William Coaker. He called himself a socialist, but the Merchants and Churches were denouncing him as an anarchist, atheist and Communist, and that was just my cup of tea!

Coaker had set himself the impossible task of organizing into a modern, powerful union, the uneducated, apathetic, poverty-stricken fishermen of Newfoundland, scattered in thousands of isolated settlements around a rugged coast. As his enemies sneered he proceeded to sign up 40,000 members in five years, win eight seats in the House of Assembly, and listen to fanatic disciples on every shore marching to the battle hymn of the man they dubbed the Moses of the North.

Would you like me to sing a verse for you?

(He waits for a cry of approval from the audience.)

All right, you asked for it.

(He leaps on a chair to sing, conducting an imaginary band.)

> We are coming Mr.Coaker, men from Green Bay's rocky shore
> Men who stand the snow-white billows down, on stormy Labrador;
> We are ready and a-waiting, strong and solid, firm and bold
> To be led by you like Moses led the Israelites of old.
> We are with the fight for freedom and the Union is our song;
> We are coming, Mister Coaker, and we're forty thousand strong.

(He waits for the applause and hops down again.)

Coaker and his rowdy out-harbour members were the sensation of the Legislature. Instead of the wing collars and morning suits worn by the city elite for the House opening, they showed up in homespun guernsey sweaters, salt and pepper caps and rubber boots.

Coaker was a brilliant debater, and in one famous confrontation over money being wasted building a bridge across the small Waterford River in St.John's, he jeered "For God's sake, I could piss half way across it".

"You're out of order" rapped the speaker.

"I must be," roared Coaker, "or I could piss ALL the way across it."

Too young to run as one of his candidates, I had to content myself with writing anonymous articles for his union newspaper, and silently cheering in the Legislature gallery, as he demanded unheard of social reforms, like minimum wages, free education, old age pensions and guaranteed prices for his fishermen. It was the first revolution in the world to succeed without firing a shot or shedding a drop of blood.

But then Coaker made his mistake. Instead of taking over the government, he decided to concentrate on Union business, trusting the politicians who promised to institute his reforms in return for union support. Compromise soon replaced resolve, concession supplanted principle, until Coaker's revolution lay in tatters.

Exhausted and discouraged, he gave up, accepted a knighthood, and entered St. John's society, learning to spend his winters in gentler climes and how to make himself rich.

The end of another hero!

Like thousands of his fishermen, I tried to fathom the reasons for the betrayal. The truth was, he had become a politician. The trouble was he had been elected as a messiah. I would never understand his problem until I had to face it myself, many years later.

And I learned another lesson; if you are given power and don't use it, you lose it.

But not to despair! Another hero was emerging. If Robert Bond was elegant and William Coaker dedicated, Richard Squires was the consummate politician, believing every handshake, every name remembered and every note of sympathy to a grieving widow would be returned a hundredfold come polling day. And he was right.

He came preaching his own new and startling revolution: to hell with the medieval slavery of Coaker's fishery. Newfoundland would be industrialized, with paper mills, factories, iron ore mines, hydro-electricity, and forced to join the rest of North America and the 20th Century!

I was hooked again!

Squires was celebrating his second term as Prime Minister, his revolution percolating along with the opening of a giant new paper mill in Corner Brook, when his political chicanery caught up with him. He was arrested and charged with grand larceny.

It's pretty juicy stuff. Would you like to hear the rest of it?

(He giggles and comes down a few steps to tell a good story.)

It seems the Prime Minister, whenever he was short of ready

cash, was in the habit of borrowing some from the week's receipts at the Government's Board of Liquor Control. He always left a cheque for each amount, he told an inquiry, and the fact that they all bounced was simply an oversight. Unfortunately, over a period of two years, Sir Richard's oversights totalled $200,366.

Squires claimed it was all a political frame-up. He never touched a cent for himself, he said, using the money to pay party expenses and bury a few pauperized constituents.

I believed him, and so did a lot of others, for two grand juries refused to indict him. But in the subsequent election, my third hero and another revolution went down the tubes.

"I know what I'll do," I told my mother. "I'll go away to New York somewhere, and get a job as a reporter on a famous newspaper, and meet some REAL social reformers ..."

"To hell with Newfoundland, betrayal, and hypocrisy!"

(And he stomps off stage as the lights fade and the sound track brings back a choir of fishermen singing a reprise of Coaker's marching hymn.)

Scene 2

(At the end of the Coaker reprise, the music dissolves to "The Sidewalks of New York" as JRS returns, dressed in a fedora with a "press" card in the hatband and a Humphrey Bogart raglan. He takes a note pad from the raglan pocket and a pencil from behind his ear and jots down a few notes, looking about furtively. Then he notices the audience, and lays the note pad on the table.)

New York in October 1920 was crowded with young people like me, come to seek their fortune. Would you believe the day after I arrived I was on my way with a job at *The Call*, the city's Socialist daily newspaper? I met real, live radicals who were convinced, like me, that things in the world weren't right, and wanted to do something about it.

Charles Erwin, our editor, called everybody "Comrade" and we endlessly debated all the crackpot causes of the times. And with my skinny energy, wild eyes behind steel-rimmed glasses, tattered clothes and frayed philosophy, I made the perfect revolutionary, and they welcomed me with open arms!

Within a month I was a regular at Socialist rallies all over New York state, as a reporter and speaker too, mouthing a catalogue of indictments against the oppressors. Some people called us Communists, but we weren't, really. We wanted revolution within the system, not anarchy outside it. And I was quick to learn how to promote that.

(He leaps up on the table, takes off his fedora to wave about, and launches into a screaming tirade.)

" ... Socialism will automatically emancipate mankind from our present degrading and devitalizing need of using himself up in the scramble to merely gather enough material things by which to live physically.
We deserve the right to enjoy the fruits of our labour.
We deserve the right to leisure and happiness. We deserve the right to share the wealth we produce. *(His voice rises to a scream, his fists shaking in the air.)*
And Socialism will let us have all these things TOGETHER."
(He jumps down from the table.)
That wasn't bad, was it?

In the next four years I had a dozen jobs and spoke at thousands of meetings, seminars and conventions all over the state, and learned how to handle every kind of heckler from right-wing intellectuals to drunken rowdies.

But, suddenly, the great days of Socialism were over in America, and I was seized with a serious bout of homesickness. I don't know if you've ever been, or ever known a Newfoundlander away from home, but we're a strange lot. We have this terrible ambivalence about the place, hating the isolation and confinement, yet yearning to go back and inhale it. Besides, I was tired of eating at automats, and pinning the huge map of my homeland on the walls of countless apartments and rooming houses.

The decision was made for me when I met John Burke, an executive with the International Paper Mill Workers Union. He offered me forty-six dollars a week to go home and re-organize his struggling locals in the paper towns. I took the first train to Halifax.

I worked like a Trojan and within six months brought the membership of Grand Falls Local 63 from one hundred members to 900. Then I left for Corner Brook to organize Local 64.

By late summer I had that done, and went on to pass two milestones in my life.

I walked across Newfoundland, and I got married.

And I didn't have to do one to accomplish the other, either.

Taking a short cut along the railroad tracks to the Union Office in Corner Brook one morning, I was stopped by a foreman and his section crew.

He was one of those original settlers from Port au Port, the French area of Newfoundland, who spoke in that fascinating back-to-front English they still use today.

(He does the accent.)

"The worst t'ing a feller can have on his house in the winter is no porch!"

That was one of their favourite sayings. Looking at me stumbling over the railroad ties, he said "it makes hard walking dere, Mr. Smallwood, because them things are too goddam close apart."

"You be de feller who make union dere in Corner Brook," he continued, "Why you not make union for us crowd?" And he told me how his crews had just been given a pay cut from twenty-five to twenty-two cents an hour.

The next day I took the train to the end of the line in Port aux Basques, held a meeting of section men, collected a joining fee of fifty cents from each one, and set out to walk the five hundred and forty miles of track to St. John's and sign up every crew along the way.

I walked for two months, and when I reached Avondale, the railway's general manager and his two top executives were on the station platform, completing an inspection tour. "What are you up to now, Joe?" they asked me. "Every section man along the line has joined my new union", I said, "and I'll close down this operation, gentlemen, at a moments notice, if you don't rescind that pay cut".

They agreed to do it on the spot. I celebrated by taking the train thirty-five miles into St. John's.

I hadn't actually walked all the way across Newfoundland island, but if you throw in the five branch lines, I'd made it across seven hundred and forty-seven miles of track, two hundred more than the main line.

I've never walked anywhere since, if I could hitch a ride on anything.

(The sound track brings in a church organ with
"Here Comes The Bride".)

When I got back to Corner Brook, I weighed only a quintal–that's 112 pounds to anyone who's never been in the fish business–and looked like a half-starved grasshopper. I also discovered my landlady, Serena Baggs, had a young cousin visiting from Carbonear named Clara Oates. She was shy and gentle, with sparkling blue eyes, and she sang and played the piano. But perhaps what attracted the solitary socialist was the fact that Clara, too, was an omnivorous reader. We talked of books and music and in a very few weeks we were engaged. That fall I completed another walk–down the aisle with Clara Oates on my arm–but it remained one of the most fortunate events of my life. Though perhaps not of hers. She never managed to domesticate me.

Anyway, now I was almost 30. I had to think about settling down and providing for a family. The question was, would this restless soul be content doing it?

(The soundtrack brings "Here Comes The Bride" in again
and he walks off as the lights fade.)

Scene 3

(JRS goes to a coat rack, sheds his "Reporter" costume and changes into a newspaper editor in shirtsleeves, armbands and green eyeshade. He comes to sit at a centre table and start picking at a period typewriter. After a moment a telephone beside him rings; he picks it up.)
    Larry? Joe Smallwood in Corner Brook. Thanks for returning my call. I wanted to talk a little politics with you ... I just heard Sir Richard Squires is going to take over the Liberal party leadership again and try for a comeback. Yeah, well, *(He looks around to make sure no one is listening in another office, then leans forward)* keep this to yourself for now, but I wouldn't mind being his candidate out here in the Humber district, myself. Yes ... been here almost two years. Married and all settled down. I've got my own newspaper started here, *The Herald*. Yeah, that's right. Bought out old Jonathan Noel. Perhaps you'd check my suggestion with the brass and call me back. I can announce this week. I'll do a front page story on myself ...
    (He laughs, then jumps up and carries the phone to the front of the desk.)
    What ...? He plans to run out here, himself? Yes, yes, I can understand why, he put the bloody paper mill here, but what about his old stamping ground in Trinity Bay?
    Well, well, well, I guess that takes care of that. What? Me go campaign manager for him? Oh, God, Larry, I don't know ... Yes ... Yeah ... I really admire his guts and all that, but ... Look, let me think about it for a day or two will you? All right, tomorrow. I'll let you know tomorrow.
    (He hangs up and sits thinking for a moment, then looks up, stands and advances to the footlights.)
    You're probably asking the same questions I did. How could Richard Squires, disgraced, charged with larceny, forced to resign as Prime Minister, make a comeback a scant four years later? The answer was simple. The electors had discovered, as they do so many times, that a political devil you know is eminently preferable to one you don't.
    Squires had been swept from power by a group of Water Street merchant reformers who claimed they were "just plain men of business", come together to "put an end, once and for all, to political graft and corruption".
    But do you know the first five things the wealthy reformers did when they met in Cabinet after their landslide election?
    (He counts it all out on his fingers.)
    They repealed prohibition ... and a sitting minister opened a brewery.
    They legalized the manufacture of margarine, and an-

other one started a margarine factory.
The Prime Minister happened to be the major shareholder in a local cigarette factory, so they raised the tariff on imported cigarettes and tobacco.
This is all true, I'm not exaggerating!
And here comes what, today, we'd call the "kicker".
They abolished the payment of Income Tax!
There were only twenty men in the whole country rich enough to pay income tax and ten of them were in the cabinet, and they voted to repeal the act.
They made off in a week with more than Richard Squires had in eight years!
This was going to be a fun election!
(He scurries behind the desk, sits, picks up the
phone and jiggles the receiver.)
Long distance, please. Hello, Long Distance, put me through to Liberal Headquarters in St. John's ... collect.
Hello, Larry? Joe Smallwood. I'll do it! Tell Squires I accept. And listen ... I've got a great campaign slogan for him. "Vote for the man who put the hum on the Humber". How's that? Fine! Call me tonight. *(He hangs up and comes to stage right.)*
I persuaded Squires to rent a Prime-Ministerial three-car special train for his arrival in Corner Brook. Then I put him on a boat and we barnstormed every fishing village in the district. "Vote for the man who put the hum on the Humber," he thundered at every stop, and when his voice gave out, I took over and did most of the talking.
After our final rally, Squires said, "Joe, the Liberal Party is going to sweep this election, but I'm worried about making it out here, myself. Maybe I should have run in Trinity?" I sat down and went through every polling station on our list. "You'll win with three thousand and fifty votes to your opponent's six hundred and fifteen," I predicted.
When the ballots were counted the next day Squires had three thousand and eleven. I was only thirty-nine votes out.
He put his hand out. "Smallwood", he said, "that was the most astonishing election forecast I ever heard. Come back to St. John's with me. I'm going to buy a new party newspaper, I'll need an editor."
(JRS strips off his arm bands and throws them aside,
grabs a coat from a coat rack.)
Within a month I moved, and besides being an editor, became the confidant, advisor, strategist, ward heeler and hatchet man for the smartest politician I'd ever known.
(He moves off.)
(The SOUNDTRACK comes in with a filtered radio
announcer's voice.)

Here is a bulletin from New York. The Wall Street Stock Market has collapsed. Financial experts are describing it as the blackest day in America's financial history. There are reports that wealthy speculators are jumping from skyscraper windows after losing their fortunes in minutes. The entire district is in chaos. To repeat ... the New York Stock Market has ...
(JRS returns dressed in a business suit and walks slowly to sit in a chair left.)
Poor Squires! He had borrowed heavily to finance his revolution and Newfoundland's quarter of a million people owed one hundred million in foreign debts. With the markets in chaos, he was not even able to raise a loan to meet the interest payments, and his government faced bankruptcy. In desperation, he tried to sell Labrador to Ottawa or Quebec. First for the $100 million debt. Then 50, then 10. There were no takers.

The last thing the already tainted Prime Minister needed was another personal scandal, but now he got one.

Peter Cashin, the Minister of Finance, rose in the legislature to announce his resignation, accusing his leader and several Cabinet colleagues of falsifying minutes of the Executive Council to pay themselves salaries. I went to see Squires; he denied everything. "It's the same old gang, Joe", he said, "they'll do anything to bring down the government".

Another inquiry dismissed the charges, but Sir Richard's political enemies smelled blood and a great rally was held in a downtown St. John's theatre. I elbowed my way to the centre of the hall as speaker after speaker demanded the Prime Minister's resignation. When I jumped on a chair shouting, "question! question!" the crowd roared. "Don't let him speak! Throw him out," But I fought my way to the front of the stage, and Chairman Eric Bowring reached down and hauled me up.

"Beware of the Greeks when they come bearing gifts", I bellowed, "And beware of Water Street merchants bringing political advice. They will stop at nothing to regain control of the government to re-line their own pockets."

As I paced back and forth, hands suddenly reached out from the wings and yanked me off the stage. I was pushed down a back stairs and, with a kick in the rear end, thrown into the alley.

The next afternoon all the stores on Water Street closed so workers could join a great protest march to the House of Assembly.

When the procession reached the Legislature grounds, hired hooligans began smashing the windows, beating down the front doors and ransacking the offices, dragging the furniture outside to set on fire.

On the floor of the House, the Speaker desperately tried to

maintain decorum, as he sat in his chair, a metal wastebasket protecting his head, with rocks and stones bouncing off it as they came crashing through the windows.
(The soundtrack brings in the shouts, smashing glass and hubbub of a rioting crowd and fades out again.)
I rounded up Police Inspector Hutchings and Clerk Jim Bindon and we ran into the Chamber, formed a flying wedge around Squires and his wife, who was an elected member, and hustled them into the adjoining Speakers Room, turned off the lights and barricaded the door.

Suddenly, someone was hammering outside:"are you there, Sir Richard, are you there?"

I signalled to everyone not to answer.

"We're afraid they're going to set fire to the building," the voice said. "You'd better let us take you out ".

We opened the door. It was Fred Emerson, a friend. He took Lady Squires out through a rear entrance. I turned up Squires' collar, took his glasses off and jammed a salt and pepper cap on his head and led him towards a side door.

Nobody recognized us as we edged out into the darkness through what was now a full scale riot. But Squires, blind without his glasses, suddenly stumbled over a piece of wrought iron fence, knocking off the cap.

"There he is! There's the bastard," someone shouted.

In seconds, we were surrounded. The mob swept us toward the front gate. "Down to the harbour with him," they yelled. "Drown the son of a bitch".

As we were carried along Colonial Street towards the waterfront, a man suddenly opened his front door to see what was going on. I pushed my way toward it. "In here, Sir Richard. Quick," and we shot through the door, and slammed it shut behind us.

I passed Squires his glasses. We raced through the house, out the back door, through a hole in a fence, across a garden and into the back door of another house on Bannerman Street. There, they let us call a taxi, while the mob boiled on towards the harbour, still thinking they had their victim.

A few hours later, with Sir Richard safely tucked away in Harbour Grace, I decided to take a look at the damage.

My two brothers-in-law came with me for protection, and I pulled my hat down over my face in case anyone recognized me, and stuffed a hammer in my coat pocket. But the crowds were too busy looting the liquor stores to pay any attention.

Squires refused to resign and called an election, and I took my first formal stab at politics, as his Liberal Party candidate in Bonavista South!

I decided if we couldn't win the election, we could at least put an end to the ruthless class, sectarian and political warfare that was paralysing our country. And so I preached a new gospel.

"Close down the House of Assembly," I shouted. "Bolt and bar the broken doors and windows of that Colonial Building. Do away with the government. Not just the government we have now, but any government. Send a petition to the King asking him for a Commission to run the country for the next five years. Party politics has become meaningless–intellectually bankrupt. We need a holiday from leadership".

I went down to inglorious defeat in Bonavista South, and Squires lost the election to his old enemies, the Water Street merchant clique. But it was a hollow victory. Unable to meet even the interest payments on the debt, they were forced to take my advice and ask London for assistance. Fearing default would jeopardize their own credit rating, the British agreed to assume responsibility for our financial obligations, on condition we accept a Royal Commission to inquire into the reasons for our fiscal collapse, and abide by its recommendations. Soon a British peer and two Canadian bankers arrived in St. John's, a trio of foreigners charged with deciding the fate of Newfoundland.

The British, of course, are experts at investigating political corruption. This is understandable, since they invented it. Did I say, "Invented"? No, the English didn't just INVENT office-buying, influence peddling, ballot-box-stuffing and vote rigging, they rewarded it with the highest appointments in the land.

They took double-dealing, gerrymandering, jobbery, inducement, bribery, blackmail, extortion, collusion and coercion and institutionalized them. Made them state of the art and art of the state! And now, with the elegant hypocrisy that is the trademark of Whitehall, their clutch of septuagenarian ninnies pronounced St. John's the Sodom and Gomorrah of the Empire, and proposed a banker's solution to our problems.

Instead of reduced interest rates, extended terms of repayment and a program of retrenchment, a British-appointed Commission of civil servants would supervise payment of all debts. Instead of a temporary suspension of political activity, our constitution would be revoked and representative government withdrawn indefinitely.

The "plain men of business" met in the House of Assembly and after defeating a motion that would bar any of them from benefiting personally through contract or appointment with the new regime, voted to a man to accept what many felt was a harsh and needless ultimatum.

It was their last and most profitable kick at the cat, and they took it joyfully.

(The soundtrack starts to softly bring in the "Ode To Newfoundland", and hold it in the background.)

The Only Living Father

I couldn't help wiping away a tear when we all crowded into a hotel ballroom to hear the "Ode To Newfoundland" play, as our last Prime Minister signed away a hard-won independence.

Never before had a people, their development paralysed for centuries by ruthless exploitation, been reviled as corrupt incompetents by the exploiters and forced to accept total blame for economic failure.

Never before in the history of the British Empire had a Colony been stripped of representative government, without even a referendum to allow the electorate to consider alternatives. But now ours was gone ...

(The soundtrack brings in a British-accented voice.)

" ... until such time as the Colony's difficulties are overcome, and the country is again self-supporting, when Responsible Government, on the request from the people, will be restored ..."

As many, including myself, suspected, it never would be.

But for now I was an editor without a paper. An idealist without an ideal. A patriot without a homeland. It was time to find another job. And perhaps another country!

(The music of the "Ode To Newfoundland" swells to a finish as the lights fade and JRS disappears in the darkness.)

Scene 4

(As the lights come up the stage is empty and we hear from the soundtrack the first verse of the Newfoundland folk song "Hard Hard Times.")

Come all you good people
I'll sing you a song
About the poor fellows, how they get along;
They'll start in the spring
Finish up in the fall,
And when it's all over, they've nothing at all;
And it's hard, hard times.

(JRS walks into the spotlight dressed in shirtsleeves, vest and battered fedora, carrying a stained lab coat and a pair of knee-high rubber boots. He throws the coat over a chair behind the centre table and sets the boots down, as he advances to the footlights.)

"Hard, Hard Times" — that was our anthem in the thirties, all right. No, I didn't go away. What was the point? There were block-long lineups of men looking for work in New York, London and Montreal. Instead, I went to Bonavista, hoping to take advantage of my organizing experience and revive Coaker's old Fishermen's Union. But if the depression created havoc in the great cities, it devastated Newfoundland. The isolation that once allowed the outports to defy British anti-settlement laws now turned out to be their worst enemy. Unable to sell their fish, whole families starved without money for the basics of flour, sugar, tea, or medical attention, the new commission government able to offer little more than token assistance.

Back in St. John's, desperate for something to keep my own family fed, I came across a volume in the library one day called *The Book of Puerto Rico*. Before the week was out, I had drafted a two-volume outline of my own *Book of Newfoundland*. Before the year was out, I'd convinced wealthy businessman Ches Crosbie to back me in having ten thousand copies printed, and I was selling them door to door for six dollars a set.

Every good writer soon learns to re-cycle his basic research, so I started a newspaper column telling stories from our history and called it "From the Barrelman", after the fellow who keeps watch in a large keg high up on the mast of a sailing ship.

Then I got an even better idea: instead of writing for the city elite, why not use the wonderful new medium of radio to tell their history to my friends on the isolated coasts of Bonavista South and the Humber district?

I went to see Bill Galgay, the manager of the government station, and within a month I had a sponsor and fifteen minutes at suppertime six nights a week. I called myself "The Barrelman" and used as my signature a sound every Newfoundlander would recognize, a ship's bell.

(He walks to a table to sit before a period microphone. Beside it is a ship's bell mounted on a small cradle, a rope hanging from the clapper. He reaches to ring it six times; ding-ding, ding-ding etc.)

F.M. O'Leary Limited presents "The Barrelman", a program to make Newfoundland better known to Newfoundlanders.

(He rings again; ding-ding, ding-ding, ding-ding.)

Tonight we start with a story sent in by Captain Jacob Mercer of Upper Island Cove:

One time, there was an old lobster fisherman and he was having a wonderful bad season. Lobsters were never so scarce. Then, to make things worse, his wife fell over the wharf and got drowned. A week later a neighbour came running up to his house. "They just found your wife's body three miles up the coast, and she was covered in lobsters," he said, "what should we do?" Replied the fisherman, "Bait her and set her again!"

(He rings the bell over the laughter: ding-ding,ding-ding.)

Soon there was hardly a settlement along any coast where people didn't stop everything each evening to listen to "The Barrelman", as I subtly encouraged the fishermen to forget their hardships, summon up their sense of humour and survival, and

The Only Living Father 277

celebrate their history of courage and endurance.

Many listeners began to use the program to exchange messages and greetings, which I usually passed on to the News Broadcast that followed me on air. But some were too good to miss: "From Daisy to her husband Bill. 'Taking on men. Took on 30 yesterday. Better come home'." Of course she was talking about the paper company hiring loggers. "From Simon Pelley in the Grace Hospital, to Melvina: 'Started walking today, will be home next week'."

I got thousands of letters and $30 pay a week, and soon became a Newfoundland institution! Joe Smallwood had found his milieu!

Ever since my attachment to our pig on the Southside Road in my childhood, I'd harboured a secret passion to be a gentleman farmer and raise these fascinating animals. So, with my new affluence, I bought a house on a few acres on the outskirts of St. John's and started a small swine-breeding operation.

And then, of course, all our lives were suddenly changed.

(The lights fade and the soundtrack cuts in with the filtered voice of British Prime Minister Neville Chamberlain and his 'Peace in our time' speech, and then into guns firing and shells exploding. JRS slips on the overalls and rubber boots, picks up a tin swill pail and comes downstage).

War has always brought prosperity to a strategic Newfoundland, and the second great World conflict was no exception. The American, British and Canadian forces were busy building bases all over the island and Labrador, but perhaps the major centre of activity was the great airport at Gander. Group Captain David Anderson, head of the RAF Transport Command Station there, was a colourful character who decided it was a shameful waste to be throwing away the tons of food left over from the military mess halls every day. So he had a load of weanling pigs flown in, hired a local man to feed them the swill, and began selling the pork to the military, with the profits going to the RAF welfare fund.

When he heard me on the radio and learned I was also a pig breeder he flew to St. John's with a business proposal. "There's enough food thrown away every day to feed 10,000 pigs, Joe", he said. "Why not come to Gander. We'll go into business together and make a fortune!" It was too good a chance to miss. I gave up my radio career, sold the farm in St. John's, moved to Gander and went into the pig business in earnest.

When the wind was northeast and blew across town I wasn't the most popular person around. And when the Smallwood family took its place in church on Sunday there was usually a wide space between us and the rest of the congregation. But the profits were good and we lived well.

And then, one day after the war ended, I heard on the radio the announcement that would change my life for the second time:
(The soundtrack again with a BBC announcer's voice).
This is London calling. Here is the news. Prime Minister Attlee announced in the House of Commons today that Newfoundland would shortly be provided with the opportunity to review its political status and decide on a future course ...

Financial stability meant agitation among local politicians for the return of Responsible Government. But the Dominions Office now infuriated them by deciding this would not be automatic. First there would be a great National Convention to examine the alternatives.

But what were they? We knew from Robert Bond's day that London and Ottawa would never tolerate an alliance with the United States. That only left Confederation with a prosperous, post-war Canada, and that seemed to be what the British had in mind. I was delighted. It would keep the merchant clique from getting their hands back in the till. And it would combine the dreams of my three heroes. It would end the economic isolation feared by Bond, bring in the social reforms of Coaker and provide money for an industrial revolution that would set Richard Squires spinning in his grave. But what politician of any standing in Newfoundland would risk his career to champion such an unpopular cause?

Would anyone, I wondered, be interested in such a movement led by a crypto-communist, left wing radical pig farmer? I decided I had to be a delegate to that Convention to find out. I would never get elected in St. John's, but the residency requirement to represent a district was only 2 years, so my pig farming adventure in Gander qualified me there. All I had to do now was get some of the old New York hell fire back into my speeches!

(He grabs the swill bucket and leaps upon a table.)

Pigs of Gander, unite. I have decided to run as your delegate to the great National Convention. Candidates are supposed to seek election uncommitted, but I will take the sow by the snout from the beginning and run as a delegate pledged to Confederation with the great Dominion of Canada. Vote for me, pigs, and I promise you free Canadian swill for the rest of your natural lives!

(There is a burst of pig snorts and oinks, as JRS leaps down off the table with his bucket and strolls off into the darkness to lively marching band music.)

Scene 5
The National Convention

(JRS strides on in a seedy suit and comes to his desk at the

The Only Living Father 279

National Convention. He is greeted by boos and catcalls and shouts of "Judas", "Quisling" and "Traitor" from the majority of the forty-five delegates. He points an accusing finger at his tormentors.)

Yes, you can call me Judas. You can call me Quisling. You can call me Traitor. But I'm going to talk to this Convention today about Confederation with Canada. And I'm going to talk about it because I was elected as a delegate committed to Confederation.

(A chorus of boos and catcalls.)

Not only that, but the people of the great district of Bonavista Centre elected me with the largest majority afforded any other member of this Convention. Do you want to hear the figures? Mr. Kitchener Pritchett, 277, Joseph R. Smallwood, 2,129. Those are my election figures. Can any of you beat them? Now I'm going to talk about Confederation with Canada as the only sensible political and economic alternative for Newfoundland, and all of you know I am speaking the truth!

(The soundtrack brings in a repeat of the name-calling. He pounds his desk furiously and shouts it down.)

Hear me, now. You will hear me. You talk of Responsible Government restored to this Colony. You talk of independence returned to Newfoundland. You prate about nationhood re-instated to this Dominion. But is it being done for the convenience and profit of the average Newfoundlander or the 21 millionaires on Water Street?

What do the rest of our people do, once your precious independence is returned? Starve, like they did before? Be proudly sovereign and poverty-stricken like they were before? Be content to eat less, wear less, use less, and accept the lowest standard of living in North America, like they did before? Or do we throw in our lot with a wealthy, progressive country and a social benefit program that can provide protection for our toiling masses when hard times come again, as surely they will?

Mister Chairman, I move that a delegation be named from this Convention immediately to travel to Ottawa and learn the attitude of the Canadian Government on the question of the Federal Union of Newfoundland and Canada.

(A new chorus of boos and catcalls erupts. He comes down front.)

The delegates voted to defeat my resolution 25 to 18. It was clear the majority were convinced Confederation should not be considered until Responsible Government had been restored to Newfoundland. But I watched and waited, and suddenly a crack appeared in the wall of opposition.

The most respected member of the Convention was a wealthy St. John's fish merchant named Robert Job. Almost 80, with silver hair and neatly trimmed goatee, he was our senior statesman. Job was obsessed with the idea of trade with the United States on a 'quid pro quo' basis. That was his favourite expression: "quid pro quo". He used it so often that when he rose for the tenth time to plead his case, a fisherman delegate moaned, "oh, my God, the Quid are struck in again".

(He strolls about, imitating Job and the pseudo-British accent of the St.John's elite of the time.)

"Mr. Chairman, the Americans hold rent-free 99-year leases on a substantial portion of Newfoundland soil. It is my firm conviction that, in return for continued use of these military installations, a delegation to Washington could secure an arrangement that would allow Newfoundland fish duty free into the lucrative American market on a quid quo pro basis ..."

His motion was soundly defeated for the same reason as mine, and suddenly I realized that the afflictions of this Job could be my salvation. I went to see him privately.

(He moves across the stage to pantomime a meeting with Job.)

"Mr. Job, I'm terribly enthusiastic about your idea of a fish deal with Washington, but it seems direct negotiation with foreign governments is considered outside the jurisdiction of the Convention. Might I suggest you move a committee of delegates be struck to meet with the Governor to find out *how* we might go about ascertaining what economic or political arrangements, if any, Washington would be interested in making with Newfoundland if and when Responsible Government is restored.

While we're at it, of course, we should include approaches to Canada and England, as well. They can't vote against that, it's part of their mandate." Next day he was beaming, as his motion passed 30 to 8.

Poor old Job! As I suspected, the Governor approved the idea of missions to England and Canada, but he flatly rejected the idea of the Convention quid-pro-quoing with a foreign country like the United States.

I had won the first and most important round!

On my return from Ottawa, I discovered the Convention proceedings were being recorded and re-broadcast each evening from nine to midnight. My old boss, Bill Galgay, had managed to place a microphone almost directly in front of my desk. The fact that he ended up head of the CBC in Newfoundland after Confederation was, of course, a coincidence. But I hadn't worked for Sir Richard Squires for nothing, now, had I?

The idea, of course, was to take advantage of my radio experience and talk over the heads of the delegates, directly to all my old friends of the Barrelman days, telling the fishermen and their wives what I'd learned about the wonderful Canadian social security system.

(He races back behind his Convention desk.)

The Only Living Father   281

Mister Chairman, I have just completed 24 days explaining to this honourable body the terms and benefits Ottawa is willing to offer regarding union with Newfoundland. I, therefore, now move that this National Convention recommend to the British Government that Confederation with Canada be added to the ballot, as a choice in any forthcoming referendum.

(A new chorus of boos and catcalls erupts as JRS races to the centre table and snatches up a telephone.)

Phil? I've been trying to reach you all day. They defeated my new motion 29 to 16. Yes, and moved to dissolve the Convention. But never mind. Here's what we're going to do. I want you to get hold of our contacts in every district and get them to deluge the Governor with telegrams, demanding Confederation be put on the ballot paper.

He's ready to do it but he needs a wave of popular support as an excuse, get it? We want fifty thousand names. I don't care where you find them.

(He races back to a radio broadcast studio.)

People of Newfoundland, I am making this special radio broadcast tonight to denounce the twenty-nine dictators in the Convention who would deny you the chance to vote for or against Confederation with Canada in the forthcoming referendum.

I denounce their vicious plot to cheat our people of the democratic right to exercise their own judgement about the future of their country!

I appeal to the fisherman in every cove, every town, every settlement,every community, every bight and every bay to support us by sending me telegrams demanding Confederation be on the ballot. Send them in the hundreds, in the thousands, in the tens of thousands, in the hundreds of thousands, and set your country free.

(He races back down to the table and switches on a radio to hear a BBC announcer.)

"Here is a bulletin just released. His Majesty's Government in the United Kingdom wish to announce that, after due consideration, they have decided it would not be right that the people of Newfoundland be deprived of the opportunity to consider the issue of Union with Canada at the referendum, and have therefore agreed that Confederation should be included as a choice on the referendum paper ...".

(JRS leaps onto a chair and throws his arms in the air.)

Yahoo! We're going to win on June 3rd. We're going to win!

(He races off as the lights fade and we hear a burst of cheering, whistles and applause followed by a lively marching band playing the Newfoundland folk song "The Squid Jigging Ground".)

Act Two
Scene 1

(The lights fade up to discover JRS standing behind the centre table in trench coat and fedora, listening intently to the following song on a radio.)

THE ANTI-CONFEDERATION SONG

A Newfie boy was leaving his home for Labrador
To fish the same old fishing grounds
His father fished before.
And as he was leaving his mother
While standing on the quay;
He threw his arms around her neck
And this to her did say.

Don't vote Confederation,
And that's my prayer to you:
We owns the house we lives in
Likewise our schooner too;

But if you heed Joe Smallwood
And his line of French patois;
You'll be always paying taxes to
That tribe up in Ottawa.

(He switches off the radio and paces back and forth.)
There it is, boys, there's the enemy! That song! That song and that sentiment being spread about by our opponents in every outport. That's their trump card; the love of independence inherent in the soul of every Newfoundlander, and that bloody, clever ditty appeals to it. How do we fight that?
(JRS fits a cigarette into a black holder as he advances to the footlights to tell us in confidence.)
I'd gathered a small group of dedicated souls around me who believed in rescuing Newfoundland from itself, and formed the Confederate Association, and I got myself named Campaign Manager. My closest associates were a sardonic, witty poet named Greg Power and a rabid young leftist writer, Harold Horwood. Soon they had us dubbed the 'three Bolsheviks'. And so we were, because, like all true revolutionaries, we revelled in the knowledge that the establishment hated, despised, and most of all, feared us.
   We set up headquarters behind Bartlett's Barber Shop on Water Street. We had no money and little chance of raising any. Our challenge was to convince the fishermen of Newfoundland

The Only Living Father 283

they could enjoy the benefits of a modern social security system, and still retain their pride and independence.
(As the soundtrack brings us the second verse, he returns
to behind the table, pacing back and forth,
smoking and listening.)

> Our life has not been easy
> Our fight was hard and long;
> But if we have faith in ourselves
> We'll stay afloat and strong;
> We want no strangers in our crew,
> Let us be on our way
> And mark your X Responsible
> When comes the polling day.

You're right, Greg. You're right. Patriotism is the last resort of a scoundrel, and that's all our opposition has to flog. Apart from that they have no policies. They're divided. They're fighting. The only personable campaigner they have is Peter Cashin, and they don't want him. Some of them are even organizing a campaign for economic union with the United States. That'll divide 'em further, but it could be dangerous. We can discredit it by telling the Orangemen they'll have to give up the Union Jack and King Billy for Harry Truman and the Stars and Stripes.

That's why, gentlemen, in this campaign, I'm going to have to be a dictator. If that's too strong a word for you, let us say I'm going to be, not the main, but the one and only strategist, tactician, coordinator, band leader and orchestra conductor.

I'm going to organize and control every last detail of the campaign at this headquarters. I'm going to decide who goes on the radio for us, and dictate every syllable they utter. I'm going to monitor every word written in our newspaper so we'll have a united story from the beginning, following a single theme. I'm going to decide when and where all rallies are to be held, who the speakers will be. I'm going to be the only campaigner outside St. John's, so our message will be plain, clear, concise and articulate.

Is that plain, concise and clear to everybody here, and does everybody accept those conditions? Good. We've got a lot of work to do. Let's get at it.
(As the soundtrack brings in a round of cheering and applause
greeting him at a rally, JRS races downstage to leap onto a
ladder and begin his first election speech.)

Ladies and gentlemen, June third, 1948 is going to be the greatest day in the history of Newfoundland, because on that day a referendum will be held to decide your political future.

There'll be three choices on the ballot paper. The return of Responsible Government as it was in 1933. Retention of the present Commission Government, and number three ... number three, Confederation with Canada.

Let me put it plainly. Commission of Government means security, but no democracy, Responsible Government means democracy but no security, Confederation means democracy AND security, and you can have both on June third!

(As a burst of applause and cheering comes, he races back to headquarters.)

Irving, I'm just beginning to realize how many of the electorate can't read. Hire the best cartoonist in Canada for the newspaper, I don't care how much it costs. And Harold, Charlie Penney is heading for Ontario, get him to find every Newfoundlander he can and have them sign a joint letter advising everyone back home to vote for Confederation, and we'll publish it.

(He races across the stage and climbs on a chair for another rally.)

My friends, let's take the ballot choices one by one. Responsible Government as it existed in 1933. Does anyone here really want to go back to 1933? The hungry thirties, the depression? Does any man, woman, sister, brother, father, mother, uncle, aunt, adult or child want to go back to starvation? To corruption? To deprivation? Does anybody here want that? If your answer is no, go out today in your thousands and vote for Confederation with Canada.

(He leaps off the ladder and races across the stage to party headquarters.)

Sorry, boys. We had two flat tires on the way in from Carbonear. We had a wonderful rally, though. Packed to the rafters. There was no radio in the car. What's the latest count? Are we ahead or behind? Or what?

(He stares suddenly about him at their faces, then looks down to see a tally of paper on the table before him. He snatches it up to read the latest totals. He lays the paper down and looks about.)

We've lost? By more than 5000 votes. That's final, isn't it?

(He sinks slowly to the chair and pushes the paper aside, staring straight ahead, hypnotized.)

They couldn't surrender their bloody independence!

(Gently the soundtrack fades in a repeat of the verse that defeated him, and the lights fade to a pin spot only on his face.)

Don't vote Confederation,
And that's my prayer to you;
We own the house we live in,
Likewise our schooner too;
But if you heed Joe Smallwood,

And his line of French patois,
You'll be always paying taxes to
That tribe up in Ottawa.

*(Suddenly, the lights flash up to full and JRS jumps
up and grabs the tally paper back to stare at it.)*
Just a minute! We lost by only 5,334 votes, and look here, 20,000 civil servants voted for Commission Government to keep their jobs. That's the best news we've had since this thing started. No, I'm not gone completely 'round the bend. There was no clear majority, there'll be another referendum in a month, Commission of Government will be dropped from the ballot, and those 20,000 civil servants stand to DOUBLE their salaries under Confederation. Harold, we've got to get a couple of Commission Government members on the radio to TELL 'EM that! Illegal? Who gives a damn! Anything goes this time.

Greg, the Responsibles are trying to dump Peter Cashin, so let's help 'em along. Spread the word he's drinking again. I know, I know, but spread it anyway.

(He reacts to the startled looks on the faces of the committee, and roars out to the front of the table.)

Irving, we need money. Get a list of everyone you think who's interested in becoming a senator or a judge. The charge is $20,000 an appointment! Firm!

Harold, most of the losses around Carbonear and Harbour Grace were marginal. Get a list of every polling station in Conception Bay and see how we can change 'em.

(He snatches up a newspaper from the table.)
What's this? *The Catholic Monitor*? What do you mean, "come out against us"?

(He rips through the paper, trying to find the editorial, and reads it out.)

" ... We alone are asked to become a nation of shopkeepers, bartering our autonomy and self-competence for a political and economic mirage. We alone are asked to measure the issues in dollars and cents. My people, Confederation is not the answer to Newfoundland's problems..".

(He tears the paper to shreds in a fury and throws it down, and stamps about.)

The bastard. We'll teach that hypocritical Archbishop to poke his nose into politics. Alright! If that's the way he wants it, the gloves are off. We'll show that outport Machiavelli, that Borgia from Branch, what it means to interfere in a campaign.

Harold, remember that headline you showed me from the *Sunday Herald* about the nuns being allowed out to vote for the first time in Newfoundland? Go out and buy every copy you can and we'll mail them out to every Protestant Church in the country. Irving has the list.

And see if he can get this brought up at a meeting of the Orange Lodge. Get a circular letter out, or something to answer this garbage. Ask all loyal brethren to rise up and take action against this ... ah ... wait, I've got it: "deliberate attempt to manipulate a free referendum on Newfoundland's future". That's good. Write that down!

(The telephone rings, he snatches it up.)

Fred, how are you? Six senators, Fred. We've got the right to appoint six. No, Fred, it's just not true we've approached one hundred and twenty-seven people. Now, if you haven't got the $20,000, borrow it! You'll be getting sixty a year for the rest of your life. There's no better investment on the market, for God's sake! *(He slams up the phone.)*

Phil, there's a secret Ottawa list of big Liberal Party donors. Get hold of it. We can put the bite on the beer and liquor companies for an exclusive franchise down here after Confederation. Don't settle for less than $100,000 each.

(He snatches up a loud hailer from the table.)

I got three rallies in Bonavista tonight. George, did you get to see Sir Leonard? Well, see him by tomorrow. Tell him if he'll come out for us before polling day he's the Lieutenant Governor. Tell Albert he can be Chief Justice. I'm off.

(The soundtrack brings in a small Otter aircraft taking off, as JRS comes downstage right and climbs on a chair, using the hailer.)

How many children do you have there, madam, eh? Yes, you— How many children? Eight, you say? You have eight children all under sixteen? And do you have trouble keeping them in boots and shoes and clothes for school? Yes, indeed, don't we all! Then let me tell you something, madam. Three weeks after the twenty-second of July coming, if you vote for Confederation, three weeks after that date, you'll receive a cheque in the mail from the government of Canada, for five dollars for each of these eight children. And five times eight is forty, so you'll receive a cheque for forty dollars. And you'll get that money every month of every year for every child until the child passes sixteen.

And it doesn't matter if you work, or your husband works, or you both work, or if you have a bad year at the fishery or a good year, you'll get that money for your children, and that's what we call the great Canadian baby bonus!

(The sound effect of a plane takes him to a Labrador community.)

People of Labrador, you all know how this coast has been neglected by every Government since the era of the great William Coaker. But let me tell you tonight, these days of neglect are over. When Confederation comes, there will be a guaranteed price for

your fish and catch insurance in years of failure. There will be old age pensions for your mothers and fathers who live with you, thirty dollars a month, each, for life. There will be pensions for widowed mothers, the blind and disabled ...
(His voice starts to falter.)
There will be ... there will be ... I'm sorry ... my voice ...
(He climbs down and the sound effect brings us the plane departing. He crosses the stage and climbs on the ladder.)
My good friends in Bay Roberts, this is my last speech because you're going to the polls in an hour. Throughout this campaign, the St. John's merchants have called me a traitor. They called me a Quisling. They called me a Judas, who is selling Newfoundland up the St. Lawrence River for thirty pieces of silver.

But, if I can keep one child here from going hungry, ever again, I will be HAPPY to be a traitor, happy to be a Judas, happy to be a ...
(His voice fades again. The soundtrack brings in cheers and applause as he comes slowly down from the ladder.)
I gave fifty-six speeches in the last two and a half days of the campaign, and by the time I got back to St. John's, late on polling night, the radio stations had shut down, and there were no returns to listen to. I dared not go home. There were always a few thugs hanging about, hoping to rough me up, and this was a night they would especially love to do it.

Instead, I walked the streets of the sleeping city, unnoticed for hours, and then, exhausted, let myself into confederate headquarters.
(He crosses to stage left, sits, and picks up a polling list and starts to check it through, then pushes it aside and his head slowly sinks forward onto his arms, and in a moment, he is fast asleep. The soundtrack brings in a radio announcer's voice.).
"Good morning, ladies and gentlemen. Here is a bulletin from our St. John's studios.There is every indication that Confederation with Canada has won yesterday's referendum by a slim majority. While all returns are not in from outlying districts, these are expected to vote heavily for union with Canada. Up to this moment, totals available were Confederation, seventy-six thousand, three hundred and forty-three, Responsible Government, sixty-nine thousand, six hundred and seventy nine ...
(The soundtrack crossfades to Prime Minister St. Laurent's speech welcoming Newfoundland into Confederation and the Peace Tower carillon playing 'The Squid Jigging Ground', as JRS rises and crosses to above centre table.)
Gentlemen, I understand it was the intention to have Newfoundland become the tenth province of Canada at one minute past midnight, March thirty-first, as a convenience to the bureaucrats here in Ottawa, whose fiscal year begins at that

instant. However, I have persuaded the Prime Minister to place the official entry at three minutes BEFORE midnight. I have no intention of being known to generations of Newfoundlanders as the man who made them Canadians on April Fool's day.
(With a mischievous grin, he pulls out a chair and sits to sign a document, as the sound track brings us a stirring rendition of "O Canada" and the lights fade.)

Scene 2

(The centre table has been turned around so it resembles a cabinet room table. As the lights come up, JRS is discovered perched on the downstage end. He looks about for a moment in silence, then at the audience.)
   The Honourable Joseph R. Smallwood, Premier of Newfoundland.
(He waits a beat.)
   I never thought I'd see the day!
   And I almost didn't. After the referenda, a movement was started to dump me. Gordon Bradley thought HE should be Premier. Others proposed several prominent businessmen and lawyers. Sir Leonard Outerbridge, designated by Ottawa to be our first Lieutenant Governor, reportedly said he wasn't going to have 'that dreadful little man' as Premier. I threatened to blow the lid off the whole campaign strategy. Tell how they'd all sold out to Confederation, for a price. Bradley settled for a federal cabinet post, the rest ran for cover.
   Then came the great Cabinet boycott. I decided to bury the hatchet and ask several prominent merchants to serve as ministers. They all refused. To heal the wounds caused by the Orange Letter, I invited leading Catholic laymen to join: Bob Furlong, Frank O'Leary, Alan Fraser, Leo Murphy. They waited a day or two, then telephoned to decline. It was clear they had sought the Archbishop's permission and the answer was, "no".
   Very well, I said, to hell with the St. John's elite. I'll recruit school teachers, union leaders, Co-Op workers and fill the ranks with good baymen and true, and I did, and we christened it Her Majesty's Outport Government.
   (And he scurries to the head of the Cabinet table.)
   Good afternoon, gentlemen. Sorry to be late. I was on the phone to Baron Rothschild. That's Anthony de Rothschild, of the famed British banking house. We've been discussing a development scheme for Labrador.
   Now, it seems the first business of Cabinet today is to accept the resignation of Mr. Russell as Minister of Mines and Resources, and Mr. Horwood from the Legislature and the Liberal Party. That's too bad. They were among my closest supporters in

the fight for Confederation, and were voted in by substantial majorities in the recent election.

But now they don't agree with my great plans to industrialize the new province of Newfoundland.

They ridicule and criticize my slogan of "develop or perish".

They disagree with my conviction that the only recourse for poor, downtrodden, backward Newfoundland, the "sport of historic misfortune", the "Cinderella of the Empire", after countless bludgeonings and beatings, with her everlasting moratorium on hope, the only recourse is to be dragged, kicking and screaming, into the 20th Century with a great industrialization program.

Well, if they don't agree with me, perhaps the best place for these gentlemen is out of my government. So the resignations are accepted? All in favour? Contrary minded? Good.

To simplify this procedure in future, on the table in front of you, you will each see your own, undated letters of resignation from cabinet. Please sign them. They will be kept in my office drawer and released to the press when and if any of the rest of you see fit to disagree with government policy.

Now, I want to introduce to you the man I have hired as the new Director General of Economic Development for Newfoundland. He is a recent Latvian immigrant to Canada, a brilliant financial planner and economist who has worked under the renowned Doctor Hjelmar Shacht, the mastermind of Germany's financial and economic resurgence in the thirties.

Please don't be embarrassed if he addresses you as "Your Excellency". That is what he likes to call me, and that is the style of address for government ministers in Europe.

Gentlemen. May I present Doctor Alfred Valdmanis.

(The soundtrack gives us the Cabinet applause of 20 people.

JRS takes the opportunity to walk downstage to sit in an armchair.)

Myself and Doctor Valdmanis spent two years travelling Europe, looking for companies, mostly German, to come and set up manufacturing plants in Newfoundland. The idea was to build and operate them with government loans until they could be sold to private interests, using the profits to start more. By 1954 we'd given twenty million dollars in grants, to build plants making car batteries, rubber footwear, chocolates, cement, gypsum, asphalt, plywood and machinery. We approved ten million more in loans and advances to finance a set-up to extract magnesia from sea water, a tannery to make gloves out of gazelle skins, and an optical factory that would use a secret process to manufacture three hundred thousand eye-glass frames and forty-five hundred thousand lenses a year, supplying the one person in five in Canada who wore glasses. I said develop or perish and I meant it.

Unfortunately, the only thing that perished was most of the new industries.

And then, one day a Latvian engineer Valdmanis had brought in tugged at my coatsleeve on a parking lot. "Mr. Premier", he said, "would it be too much to ask if we could get inside your car and talk?"

We drove into the countryside. "Has Doctor Valdmanis ever made a contribution to your Liberal Party, Mr. Premier?" the man asked.

"No, of course not. Why should he?"

"Have any of your new industries given donations?"

"Never!"

"Are you aware then, Mr. Premier, that Valdmanis is collecting substantial commissions, allegedly for your Liberal party, on contracts negotiated with German companies?"

Back in my office in Confederation building, I made one of the hardest decisions in my life and called RCMP Superintendent McKinnon. A few days later, Alfred Valdmanis was arrested in Montreal on a warrant issued at my request, charged with extortion, pleaded guilty and sentenced to four years in prison.

Later, I heard a murky tale of intrigue in which he was supposedly paying blackmail to two Jewish refugees in New York to keep them quiet about his connections with Hitler and the Nazis.

(He stands before the chair.)

All this, of course, brought me the derision of my political opponents, and especially the local humorists when they discovered an enterprising lady from Montreal, named Germaine Plante, had set up a house of ill repute in St. John's to cater to the new industrial elite. *(He picks up a paper to read it.)*

> Joe said he'd build new plants and fact'ries
> From St. John's to Nain,
> But in a few short years we found
> One thing was very plain:
> The only plant to really make a profit was Germaine;
> She left for Montreal with forty grand;
> The country's in the very best of hands!

My plan to take up where Richard Squires left off and free Newfoundland from the curse of dependency on one resource was in a shambles. Perhaps the answer was to go back to that one resource and take up where William Coaker had left off.

(JRS crosses back to the Cabinet room and the head of the table, changing bow ties as he goes.)

Good morning, gentlemen. Sorry to be delayed. I've just been on the phone to one of the most important men in Ottawa, the Clerk of the Privy Council, Jack Pickersgill. I remember, the first time I met Jack was at a cocktail party he was giving in Ottawa in honour of the new British High Commissioner to Canada.

"Joe", he said, "I'd like you to meet Sir Peter Clutterbuck". What strange names, I thought as I shook hands, Pickersgill and Clutterbuck when, suddenly, Jack turned and said, "Now, Joe, I'd like to present the new American Ambassador to Canada, Charlie Wigglesworth".

(He takes a letter of resignation from his pocket, working himself slowly into a frenzy.)

But first, gentlemen, I am releasing to the press today a letter of resignation from the Minister of Public Works, Doctor Herbert Pottle. It seems he has decided this government should be investigated for corruption.

I think this is simply a case of the Pottle calling the kettle black? Wasn't he the member of the Commission Government who went on the air during the referenda and campaigned in favour of Confederation to swing the civil service vote to our side so he could be rewarded with a post in this cabinet?

Perhaps Dr. Pottle should be investigated for corruption?

Well, I can assure the ex-honourable Doctor, there will be no investigation, now or at any other time, of this government, because there IS no corruption in this government. I take it the resignation is accepted. Good.

(He simmers down.)

As far as our industrialization campaign is concerned, gentlemen, we go down one road, and if it doesn't lead us anywhere, we abandon it and try another. Newfoundland cannot stand still. We must go ahead, or go astern.

With that in mind, I want to announce to you today the inauguration of a great new Fisheries Revitalization Program. My plan is to spend one hundred million dollars revolutionizing Newfoundland's basic industry.

We have ten million dollars left of the treasury surplus on hand when we entered Confederation. Mr. Pickersgill will try and persuade Ottawa to supply the other ninety million dollars. If they won't, we'll borrow it and use their credit!

I don't mind admitting that perhaps we should have started out modernizing the fishery instead of trying to industrialize Newfoundland. And I don't mind it when people say the reason was Joe Smallwood always hated the fishery. Did everything in his power to turn his people away from their traditional link with the sea. Perhaps that's true.

I know I've always hated what it did to our people. I hated the odiferous pall of poverty that surrounded it. Hated the miserly pittance of a few cents a pound the fishermen received after standing up to their knees in the stench and guts and gurry of it from morning till night.

Well, that will all change! We're going to make up for that.

We'll build new trawlers, new plants, put white coats on the fish gutters, and sterilize the splitting tables with steam hoses. We'll bring the fishermen from thousands of isolated outports to centralized growth areas, teach them the latest catch technology from Norway, Iceland and Denmark, introduce hands-off vacuum unloading and devise new marketing strategies for the fresh fish trade.

I would now like to introduce the man I have hired to take charge of this great new program. He is a brilliant economist from British Columbia, a celebrated oceanographer and technologist, and founder and current Secretary General of the Fisheries Council of Canada. Gentlemen, Mr. Clive Planta.

(The soundtrack brings in the cabinet applause, as JRS exits and comes back down to his chair.)

Ottawa refused to go along with my fisheries program, so we tried it on our own. We doled out thirteen million dollars in loans to build numerous private fish plants. None of it was repaid. Soon, we ran out of money and had to abandon the scheme, leaving the Grand Banks once again to the Russians, the Spanish, the Portuguese, and the French.

Following revelations he had accepted personal loans from some of the Fish Companies to which we gave assistance, Mr. Planta left Newfoundland in disgrace.

(He rises from his chair.)

But, finally, in the midst of failure and discouragement, a triumph. A triumph that combined the greatest moment of my life with the greatest accomplishment of my political career.

(He crosses back into the Cabinet, changing bow ties again.)

Good afternoon, gentlemen. Sorry to be behind schedule. But I have just been talking with my good friend from New Brunswick, Lord Beaverbrook.

But first, it is my sad duty, today, to accept the resignation from Cabinet and government of the Honourable Gregory Power. He was my closest confidant, ally and friend in the great fight for Confederation. I have no further comment.

(He glares about him, daring anyone to speak, then proceeds.)

Gentlemen, the idea of forming a consortium to develop the seven million horsepower potential of Labrador's great Hamilton River has been on my mind ever since I first visited England in the 1920's. But the project has always needed the endorsement of some world-renowned figure to spark interest in the enterprise. I'm leaving for London tomorrow. Beaverbrook has gotten me an appointment with Sir Winston Churchill.

(The cabinet applauds dutifully in a standing ovation as JRS comes back downstage.)

Churchill met me at the door of 10 Downing Street with his usual glass of brandy and cigar and waved me to a chair. "You'll have a drink?" "No sir, thank you, I don't drink".

"You'll have a cigar?"
"No Sir ... but if you don't mind, I'll have a cigarette."
*(He stands, fits a cigarette into his holder,lights it
and paces about as he tells the story.)*
I leapt in with both feet.
"Labrador, Prime Minister, is the Alaska of eastern North America. Timber, iron ore, hydropower, a treasure-house all on its own. But developing it is too massive a project for any single company, any single government, any single country!
What we need is the greatest syndicate of business firms ever put together in the world: Industrial, mining, electrical, financial. I'm thinking of something like the old East India Company, sir, or Hudson's Bay ... a vast pool of commercial talent to launch a magnificent program of what you might call 'industrial colonization'. And it must be done at once!
*(He waits, staring at Churchill, then sits quietly, a little
embarrassed at his outburst, snuffing his cigarette.)*
After a long silence, he looked at me. "It is a grand imperial concept," he growled, "and I don't mean imperialIST".
"Thank you, sir. And, of course, we're going to name the project after you."
I wasn't back at my hotel more than an hour when the telephone rang. It was Anthony de Rothschild, inviting me to lunch. "Do you want us to put this thing together for you, Smallwood?" he asked.
"Yes, yes ... by all means." I said.
I knew I had changed the course of Newfoundland history for the second time.
But then the CURSE of Newfoundland history set in.
The Rothchilds formed the British Newfoundland Corporation to develop the power at what we now called Churchill Falls, and Consolidated Edison of New York agreed to purchase most of it. But the only way to get it down there was to feed it across Quebec. The newly nationalistic negotiating team headed by René Levesque insisted the only way they would permit that was if all power were sold to Quebec at the border, and at a low enough price to re-sell half to Con Ed for a profit. In addition they demanded changes in the Labrador boundary, 4000 French workers be guaranteed jobs at the site and all Quebec materials used. It looked like a stand-off, and everybody gave up on the project.
But I kept on fighting, arguing, negotiating, praying, bluffing. I threatened to have Prime Minister Pearson declare the project one of national interest, allowing Ottawa to seize the power corridor lands as federal territory. He was terrified. I had engineers survey an "Anglo-Saxon Route" across the Strait of Belle Isle, down Newfoundland's west coast, and back across the gulf to the Maritimes. It was too expensive.

Finally, on May 12 ... I'll never forget the date ... by May 12 1969, we had settled all disputes and agreed on a price that would make the project feasible to all sides. Quebec contracted to take delivery of 29 billion kilowatt hours a year for 40 years with an option to renew for another 25. The rest we could keep for ourselves. *(He sits, exhausted by the memory.)* I had been at it morning, noon and night for SEVENTEEN years!
(He suddenly sits bolt upright.)
Oh, I know what you're thinking. *(He rises again.)* I know what you're thinking. It was a lousy deal for Newfoundland in the long run. Joey Smallwood's greatest blunder. His biggest sell out! Well, let me tell you something, when that contract was signed no one said a word about oil prices going from $1.50 a barrel to-what are they today - $25? $30? Not a word. And no one even remotely suggested that as a result, Quebec would be buying our power for 2 mills and selling it for 70!
Among the greatest business brains in the world that we had assembled to launch the project, among the most sophisticated civil servants, the most experienced negotiators, not one single, solitary soul imagined Quebec could quadruple, quintuple, sextuple its profit within 5 years. No one had an inkling ... an inkling, that might occur. Not one!
And when the contract was ratified by the Newfoundland Legislature not a member of my cabinet, not a member of the Opposition voiced a syllable about putting in a re-opener clause. No one said a word. Of course, neither did I. Not a word. Why should I?
But when the poorest province in Canada ended up subsidizing one of the richest to the tune of a billion dollars a year, guess who got stuck with the blame?
Me, that's who! Joey Smallwood! No one else. Not Donald McPharland, who signed for the Consortium, not René Levesque, who refused the power corridor, not Anthony de Rothschild, not Con Edison, not Ottawa, not the British Government, but me alone! Joey. The idiot! The ersatz economist! The Gambo Galbraith. Not the great corporations who backed the deal: Klienwort-Benson, Prudential Insurance, Rio Tinto. Not my brilliant young lawyers in the Cabinet, John Crosbie and Clyde Wells. No. None of them. Just me!
(He plunks himself down in his chair in disgust.)
It's enough to make you vomit!
(He stuffs a cigarette in his holder while he calms down, then rises again to pace about.)
Well, there it was.
My greatest triumph turned to my greatest disappointment, as the economic breakthrough I had envisioned for Newfoundland never materialized. Once the construction jobs petered out,

we were in the same old rut, garnering a miserable pittance from our greatest natural resource while someone else raked in the profits.

But still I refused to accept defeat. I launched the exploration of the great iron ore field of western Labrador. I started sheep and cattle-ranching ventures. Shipyards. Gold mines. I even had the idea of lining the first twenty miles of the Trans Canada Highway eastward from Port aux Basques with flowering trees and shrubs that would come into blossom in succession throughout a period of several months each year. We would advertise it as the "world's longest Lovers Lane".

And then I had a revelation.

A revelation that for 20 years I'd been working virtually alone, eighteen hours a day at a pace that would have killed most men.

A revelation that, although I would never surrender my belief that Newfoundland could be rescued from economic isolation, suddenly I was tired, and couldn't summon up the old energy and imagination any more. A revelation that many of my old friends were gone; some alienated, many dead, the rest tired of my impossible posturing.

(He walks up to the cabinet table, sits behind it and picks up a phone and dials.)

Hello, Greg? Joe Smallwood. No ... don't hang up. I've got some news. I'm going to retire. Yes, it's true. I've finally realized I'm not Joey the revolutionary, the people's leader, the little fellow from Gambo any more. It's Joey the little tinpot dictator. The paperback Mussolini, the bayman's Schicklegruber.

(He laughs at Power's reply.)

I know. You told me that long ago. I can look forward to us getting together when I'm settled away, can I? Thanks.

(He hangs up, thinks a moment, picks up a volume of poetry, and comes back down to his chair.)

Greg Power! I'd always admired and envied his talent. My writing was propagandistic, confrontational, full of arguments and statistics. But Greg could be touchingly effective while driving the same message home in a few lines of verse.

I went home that evening and picked up a favourite poem he'd published as a young man. It's as good as anything Frost or Whitman ever wrote. Let me read you a fragment. It's called "The Price of Bread";

> On Sunday afternoon we went
> Around the cliffs to see the wreck ...
> We climbed her stranded hull and spent
> The sunshine on her splintered deck ...
> We watched the unrelenting sea
> That claimed so many of our dead
> And wondered why the gods agree

On such a dreadful price for bread.
(He lays the poetry aside.)
General Wolfe said, as he lay dying on the Plains of Abraham, that he'd rather have written Gray's "Elegy" than taken Quebec. And I began to feel I'd rather have written those lines than be Premier of Newfoundland.

It was time to get out. Patch things up with Greg. Reminisce about the great Confederation battles, and try and write something like that. "Don't wait to be kicked out, Joe", he'd always said. "Make the graceful exit, if it kills you".

But when word leaked out I was considering retirement, one of the bright young men I'd brought into my government couldn't wait. John Crosbie decided to stage a revolt with his colleague, Clyde Wells, over a $5 million bridge financing plan for my latest project, a great oil refinery at Come By Chance. When they both threatened to resign from Cabinet, I pulled the old trick on them. "No, you won't get that opportunity, because here are your resignations" and I pulled them from my pocket and threw them on the table. That night I had their House of Assembly desks moved across with the opposition benches. When they walked in the next day and tried to lug them back to the government side, they couldn't move them. I had the desks nailed to the floor.

The refinery ended up as the greatest bankruptcy in Canadian history.

Crosbie used this as an excuse to demand my resignation. I announced a great Liberal Party leadership convention that would, hopefully, endorse the man I chose to succeed me, not him.

(He jumps up.)

Let's see, now; who would I like to see in my place? Ed Roberts? Smart, experienced, but no imagination. No common touch. Billy Rowe? Too young. A lightweight. Richard Cashin? A Catholic. Don Jamieson? Would he leave a high profile cabinet post in Ottawa? Someone had to stop John Crosbie! That bully boy son of a merchant prince! That political climber! That grasping traitor wasn't going to take over MY Newfoundland. Rather than see John Crosbie premier, I'd run again myself!

(The lights dim almost out as the soundtrack brings in a stadium crowd chanting "Joey, Joey, Joey," and JRS rises and walks offstage for a costume change, and the soundtrack crossfades to an announcement over a P A system.)

Ladies and gentlemen, the results of the balloting to elect a leader of the Liberal Party are as follows.
Randy Joyce, 13. T. Alex Hickman, 187. John C. Crosbie, 440. Joseph R. Smallwood, 1,040.

(The soundtrack repeats the delirious chants of "Joey, Joey, Joey," and then dissolves to a band playing his new theme song,

The Only Living Father

"Hello Dolly". As the lights come up on stage, JRS re-appears in a white tropical suit with purple shirt and matching tie and steps into a spotlight to acknowledge the cheers with a prize-fighter gesture, arms over his head. After a few moments, he walks down to the audience, showing off his suit.)
What do you think ...?
This is what a Toronto Public Relations outfit I hired did to me! Let's see if it's going to work.
(He crosses the stage and climbs on his ladder.)
My friends, I have called an election for October 28, and I come to seek your support once more. October 28 is the feast of Saint Jude, the patroness of hopeless cases, but I am not a hopeless case, as some would have you believe. I am a leader of experience, vision and success. Seventy-five years old, but vigourous and strong as ever, ready to serve a full five year term as Premier of Newfoundland. A full five year term!
(Cheers and applause from the soundtrack change to boos and chants of "Ho, Ho, Ho chi Minh" as he crosses to another area for another rally.)
Oh yes, you young people mock me now, and taunt me with cries of Ho Chi Minh. Very well. That is your right. You are like young people everywhere, it's easy to get you to turn against something. It's harder to find out what you are for. Your leader, John Crosbie, has finally shown his true colours by joining the Tories. But let me tell you tonight, I did not wrest Newfoundland from the greedy claws of the merchants in 1949 just to hand it back now, on a silver platter, to their sons like Frank Moores and John Crosbie. Not on your life.
(Cheers and applause from the soundtrack as he crosses the stage to another rally point and mounts a chair.)
Voters of Fogo district, an old friend calls on you tonight for one last favour. After what we have been through together, this past quarter century, I think you owe me that. God bless you for your support in the past, now let me have it one more time. Make one last trip to the ballot box for Joey.
(The soundtrack band strikes up "Hello Dolly" again as he climbs down and races off and we hear a TV announcer's voice.)
Ladies and gentlemen, the CBC decision desk tonight can reach no decision, because the Newfoundland election has resulted in a virtual tie. The Tories under Frank Moores have won twenty-one seats, Joey Smallwood's Liberals have won twenty, and there is one independent member who could support either side. Premier Smallwood has refused to resign.
(JRS marches on, still in his white suit, and comes to the centre table and picks up a ringing phone.)

Resign? If I fail to get a majority when I meet the House of Assembly I'll resign. Until then, I'm still the Premier of Newfoundland, remember that. *(He hangs up the phone.)*. How the hell did they find out I was in Florida?
(He rubs his hands together, gleefully.)
Resign, with a tie election on the go? For God's sake, this is just my cup of tea!
(He yells off stage as the phone rings.)
Steve? Get in here. Quick. *(He grabs up the phone.)*
Gerry? I've been trying to get you. I'm at Al's condo. Listen, we lost your St.Barbe district by only eight votes. I need some time to manoeuvre, so file for a re-count. But we want it delayed for a few months, so something's got to happen to a few ballots before the court seizes them. What? I don't know. Use your imagination. Richard Squires used to call it spontaneous combustion.
(He bangs up the phone.)
Idiot!
(He turns to meet Steve, and start pacing back and forth, the old adrenalin flowing again.)
Steve. Our little independent Member for Labrador is starting to shoot off his mouth that he's the king-maker. Holds the balance of power. John Doyle's private jet is in Lab City. I don't care how you do it, but get Tom Burgess on that plane and down here. We've got to find out what he wants. A cabinet post. Money. Whatever. He's got to support our side, give us a tie and force a new election.
(The phone rings, he grabs it up.)
Joe? I'm having Burgess flown down here. Sort of take him to the mountain top, you know. What? He's decided to go with Crosbie and Moores? For how much? They would? I don't believe it.
(He bangs up the phone and yells off.)
Damn! Twenty-two to twenty. Now they can elect a speaker and have a majority.
Steve! I want a list of every Tory candidate elected. How much money they owe and to who, mortgages, personal guarantees, you name it. And the alcoholic one? Put Ed onto him. When the House opens, we want his seat empty.
(He comes down to the audience.)
When officers of the Supreme Court went to seize the ballots in St. Barbe South, they discovered Mrs. Olive Payne, the returning officer at the polling station in Sally's Cove had mistakenly burnt hers in her wood stove before going to bed on election night. So help me God, I had nothing to do with it.
But I immediately requested that district election be declared null and void. Then I got hold of young Ricky Cashin, President of the Fishermen's Union, and promised him the Premiership if

The Only Living Father

he'd run in a by-election.
(A sound effect of a radio flash, as JRS goes back to the desk.)
Here is a bulletin. The Newfoundland Supreme Court has declared the controversial election in the district of St. Barbe South valid, and the Tory candidate elected. Damn! Damn! Damn! Damn! Damn!
(The phone rings, he snatches it up, then leans back.)
Well, well. Mr. Burgess. Welcome to Florida. You're leaving the Tories? You and Hughie Shea, together? Oh, yes, I'm definitely willing to talk. I'll have my car pick you up this evening. Here's something to think over in the meantime. I'm willing to announce my resignation and call a leadership convention for February. You can win with my support and money. Then dissolve the House and ask for a new election. The momentum should guarantee you victory and the Premiership. How's that sound? Great. At eight? Looking forward to our chat.
(He hangs up the phone.)
Steve! You know the crackpot elected for the Tories who owns the grocery store? He's crossing the floor with Burgess, because they won't give him a cabinet post. Get hold of him. Tell him I'll make him Minister of Supply and Services. *(He rubs his hands.)* 22 to 20!
(The phone rings.)
What? When? Damn! *(He slams down the receiver.)*
Gus Oldford resigned today as Liberal member for Fortune Bay. They got to him.
(The phone rings. He grabs it up again.)
Bill? Bill Saunders. How are you. Thanks for returning my call. I'm just checking up on my caucus members, getting ready for the House opening ... What do you mean, you're not going to show up? *(He listens a minute.)* Now, look, Bill, we go back a long way you and I. You were one of the first confederates in Bay de Verde ... now, listen, Bill, Gus Oldford just quit, we can't afford to lose' another Liberal seat. What are they offering you. I'll match it ... Bill ... wait! *(He bangs up the phone and leans back, exhausted.)*

(The lights slowly dim on JRS and he exits for a costume change as the CBC TV announcer's voice comes back.)
As the House of Assembly met today the seat of another Liberal MHA was mysteriously empty. No one could explain the absence of William Saunders, recently re-elected in Bay de Verde, who stands to lose a sessional indemnity payment of $10,000 and a pension from the House for life by not showing up. Meanwhile, Independent member Tom Burgess announced he would be supporting the Tories, giving them twenty-one seats to

the Liberals nineteen. Premier Frank Moores has announced his intention to formally request the Lieutenant Governor for a dissolution of the Legislature, and a new election if Saunders resigns as expected.

(The closing theme music starts and fades to background as JRS comes slowly down to sit in his chair. He wears a dressing gown over black trousers and carries a biography of John Wesley.)

How silly we are not to know when the time has come to go. But that's the hardest decision any successful politician has to make. And I think I was a successful politician, at least. Anyway, I had the satisfaction of giving those Tory buggers a run for their money.

I retired to my farm on Roche's Line, pretending that I would enjoy my new-found tranquillity, telling the newspapers I was delighted, at last, to have the time to read a new biography of John Wesley. *(He throws the book aside.)*

Does anyone realize what a boring life John Wesley had?

(He jumps up and strips off his dressing gown and flings it over a chair, goes to his coat rack to put on his homburg, black coat and silk scarf as he talks.)

No! Retirement was not for me!

I decided I'd fulfil a long time ambition and travel. I toured China, Cuba and visited Russia with Richard Nixon, who was also recently out of a job. As the Only Living Father of Confederation, I collected honourary degrees from a dozen Canadian Universities, and became a celebrated after dinner speaker. I especially enjoyed several engagements in Germany, where the custom is to list ALL the guest's honourary degrees.

(He comes downstage in his "Premiers" outfit, counting the titles off on his fingers.)

So I would be introduced as Doctor, doctor, doctor, doctor, doctor, doctor, doctor, doctor, doctor, doctor, doctor, doctor Smallwood.

Back home, I decided to start on a long cherished dream, writing an Encyclopedia of Newfoundland: three volumes, maybe four or five. And then, what about a complete, updated history of the province, perhaps a new autobiography, telling all ...

And then ...

(There is a sting of music to denote a stroke he suffered shortly after retirement. After a moment it fades to silence, and in the distance we hear, faintly, that Christmas chorus singing "Angels We Have Heard On High" again, and it gradually comes to full volume. JRS walks to centre stage as the carol fades again.)

Well, well, another Christmas here again ... and so soon? Another birthday. One good thing about being born on Christmas Eve, is I'll always be remembered for that, won't I?

The Only Living Father

When they're celebrating in Newfoundland, even a thousand years from now, there'll be someone who'll remember and say ... "Joey was born on Christmas Eve too, wasn't he?"

What else will I be remembered for, I wonder? I enjoyed being "The Only Living Father of Confederation"? That was a nice title, but, of course, it demands certain qualifications. My Centralization scheme? Breaking the IWA strike?

Unfortunately, like most politicians, I'll probably be remembered for my mistakes. Not for the bridges I built, the hospitals I opened, or the hope I put in a hundred thousand hearts.

(The Christmas carol is replaced by the closing theme music as
  JRS takes off his black coat, silk scarf, homburg and horn
  rimmed glasses, and lays them on the table's front edge.)

Ah, well, maybe I should have stayed a reporter and a writer. Writers have it better than politicians. Their mistakes remain unpublished and only their success is noted.

I really haven't done enough serious writing to be remembered for that. But I did start my encyclopedia, and I'm sure they'll finish it for me.

And perhaps, some day, some young student at the Smallwood Institute for Newfoundland Studies at Memorial University — my University that I built — perhaps they'll be looking something up and turn to a friend and say:

"This writer fellow, Smallwood. He was in politics for a while, too, wasn't he?"

(And he turns and walks off into the darkness, as the music
  swells and the lights fade to a pinpoint on his trademark
  bow tie, homburg, glasses, white scarf and black coat.)

Curtain

Tomorrow Will Be Sunday

1992

Adapted and Written by

Des Walsh

Production History

This adaption of Harold Horwood's novel *Tomorrow Will Be Sunday* was commissioned by Rising Tide Theatre, Donna Butt – Artistic Director, and workshopped and developed through Rising Tide Theatre's New Play Development Program in June, 1992. This adaptation was given a public reading on June 28, 1992.

Performers: Rick Boland, Brian Downey, Randy Follett, Charles Herriott, Amy House, Ed Kielly, John Ryan, and Berni Stapleton.

Dramaturge: Guy Sprung

The world premier of this adaptation of *Tomorrow Will Be Sunday* was a co-production of Rising Tide Theatre and the Division of Cultural Affairs and was presented at the St. John's Arts and Culture Centre, St. John's, Newfoundland, September, 1992, with the following cast:

ELI PALLISHER	Mark Critch
ELIAS PALLISHER	John Ryan
MARTHA PALLISHER	Berni Stapleton
JOSHUA MARKADY	Michael Wade
BROTHER JOHN MCKIM	Rick Boland
VIRGINIA MARKS	Janet Edmonds
CHRISTOPHER SIMMS	Brian Downey
CROWN LAWYER	Todd Hennessey
DEFENSE LAWYER	Glenn Downey
JUDGE	Michael Chaisson

SISTER LEAH and other members of the congregation were played by members of the cast.

Directed by Guy Sprung
Set Design by Gerald Squires
Lighting Design by Peter Conroy
Sound Design by Paul Steffler
Costume Design by Marie Sharp
Stage Managed by Neil Robbins

TOMORROW WILL BE SUNDAY

Act I
Scene 1:
Wharf In Outport Newfoundland (*ca.* 1940's.)

(ELI PALLISHER and his father, ELIAS, are standing on a wharf. ELIAS is putting fuel in a drum, he is preparing for a trip ... sounds of the seashore are heard, there is a strong wind ... then the unmistakable cry of an eagle.)

ELI: Look at the eagle, father ...
(There is a pause here for the audience to watch both father and son silently study the wheeling arc of the predatory bird making its looped survey of the hills around the harbour. To ELI, its search for food not unlike their own; to ELIAS, an omen. He continues with his work while ELI's eyes are fixed on the bird.)
ELIAS: I caught one on a baited hook just off here when you were just a baby ...
ELI: What did you do with it?
ELIAS: Nothin' ... you couldn't tame it. Jabez Squire's dog fought it to the death ... That was some sight, I'm tellin' ya ... the dog was tore up somethin' pitiful and he wasn't any use after that ... but he killed that eagle fair and square ...
ELI: That's terrible ... it wasn't fair ... he was caught with a hook and line ... why didn't somebody try and stop it?
ELIAS: And why should they ... what good is an eagle, boy? Like I said, one of the devil's birds ... it even hissed like a snake when the dog tore out its windpipe ... death is not far if you see an eagle ...
(A woman's voice is heard calling.)
MARTHA: Elias ...
(ELIAS looks up to see his wife, MARTHA, approach. She carries supplies. ELI continues his observations of the eagle while pondering the words of his father.)
MARTHA: Shouldn't you wait till the sea goes down ... you're foolish to put out in this.
ELIAS: I've been out in worse ... and for worse reasons, too. Somebody got to go for the nurse and that's all there's to it.

MARTHA: Well ... here's a lunch, and the kettle ... a change of dry clothes are in there, too ...
ELI: Is the Pike baby gonna die?
MARTHA: That'll be up to the Lord, Eli, not us ...
ELIAS: Make sure you finish with the wood, Eli, and see to it that the ...
ELI: (*Interrupting.*) If I'm as good on the water as you say I am, why won't you take me?
MARTHA: 'Cause I'm not goin' to lose me whole family the same day.
ELIAS: You're to stay here with yer mother Eli ... I've told ye ... finish with the wood and be sure to salt those fish and don't interrupt when I'm speakin', do ya hear?
ELI: Yes father ...
    (*ELIAS turns and continues with his labour.*)
MARTHA: Help your father put his things aboard ...
    (*ELI silently passes items to his father. He will do what he's told.*)

Scene 2:
Joshua Markady's House

(*JOSHUA MARKADY, an older man with years of experience at sea, and ELI are seated at a table. There is a well-stocked bookshelf behind them. This is a modest, yet comfortable, environment. ELI notices a book on the table.*)
ELI: Lord Jim ... by Joseph Conrad ...
JOSHUA: That's a good book ... do ya read much?
ELI: Yes sir ... all the time. I fell asleep reading the other night and burned the wick out of the lamp ... I had some quick trimming to do in the morning I can tell you that.
JOSHUA: Take it and read if ya like ...
ELI: I'll bring it back as soon as I'm finished it ...
JOSHUA: There's just one more little bit of business.
    (*ELI is confused as JOSHUA takes a wrapped bundle of brown paper about four or five feet long and places it on the table in front of him.*)
JOSHUA: Well go on ... open it.
    (*JOSHUA is delighted with the game as he watches ELI unwrap the parcel and produce a brand-new, single-shot, twelve-gauge breech-loader; with it, a box of shells.*)
ELI: My God ... it's beautiful ...
JOSHUA: Look at the name on the stock ...
    (*ELI looks at the gleaming brown stock. His delight is heard in his voice.*)
ELI: Eli ... it says Eli Pallisher!
JOSHUA: That's fer savin' me from being wrapped up in kelp ...

ELI: I only did what was right ... I don't expect to be paid for that.
JOSHUA: Well you had the sense to crawl out to me with a ladder after me goin' through the ice. That fool Jehu Gilmore, rantin' and ravin' from the landwash, watching a young boy do what he should've done.
(Pause.)
(JOSHUA laughs.)
JOSHUA: There he was bawling out, "the hour be at hand an' the wrath of God be terrible upon the heathens." That's what you wanna' hear when you're after goin' through the ice twenty feet from the shore ... no, my son, it's not payment, it's more of squarin' up.
ELI: He wasn't thinking, I suppose ...
JOSHUA: By Christ, Eli, you're a forgiving soul, brave like your father but just as damn forgiving. I'm calling for the man to throw me a rope 'til I see you, and I'm shoutin' "Jehu Gilmore, by the bleeding Christ, when I get ashore I'll ram that Goddamn bible down your hymn-singing throat".
(There is a silence. JOSHUA senses ELI's discomfort.)
JOSHUA: They're just words, boy, like any others ...
(ELI stands in amazement and places the stock to his shoulder.)
ELI: The feel of it is unbelievable ... not as heavy as the old one I'm using.
JOSHUA: I trust ya with it. I'm sure ya can handle it ...
ELI: ... "thank you" doesn't seem like enough.
JOSHUA: It certainly is ... I expect no more than that about it.
*(ELI studies the gun and is proud. He has won the
respect of JOSHUA.)*

Scene 3:
Twine Loft

*(ELI and his father are mending a net. ELI shows the same
dexterity, as both move quickly with the wooden needles.)*
ELIAS: I was puttin' away to buy ya one meself ...
ELI: I know, father ... but where he went to the trouble of putting my name on it ... anyway, now you can use that money to start saving for yourself. Maybe you and mother take a trip ... the Boston States ...
(ELI and his father laugh.)
ELIAS: That's just where I need to go now ... the Boston States. 'Though I s'pose if I turned starboard off Lattice Harbour point and kept goin' I'd get there.
(Both share the humour then continue silently with their task.)
ELIAS: Careful with where your line is crossin', you've got it doubled there now, you won't tie off in the right spot and ye'll make a mess of it ...

(ELI sees the mistake and quickly corrects it. They quietly continue with their work.)
ELIAS: It'll soon be time fer ya to get shares in the boat with me, I s'pose.
(ELI can hardly believe what he hears. He does his best to contain his excitement but bursts out with glee.)
ELI: Do you mean it, father? Can you afford to ... my own shares ... I'd send away for things ... I could order books ...
(ELI calms himself, aware of his father questioning the outburst.)
ELI: I'm sorry, father, ... it's just that I'll be the first one in the harbour my age to get his own shares ...
(ELIAS smiles.)
ELIAS: Well, boy, ya certainly did yer share of the work this season ... and if ye weren't with me, I'd have to be payin' someone, and I'd rather give the money to me own ...
(ELI tries to contain his pleasure. This is an entry into the world of pay, his initiation is over.)
ELI: I don't expect it, father ... I'm not doing it for money.
ELIAS: I know that, son, but 'is not right to work and not be paid ... but yer bills will be yer bills, mind ya ... and don't you take anything on credit from Solomon Mark's store, just because ya think ya got money ... be in debt to no man, ya understand?
ELI: Yes, father.
(Both continue with their net-mending. ELIAS studies his son's work, to see it's being done properly.)

Scene 4:
Pallisher House

(ELIAS, ELI and MARTHA are seated at the kitchen table for the evening meal. ELI is reading as he eats.)
MARTHA: Accordin' to Ida, he's arm is swole up like an apple ... and, Eli, you with a horse stinger for a pet last year ... feedin' it house flies in a gallon jar.
(ELI doesn't look up from his book.)
ELI: They're called dragonflies and they don't sting ...
ELIAS: Dragonflies ... who told ya that?
ELI: I read it in a book on insects.
MARTHA: Was that the book with the pictures of those spiders that eat each other?
ELI: They're called black widows, mother, the female eats the male after they ... ah ... after ... well she eats him.
MARTHA: And what about those long, skinny things that pray?
(ELIAS is getting impatient with the conversation, one that he's not part of.)
ELI: That's the praying mantis ... the Latin name is *mantis re-*

ligiosa ...
ELIAS: Never mind yer Latin my son ... an insect prayin' ...
(ELI demonstrates the position of the mantis and raises his arms, putting his hands together.)
ELI: They look like this ... their front legs look like they're praying ...
ELIAS: Well, I'd say it's time to get yer nose out of a book that teaches ya that 'cause it's foolishness and makes a mockery ... and as fer yer dragonflies, that person that wrote the book was never around here 'cause if they were they'd know they were horse stingers and could leave a bump on ya as big as a turnip.
MARTHA: There's no harm in a book on insects, Elias, and sure you know yourself some calls an emmet an ant ...
ELIAS: Can we eat our suppers without talkin' about insects prayin' and eatin' each other?
(ELI and MARTHA smile at each other but continue quietly with their meal.)
ELI: You know the new minister, don't you father?
ELIAS: Brother John McKim ... I've heard of 'em.
(All are silent again.)
MARTHA: They say he talks to God.
ELIAS: They say he has a special gift. And that's what this harbour needs, someone to talk to God before He turns his back on us all.
ELI: How did Pastor Tishrite get sick so fast? I saw him just before he left and he looked fine ...
(ELIAS and MARTHA look at each other.)
ELIAS: Eat your supper.
(The Pallisher family finish the meal in silence.)

Scene 5:
Government Wharf

(As many of the cast and any extras that can be used are on the wharf to meet the new minister. Suitcases and boxes are on the dock. BROTHER JOHN McKIM steps into the circle of the curious onlookers, behind him SISTER LEAH, a cold, stern-faced woman who says nothing.)
BROTHER JOHN: And He shall send His angels with a great trumpet to gather the elect from the four winds. To the chapel brethren. I want to meet ye in the house of the Lord and now's as good as time as any.
(BROTHER JOHN sees ELI.)
BROTHER JOHN: Come along with those cases, boy ...
(ELI is seen picking up a suitcase as the gathering, sheep-like, follow the new minister to the chapel. He is pulled aside by VIRGINIA MARKS, the merchant's daughter.)
VIRGINIA: I know why Pastor Tishrite had to leave and why we

got him ...
ELI: He got sick and had to go ... everyone knows that ...
VIRGINIA: Not likely, Eli ... have you seen the stomach on Bertha Penchley lately ... half of what's in there belongs to Pastor Tishrite.

Scene 6:
Chapel

(BROTHER JOHN McKIM, the new minister, is giving his sermon in the small chapel. ELI and his father and mother are there, as well as VIRGINIA MARKS, only a few years older than ELI. Here we see her uninterested and bored during the service, a contrast to the others.)
BROTHER JOHN: Behold the Lord cometh, burning with anger, his lips full of indignation, and his tongue a devouring fire ... the Lord cometh, not in some far-off future time, but now, here, in *this* place and time. That is the message I bring ye—the imminent coming of the day of the Lord.
(ELI and his parents and any extras shift a little as BROTHER JOHN's voice increases its range.)
BROTHER JOHN: God in the form of the awful shape of Justice come to judge the earth, his eyes burning with coals of fire, his tongue a river of flame, licking over the forests and the mountains and the isles of the sea ... for behold, the day cometh when the mountains shall flow down like wax and the slain of the Lord shall be at that day from one end of the earth even unto the other. They shall not be lamented, neither gathered nor buried. They shall be dung upon the ground. And the stink shall come out of their carcasses, and the mountains shall be melted with their blood, and the heavens shall be rolled together as a scroll, and the stars fall from their places.
VOICES: Even so, come Lord Jesus ... save us Jesus ... we hear you Lord ... Amen ...
BROTHER JOHN: For these things are to happen here upon the earth, not in some far-off day of judgement beyond the grave, but right here, in the land that we know, and in our own day ...
(BROTHER JOHN pauses. VIRGINIA is bored.)
Look ...
(He points to a single church window, which dimly lit until now, illuminates itself more clearly to the audience.)
Think of the day when *these* mountains shall melt, and *this* forest shall go up in a puff of smoke like a feather dropped in a fire ...
(His voice calms itself.)
Yea, as I shall show ye, the year and the hour is upon us when the Lord shall descend from heaven with a shout and with the voice of the archangel and the great sound of a trumpet, for I am sent

Tomorrow Will Be Sunday

unto you even as was John the Baptist to the lost sheep of the House of Israel, to proclaim the coming of the great and terrible day of the Lord.

VOICES: Yes, Lord, we hear you ... shine your light Jesus ... we praise the word.

(The lights go down on the congregation.)

Scene 7:
The Pallisher House

(BROTHER JOHN is at Eli's house; ELIAS is there as are two or three other elders of the harbour. They are sitting around a table. ELI has a pencil and paper. We see MARTHA busying herself with other work. She is off to the side, aware but not participating in the conversation. She watches her son with pride.)

BROTHER JOHN: Ye see it, do ye not?

(ELIAS and ELI look over the piece of paper.)

From the time of the Abomination of Desolation ... and ye take forty years and add that ...

ELIAS: The years between Adam's creation and the crowning of King David, from those between Noah's flood and the birth of Christ ... do you have the figures, Eli?

(ELI is busy with his pencil and paper. He looks at it for a moment, then passes it to his father who in turn passes it on to BROTHER JOHN.)

BROTHER JOHN: There it is ... the year of the antitypical flood, the great Time of Trouble that should overwhelm the world, and to the crowning of the antitypical David, the Lord in glory.

ELIAS: It is, indeed ... there's no getting around it.

BROTHER JOHN: Ay, brother, the Lord has opened yer eyes. The years from the Babylonian captivity, when the Lord's favour was withdrawn from the House of Israel accordin' to the flesh, to the date when all things should be fulfilled in the consummation of Israel according to the spirit ... what figure do you have, boy?

(ELI busily scribbles on his paper, then looks up.)

ELI: It's the same year ...

ELIAS: So it is, it's prophecy.

BROTHER JOHN: Are you sure, lad?

ELI: Yes, sir ... I did it two different ways to check.

(BROTHER JOHN lays his hands on ELI's shoulders.)

BROTHER JOHN: You seem to be a very likely boy, Eli ... smarter than any I've seen for quite a time. Ye have more than your share of talents from the Lord, seems to me. Pray ye use them wisely child, for the Lord will demand an accountin' of every gift ...

(We see MARTHA's pleasure at the recognition of her son's abilities.)

ELIAS: He's a trusting boy ... we're hopin' for him.
BROTHER JOHN: He's old enough for conversion, Elias. He should think about seeking the Lord ...
(BROTHER JOHN looks at the piece of paper again.)
BROTHER JOHN: That's it, then ... the fulfilment of the prophecy will be a week from Wednesday coming.

Scene 8:
Joshua Markady's House

(We see JOSHUA there alone, reading, when VIRGINIA MARKS, the girl from church and a neighbour's daughter, comes in.)
JOSHUA: Hello, Virginia, ... and how are we today?
VIRGINIA: Bored as always ... did ya hear Eli's story about Sister Leah ... Brother John's wife ... and the bear?
JOSHUA: What bear?
VIRGINIA: She told Eli that when her and Brother John were down the coast, she caught a black bear this one morning, out on a flake, helping himself to the fish. The women barred themselves and the children inside, and it seems Sister Leah, having nothing more than a broom, drove him off ... I'd say it's a pack of lies.
JOSHUA: Do you believe it, Eli?
(VIRGINIA looks around the room, startled.)
JOSHUA: I know you're outside the door, Eli, I saw you look in through the window ... now c'mon in here and stop eavesdroppin'.
(The door opens and in comes ELI. He has a book in his hand.)
ELI: I was bringing back your book ...
VIRGINIA: Why you little sneak ...
ELI: And you're calling Sister Leah a liar ...
JOSHUA: I can well believe if that woman got mad it'd take more than a bear to stare her down. You mark my words, Eli, if that woman ever gets into heaven the Lord God will either have to mend his ways or move out ... Sister Leah the Pure.
VIRGINIA: See ... old Josh thinks she's a liar ...
JOSHUA: That's not what I said, Virginia, and, for Christ's sake, stop callin' me old Josh ... not out for any birds today, Eli?
ELI: No, sir, ... I'm getting ready for the service tonight ...
VIRGINIA: That's not what I'd call it ...
JOSHUA: I've heard pretty well everybody in the harbour is plannin' to meet out at the graveyard tonight to wait for the end of the world, practically under my window.
ELI: Aren't you a little bit scared ... what if it's true ... the prophecy?
VIRGINIA: Boo!
(Eli and JOSHUA jump.)

JOSHUA: The only thing I'm concerned with, boy, is a crowd of ignorant fools in this harbour. I wouldn't do any of 'em any harm, and in the ordinary way I'd trust them with me life. But I was never one to take chances with a mad dog, even if it was me own.
ELI: Nobody'll bother you, you know that ...
JOSHUA: Most likely not, but you see that you tell your father that there's a good hundred and fifty feet of clear space between my house and the graveyard road and that any man sets a foot on the property between now and tomorrow noon is liable to be shot like a seal.
VIRGINIA: Sure you might be blamed for it if the Lord decided not to show tonight ...
(JOSHUA looks annoyedly at VIRGINIA then directs his attention back to ELI.)
JOSHUA: Just tell yer father so as he'll tell the others.
ELI: Yes, sir ...
JOSHUA: I don't mean to scare ya any more than you are, Eli, I'd just as soon have you at the house with me, away from it all, but that would cause a row for sure ... Good Christ, there's not a man on this coast will be able to tell a sail from a bedsheet ... only quote the Bible and accuse his neighbour ... come see me tomorrow when all this foolishness is over ... I'm thinkin' about buildin' a new boat this year and I'd like you to help me with her ... you seem the only one left around here who got any interest ...
ELI: Being pure like Sister Leah isn't bad for any of us.
JOSHUA: Not at all, boy. But if the world was ruled by those blind, the pleasure of sight would be counted a mortal sin. No, my boy, you go ahead and be as pure as ya can manage, but if ya find yourself slippin' into a small sin now and then, don't let it prey on your mind. Many a saint have sinned without losin' his immortal soul.
VIRGINIA: Brother John callin' out to me, "the harvest is past, the summer is ended, and we are not saved". He scared the friggin' life out of me ... I don't know how ya can stand it, Eli, Brother John over to your house all the time ...
ELI: You haven't even talked to him, Virginia, you don't know what he's like ...
VIRGINIA: He's like all of them ... and Sister Leah, I'm not goin' to bow and scrape to her I can tell you that ...
ELI: It's all right for you to get on your high horse ... you're a girl.
VIRGINIA: And what's that got to do with it?
ELI: You don't have your father standin' over you.
VIRGINIA: Ha ... you don't know my father as well as you think, young Eli Pallisher. He mightn't belt me but he'd lock me up and feed me on bread and water till I crawled on my belly if he wasn't afraid I'd be more his match in the end. Even when I was younger than you are now, I knew you couldn't let people shove

you around.
          (JOSHUA gets up from his seat.)
JOSHUA: Is this what the two of you come here for, to have me listen to ye squawk?
          (ELI and VIRGINIA ignore him and continue.)
ELI: You're not much older than me, Virginia, and nobody's shovin' me around, but it seems we might all be in the Kingdom before any of us have much to say about it ...
VIRGINIA: You don't really believe all that nonsense about the end of the world, do you?
ELI: They got me to add up all the dates for them, and it really did work out ... six or seven different ways, too ...
JOSHUA: Well, well, well ... the end of the world. That's it, you two out of here and go on about your business. I've got to make a lunch and prepare to meet me maker, I suppose ...

Scene 9:
Pallisher House: Part Scene/Part Dream Sequence

(This scene will utilize pre-recorded sound to enhance the mood and the surreal ambience needed.)
ELIAS: There'll be no more talk about it ...
ELI: Mother ...
MARTHA: The wind has turned, Eli ... it's going to be a miserable night and there's no need of it ... besides, if the prophecy is true, I don't want ya enterin' the Kingdom with double pneumonia. It's a ceremony for the elders mostly ...
ELI: There's lots my age going ...
MARTHA: You'll get a cold and miss school and I'm not havin' it ...
ELIAS: The stove is well stoked and there's an extra blanket under the foot of the daybed ...
MARTHA: You can leave the lamps on 'til we get home if you like ...
(The parents move toward the door and exit. ELI looks around the room, then turns the lamp up a little brighter before settling down on the daybed. The sound of the wind picks up suddenly, the panes of glass rattle in the house. ELI sits up, looks around, then tries to comfort himself in the large blanket.
He drifts off to sleep.
ELI is dreaming. He is on a ship at sea ... we hear the wind, the scream of birds, the creaking of the deck. In his dream, he sees the Captain. It's BROTHER JOHN.)
BROTHER JOHN: *(Voice over.)* These stones shall be made bread! Touch them not!
(The sounds of the sea, the birds, the creaking, continue.)
BROTHER JOHN: *(Voice over.)* Lift up thine eyes, Eli ... lift thine eyes to Heaven and look. Behold! The elements do melt with fervent heat. The earth being on fire is dissolved! The heavens

are rolled together as a scroll and the sea is no more ...
(The sounds of fury suddenly stop. A clock strikes midnight. ELI bolts straight up in the daybed, looks around and settles back down to sleep. The startled cry of gulls, babies, adult voices ... the sounds of a roaring fire.)
BROTHER JOHN: *(Voice over.)* For in those days, men shall seek death and shall not find it, and shall desire to die and death shall flee from them, for there shall be a great earthquake, and the sun shall be black and the moon shall be as blood and the stars of heaven shall fall upon the earth ...
VOICES: *(Voice over.)* Amen, Lord Jesus ... come Lord ... our sweet saviour ...
BROTHER JOHN: *(Voice over.)* Then all they that are drunken with the blood of the martyrs of Jesus ... all the kings and the captains and the mighty men, shall hide themselves in the dens and the rocks of the mountains, and shall say unto the mountains, fall on us, and hide us from the face of Him that sitteth upon the throne, for the great day of His wrath has come, and who shall be able to stand?
VOICES: *(Voice over.)* I will stand, Jesus ... I will stand ... praise God ... come, Jesus, come ...
(The sounds of fury increase.)
BROTHER JOHN: *(Voice over.)* Eli ... Eli ... have ye washed yer robes an' made them white in the blood of the Lamb? For He shall appear in a moment ... and those that have kept their robes spotless, shall rise with the Lord, as the stars come down on every hand, blazing and going out, and swallowed into everlasting darkness ...
(The sound of wind, waves, fire, birds, the screams of children ... ELI tosses and turns in his sleep.)
BROTHER JOHN: ... with the awful sound of the trumpet ripping the sky apart, while sinners and unbelievers, left behind, shall writhe and scream in the ocean of flame that shall wrap the earth from pole to pole ... a mere taste of the tortures of hell-fire that shall be their lot from henceforth ... forever and ever ...
(As the feverish pitch rises to a frenzy, it stops as suddenly with the opening of the door in the Pallisher home. ELI jumps up as ELIAS and MARTHA come into the room. ELI is visibly shaken. ELIAS and MARTHA are soaking wet. They appear almost comical, their clothes drenched, their hair tight to their heads from the weight of the water.)
ELIAS: What is it, child? ... it's only us ...
MARTHA: Are ya sick, Eli?
ELI: I had a dream ...
(The three are quiet ... only the ticking of the clock and the low, subsiding wind.)
ELIAS: We must have been mistakin' in the chronology ...

(Another long silence.)
MARTHA: Let's all go to bed ... the new teacher arrives tomorrow, Eli, you need to be your best.

Scene 10:
Landwash

(CHRISTOPHER SIMMS, the new school teacher, and ELI are on the landwash. CHRISTOPHER looks at the evening sky.)
CHRISTOPHER: "Henceforth I ask not good fortune ... I myself am good fortune; henceforth I whimper no more, postpone no more, need nothing, strong and content, I travel the open road. The earth, that is sufficient; I do not want the constellations any nearer; I know they are very well where they are; I know they suffice for those who belong to them."
ELI: Is that a poem? It's beautiful ... did you write it?
CHRISTOPHER: *(Laughing.)* No, no ... that's Walt Whitman, an American poet.
ELI: What did he mean about the constellations?
CHRISTOPHER: The evening stars ... we've watched them for centuries, made up myths and stories about them, set calendars by them, and they're not ours, they're not even Gods ...
ELI: Don't say that in school or you won't have a job long.
CHRISTOPHER: I'm a teacher, Eli, and I teach the facts, but maybe I'll teach only *you* the real origins of the universe ...
ELI: Evolution..? Most here think it a delusion of the devil ...
CHRISTOPHER: What do you think?
ELI: I've never talked about it.
CHRISTOPHER: Well you should start ... Joshua says you come over to his house a lot to read ...
ELI: Yes, sir, ... Mr. Markady's been good to me. He's got the only collection of books in the harbour.
CHRISTOPHER: I had to send away for books when I grew up here ... how did you start?
ELI: I suppose Mr. Markady's stories about his foreign-going days started me off. I began reading stories of exploration, travel, stuff like that ...
CHRISTOPHER: You borrow the books ... bring them home?
ELI: Well, sir, ... some books I do, some I don't.
CHRISTOPHER: Call me Chris, Eli. Is it your parents? ... Do they think books are evil?
ELI: Not really ... mother hopes I'll get a shore job, working as a clerk or something. She never did like the sea. I guess it's more the kind of books I read at Mr. Markady's, you know, the Outline of History, things like that. Father can read, too, and, if he found a book like that in the house, he'd burn it, no matter who owned it.

CHRISTOPHER: Because it doesn't start off with the story of Adam and Eve and the serpent ...
ELI: It doesn't just leave it out ... it makes it look silly. I respect his faith and what it brings him but, if I said I doubted a single verse of the Old Testament, and I'm not sure how much of it I do, he'd likely come after me with a boat hook.
CHRISTOPHER: Then you've transferred your faith from the Bible to the Outline of History, is that it?
ELI: No ...
CHRISTOPHER: What then?
ELI: There's a difference between science and superstition. But, I suppose, faith isn't superstition ... it's something more personal.
(CHRISTOPHER is amused.)
CHRISTOPHER: My God ... amazing ... someone in this harbour is thinking. C'mon, let's walk around the cove.
(CHRISTOPHER bends over and takes off his shoes and socks to go barefoot. We see VIRGINIA off to the side in the alders. She's been watching but doesn't want to be seen.)
ELI: I'd say you're the first teacher to walk barefoot in Caplin Bight ... someone in the harbour will talk, that's for sure.
CHRISTOPHER: Let them talk, Eli, ... it's what they do best.
(They head off for their walk.)

Scene 11:
Joshua Markady's House

(VIRGINIA is in Markady's house when ELI arrives.)
VIRGINIA: Where's your little teacher friend?
ELI: How would I know?
VIRGINIA: Oh, listen to him ... sure you've only been around him every day since he came back to the harbour ...
ELI: What are you on about now ...
VIRGINIA: It's plain enough to see you're in love with him, but you might as well start gettin' over it because that sort of thing only leads to trouble ... do you like trouble, Eli?
ELI: We've become good friends, what's wrong with that?
VIRGINIA: Friends ... ha. He's the school teacher for God's sake and, anyway, you can't have him, 'cause I mean to have him for myself.
ELI: You can't be serious ... you don't mean that you're jealous of me ... I can't believe it. Virginia Marks is jealous of me.
VIRGINIA: Jealous of a young pup like you ... you listen here, I've been in love with Christopher from the moment he stepped ashore. And it's like I'm waitin' for him to pounce. Does that make any sense?
ELI: No, it doesn't.
VIRGINIA: Well, he gives me the chills and I don't want anyone

laying the slightest claim to him. If Christopher had a dog that he was fond of, I'd shoot the dog ... and he likes you a good deal more than any dog.
ELI: This is nonsense, Virginia. If you're so mad about him then go ahead if you can get him, but don't bring me into it.
VIRGINIA: Sometimes I think you're as innocent as you look ... what a baby you are, Eli Pallisher.
(ELI is angry.)
ELI: I don't have to listen to this. You're just thinking things up in your own mind. I don't care what the two of ye do ...
VIRGINIA: Ooh my ... I like it when you're a little mad, Eli, or when you're lookin' like a lost calf, which is the way you're lookin' now ... but that doesn't change what I said about Christopher.
ELI: Will you cut it out and be sensible ...
VIRGINIA: You're the one that's got to be sensible, my son, before the whole harbour starts talkin' about ya.
(ELI goes to the door.)
ELI: Let them talk ... that's what they do best ...
(ELI leaves.)

Scene 12:
Pallisher House

(ELI is sitting at the table finishing homework. His father and mother are with him.)
MARTHA: Yer sharp with figures aren't ya, Eli, it is a gift like Brother John says ...
ELI: This is algebra ... you use letters instead of numbers.
ELIAS: Letters ... what kind'a nonsense is that?
ELI: It's still sums, but you don't know what they mean until you reach the end. This way you can do difficult problems that you couldn't do with figures alone.
ELIAS: An' be it of any martal use to anyone?
(ELI sighs.)
ELI: Oh, father ... of course it is. Look, suppose you wanted an eighty-gallon tank in a boat, to fit in the bow, where she begins to turn in. The shape would be so odd you wouldn't be able to figure it out with figures, but you could with this.
(ELIAS laughs.)
ELIAS: An' who'd be such a fool to put a tank up farward in a boat. The tank'id go in the starn where's there's lots a' room.
(ELI rolls his eyes.)
MARTHA: It's alright, Eli. I've asked Mr. Simms to teach ya bookkeepin' as part of yer school work ... Solomon Marks might take ya on fer a month or so in the winter.

Scene 13:
Joshua Markady's House

(CHRISTOPHER and JOSHUA MARKADY are enjoying a few glasses of rum. ELI is off to the side, reading.)
JOSHUA: Bookkeeping? What in the name of Jesus do ya want to learn bookkeeping for?
CHRISTOPHER: He says it'll help him get a job ... it's his last year of school and he wants to prepare for the world.
(ELI looks up at the two of them for a moment then returns to his reading.)
JOSHUA: Those Bible-readin' parents of his want to make him into a goddamn clerk. They see a white collar the same way that imbecile John McKim sees a halo.
CHRISTOPHER: But what can I do ... I'm his teacher for Christ sake ...
JOSHUA: *(Turning to ELI.)* If I had a choice to teach ya to be a bookkeeper or for ya to sharpen yer skills on the water, I'd see to it that ya stayed in a trap boat until yer arse grew fast to the taut!
(More drinks are poured. Their voices reacting accordingly.)
CHRISTOPHER: But it's what Elias and Martha want ...
JOSHUA: Why in God's name do parents have to try their best to cripple their children for life? What makes people such fools? But I s'pose when you've lived as long as I have, ya should be less astonished at foolishness ... who's not a fool is generally a rogue, and it's rarely ya find one that's not the other ...
CHRISTOPHER: He should go on to college ...
JOSHUA: Or sail to the West Indies ...
CHRISTOPHER: Or Spain and Portugal ...
JOSHUA: Around the Horn ...
CHRISTOPHER: Search for the Grail ...
JOSHUA: The Arc of the Covenant ...
CHRISTOPHER: Beats singing hymns ...
(They look at each other. A silence. JOSHUA bursts into song.)
JOSHUA: What a fellowship, what a joy divine
Leaning on the everlasting arms,
What a blessedness, what a peace is mine,
Leaning on the everlasting arms.
Leaning, leaning,
Safe and secure from all alarms
Leaning, leaning,
Leaning on the everlasting arms.
(CHRISTOPHER joins him in the singing. Their voices rising in the room. ELI attempts to shut out their revelry by burying himself deeper in his reading.)

JOSHUA AND CHRISTOPHER: (*In unison.*)
Oh how sweet to walk, in this pilgrim way,
Leaning on the everlasting arms.
Oh how bright the path grows from day to day,
Leaning on the everlasting arms.
Leaning, leaning,
Safe and secure from all alarms.
Leaning, leaning,
Leaning on the everlasting arms.
(*Lights go down on this two-man, drunken choir.*)

Scene 14:
Joshua Markady's House

(*We see JOSHUA feeling the pain of last-night's revelry. A knock is heard at the door. He goes to answer it and, on opening, sees ELIAS Pallisher.*)

JOSHUA: Come in, Elias, ... there's no need of you to knock, you know that.

ELIAS: I want to talk to ya about Eli.

JOSHUA: What about him?

ELIAS: He's spendin' too much time over here.

JOSHUA: You know where he is when he's here and what he's up to. He reads and talks ... that's about the size of it. I'm sorry if you're losing sleep over it. It should please you ... the boy is extremely bright.

ELIAS: He knows the rule about comin' home at a decent hour. And I don't need you to be worried about my sleep or tellin' me about me own boy. I know 'em well enough.

JOSHUA: Ya don't sound very friendly, Elias, that's hardly a civil thing to say comin' in to a man's house.

ELIAS: 'Is not a civil thing a young fella not under 'es own roof at night.

JOSHUA: Give 'em a tongue lashing and make 'em feel like he's done something wrong if it makes ya feel any better. But mark my words, you'll lose whatever respect he has left for ya.

ELIAS: Don't ridicule me, Joshua, ... I won't stand for it ...
(*ELIAS is angry. JOSHUA is silent.*)
Listen here, Joshua, ... you're turnin' his head with all them books yer givin' 'em and ya shouldn't gave 'em that gun either. If the boy needed a gun, it's his father shoulda' give it to 'em.

JOSHUA: Look ... I'm not gonna fight with you like two youngsters on this but Eli has as much right in this house as he has in yours. He's got a mind of his own and you gotta let him use it in his own way. Nobody is trying to lead him into evil ... not here, anyway.

ELIAS: Ya tellin' me what to do about raisin' me own son?

JOSHUA: The time is past for that.

ELIAS: He's not too big to be made to mind, even if I have to skin the young whelp with a horsewhip.
JOSHUA: That'd do the boy no good and ya know it.
(Both men are quiet.)
ELIAS: Ya may have a grain of right on your side, Josh, and perhaps ya do mean well, though Brother John has declared ya an agent of the devil.
JOSHUA: Let him save his words for the pulpit ... I know he's behind this visit. He's an ignorant man, though no doubt one with some good in him. He might have been a better man if he'd had the chance that I'm askin' you to give Eli.
ELIAS: Whaddya mean by that?
JOSHUA: I mean John McKim is a person with a clever mind and almost no learning ... because he was most likely denied his rights growin' up I'm tellin' ya. Twenty years ago he was the age of Eli, probably with a mind like Eli's.
ELIAS: He's a man of God and curse ye that speak bad of 'em. Ya have yer own ways and I don't bother ya about 'em. I expect ya to do the same for me. The boy will learn to walk a good road from Brother John McKim.
JOSHUA: McKim was cooped up in a little harbour with nothin' but rocks and Bibles and hymn-books to feed his mind. Like most of us, he never had the chance that Eli's got.
(ELIAS is quiet with what he's heard.)
ELIAS: Ya really believe the boy has somethin', don't ya?
JOSHUA: You're damn right I do ... he can do or be anything he wants ... if he has the right guidance and the chance to do so.
(ELIAS goes to the door and opens it. He speaks with his back to JOSHUA.)
ELIAS: Everything of importance a man must do or discover for himself ...
(ELIAS pauses, then turns to face JOSHUA.)
... and that's one of the reasons the world is such a lonely place.
(ELIAS closes the door behind, letting the truth ring in JOSHUA's ears.)

Scene 15:
Pallisher House

(ELI, MARTHA, BROTHER JOHN and ELIAS talk about a trip in the woods. BROTHER JOHN is off to one side. He is reading, but listens to the exchange. There is a plot here on the part of Brother John and Eli's parents. ELI is unaware.)
MARTHA: Have you decided on next week, Eli?
ELI: I'm still thinking I might go in for a moose or caribou ... maybe a few partridge.
MARTHA: Haven't found no on to go with ya?

ELI: No ...
ELIAS: Well, whoever goes has to be someone who knows what they're at, 'cause you'd have to kill it near the water where ya could get a boat, or near enough to a path to get a horse in.
MARTHA: Pleman Pike can't go?
ELI: Christopher says he can't afford to miss any school if he's goin' to pass.
ELIAS: I can't go ... not this time ... I heard tell moose are scarce anyway.
MARTHA: Three men from Lattice Harbour came out by Main Brook yesterday and seen no more than two or three ...
ELI: I was thinkin' of goin' farther down the coast ... I suppose I could go alone.
MARTHA: Not likely ...
ELIAS: And that's what you won't. Listen to yer mother ...
BROTHER JOHN: I'll go with ye ...
(MARTHA and ELIAS pretend to be surprised, no one knowing exactly how to react.)
BROTHER JOHN: I was thinking of going up country come Monday ... trouble is I don't know the country well enough. I wouldn't know where to put up for the night.
MARTHA: Well, Eli's been all over the handy part of the country with 'es father, an' even farther with Joshua Markady. All the way back to Wolf Pond last October ... and that's a fair piece in, I'll tell ya that.
ELIAS: What do you think, Eli ... could you make a trip in with Brother John?
ELI: Well, ... sure, why not. We'd go by boat as far as the barachois at the mouth of Wolf Pond Brook, and then walk in, it's about six miles into the falls ... that's where Mr. Markady has his cabin.
BROTHER JOHN: Ya make it sound easy, Eli ...
MARTHA: You'll have no trouble with Eli ... he can carry a load the same as another ... and he's sensible with a gun, too. Not like half of what's in this harbour.
BROTHER JOHN: Right then ... it's settled ... Monday?
ELI: Monday ... soon as it's light.
(Lights go down on the Pallisher kitchen.)

Scene 16:
Open Meadow

(CHRISTOPHER and VIRGINIA are sitting. Their discussion is warm and somewhat seductive on both parts.)
VIRGINIA: I just can't be bothered with the nonsense I see in this place ... all around me, all the time.
CHRISTOPHER: It's classic rural life. Everyone follows a path that's laid out, there's nothing unique about Caplin Bight in that.

VIRGINIA: Well, I won't do it. If people won't take me the way I am, to hell with them ... and that goes for you, too, Christopher Simms.
(CHRISTOPHER laughs.)
CHRISTOPHER: You can be as lascivious as you want with me, Virginia.
VIRGINIA: La what ...? What does that mean? Is that good or bad?
CHRISTOPHER: Forget it ...
VIRGINIA: I won't forget it ... what does it mean?
CHRISTOPHER: It means to express sexual lust ...
VIRGINIA: Ooh ... I like that.
CHRISTOPHER: There's nothing in you I want to change ... you've survived with your heart, soul and mind intact.
VIRGINIA: The wonderful trinity of heart, soul and mind. Like you, Eli and myself ... now there you are, who's who. I think Eli could be all three.
CHRISTOPHER: *(Playfully.)* So it's Eli you're thinking of now, is it?
VIRGINIA: Are you jealous ... like Brother John?
CHRISTOPHER: I don't know ... kiss me and I'll tell you.
(They kiss. CHRISTOPHER's hands search for the flesh beneath VIRGINIA's sweater. A soft light shows us ELI watching them.)

Scene 17:
Back Country; Several Miles In The Woods

(BROTHER JOHN and ELI pause to view the panorama before them. They lay down their packs.)
BROTHER JOHN: It's as beautiful as you described, Eli.
ELI: See there, where the river runs out from the bottom of the lake ...
BROTHER JOHN: Beyond the first knall ...?
ELI: Just before it ... the stand of pine ...
BROTHER JOHN: Yes ... yes. I see the pine.
ELI: Beyond where the river runs out, there's a small point of land that juts out into the lake. The cabin's on that.
(Both study the vista. Sounds of the woods. Then the cry of an eagle. ELI is excited and looks around to find it.)
ELI: An eagle ... do you see it?
BROTHER JOHN: No ... I heard 'em, like yerself, but I don't see 'en.
(ELI searches the sky.)
ELI: It's nearby ... somewhere in against the hill.
BROTHER JOHN: Eagle or no, Eli, we best be movin' on ... be dark soon. There's the better part of two hours to get to where ye

pointed.
(BROTHER JOHN moves on ahead. ELI searches for the bird in a last attempt at securing a look at his winged obsession before following the minister along the path.)

Scene 18:
Joshua Markady's Cabin

(ELI and BROTHER JOHN are settled in for the night in the sparse but warm one-room cabin.)
BROTHER JOHN: If all men could live in a place like this, breathe the air of God's wilderness as we've been doin', there'd be no evil in the world.
ELI: None at all? ... I doubt it.
(They are silent.)
BROTHER JOHN: Eli ...
(ELI looks at BROTHER JOHN but says nothing.)
You haven't sought the Lord yet. What's holdin' ya back?
ELI: I guess I haven't been called ... I go to service regularly and to weekly prayer, you know that, but there's no use pretendin' to have a change of heart if ya haven't. Is there?
BROTHER JOHN: No, boy ... no, certainly not. There'd be some would do that, but they call down damnation on themselves, not blessin', for the Lord reads the heart, not the lips. If he don't speak to ya, it'd be blasphemy to say He did ... yet I'm wonderin' there must be some reason in yer own soul if He don't speak. Evil companionships keep many a soul from the Lord, ya know. That Simms fella that ya spends so much time with ... he don't know God, and the Bible teaches us that the devil often shows hisself as an angel of light.
ELI: Christopher is not a soldier of the devil, Brother John. He's the best friend I've ever had, even if he isn't the same kind of Christian that we are. You'd like him if ya knew him better.
BROTHER JOHN: Ain't a case of likin' or dis-likin'. I just think the devil may be makin' use of 'em to lead ya away from God. All the worldly knowledge ya could ever get wouldn't be worth that, boy. If ya spent more time with me an' less with an unbeliever, ya might hear the Lord speak to ya.
ELI: But a path of knowledge is not an evil one ... there's been great books written on the history of Christianity, the history of civilization ...
BROTHER JOHN: ... and what of the other books ... the ones that denounce the Lord and praise the ones that do 'em wrong?
ELI: Then you have to trust yourself to believe or not believe ... you can't just dismiss it like a plague because it's not a plague and books shouldn't be treated like that.
BROTHER JOHN: A book is not as important as God!

ELI: I didn't say that, Brother John ... you have to listen to what I'm saying if we're to be friends. You have to give me a chance to be heard, to explain how I feel about God, love, books, the salmon in the pools, the eagles ... all of it. But you have to listen.
(ELI falls silent. Both look around the room, their silence becoming each other's defense.)
BROTHER JOHN: I'll tell ya the truth, Eli ... I'm very fond of you, boy. It was no accident that I was by you're house the other day. I heard from your parents that you were talkin' about makin' a trip and that yer father couldn't go with ya. So I thought it'd be a good time for us to get to know one another better. I'd like to be your friend and the Lord might work through our friendship like he did with David and Jonathan.
ELI: Our love of the country and the water is enough to build a friendship on, but to have it last there has to be trust and understanding ... like myself and Christopher.
BROTHER JOHN: I don't want ye to compare us to yerself and the teacher, ... Anyway ... enough for the night. It's time we turned in. Let's bow our heads ... we thank thee Lord for all thy many blessings, for the beautiful earth, for the birds and the beasts which thou have put in subjection under us. We thank thee for each other, and for the love which thou has put into our hearts. Forgive us our sins and lead us into the light of thy holy countenance. Amen.
(They both lie down and get under their blankets.)
BROTHER JOHN: Good night, Eli.
ELI: Good night, Brother John.
(The lights go black on our hunting companions.)

Scene 19:
Landwash

(CHRISTOPHER and VIRGINIA are seen walking along the landwash. They stop and kiss passionately. They begin to remove their clothes. There is no dialogue here, merely a scene contrasting the previous one.)

Scene 20:
Joshua Markady's Cabin

(We see the empty cabin then hear the sound of shotguns. We hear BROTHER JOHN and ELI call to each other. These voices are off stage. We don't see the characters. We hear the sounds of the woods, birds, the seductive rustling of wind in the trees, the rattling of a brook etc.)
BROTHER JOHN: *(Offstage.)* Good boy, Eli, ... one shot. I'd hate to have ya gunnin' for me.

ELI: *(Offstage.)* Across the marsh ...!
(Another shot.)
ELI: *(Offstage.)* Good yourself, Brother John, ... ya haven't spent all your time in the pulpit.
(Shouts of satisfaction are heard from our two hunters as the lights go down and the voices fade. We hear only the sounds of the forest and the haunting beauty it creates in our memory.)

Scene 21:
Joshua Markady's Cabin

(ELI and BROTHER JOHN are back in the cabin after their day on the barrens. They are cleaning and cutting up a bird for the next day's meal.)
BROTHER JOHN: Well, lad, if I were wearin' a hat I'd take it off. A caribou and four brace of partridge ...
ELI: I saw a small covey go into a tuck of spruce and, when I flushed 'em out, the air was full of birds. You couldn't miss if ya tried.
BROTHER JOHN: 'Twas great shootin' all the same.
ELI: This is the messy part ... but they'll be all ready for the pot tomorrow. A few onions and potatoes and turnip and we'll have a feed never seen in this part of the country ... ahhh, now I've done it.
(ELI cuts himself with the knife and quickly puts his finger to his mouth.)
BROTHER JOHN: Is it deep ... let me tend to ye.
ELI: It's okay ...
(ELI looks quizzically at his fingers then returns them to his mouth.)
ELI: Funny ...?
BROTHER JOHN: What ... cuttin' yer finger?
ELI: No, no, ... the taste. I can't tell the difference between my blood and the partridge.
BROTHER JOHN: The blood of the lamb of God is said to be sweet as honey ... is it sweet?
ELI: No.
(ELI puts the work away, washes his hands, then sits on the sleeping bag on the floor and begins rubbing his feet. BROTHER JOHN notices and moves closer.)
BROTHER JOHN: Here, Eli, ... let me do that. A man can't warm his own feet.
(He takes ELI's feet in his hands and begins to rub them gently.)
BROTHER JOHN: That was some of the biggest caribou I've ever seen ... and you ... sure a box of slugs should last you a lifetime.
ELI: I don't feel proud of it at all. Sometimes like I've done some-

thing wrong, like smashed out a window or something. I felt the same way when I shot a moose last fall. Do you feel like that?
(BROTHER JOHN continues with his caressing.)
BROTHER JOHN: Can't say as I do ... the Lord put them here for us to use.
ELI: It still seems wrong somehow, to take the life of any animal.
(BROTHER JOHN stops his massage and stretches himself out next to ELI and pulls the cover over the two of them.)
BROTHER JOHN: It's colder tonight ... we'll be better off under the one cover. Blow out the light, Eli.
(ELI leans over and blows out the kerosene lamp. The stage is dark. We see the two silhouettes of our hunters lying next to each other. There is no sound for the longest time, perhaps the cry of a loon. We see one of the figures move his arm around the other, the blankets move.)
ELI: Don't do that ...
BROTHER JOHN: I'm sorry ... I was just tryin' to get warm ... I didn't mean any harm by it.
(Both lie still. Night sounds are heard. We see a figure turn again.)
ELI: Your hands ... they're cold.
BROTHER JOHN: It's okay, Eli ... just close your eyes. It's okay.
(We hear the sounds of paced breathing, shifting of bodies.)
BROTHER JOHN: Do you like how that feels?
ELI: I don't know ...
(More breathing.)
BROTHER JOHN: Give me your hand ... there you go ... that's it ... just go slow ... that's it ...
(The breathing becomes more intense, a guttural groan is heard, then complete silence.)

Act II

Scene 1:
Landwash

(ELI and VIRGINIA are walking along the beach.)
VIRGINIA: Well, you better watch your step, that's all I'm sayin', Eli, or your likely to fall in a cellar. They say you and Christopher are practicin' what the hymn-singers call unnatural sin.
ELI: It's crazy ... there's not a word of truth in it. We're friends. Can't two people be friends?
VIRGINIA: I know that, bye, ... sure I'm the one he's chasin' all over the harbour ... but I got a feelin' there's gonna be trouble. I know what happens when this crowd starts talkin'. Mildred Pike

was tellin' me and she said she even heard ole Abram Squires talk about it.
ELI: How do stories like this get started?
VIRGINIA: Someone plants 'em. Like every other bit a gossip that poisons this place. It's not the lobsters crawlin' up on the landwash snappin' their claws I can tell you that.
ELI: But who ...?
VIRGINIA: I'd say yer fine friend, John McKim.
ELI: But why would he do that?
VIRGINIA: Because he's jealous, that's why.
ELI: Jealous of what?
VIRGINIA: My God, Eli, I love your innocence ... ever since ya both came back from that huntin' trip, Brother John has been a changed man. He's been takin' ya around ... took ya over to Lattice Harbour ... he's bought you things ... but you keep spendin' most of your time with Christopher.
ELI: That's nonsense ...
VIRGINIA: Open your eyes, Eli ... you and Christopher off swimming every other day, reading each other poetry in Pike's meadow, two of you on long walks, helping ole Josh with his boat.
ELI: But Brother John's been good to me ... he's become my friend too, not a friend like Christopher, but someone I can trust. He wouldn't do anything to me ... to hurt me, I mean.
VIRGINIA: It's not you he's doin' it to ... it's not you he wants to hurt ... it's Christopher.
(ELI turns and walks away quickly. VIRGINIA watches him go as the lights go down.)

Scene 2:
Chapel

(BROTHER JOHN is preaching a sermon. ELI and his parents and any extras are there.)
BROTHER JOHN: He that has love, let 'em keep and express it. What man is fit to declare the excellence of its beauty? Love and charity unite us in God, they endure all things. There is nothing base and morbid in love and charity, they are not seditious. By love and charity, we're all the elect of God made perfect. Without them, nothin' is pleasin' and acceptable in the eyes of the Lord.
(The parishioners are surprised. They look at each other. This is not BROTHER JOHN's usual hell, fire and damnation delivery. He is soft, his voice reassuring to the listener.)
BROTHER JOHN: All the ages of the world, from Adam even unto this day, are passed away, but they who've been made perfect in love, have by the grace of God, obtained a place among the righteous and shall be made manifest in the glory of love and

charity. For it is written, enter into my chambers those that love, till my anger and indignation shall pass away. And that is my message to ye here tonight, happy, then, shall we be, in the unity of love so that through love, our sins may be forgiven us.

Scene 3:
Chapel

(The rest of the parishioners leave the chapel. ELI stays behind to be alone with BROTHER JOHN.)

ELI: That was a different sermon ...

BROTHER JOHN: The Lord talked of love in his day ... 'is not a thing the harbour shouldn't hear about. The love I have fer ye is a blessin' to me ... but I've not seen much of ye, lately. God's will is for us to be as we are.

ELI: Have you heard any of this talk in the harbour about myself and Christopher?

BROTHER JOHN: Of course there's talk. Why not? I warned ya to stay away from 'em but ya wouldn't listen.

ELI: It's all lies and you know it.

BROTHER JOHN: He's an evil young man and you're to leave 'em be. If ya do that, I'm sure the talk will stop.

ELI: He's more of a Christian than most of the people in this harbour ... more than you are as far as that goes.

(The accusation stings.)

BROTHER JOHN: Indeed, ... indeed, now.

(His tone becomes harsher.)

And who gave you leave to sit in judgement ... you who are not among the saved. It's for you to mind your place and seek the Lord humbly, and ask for forgiveness before ya find yourself consigned to hell-fire. That teacher that you're so fond of has brought evil to this place, settin' the hearts of the children against their fathers as the Lord foretold. He's a false prophet and the Lord will let him go just so far before He'll cut 'em down in his wickedness ...

(ELI explodes.)

ELI: *(Loudly.)* Stop it ... don't you preach to me about wickedness ... what they're all sayin' is true ... it's just that they got the names mixed up ... it's you and me.

(BROTHER JOHN is anxious, frozen into stillness, then he speaks with terrible, icy calm.)

BROTHER JOHN: What are ya talkin' about ... what do ya mean, you and me? We haven't done anything sinful. You watch your tongue boy or it'll get ya into far more trouble than ya can handle.

ELI: Don't you threaten me ... I thought we were friends. I was wrong.

(ELI turns to leave.)
BROTHER JOHN: Eli ...
(ELI doesn't stop.)
BROTHER JOHN: Eli, ... come back here.
(ELI is gone. BROTHER JOHN is talking to himself.)
BROTHER JOHN: Don't go, Eli ... please don't go. I'm sorry, I'm only doin' what's best for ya, boy ... it's only what's best.
(BROTHER JOHN stands alone in his church.)

Scene 4:
Open Meadow

(CHRISTOPHER and ELI are seen coming out of the water after a swim. They dry themselves with towels. CHRISTOPHER stretches his arms to the sky and howls.)
CHRISTOPHER: Yaaooo! Here we are, Lord ... the flesh heathens. Strike us down in our naked beauty!
(ELI doesn't share in the revelry.)
ELI: Stop it ... someone will hear us. I think we should get dressed ...
(CHRISTOPHER playfully whips ELI with his towel.)
CHRISTOPHER: What's wrong ... afraid God will hear us, afraid he'll do it?
(ELI doesn't respond. He begins putting on his clothes. CHRISTOPHER grabs up his pants and shirt and holds onto them.)
ELI: Give them to me ...
CHRISTOPHER: What's wrong, Eli?
ELI: It's too quiet lately, at least when they were all talking I knew what was going on.
CHRISTOPHER: "Agonies are one of my changes of garments, I do not ask the wounded person how he feels, I myself become the wounded person."
ELI: I've got to get out of here ... somewhere where nobody knows me. Somewhere I don't feel eyes burning in the back of my head.
CHRISTOPHER: You've changed ... Virginia's the one who notices most. You're starting to unshackle Caplin Bight from your legs and beginning to see you can walk to the end of the world on your own.
ELI: You don't know what I've been through lately ... I've got to talk ... not talk ... I mean I need to ... it's church. I can't go to church anymore.
CHRISTOPHER: That's easy ... don't go.
ELI: It's not that simple ... something's happened ... I feel ...
CHRISTOPHER: C'mon, Eli. Talk to me. We made a vow never to hold back from each other.
ELI: Never mind ... forget it. Not now ... some other time.
CHRISTOPHER: Just like that. I'm afraid that won't do. Now

what is it?
(ELI shows his first signs of anger toward CHRISTOPHER.)
ELI: I said forget it ... you can't talk about everything and heal every wound in everyone you meet ... just forget it.
CHRISTOPHER: Don't turn on me, Eli ... and don't accuse me of Franciscan attitudes in dealing with those I love ... like you.
(They fall silent. Each searching for the right moment to move on.)
CHRISTOPHER: Virginia and I are getting married.
(ELI is surprised, almost hurt.)
ELI: What?
CHRISTOPHER: We're going to be married next month. You're the first person I've told.
ELI: I'm not surprised ...
CHRISTOPHER: Nothing will change. We'll all be friends forever ... you've got to believe that. Things have to evolve, turn upside down, but friendships, love, the glue of the world ... that lingers forever.
(They both pause to listen in on the sounds around them.)
CHRISTOPHER: Things move so fast ... you'll leave here soon, like I did. Travel around ...
ELI: I'd like too ... like Josh Markady ... Barbados, Trinidad, Oporto ...
CHRISTOPHER: But I think you'll come back, too. You can never forget. None of us can.
ELI: "If I forget thee, O Jerusalem, let my right hand forget her cunning ... if I love not Jerusalem more than all the joys of the earth ..."
(CHRISTOPHER grabs ELI playfully and wrestles him to the ground where he sits on the boy, pinning ELI underneath him, while he tickles his younger adversary. As he does BROTHER JOHN is seen off to the side, he has come upon the two friends.)
CHRISTOPHER: You better not forget me, you little snake.
ELI: *(Laughing.)* I won't, I promise ... let me up. I won't forget you, ever.
CHRISTOPHER: *(Laughing.)* Say you love me and you've loved our time together or I'll kiss you right on the mouth ...
ELI: I love you ... I love you ...
(BROTHER JOHN practically leaps from his hiding place, startling ELI and CHRISTOPHER.)
BROTHER JOHN: Eli! Have ya no shame, boy? Get up from there and come with me, this instant.
(CHRISTOPHER is furious.)
CHRISTOPHER: You bastard ... you've been spying on us, haven't you? Who do you think you are, anyway ... shouting out your orders. He doesn't have to go anywhere.
(BROTHER JOHN steps threateningly toward

CHRISTOPHER.)
BROTHER JOHN: Don't raise yer voice to me. Ye have stained this boy's soul, discolored it and made it foul. Comin' back to this harbour with all yer worldly knowledge, thinkin' ye can fool those around ye, but ye haven't fooled me. I've seen yer poisonous kind before.
CHRISTOPHER: What do you know of the world, McKim? What do you know of Elis' soul?
ELI: It's alright, Christopher ...
CHRISTOPHER: No it's not ... it's got to stop.
BROTHER JOHN: I agree there ... it is going to stop. I wonder at your gall, Mr. Simms, I really do. You are a black-hearted villain and a shameless agent of the devil, leadin' this boy down the broad road of vice that leads to destruction. The two of ye, for that matter, wrestlin' around, holdin' each other like that, in the sight of the Lord, without shame. It's whipped ya should be ... in the days o' King Hezekiah ye'd be taken out an' stoned.
CHRISTOPHER: I'm sick of threats of the devil and we're not in the days of Hezekiah ... and we've got nothing more to say to you.
BROTHER JOHN: How can ya do it, Eli?
ELI: Do what? We're not doin' anything. There's nothing wrong here ...
BROTHER JOHN: *(Loudly.)* Wrong! I know what ye was up to ... I know what ye was about to get on with ... now come on, you're comin' with me.
(BROTHER JOHN moves toward ELI and takes him roughly by the arm to lead him away. CHRISTOPHER grabs him and throws BROTHER JOHN aside convincingly. BROTHER JOHN slips to the ground.)
CHRISTOPHER: Get up and get going, McKim. And if you ever try and lay a hand on Eli I'll break that hooked nose of yours so it will never be straight again.
(BROTHER JOHN stands for a minute in defiance, looking as if he's going to strike CHRISTOPHER, both men in a stand-off. ELI is scared.)
BROTHER JOHN: The Lord says to turn the other cheek, though it's a mighty hard thing to do at times. You've no cause to threaten me. I'd no intention of hurtin' the lad, but it's my Christian duty to admonish 'em when I see 'em slidin' into the bottomless pit of vice.
CHRISTOPHER: No more talk of vice ... it's you who's been spreading these Goddamned lies about me and Eli, I'm sure of that. And, by Christ, if they don't stop you'll get more than a shove in the woods the next time I see you ...
(BROTHER JOHN turns and walks away, speaking as he does.)
BROTHER JOHN: You'll be sorry for this, Simms.

(He disappears offstage leaving ELI and CHRISTOPHER to themselves and the lingering discomfort of the confrontation.)
ELI: He scares me ...
CHRISTOPHER: Don't worry about it ... come on, I'll race you back.
(CHRISTOPHER starts off in a dash. ELI simply walks away slowly.)

Scene 5:
Pallisher House

(ELIAS and MARTHA discuss ELI.)
MARTHA: Is it right to be so hard on the boy ...
ELIAS: The boy is a man, he's almost sixteen ... it's time he started behavin' like a man ...
MARTHA: Brother John thinks he might get called ...
ELIAS: There's nothin' wrong with that ... if he gets touched by the Lord, the sooner the better.
MARTHA: Who knows, Elias, maybe he should go on to college and keep clear of here. He don't want no clerk job. That way he'll not be tempted to the water.
ELIAS: Do ya' not think it a good life ... I spent all me life on the water, even if 'es to be held in the arms of Jesus. At least, he'd be away from the sinners where he'd be safe and looked after?
MARTHA: Of course fishing is a good life ... but I'm not sure if it's a life I want for Eli. And as for the Lord, you can still be in the arms of Jesus without wearing his clothes ...
ELIAS: The boy needs an anchor, I'm tellin' ya, and the Lord's as good an anchor in this world as you're gonna get.
MARTHA: My faith is as strong as it ever was, Elias Pallisher, and I know what the Lord has given me ... I want the boy to make up his own mind.
ELIAS: There's talk about that school teacher ... bad talk. I'll not have that boy go down the wrong road and that's all there's to it ... I don't care if he doesn't live with the Lord but he has to walk with 'em. A man doesn't spend his time on this earth to have it flicked back in his face ... the boy will do what's right. If it's not with the Lord, it'll be somethin' that's proper and has respect.
(ELIAS leaves.)

Scene 6:
Joshua Markady's House

(JOSHUA is alone when ELI comes bounding through the door.)
ELI: You've got to help ... you've got to do something ...
JOSHUA: Help who?

ELI: I mean, it's too late ... ya can't do anything now, they're gone ...
JOSHUA: What are ya on about, Eli, slow down my son, help who ... who's gone?
ELI: Christopher ... Christopher's gone ...
JOSHUA: Gone where?
ELI: They've arrested him ... a policeman came on the steamer ... he walked right up to Christopher, asked him his name and then he said somethin' about a lawyer and he took him away to St. John's for trial.
JOSHUA: Arrested him for what? Not goin' to church? Make some sense to me, boy ...
ELI: Something about indecency and ... and sex acts with a minor ... me! They're talkin' about me ... that he did it with me.
JOSHUA: Ya can't be serious. Who was there ... was Virginia there?
ELI: No ... she wasn't on the wharf and they wouldn't let him see her. Pleman Pike told me her father had her locked in her room and he could hear her screaming from his father's garden ...
JOSHUA: Was John McKim there?
ELI: Ya ... ya, he was, why?
JOSHUA: 'Cause you mark my words, that son of a bitch is who's behind this ... that meddlin' no good for nothin' bible beater started this whole goddamn racket.
ELI: He wouldn't do that ... I mean, he didn't like Christopher, but he wouldn't lie and have him arrested ... I can't believe that, he's the Minister.
JOSHUA: For Christ's sake, get yer head out of the flour barrel, Eli ... he may have gone out in that gale last fall and saved those four men from drownin' and he may have pulled the young Gilmour boy eighteen miles on a sled to see the Doctor, but, mark my words, deep in his soul that man is brooding. He had it against Christopher right from the start. He said he'd get 'em and this is the way he's done it.
ELI: I swear to God ... we never did anything wrong. It's all lies.
JOSHUA: I know ya didn't, boy, ... sweet Jesus, the whole harbour has gone mad.
(The lights go down.)

Scene 7:
Chapel

(BROTHER JOHN is bidding good-day to his congregation. ELIAS, MARTHA and ELI leave the chapel. BROTHER JOHN pulls ELI aside as his parents continue on home.)
BROTHER JOHN: Eli ...
ELI: I hate you, Brother John. I hate you! Every night I pray to God that you'll die.

(ELI leaves and goes to the landwash where he meets VIRGINIA.)

VIRGINIA: I'm on the side of the sinners and I intend to stay that way. I love Christopher and I'm gonna marry him, and they aren't gonna stop me ... especially not John McKim. How can you go inside that stinking church after what's happened?

ELI: I'm still under my father's roof. I don't have much choice.

VIRGINIA: Choice, is it ... I'll show those hypocrites something. Even if I have to do it alone.

ELI: I'm sorry, Virginia ... what can *I* do?

VIRGINIA: You must be more of a child than I thought ... and I wanted to kiss you once. Good God. If you don't know what you should do then what's the use of me tryin' to tell you. Go back to church, Eli, it's where you're most comfortable and can do the less harm.

(VIRGINIA leaves ELI on the landwash. He is dejected and ashamed.)

Scene 8:
Pallisher House

(MARTHA, ELIAS and ELI are home. Their lives have been changed forever, and they all know it.)

ELIAS: What do ya think it was all for ... answer me that. Every day of me life since ya was born ... when the fish was gone and half the bay was on the dole, I was the only man afloat ... the only one to pay his bills, 'cause I worked, in any weather, to make yer life as good as I could. And this is the thanks I get fer it ...

ELI: Why won't you believe me?

ELIAS: Believe that a man o' God is lyin' ... what's John McKim got ta' gain from makin' me the talk of the coast. This family and our families before us have built a respect over the years and now we're down to this ...

MARTHA: Ya can't go to court, Eli ...

ELI: You still won't listen ... Brother John is lying. If I don't go, there'll be no one to speak in Chris' defense. I can't just ignore it like nothing happened.

ELIAS: If we say yer not goin' to court, there'll be no more talk of it.

ELI: You heard what the lawyer said. Even if I didn't want to go myself, the court can order me ... is that what you want? More police coming to the harbour with court orders to haul me off to St. John's, too ...

MARTHA: Why couldn't ya see it comin', Eli? Why didn't any of us see it comin'? I heard some of the talk but I was sure it was idle.

ELIAS: I seen it comin' then, but in my heart I thought he had more sense and would come into 'es own and would see it hisself.

Why da ya think I was ready to give ya half shares in the boat if I didn't think all the foolishness of a youngster was goin' out of ya?

MARTHA: Why didn't ya come and talk to me. We always did before, about everything else. There's not a mother in this harbour talked with their boy like you and I have this last while. Where does all this come from?

ELIAS: It comes from the likes of Christopher Simms and his fancy ways of seein' the world. Well, I'll tell ya this, if yer goin' to that court in St. John's, I'll be there, and so will yer mother, to make sure that there's no more trickery by the likes of that school teacher or any other ... because like it or not, this is a family and by the word of God I'll see to it that it stays that way ...

MARTHA: Yer father's right, Eli ... we have to go and be with ya and when it's all over, we'll settle down to what we were before all this started.

ELI: I don't know if we can, mother ... because I don't know *what* we were before ...

Scene 9:
Court Room

(ELIAS, MARTHA, ELI, JOSHUA MARKADY, VIRGINIA, CHRISTOPHER and JOHN McKIM are in the court room. Christopher's lawyer is seated as the Crown questions BROTHER JOHN. A JUDGE looks on. Our focus is ELI, his uneasiness in the courtroom and his awareness of all eyes on him and his life.)

CROWN LAWYER: And what were they doing?

BROTHER JOHN: They were engaged in the act o' sodomy.

CROWN LAWYER: And then what happened?

BROTHER JOHN: They jumped apart when they heard me approach, an' the guilty jumped up and threatened me, an' used violence ...

DEFENSE LAWYER: Let me remind the court that Christopher Simms is not guilty until such time as found guilty ...

JUDGE: So noted.

CROWN LAWYER: Now, Brother John, how much violence did the accused use, if accused is a word allowed by this court, that is.

BROTHER JOHN: He struck me an' knocked me down.

CROWN LAWYER: Did you strike back?

BROTHER JOHN: No, sir ... I am a servant of the Lord, bound, as He commands, to turn the other cheek.

CROWN LAWYER: And what threats did Mr. Simms use?

BROTHER JOHN: He said he'd, and these are his exact words,

he'd break me hooked nose so it'd never be straight again ...
(VIRGINIA laughs ... JOSHUA MARKADY laughs.
BROTHER JOHN shoots them a cold glance.)
CROWN LAWYER: No further questions, your Honour.
(The JUDGE is seen scribbling notes.)
JUDGE: The defense may proceed.
(Christopher's lawyer approaches BROTHER JOHN.)
DEFENSE LAWYER: Now, this act of sodomy as you call it ... please tell the court exactly what you saw, what they were doing, that is.
BROTHER JOHN: They were ... embracin' ... in an indecent way ... ya know, like man and wife!
DEFENSE LAWYER: Describe their positions exactly.
BROTHER JOHN: They were lyin' on the ground ... with the guilty ... with the teacher on top ... as ya might expect.
DEFENSE LAWYER: And the boy was how ... describe his position.
BROTHER JOHN: Face up ... 'twas he looked over and saw me first.
DEFENSE LAWYER: Not face down ...
BROTHER JOHN: No sir.
(The LAWYER pauses and consults his notes.)
DEFENSE LAWYER: Now, about this alleged assault the defendant made upon you. Did you threaten him in any way?
BROTHER JOHN: Most certainly not!
DEFENSE LAWYER: Did you threaten the boy?
BROTHER JOHN: No sir.
DEFENSE LAWYER: Think a minute. Did you order the boy to go with you, and start toward him in a threatening manner?
BROTHER JOHN: I admonished 'em, as was me Christian duty, not to do the horrible thing he were doin' ... maybe I stepped forward to plead with 'em.
DEFENSE LAWYER: Did you raise your hand?
BROTHER JOHN: I don't remember ...
DEFENSE LAWYER: You remember everything else ... was it then Mr. Simms pushed you?
BROTHER JOHN: Maybe so ... listen here, Solomon Marks already told ya how he had seen the both of 'em behind his shed late at night indecently exposed and in a shameless embrace ... the whole harbour knowed about 'em and the whole harbour is behind me. I'm not on trial here ... he is.
(The lights go down on BROTHER JOHN's tirade long enough to sense a passing of time. They come up to show CHRISTOPHER on the stand. BROTHER JOHN joins the assembled in the court room.)
DEFENSE LAWYER: You worked away from home for a number of years. What led you to return?

CHRISTOPHER: The school had been without a regular teacher for two years, and had actually been closed all one winter.
DEFENSE LAWYER: It was a small school?
CHRISTOPHER: One room.
DEFENSE LAWYER: You had taught before?
CHRISTOPHER: Yes sir ... first as a grade teacher then as vice principal in a six-room school here in St. John's.
DEFENSE LAWYER: When did you first meet Eli Pallisher?
CHRISTOPHER: On the day of my arrival. He was with Joshua Markady on the wharf. Joshua mentioned him in his letters as a brilliant youngster having promising prospects, provided he received proper instruction.
BROTHER JOHN: Is that what you call what you gave 'em ... proper instruction?
JUDGE: Order please ... continue.
DEFENSE LAWYER: Describe your relations with the boy.
BROTHER JOHN: I already did ...
JUDGE: One more out burst and I'll clear this room. This is a court room, not a stage head ... continue, please.
CHRISTOPHER: Aside from Joshua Markady and Virginia, he was the only intellectual companion I had in the harbour.
DEFENSE LAWYER: Your relations were entirely intellectual?
CHRISTOPHER: Oh no ... we ...
(BROTHER JOHN interrupts.)
BROTHER JOHN: Ha ... there it is ...
JUDGE: Mr. McKim ... this is my last warning to you.
DEFENSE LAWYER: Mr. Simms ...
CHRISTOPHER: We developed a deep emotional attachment. He's like a son to Joshua Markady and like a younger brother to me. A companion and friend for whom I have the deepest affection and the highest hopes.
DEFENSE LAWYER: Do you have the same sort of relationships with the other students as you did with Eli Pallisher?
CHRISTOPHER: If you mean do I love them, yes, I do. And they knew it and trusted me and worked hard because of it. But none of the others had the brilliance of mind and spirit that I found in Eli, or the same emotional responses.
DEFENSE LAWYER: You mentioned a Virginia?
(VIRGINIA straightens in her chair at the mention of her name.)
CHRISTOPHER: Yes, Virginia Marks, my fiancée. She's the daughter of the Mr. Marks who testified here this morning.
DEFENSE LAWYER: How did her father feel about your marriage plans?
CHRISTOPHER: He tried to break it up, with threats and intimidation.
DEFENSE LAWYER: Now, I believe that nearly all the people in

Caplin Bight belong to a certain religion ... the Church of the Firstborn?
CHRISTOPHER: Except for my father and Joshua Markady.
DEFENSE LAWYER: You refused to join ...
CHRISTOPHER: I was never asked ... but in any case, it's nothing more than a sect of pure hypocrisy.
(As before, the lights go down to give a sense of time. When they come up the Crown is questioning CHRISTOPHER.)
CROWN LAWYER: Are you a Christian, Mr. Simms?
DEFENSE LAWYER: Objection!
JUDGE: Sustained.
CROWN LAWYER: But, my Lord, my learned friend has already questioned his client about religion.
JUDGE: That was to establish that Mr. Simms did not belong to the same faith as the majority of the people in Caplin Bight. Beyond that, his religious beliefs are irrelevant, objection sustained.
CROWN LAWYER: Well Mr. Simms's religious faith, or lack of it aside, his attitudes toward love as he calls it are certainly relevant ... answer me this Mr. Simms, would you call this Christian love, between you and Eli Pallisher?
CHRISTOPHER: What I'm talking about is precisely the compassion taught by Christ ... to the denial of one's self interest.
CROWN LAWYER: But the lover, if you'll pardon the expression, gets nothing out of it at all.
CHRISTOPHER: On the contrary ... the emotional dividends from this sort of investment are enormous.
CROWN LAWYER: Ah, yes, the emotional dividends. But of course there's no dirty sex mixed up with it, or am I wrong? Did you admit earlier that there was?
CHRISTOPHER: Sex is not dirty, sir ... except in your mouth.
CROWN LAWYER: You regard it as sacred, perhaps, beyond all human regulation.
CHRISTOPHER: If a sexual relationship has no love in it, then it is entirely vicious, and it makes not the slightest difference whether it is blessed by some church or not ... look, maybe John McKim is honestly mistaken, maybe he believes he isn't lying and in his religious zeal and his Puritan horror he misinterpreted what he saw. He was probably carried away by his shock of seeing a couple of undraped bodies, jumped to the conclusion that he was witnessing a sin against nature, and then built his suspicions into a dead certainty.
(The lights give us our passage of time again. When they come up, ELI is on the stand.)
ELI: We were never behind Virginia's father's shed ... it's a lie.
CROWN LAWYER: And you didn't think it unusual to be rolling around in the grass with your teacher?

ELI: Of course not ... and we weren't rolling around in the grass ... we were wrestling ... that's all we were doing, wrestling ... a sexual act is a consummation of love and that doesn't happen in wrestling and playing around. Christopher was teasing me, that's all ...
CROWN LAWYER: Teasing you? Not something that the school board of the area would approve of, I don't think ... the teacher in the grass teasing a pupil?
ELI: Not teasing in that way ... there was nothing sexually demonstrative ... my God, we were simply having a laugh.
(The LAWYER scans his notes. ELI is becoming uncomfortable. He's afraid of saying the wrong thing.)
CROWN LAWYER: Those nights you spent with the accused at the Markady house, what did you do there?
ELI: We read and talked ... history, science, literature, even some philosophy ...
CROWN LAWYER: You were seen on numerous occasions leaving the Markady house very early in the morning ... three, sometimes four o'clock ... is this true?
ELI: What are you saying ... what crime is that?
CROWN LAWYER: Is it true or isn't it?
(ELI begins to show some strain.)
ELI: Why are you asking me that ... what does that have to do with anything?
JUDGE: Just answer yes or no ...
(ELI looks around the room. Things are closing in.)
ELI: Yes ... there were nights when I stayed late.
CROWN LAWYER: As I understand, against the wishes of your father and mother ... did Mr. Simms encourage you to stay?
ELI: Lots of nights I wasn't aware of the time, that's all ... Mr. Markady would cook up some food and I'd stay and ...
CROWN LAWYER: Mr. Markady would encourage you to disobey the wishes of your parents, as well?
ELI: No..that's not what I said ... that's not what you asked. You asked if Christopher did ...
CROWN LAWYER: Well, who did then ... was it Mr. Simms, Mr. Markady ... who?
(ELI looks directly into the eyes of the CROWN LAWYER, then into the eyes of JOHN McKIM. Something transforms him. He sits straighter in his chair.)
ELI: No one ... no one made me do anything. I stayed because I wanted to stay ... you're trying to get me to say things ... you're trying to confuse me ...
CROWN LAWYER: Okay, okay ... let's leave that ...
(The LAWYER pauses.)
CROWN LAWYER: What are your feelings toward Mr. Simms, now?

ELI: The same as they always were ... I love him like a brother.

CROWN LAWYER: I find it a concern that a boy of your age should be unusually familiar with sexual matters. Where did you learn these things...?

ELI: The theoretical part I learned from Christopher and Mr. Markady.

CROWN LAWYER: Ah! The theoretical part! And what about the practical part? Where did you learn that? Isn't it true that Mr. Markady has his old schooner tied up to his wharf?

(ELI's confused.)

ELI: Yes ... why?

CROWN LAWYER: And doesn't that schooner still have bunks in it?

ELI: Yes ... up forward ...

CROWN LAWYER: Well forward..away from the companionway in a schooner that hardly anyone goes aboard of anymore. Except by one witness account of a night when you and Mr. Simms were seen going aboard and not leaving until the small hours of the morning and that is where you learned the practical part and you were taught by Mr. Simms, your teacher.

(ELI doesn't answer. VIRGINIA moves as if to go to him. ELIAS, MARTHA and the rest of the room watch a young man in the most difficult time of his life look suddenly at ease, almost serene, as if a weight had been lifted from his life.)

CROWN LAWYER: Well ...

(ELI speaks quietly but very clearly.)

ELI: That's not true. It's a lie ... he's turned the whole harbour against us ... the three of us.

(ELI looks at CHRISTOPHER and VIRGINIA. He doesn't see anyone else. Suddenly his eyes focus on BROTHER JOHN, himself reacting to the scene in front of him.)

ELI: Brother John ...

CROWN LAWYER: Pardon?

ELI: The practical part I learned from Brother John McKim, the pastor of the Church of the Firstborn, who testified on the stand this morning.

(The courtroom is quiet.)

CROWN LAWYER: You mean that your pastor gave you instruction in the practical affairs of life ... leading toward marriage and so on.

(ELI is very clear and methodical in what he says.)

ELI: No. I don't mean that at all. I mean I slept with him, more nights than I can count, and we did together the very things that Christopher Simms is wrongly accused of.

(The room is in shock.)

JUDGE: The Reverend Mr. McKim is not on trial. It is a very serious thing to accuse a man of such a crime, especially under

oath, and without corroborative testimony.
ELI: I know that ... but it's the truth ...

Scene 10:
Pallisher House

(ELIAS, MARTHA and ELI are seen in the kitchen. They look as if they're preparing to go out the door, except for ELI who sits quietly at the table.)
MARTHA: Hurry, Eli ... we'll be late.
(ELI doesn't respond.)
ELIAS: Did ya hear yer mother, boy ... get yer coat.
ELI: I'm not goin'.
MARTHA: What's wrong, Eli ... are ya not feelin' well.
ELI: I feel fine ... but I'm not goin' to church. Not now or ever again.
ELIAS: I'll only say this once. The teacher was found guilty and got what he deserved ... he's in jail.
ELI: No one believed me ... the jury, you, and not even you, Mother.
MARTHA: It's all over, Eli ... you gotta stop harpin' on it. C'mon to church, it'll be good for you ... to see your friends.
ELI: My friends don't go to church ... I don't believe in the God you worship and I won't pretend to pray to him.
(ELIAS sits down very slowly. The room is quiet.)
ELIAS: I should whip the daylights outta ya.
ELI: Try it ... go ahead and beat me if ya think ya can do it. But I'm warnin' ya, I'll hit ya back.
MARTHA: Eli! Don't talk to yer father like that. Elias, you leave him be now, he's not at fault. He'll be better of this soon. I'll stay home with 'em.
ELI: Go on to the meeting ... nothing makes any difference, nothing you can say or do. It's all been done.
ELIAS: I'll not shelter a blasphemer under my roof, do ya understand. Ya can think it over for tonight, ya needn't go, but we'll talk of it tomorrow.
ELI: All the talkin's been done. I should have had this out a year ago. I'm never goin' to darken the door of that damned church of yours again so long as I live.
(This is too much for ELIAS. He rises and starts toward ELI who jumps up and grabs a heavy iron poker.)
MARTHA: That's enough, Elias ... Eli, sit down, now! Lord, Lord, what have I done to have me own fightin' like murderers ...
ELI: I'm leavin' this place.
ELIAS: If ya do you'll not come back ...
ELI: I'm not plannin' to.
(ELI gets his coat and heads for the door.)
MARTHA: Your father means it, Eli. He'll lock ya from the house ...

(ELI walks out the door.)

Scene 11:
Joshua Markady's House

(ELI and JOSHUA are seated at the table.)
ELI: I can't go home ... there'd be nothing easier for me than to go up to the mercy seat in the church, confess I'm a sinner and be taken back and prayed over but I can't do it ...
JOSHUA: You needn't explain it to me, my son.
ELI: But you, too ... .you got dragged into this.
JOSHUA: Sure, now they're all right that you're livin' here ... they figure they've got the heathens together under one roof ... we've gone out to the Evil One like the scapegoats from the Children of Israel, and we're to be left to Satan in the outer darkness.
(A knock is heard at the door.)
JOSHUA: Come in at yer peril ... it's been open for the last sixty-odd years ...
(BROTHER JOHN McKIM enters the house.)
JOSHUA: Well, well ... what's this, the sheriff comin' to serve summons. You've more brass than a ship, McKim. What brings you to the house of the devil?
BROTHER JOHN: Ye can save the civilities for your friends, Mr. Markady. I've come to have a word with Eli.
ELI: Here I am then ...
BROTHER JOHN: I'd like to speak to ya alone.
ELI: Anything ya have to say to me, you can say in front of Mr. Markady. But ya should know I've nothing to say to you at all.
BROTHER JOHN: Eli ... we were friends once, remember? More than ever I want to be yer friend. I prayed for ya last night. The whole harbour is prayin' for ya.
ELI: Yes ... I heard ... and I hope your prayers get as far as the ends of your noses.
BROTHER JOHN: Don't hate *me*, Eli. *I* always treated ya with great favour an' believed the Lord would speak to ya through me. What I did was for your own good and for the greater glory of the Lord. You've been trapped and snared by the devil ... a brand that had to be snatched from the burnin' ... I did it from the Christian love that's in me heart, seekin' the sheep that are lost, like the Lord says in the parable.
(JOSHUA has heard enough.)
JOSHUA: McKim ... you're not just a hypocrite, you're worse. I'm goin' to have to shoot ya ... and it's a pity, 'cause I know you're an able man and in some other time or place ya might've turned out different ...
BROTHER JOHN: Eli ... ya can't hate me. Come back to me, boy.

I know you're not wicked. The Lord sent me to ya with a purpose. I'd be willin' to forgive ya, Eli ... and you forgive me, too, if I've done ya wrong ...
ELI: It's not me ... you didn't force me to do anything. I trusted you ... it's what you've done to Christopher.
JOSHUA: I never killed a man in me life, McKim, but I'm not too old to start ... the very first time I catches ya in the woods, or out in a boat, or any other place where it can be made into an accident, I'll shoot ya like the dog that ya are. The first time I get a chance I'll put a bullet through ya or ram yer skiff and drown ya ... an' in case ya think I'm makin' an idle threat in the heat of the moment, I swear it to ya on the blood of the Lord Jesus.
BROTHER JOHN: Would ya be party to murder, Eli? Is this how far you've strayed from the Lord?
ELI: Was it murder when the Lord sent fire upon Sodom?
JOSHUA: Go yer way, McKim ... an' leave this lad alone. It isn't the Lord that speaks to you, it's the lust of the flesh speakin' out of your own evil heart. It's enough you've done to him already.
BROTHER JOHN: Please don't hate me, Eli ...
(BROTHER JOHN leaves.)

Scene 12:
Open Meadow

(ELI and VIRGINIA are sitting while they talk.)
ELI: St. Paul had a phrase for what happened to Christopher ... crucifying Christ afresh.
VIRGINIA: Oh, forget about the Scriptural allusions, Eli, you sound like John McKim.
ELI: They come naturally ... they were bred into me. I sucked them in with mother's milk.
VIRGINIA: You know what I'm trying to say. We've spent so much time together lately ... just talking. I love it. I mean I love Christopher, I'd die for him, but I never feel as free as when I'm with you.
ELI: Like eagles ...?
VIRGINIA: Ya ... like eagles ...
(They listen to the sounds of the earth.)
VIRGINIA: I never believed in any of it, not really, none of the things we were taught. From the day I started to grow up I was trapped and put in a cage. It was all, 'Virginia do this', 'Virginia do that', 'Keep your knees covered, dear'. I mean, wouldn't it make you want to spit? And what's the use of them telling you about purity of heart when God plants the apple of temptation right in your own body ... and they talk about salvation and robes of righteousness and stuff like that, when all the time you know what your salvation is.

ELI: What is our salvation ... yours and mine? Is it here in this place?
VIRGINIA: You have your salvation, Eli ... it happened in that courtroom.
ELI: And what do I do with it ... my salvation ...?
VIRGINIA: You take possession of your own soul, that's what. Our spirit may be damned to hell and good luck to it if it is, but our bodies will be redeemed forever and ever.
ELI: Nothing very wicked about that ...
VIRGINIA: No, there isn't, but sometimes I want to coax the world into sin. I can't stand the smell of righteousness, it makes me sick. I want to dance like the tribes of Africa, I want to wrap myself in lust and madness. They used to tell us about the perfect liberty of the children of God, but it's the children of the devil who have the real liberty. Once you're passed all salvation then you're truly free.
(ELI is silent. VIRGINIA moves closer to him. ELI says nothing as VIRGINIA leans into him and kisses him passionately.)
VIRGINIA: We love each other ... the three of us. You, me, Christopher ... we'll all be damned together.
(They make love.)

Scene 13:
Chapel

(BROTHER JOHN is in the middle of his sermon.
ELI is not there.)
BROTHER JOHN: ... the well-worn path of the wicked is clearly marked, and stained with the honey-sweet blood of the lamb, it clings to the fern and calls out as ye pass, taste me, taste me, and ye shall feel the beauty of sin, yet the Lord says, ye that have sinned belong to the fires of hell, and the wax that melts from the burning shall scorch yer feet, no sinner shall walk without wounds and the breath of angels not cool their fiery souls ...
(BROTHER JOHN stops.)
... the cool breath of angels ... I want to feel it again. Dear Jesus, let me walk with you, don't throw me out. Let me drink the cool waters of forgiveness ... do ye hear me, Lord ...
(The congregation witness the unravelling of a man of God.
They shift uneasily in their seats, uncomfortable
with what they hear.)
... what have I done to be thrown from the steps of the saved ... where is your mercy now? Hear me brethren, it is to ye and not the Lord I confess.

Scene 14:
Chapel

(ELI has come into the chapel and stands silently. He is in deep thought, we see the pain on his face, we see the memories. BROTHER JOHN walks in.)

BROTHER JOHN: I guess you heard what took place here last night.

ELI: Yes, I did ...

BROTHER JOHN: I'm leavin' ... I've told the congregation and I told yer parents what really happened ... not all of it, mind ya. Wasn't easy, lad, but then nothin's been very easy this last eight or nine months, has it?

(ELI looks on quietly.)

BROTHER JOHN: If ya ever wish for a taste of hell, Eli, just try and live like I did this last while ... the life of a sinner. I did ya wrong ... it's a hard thing to always choose the right road, with the voice of the flesh speakin' so guileful ... I'm sorry for what I've done, is what I'm sayin'. I'm cursed and cut off from the Lord's elect an' my name will be blotted out of the Book of Life. I'm cursed in the eyes of the angels of God an' the four beasts that guard his throne.

ELI: Don't preach to me again, Brother John ...

(There is an uncomfortable silence in the chapel.)

BROTHER JOHN: Word has gone to St. John's about Mr. Simm's innocence. What's gone on between the teacher and me, there's no forgiveness. But the wrong I've done you, Eli, say ya forgive me for that.

ELI: I've told you before ... what went on between us was between us ... but I forgive you if forgiveness is what you want. But I won't pretend that it's easy for me to forgive putting a friend in jail ... for a long while I've hated you with bitterness and contempt, but that's all over now. I'll hold nothing against you for what we did together.

BROTHER JOHN: Thank you, lad ... you've a kind heart, I always knew that. I was tormented that I might have been the instrument that put out the flame of charity in your soul.

(BROTHER JOHN begins to leave the chapel.)

ELI: Where will you go?

BROTHER JOHN: Oh, I don't know ... in a strange way I feel a cleansin' somewhere inside of me. Like when I first testified and was saved. The Lord's heart is even bigger than I thought ...

(BROTHER JOHN looks once more into ELI's eyes.)

BROTHER JOHN: I still love you, Eli ... try to think of me kindly sometimes.

ELI: I know ... and I will.

BROTHER JOHN: Good-bye, lad.

(BROTHER JOHN leaves while ELI stays and looks around. He sits in a pew. The lights go down.)

Scene 15:
Open Meadow

(VIRGINIA and ELI talk.)
ELI: I feel sick about it, that's how I feel. I love you more than anything I've known ... and I know you love me.
VIRGINIA: I do, you know I do ... don't ask me to explain my life, I can't do that ... your love has kept me all this time and I'll keep that warmth in my heart forever.
ELI: So I was someone to entertain you while Chris was in jail ... someone to get you through the hard times.
VIRGINIA: Don't drive knives into me, Eli ... it's not like you ... you've helped me when I needed it most and I know I'm a better person because of you. You've got to leave. It's the way it's got to be ... this is the way I want it to be ... you've got to leave here ...
ELI: My heart is broken ... you know that. Things will never be the same, even if the three of us were to meet on the street in St. John's ... we'll never look or talk to each other the same way ... I want to cling to you forever and I know, in a way, that's impossible and what you say is right but it doesn't make it any easier. My only protection has been in your arms, your mouth on mine ...
(VIRGINIA looks at him and begins to stroke his face.)
VIRGINIA: My sweet, sweet little Eli ... how I envy the world for being with you longer than I will.
(She begins to unbutton his shirt then kisses him. He responds as before, he kisses the woman he loves. They begin to undress.)
VIRGINIA: One last time, Eli ...
(They slowly go to the ground, their lives entwined, their hearts on fire.)

Scene 16:
Joshua Markady's House

(ELI and JOSHUA are at the table.)
JOSHUA: The steamer's well off Lattice Harbour Head by now and what would you say or do if ya could talk to her. Soon as she got that wire from Christopher, she was hell bent on goin' to St. John's, sure, she told ya that.
ELI: Christ Almighty ... I thought she'd see me first.
JOSHUA: Good Lord, he's startin' to swear ... listen here, do you think it'd be as easy as that for Virginia to just stroll in and ask ya to walk her down to the wharf and say so long to ya after the summer you two have had ...
ELI: But love ... what about love?

JOSHUA: Love between a man and a woman is a thing ya can do little about. It takes possession of ya and there ya are ... I can see well enough that you're in misery, but these things just don't obey the rules the way they ought to.
(ELI stands up and paces the floor.)
ELI: But she's going to have our child, my child ...
JOSHUA: Christopher knows that, but listen here, nobody owns a child, Eli ... if there's a human claim on it, it comes later, by those who nurture it, love it and help it grow.
ELI: Love is harder than dying, it must be. Such sudden and bitter changes ... your whole life, everything you've loved disappears after childhood.
JOSHUA: Well, I'm glad you found that out for yourself. Everyone who's goin' to transcend their childhood has to watch it be killed ... but the pain is worth it, boy, 'cause it's also a kind of rebirth.
ELI: What do I do now?
JOSHUA: Do what's best fer ya ... get yourself ready for college and get that education you always said you wanted ... see the world and then come back and straighten this place out, 'cause for all it's faults, ya know, it's worth savin'.
(There is a long pause, it's all been said. ELI goes to the door.)
ELI: I'm gonna go in and check the salmon pool ... see if there's anything running yet ... I'll see you later.
JOSHUA: Oh I'll be here, my son. I'm not goin' anywhere.
(ELI leaves.)

Scene 17:
Open Meadow

(ELI, on his way to the salmon pool, stops for a moment where he and CHRISTOPHER swam and where he last held VIRGINIA. Then he hears it, the unmistakable cry of an eagle somewhere overhead. He hears VIRGINIA's voice somewhere in the sky above.)
VIRGINIA: *(Voice over.)* Like eagles, Eli ... free as eagles.
(He takes off his clothes and stands with his arms outstretched.)
ELI: *(Shouting.)* Here I am, Lord ... your obedient servant. Strike *me* down in all your righteous glory. If not, let me walk to the end of the world alone.
(ELI dives into the water.)

Curtain

Woman In A Monkey Cage

1993

Written by
Berni Stapleton

WOMAN IN A MONKEY CAGE

(Woman has been locked up for thirty days).

DAY 30
Lights Up

WOMAN: What are you lookin' at?
What are you lookin' at?
See anything you like?
I'm sick and tired of you all the time lookin' at me.
(Pause.)
Look at me. Can you smell me? Would you like to smell me? I smell good ... I used to smell good.

See my arms? And my legs ... I've had my arms and my legs kissed, and my lips too. One time, I kissed a woman. It was only the one time.

Would you like to touch me? It's easy, all you have to do is open the door and ...

I'd kill for a smoke. And a nice brandy, in a snifter, a nice heated snifter filled with Remy, brimming over with Remy, I could lick the drops off the side of the glass and smoke and kick back ... this is not a non-smoking cage, is it?

I know what you want. There's no avoidin' the future if you knows what's gonna happen.

After all this time, surely to God you could say something. You want to know my name. I know you do, you're just dyin for me to say but ... not yet.

You look like a tree. The way you move, you remind me of the nursery rhyme, that one "bend and stretch ... bend and stretch, reach for the sky" 1, 2, 3, 4, 5, 6, 7, 8, 9, 10!

Blackout

DAY 34:
Lights Up

(Woman is dancing. There is no music. She glances out and sees watcher. She stops for a moment, then closes her eyes and resumes her dance.)

Blackout

DAY 35:
Lights Up

WOMAN: Listen. I appreciate the larger cage. At least I can see some of the other cages from here. I can see that smug little monkey. Still ... it's too bad about the elephant. No more elephants. But that just goes to show you! I mean, survival is everything, right? And *I'm* still here, right? And if that's what it takes to get a few creature comforts around this place, well, I can watch them all drop dead. Jesus God-forgive-me. But, if we're all gonna get bumped up one, if we're all gonna move up the corporate ladder, so to speak, then *I* should have gotten the *zebra* cage! You know, the elephant dies and you switch us all around and you move the monkey into that great big zebra cage and you go and stick me in here in the monkey cage and you haven't even changed the sign! It still says monkey, but it should say—that should say Woman!

No more elephants. No sense cryin, is there? Tears'd be wasted on you.

Must have been the stress got to it. Now, me, I'm used to stress. I'm a hair stylist. Beauty is a very stressful business. I could have a perm, a colour and a wax and peel goin' at the same time, and believe me, a wax and peel isn't easy, you can haul the face right off someone ...

It's sick, what you've done. Having the elephant stuffed and animated and up walking around like that. It's like some kind of ghost wandering around out there. I know it's dead. I saw it die, for Christ sake. What's it doing up walking around like that. If you're dead, you should go lie down somewhere! Gives me the willies.

I know what you want.
(She starts to dance.)
I'm flyin'. I'm flyin'.

Fuckin' dingbat. Locked up like a filthy animal! Quit flyin' and get back in your own head and smell your own stink!

Fuckin' dingbat. Talk to Watcher half-way decent and we might get outta here!

That's funny. Why do you think it's a he?
I know why, you want it to be a he!
Because you're horny!
You are so!
You don't have to be horny, you know. Just look around you. All these lovely ripe bananas.
I bet you'd sleep better at night.
So what? Let it look! It's just a stupid elephant who starved itself to death because it couldn't cope.
Ha! You don't do disgusting stuff! Then what's that all over your fingers, huh! What are all these little cuts you got all over your fingers! Huh!! Sex'd be better for you than slicin' your fingers open!
You started doin' that when a bad man got you in an alley. Now a bad thing's got you in a cage!
You can't cope out there, that's how come you're in here in the first place. Relax. Have sex with a banana.
Daddy's little girl, daddy's little girl.
Get a grip! No sharp objects in here, huh?
Bad man's in the alley and your kid is in the street.
What was your kid doin' in the street in the first place?!
CUTTIN' AT YOUR FINGERS EVERY OTHER DAY!!!!
SHUT-UP SHUT-UP SHUT-UP SHUT-UP SHUT-UP!!!!
1, 2, 3, 4, 5, 6, 7, 8, 9, 10!!!

Blackout

DAY 35-A:
Lights Up

WOMAN: Sex, sex, sex was, well, you know, the man and the woman would ... or it could be two men, or it could be two women, or it could be two men and a woman, or it could be two women and a man, or, and, well, shit, sex was like riding a bike, once you got the hang of it, it could be very pleasant and therapeutic and you never forgot how. Women could go for bike rides and think about anything at all, whereas men were very bike obsessed. Women could go for long bike rides, and men went for short bike rides, and if you fell off the bike, you got pregnant. Now record that and stick it up your arse, I'm really glad you're here, now fuck right off.

Blackout

DAY 35-B:
Lights Up

WOMAN: I am normal. I am me. I am me.
I am me.
I am me. I have a name.
Listen. You got the right idea. A place for everything and everything in its place. Woman in the monkey cage and all is right with the universe. You thing I give a fuck? Hey. I'm safe. I'm safe in my place 'cause I know where my place is. All I want is for that Jesus-God-forgive-me sign to get changed.
I'm safe, we're all safe, nobody gets hurt. I'm safe, we're all safe and nobody gets hurt. I'm safe, we're all safe and nobody gets hurt.
Just pass over your wallet, lady, and nobody gets hurt. Don't make it hard on yourself, lady, don't move and no need to get hurt, see, keep your trap shut, you just pull up your skirt, that's nice, yeah, just like that, lady, oh lady, yeah, that's nice, don't make me have to hurt you now, don't make me have to hurt you now... you a townie, lady? You looks like a townie ...
1, 2, 3, 4, 5, 6, 7, 8, 9, 10!!!
I know what you want. Don't say I never gave you nothin'.

Blackout

DAY 36:
Lights Up

WOMAN: What are you lookin' at?
What the fuck do you think you're lookin' at?
I know what *I'd* like to look at. I'd like to look at me. I can't remember what I look like. Sometimes I close my eyes and I try to picture my face, but all I see is Michelle Pfiefer. She had good hair.
Everything is alien here. Even me. Especially me. I'd like to shave all the hair off my body so there'll be nothing ... animal about me. God, I've got hair comin' in on my legs like weeds and bushes growin' under my armpits and my eyebrows are takin' over my face. I'd like to scrape myself bald from head to toe, everywhere, just to feel... human... just to feel soft again and smooth and clean ... I wish I had a mirror ... afraid I'll hurt myself?
You remind me of Joe. He never talked much, either. I could talk to Joe 'til I was blue in the face, I'd come home from work and go, "Joe, you shoulda been in the shop today, Joe, Mrs. Rose came in and wanted a bleach job on top of her perm and I told her

it wouldn't work and I turned her hair green, Joe" and Joe would just sit and read the paper and nod ... or sometimes, you know, I'd be talkin' about something real important, something real meaningful to me, and he'd just, I'd be right in the middle of a sentence and he'd say, "What's for supper?" or, "Pass the butter." And there I'd be, with all me feelings hanging down around me ankles. Don't get me wrong, though! We had a good marriage. The only reason we got divorced is ... he moved away.

Are you the boogey-man? You look like the boogey-man. When I was little, I was afraid of the boogey-man. When I was really little, the boogey-man lived under my bed, he did. He crawled out from underneath my bed at night, but I flew away so he couldn't get me!

When I was little, you know who I wanted to be when I grew up? Amelia Earhart. She flew away but she never had to come back. She made the world smaller. She took the ocean and shrank it to the size of a single newspaper headline. 'First woman to solo across the Atlantic'. My grandma saved the old clipping and gave it to me and I could take all them miles and miles and just fold them up and put them in my pocket. I took flying lessons one time, in a plane. This old guy, he had a bush plane even more racked up than he was, the pair of them were bushed. This old guy, Cyril, he takes my money up front, and then he tells me there's no refunds, no-where-no-way-no-how! And then he looks at my chest. And, he's lookin at my chest like, where the fuck are her tits? I nearly apologized to him, he looked that offended. I wanted to say, "I'm sorry my tits are so small". He loved his plane though. Loved it, stroked it, petted it, called it honey, baby, sweetie, she, her ...what a hoot! He treated women like objects and planes like women. I never did get my pilot's license. Cyril crashed in his honey. Smacked into the side of a mountain. Love is blind, right? So, gettin' a refund was definitely out of the question. Amelia Earhart went down, too, but her plane wasn't the woman, *she* was the woman...

Wish I had a smoke. I could eat a cigarette. You got cable here?

>Little girl, little girl, fly away home
>The boogey-man's waitin' and he's all alone
>Little girl, little girl, fly or be dead
>The boogey-man's crawling right into your bed!

I bet you're pissed off. The elephant tricked you, didn't it? It didn't give you what you want. It never made a peep the whole time it was alive, so you couldn't record it. You've got no voice for your ghost. But I know what you want. You want me to tell about ... me, so you can record it. You want my voice. I'm full of voices, voices in my head, comin' out of my mouth all the time.

Oh God ... shit... my stomach, damn that hurts! Listen, I got

really bad cramps in my stomach. Oh, no, I got a really sharp pain right here ... uh ... help me, it hurt so much, please do something, it's all those goddamn bananas, I'm poisoned, get me the fuck out of here, I'm sick!!!
(Pause.)
O.K., I was faking.
(Pause.)
(She begins to make monkey sounds.)
eee! eee! ooooh!
EEEE, EEEE, EEEEE, E, E, E, OOH, UH, OOH, UH, OOOHOOOHOOOHOOOHOOO, EEEEE, E, E,
EEE, EEE EEEEEE, OOHOOHOOH, EEE, E, E, E, !!!!!!!
WHY ARE YOU STILL GIVING ME BANANAS! WHY HAVEN'T YOU CHANGED THE MONKEY SIGN! I'M A CIVILIZED HUMAN BEING! I WANT MY OWN SIGN! ARE YOU TRYING TO CONFUSE ME!!!!
I'm so hairy. I'm so goddamn fucking hairy I sit around all day growing hair and gibbering like a monkey. I don't know what I look like. I could live here for a million years and get wrinkles and turn grey and have dirt all over my face and not even know I'm an ape, I'm an ape!
I'm ape over you,
I was born in the zoo,
with the monkey and the elephant.
I'm a monkey.

Blackout

DAY 37:
Lights Up

WOMAN: Oh great spirit
who flew in on the wind
you haven't used your wings in ages
it's time now to begin
you can't dream on stars
there's things in space
but you can fly to another place
here is the door
I've cut it wide
now use the door ...
now spirit leave this body to herself and fly, now spirit leave this body to herself and fly, now spirit leave this body to herself and fly and fly and fly ...
Mom was Inuit. Out of Labrador. When I was little, the welfare crowd came to the house one time and tried to take me

and my brothers away. We were after goin' to school with cuts all over our fingers. We had the croup and mom took us to the doctor, but she also took a little knife and made little nicks on our hands. She was lettin' out the bad spirit that was makin' us sick.

Mom was an angel. And now I've met the devil.

Mom was an angel. She had long hair, shone like fresh tar and her skin was brown, like that expensive panelling. Daddy was Irish Red. He worshipped the ground mom walked on, 'cause she gave him all those sons. Daddy loved his sons. Daddy loved mom. I had that with Joe, too, at first, and I'm tellin' you, once you've had that kind of love with someone, anything after is just a faded colour, like a shirt washed out too many times.

Mom told me, she said, "An ignorant man is a man with his eyes closed. He cannot see. You are only what you are. But you can see. And that is a brighter gift than bright hair and skin. When I was young, I was walking by the woods one day. And a bear ran out of the woods at me. He ran like he was in a dream, strong and fast, his muscles rippling like a brook over his bones. I raised my rifle and waited for the sure shot. I watched him as he ran at me. He saw my rifle and smelled my fear and knew me for what I was. I saw his eyes and his teeth and I knew him for what he was. And then I blew his head off. There was blood on me, to mark me with respect. When I told my good father what had happened, he swooned with fear and told all his friends how lucky I was to escape with my life. And then he sold the bear skin. But now, I will tell you, I was not lucky. I was strong. My father was the lucky one. He got a skin for free!"

There's no avoiding the future if you knows what's gonna happen. You're gonna let me out. You just can't see yet. You don't know me for what I am. I'll help you to see ... what it's like to be me.

Blackout

DAY 38:
Lights Up

WOMAN: For God's sake, keep it away from me, I woke up and it was out there lookin' in at me, dear Jesus-God-forgive-me, it's dead and it's lookin' in at me, I'm afraid of it, yes, I am and I don't care, daddy told me there was no such thing as ghosts but daddy blew up with the rest of the world ...

The only thing that's free to walk around in this place is the elephant and it's dead! It opens its mouth and no voice comes out, it's got no voice. Can't you see how nervous it makes everybody, the monkey, the lion, the ... everything just freaks out when it comes near ... stupid, stupid elephant! I want to comfort them 'cause I know how scared *I* get.

I dream a lot. I dream of earth. I dream I get out of here and walk out into that big grey space. Last night I dreamed I was a monkey. That was a nightmare. Maybe the monkey has nightmares too, maybe it dreams it's a woman and wakes up screaming.

Maybe the elephant's soul is trapped in that body.

Keep it away!

Do you know, do you know what it's like to be just standing on the street. To look up and the sky is filled with big red space ships, like big red balloons just hangin' in the sky, like some giant is havin' a birthday party. People screaming and cars crashing. That car's comin' too fast. Too fast! Grab my hand. Grab my hand, jump! Jesus, jump! Grab my hand, I CAN'T REACH YOU, GRAB MY HAND!!!! 1, 2, 3, 4, 5, 6, 7, 8, 9, 10!

And now you are my keeper. You are my Watcher. I like it when you look at me. I miss you when you're not here. Can't you, could you, just once, open the door? Just open the door and let me touch you, just a touch, I need someone to touch me. We could stand beside each other, side by side and just barely feel ... your skin looks like leather, I wonder if it feels soft like leather. You could sway next to me, bend and stretch, and I could bend and stretch with you. We could almost dance, you and me ...

(She dances)

No-one had asked me to dance all night. I was spending all my time in the bathroom so no-one would know I was a wallflower. I went to the bathroom twelve times in one half hour. And then the band played 'Sweet Dreams'. And Joe came over. And all while we were dancin' I could smell his sweater. It smelled good. Like it just came in off the line.

It's not that I don't feel safe here. I do. You don't judge me.

I had a child. On earth. He was four. I can't say his name out loud. If I say his name out loud I'll go insane.

I think I was a good mother. Sometimes, after the divorce, I'd be too tired to cook and I'd give him Cheerios for supper but, I think I was a good mother. He had dark eyes ... elephant eyes.

I wish you'd been able to save another woman. I should be wishing for a man, I suppose, but ... another woman would understand me! I haven't had a period since I got here, did I tell you that? A woman would understand. When I got my first period, I called up my best friend and told her I thought I broke something inside me when I jumped on my bike too hard. And she laughed to kill herself and told me I didn't have to go to gym anymore when I was on the rag and I could hang out behind the school and smoke with all the others. I felt like I'd joined a club. I wanted to send out announcements. I wanted to walk up to strangers on the street and say, "I got my period!" Course, it don't take too long to figure out what's up, they tell you it's a wonderful gift, called the curse! And mom got me the big blue Kotex box. And the pads were these big long things with strips on each end you had to hook into your underwear. And when you had this big canoe in between your legs, sure, you waddled around like a duck! Shitbaked, you know, hopin' no boys would notice. Hopin' everyone else *would*, so they'd know, a real woman waddled among them ...

Your silence is killing me. Jesus, I'd even welcome Joe at this point. Daddy would laugh if he could hear that. When I told daddy I was divorcin' Joe, he said "What for? He don't drink, or beat you up! You don't know how good you got it! It's a sin!" he said. That's the only time in my life I never listened to daddy. Maybe if I hadn't got divorced the world wouldn't have ended and I wouldn't be in a monkey cage.

I wonder ... I wonder if the elephant was female ... if it had any children. Maybe that's what happened to it. Maybe it said its child's name out loud and went insane, maybe that's what happened. There's things you can do, you know, to stop from thinking about stuff you don't want to. Like, whenever I start thinking about stuff I don't want to, when the voices in my head get too loud, talking about stuff I don't want to hear, I just start countin', out loud, as fast and as loud as I can. It works! 1, 2, 3, 4, 5, 6, 7, 8, 9, 10! It works! 1, 2, 3, 4, 5, 6, 7, 8, 9, 10, grab my hand, 1, 2, 3, 4, 5, 6, 7, 8, 9, 10, never comin' home, never comin' home, it works, grab my hand, 1, 2, 3, 4, 5, 6, 7, 8, 9, 10! 10! 10! 10! 10! 10! 10! 10!

Who am I? I don't know who I am. You don't understand, I'm not supposed to be by myself, I've never lived by myself, I'm someone's mother, someone's wife, someone's daughter, someone's hair stylist. Now that I'm not anybody's anything, I don't know who I am.

I had a dream. In my dream you talked to me. You told me that when I had given you everything you wanted, you'd let me out. Or you would kill me.

Blackout

DAY 40:
Lights Up

WOMAN: ... now, spirit leave this body to herself and fly, now, spirit leave this body to herself and fly, now, spirit leave this body to herself and fly and fly and fly ...

I need a razor blade.

See this little half-moon scar, here? Right in between my toes? I was four, I was jumpin' off a pump-house with garbage bags tied on to me ... tryin' to fly. I was so sure if I could fly in my head, then I must be able get my body up there, too. Didn't work. I landed on a piece of glass. I was half hopin' my big toe was gonna come off. And look here, I got this little bone sticks out funny on my ankle. I was eight, dancin' in a Christmas concert with Jerome Hickey and he kicked me right in the ankle. I was hoppin' around so much, everyone thought we made up a new step. We got a standing ovation. After the concert I kicked him right back. And then I clapped and asked him how *he* like it! Daddy clocked me one for that, but I didn't care. And here, I got this burn mark on the back of my knee. I got a bit too close to a bonfire the first time I got drunk. I was thirteen. Climbed out my bedroom window and sneaked off to the Protestant graveyard. Drunk Catholic kids and dead Protestants, all the sinners in the one spot.

If you're dead you should go lie down somewhere!

Fuckin' elephant.

Want to see my stretch marks? You can still make 'em out, from when I was pregnant. And I got a little lump in my right ear. My cousin pierced my ears with an ice cube and a darning needle. I passed out halfway through. Hit the floor like a cold junk. I got a mark on the back of my head from that, but you can't see it, it's under my hair. See? I don't have to tell you nothin'. My whole life story's written all over my body.

And see all these little scars on my fingers? That's from times when I felt bad and I had to let out the bad spirits.

(She counts the scars.)

1, 2, 3, 4, 5, 6, 7, 8, 9, 10 ... 11, 12, 13, 14, 15, ...

(She dances.)

I'm flyin'. I'm flyin'. I'm not even here.

Blackout

DAY 47:
Lights Up

WOMAN: I am still sane. I am still sane. I am still sane. I am still sane. I am still sane, still sane, still sane! I am still sane and I've got the lipstick to prove it. Being saved from certain death and put in an intergalactic zoo is the very best thing that ever happened to me.

A woman with lipstick is the very picture of sanity.

Where are you? WHERE ARE YOU!?

You're not playin' by the rules, you fucking ugly Jesus-God-forgive-me ... I'm talkin', I'm talkin', you're supposed to be here! I'm talkin', listen, listen, listen, I'm giving you what you want! I'll tell you somethin juicy! I, I, I, I like to look pretty. I can't help it, it's a flaw in my feminism. On earth, I had sixteen different shades of lipstick and shoes that matched! One time, I marched down to the bank and told off the bank manager because he wouldn't give me a loan unless someone co-signed it with me! And Joe was gone then, and I was doin' just fine, payin' the bills and puttin' the grub on the table. So I went in there and I looked that three piece suit right in the tie and I said, "Now you listen here, buddy! I've been workin' since I was fifteen years old and my little bank account here, may not mean much to you, but right after I closes it, I'm gettin my best friend Eileen to close her's and then I'm getting Carla to close her's and then I'm gettin the girls at the Wash&Spin to close their's and then I'm gettin Marla to close her's and she sells Mary Kay and drives a pink Mercedes!" I did! I swear to God, I did! I got the loan! And I know, I know in my heart and soul that what gave me the confidence to go in there and do that was the fact that I was wearin' Revlon Purple Passion Creamy Fresh Lip Lustre #2!!

I'm a winter. That was my specialty, at the shop. Doin' colours. So I know, I'm a winter. I look best in a burgundy or deep red.

Got a light?

Blackout

DAY 50:
Lights Up

WOMAN: I fished with my daddy. I loved my daddy. I fished with daddy one summer when I was ... eleven. And then, when I was fifteen, I quit school and went at it for years, until they closed the fishery down and I had to get retrained. See, I had one brother was up on the mainland, and one brother in the pen, and one brother couldn't get on a boat to save his own life. He used to get seasick is what I mean. If the T.V. so much as started to roll, he had to go lie down. And daddy had his bad arm. What choice did I have, I did what I was told. So, I went on the water. But you want to know something? That was the next best thing to flyin', sittin' on top of the water. I was goin' out with Joe then. Times were good then. It's a funny thing, you know, when I met Joe, I forgot all about the boogey-man. Joe said, "A woman wantin' to fish, I s'pose you'll want to pee standing up next thing." I said, "I don't want to piss in the wind, my son, I'd rather sit down to pee anyday, it's much more dignified and it keeps your hands free."

Joe laughed at that. And me and daddy and Joe fished together. They were good years, but that's some hard work. And the first year, the government wouldn't give me me unemployment in the off season. Said there was no way little old me was out haulin' in fish with the men. They changed their minds, though. Daddy and Joe went and dumped a truck load of fish guts on the front steps of the unemployment office. That's when I knew daddy really loved me. And me and Joe had ... a son.

But Joe stopped talkin' when they closed the fishery down, and then it was like I couldn't shut-up at all, like I had to fill in all the gaps with words, all the voices came spillin' out of me to eat up the silence. I got retrained. I had a choice. I could be a home care worker or I could be a hair stylist, the world is my oyster, right? So I went to beauty school. But Joe wouldn't have no retrainin', he went off to the mainland to work on a factory line. And *I* wouldn't have none of *that*, so I got a divorce. And I did just fine. But then, one day some son-of-a-bitch got me in an alley ... and then, I'm starting to remember about the boogey-man ... and then ...

... I'm small.
I'm way small.
I'm a girl.
I'm a ugly stupid smelly stupid girl.
The boogey-man lives under my bed, he do.
He got eyes that glows in the dark.
He gets on top of me and makes me choke.
I think my insides are all broke.

Whee! Whee! I'm flyin', I'm flyin' ...

... I had to bar myself up in the house day after day after day. And I sent ... our son out to play by himself, and I watched him from the kitchen window. I'd give him a bowl of Cheerios and a big kiss and a hug and ... I'd watch him from the kitchen window.

Joe showed up on my doorstep, and wanted to try again. And me, with all my talk and all my voices, I couldn't think of one single thing to say to him.

Joe? ... Joe? ... The spaceships came, Joe, honest to God, Joe, like in some kind of movie, and one minute I was just standin' there and the next thing I know I'm floatin' up, up, up, in the air, and I looked down and everything was gettin' smaller and smaller ... and I tried to grab him, Joe, I tried to reach him ... do you blame me, Joe? My answer was, yes. Yeah. I would have liked to try again ... Watcher? Watcher? My answer is, yes, please, come back, come back and we can try again. O.K.? O.K.?

Blackout

DAY 56:
Lights Up

WOMAN: ... and the men were very upset with me. They thought I was crazy. Not because I was hearing voices and they couldn't. And not so much because I was pretending to be a man. But more so because they said I was causing trouble. If you look at war as trouble.

And the men said to me, "JOAN OF ARC! FOR THE LAST TIME! WE IMPLORE YOU! RENOUNCE THE VOICES! GO BEFORE THE PEOPLE AND RENOUNCE THE VOICES!"

It's true.

They said, "RENOUNCE THE VOICES AND WE WILL RELEASE YOU FROM YOUR CAGE!" ... no, it wasn't a cage, they didn't have me in a cage ...

"RENOUNCE THE VOICES AND WE WILL SET YOU FREE!"

I'm, I, what was I sayin'... oh, yeah, and it's true, because I was there, at the movie when it happened is what I mean, and Ingrid Bergman, she had all her hair cut off. She looked so beautiful. She didn't look like no boy. I look like a boy. When I was little, I had really long hair, and I took the scissors and cut it all off. I had the itch, you see. And the nuns went and put lye all over me head and burnt off half me scalp, so I went home and finished the job ... and daddy used to torment the life right out of me, callin' me 'young fella' all the time. I went around with a stockin' cap on me head, sure, I looked just like one of my brothers, except they were dark and I wasn't. I bet Ingrid Bergman never had the itch ...

Oh, it's true, so true, they tied me to a stake and they were going to burn me alive, and I said, "OH GOD, MY GOD, WHY HAVE YOU FORSAKEN ME" no, that was Jesus. He heard voices too, only he got nailed to a cross.

They burned me alive and my ashes flew and flew and flew ...

I forgot what I was sayin'.

I was ... oh, yeah, I had no hair, and daddy loved me when I was a boy, I ran around throwin' rocks at the Protestants and stealin' plums out of trees. And then, one day daddy come in off the boat and said they needed a young fella to go on board for a bit, 'cause John Kelly's boy lost three fingers in a winch and got the gangrene. And daddy asked around the harbour, but it was too late in the season and he couldn't get neither young fella to go on board. So one day after supper, daddy looked at me and winked and he said, "How about it, young fella?" And I winked back at him.

That was the best summer of my life, the summer I was a boy! The boogey-man went away, 'cause I was fishin' with him and I never lost no fingers in a winch. You don't have to sit with your knees together and you don't have to stay clean all the time and you can piss in a beer mug when no-one's lookin'! The seagulls followed the boat, lookin' like a big white cloud, all white and pretty and shittin' over everything. Their screechin' was voices, callin' out to me, "YOU'RE A BOY!" And I call back, "I'M A BOY!"

The fall after that was the worst. I got beat by the nuns that many times 'cause they just didn't get it! "I'm a boy, sister, I'm a boy, I'm not wearin no fuckin' skirt! Ow! Sister, ow! Lay off! I have got a dick, have so, wanna see? I'm goin' on the boat with my daddy again next summer and then ye'll all see who's a boy. I'm free. I'm even gettin' me own stitch! If you're on a boat, you got to get your own stitch knit into your sweater. That's in case you falls overboard and gets drownded, and the fish eats the face right off ya, when you washes up on shore they can tell who you are by what stitch you got knit into your sweater! Why do you think they calls 'em fishermen's knits?! Stitch, stitch, I got me own stitch! Stitch, stitch—ow!! Mom! I got a stitch in me chest, Mom. MOM! There's somethin' wrong with me chest, it's all swoled up, there and there ... mom? What's that? ... I'm not wearin' that ... DADDY! Mom's makin me wear a bra! ... Daddy! ... Daddy? ... Yeah, daddy ... I guess I'm a young woman now ..."

Oh, how he broke my heart when he told me that. He told me I was a young woman, now, and I cried and cried, 'cause I knew for sure then. I was a girl. I had to go babysittin' for the Kearly's. And he started crawlin' into my bed again at night, 'cause he knew for sure I was a girl, too.

Funny. How I became a beautician. And how I miss my period now.

I RENOUNCE THE VOICES! There. Will you let me out now?

Blackout

DAY 57:
Lights Up

WOMAN: We are so sorry we could not save your planet from exploding. We did send a warning to your very intelligent cat life forms, but instead of listening, you kept putting the cat out. It is beyond our means at the moment to correct terminal atmospheric damage, such as occurred to your late planet. We did attempt to help. We have read your most popular world-wide best selling novel, The Bible, by Mr. Gideon. We see you have had trouble with the world ending before, although not with this severity. So, we decided to save two of everything. Unfortunately, due to a computer malfunction, we were only able to save one of everything. Please forgive this inconvenience. Watcher, the one who watches, will record what you are. This record will be kept forever. Please co-operate in the matter. Thank you.

I'm the only one they managed to save and I'm a fucking lunatic.

I put the cat out. I thought it was in heat. I took it to the vet and had it fixed!

Blackout

DAY 60:
Lights Up

WOMAN: So just remember! When you're rollin' your perm, the secret is all in the size of the rods and keepin' your ends neatly wrapped. You don't know how many women I've seen walkin' out of other hair salons lookin' like they just had their hair done with a mix-master.

I ran a good business. I learned from daddy. Daddy always told me I was smart. Well, what he used to say was, "Smarten up or you'll get my knuckles across you head." Daddy used to say, "Don't get your fingers nipped off in the winch and put me to shame." I think daddy kind of thought Joe was gonna turn out to be a winch. But then, after the divorce, daddy kept sayin' I didn't know how good I had it. And daddy was right, wasn't he? All the bad stuff came after the divorce.

Now, with the eyebrow, when plucking, just follow the natural arch, like so. And pluck in the direction that the hair is growin' in, that's very important. Don't fool with the natural arch or you'll end up with a woman lookin' permanently stunned.

Daddy loved mom. She gave him all those sons, well, she gave him me, too, but he never held that against her. Mom said there's voices everywhere, in nature and inside everybody, you just got to listen. Dad's voice was boss in our house, and *everybody* listened when he roared. Mom did her best. We'd come in off the water and she'd have supper cooked. Salt beef and cabbage and peas pudding, and the steam'd be drippin' off the windows, she'd be after boilin' everything that much. I used to do her hair to go to bingo. Mom had good hair.

Just now I looked out and I thought I saw the water ...

This is how you stands in a boat. You got to roll with it, don't fight the swell, or your stomach is gonna let you know some fast. And then you grabs on to that net, and haul it in 'til your back is crackin' off. And pull! Hand over fist, and all the time the sea is rollin', now that's my kind of rock and roll.

SHIT! Goddammit!!! I just broke off my goddamn nail! I finally get my nails just the way I want 'em, and I go and break one off just by doin' nothin'!
IS THERE NO JUSTICE IN THIS PLACE!!
Did I use aerosol spray cans? No! I recycled! It wasn't me that frigged up the friggin' ozone layer that frigged everything up!!

I survived the boys and the bay and the booze and the bad spirits, and I survived rape and religion and poodle perms and polyester, and goddamn fuckin' voices in my head, and I survived daddy, and I survived lookin' up into the sky one day and seeing all them goddamn friggin' space ships and I survived floatin up into a fuckin' space ship and being burped out into an intergalactic zoo, so tell me, how come I can survive all of that and I can't have my fucking nails the way I fucking want them !!!

You listen and you listen good, I am not a monkey. I hate your guts, you puking ugly leather pompous boogey-man who won't even talk, go suck on a banana peel! You won't talk 'cause that's how you get me to talk, you think I didn't work that out a long time back? You think I'm stunned, or what? OR WHAT! I MIGHT BE FUCKING CRAZY BUT I AM NOT STUNNED! If you know what's good for you, you'll never let me out of here, 'cause if you do the first thing I'm gonna do is I am gonna fuckin' kill you!

(She retreats.)

What's goin' on? What's goin' on? How come I'm here? I don't know what's goin' on.

(She screams and screams.)

Blackout

DAY 61:
Lights Up

WOMAN: I had a dream.

In my dream, I was walkin' down a long road. It's a gravel road with the dust flyin' up off it in the breeze, and bushes and trees crowdin' in on it, touchin' against me as I walk by. And I'm tired and hot. I come to this rock by the side of the road, so I sit down on the rock to have a rest. Suddenly, I hear this voice. It says "GET OFF!" I go, "Who's that? Who's that talkin' to me? I'm frightened!" And the voice says, "It's me. It's the rock." And I say, "Rocks can't talk." And the rock says, "I have been here for a long time, and I have been just fine. But then you come along and you sit on me, and that is not fine. So I told you to get off. The only time to make yourself heard is when you've got something to say".

And I go, "Thank you, Rock". And the rock says, "Thank yourself. Now get off". So I get off ...

And then I wake up. And I'm still in here. And I still hear that voice.

Mom said to me, "One time, I wrote down the story of my life so far for the reverend. He asked me to do it. It took a long time as I do not read or write too good. But he lost it. This does not mean my life is lost. But this means that now I will only give you a little bit of my life. The less I give, the more you will keep. The more I give, the more there is to be lost".

I told Mom I wanted to be a strong woman, like her. She told me all women are strong. They just have to know it's safe to show it.

Mom ... Mommy ... I can see you! See me, Mommy? I'm a little girl. See how clean and smooth and clean and clean and clean I am? I'll be a girl, o.k., Mommy? Can't you hear me, Mommy? Pick me up and swing me round. Grab my hand ... Mommy, grab my hand, grab my hand, GRAB MY HAND, OH, JESUS, JESUS, GRAB MY HAND, JUMP! JUMP! JUMP OUT OF THE WAY, FOR JESUS SAKE, I CAN'T REACH YOU THAT ... I tried to reach him. I couldn't reach him.

Here. This is a tear. You can have it. It's a part of me, too.

Blackout

DAY 62:
Lights Up

WOMAN: this bird flew too high
            chasin' clouds
            wantin' to land in 'em.
            this bird fell hard
            before learnin' about clouds.
            this bird looks up at an alien sky
            and glides.
            this bird flies with a heart of stone.
            amelia earhart's never comin' home.

Blackout

DAY 63:
Lights Up

WOMAN: The thing about Amelia Earhart is, you know, she went down in the Pacific somewhere, no-one knew where, for a long time. But people looked for her, they always looked for her, they just couldn't let it be. Amelia didn't want to come back. The last thing I heard was this bunch of explorers were holding up her shoes on the news ... that's a sin. People should just let go.

'Cause, all that time and money spent lookin' for Amelia, and, some guy in an alley with a knife, he could just disappear forever ...

It's like the elephant. I watched the elephant. It just stopped eating. They tried all their fancy technology on it. They tried to force feed it, they stuck it with needles, they tried to trick it into eating. Still. The elephant starved itself to death. I saw it all. You see? I've been watching. I'm a watcher, too. They stuffed it and animated it and got it up walking around. But I saw how it didn't always go where it was supposed to, how it came up and stared in at the rest of us with it's black eyes ...

Yesterday, it walked right up to me and looked in at me, and for a moment I thought ... I heard it's voice. It spoke its child's name to me.

My son's name was Matthew. He was four. I dreamed I was on the earth again. And the space ships came. But this time I grabbed him up in my arms and we floated up here together. I'm not sad.

I dreamed the door opened and I was afraid to walk out.

I dreamed I was an elephant.

I wonder how they'll all get bumped up this time.

I haven't eaten anything in such a long time ... feels so good. You know that? My period started again today. Isn't that the damndest thing? The ... essence of me is just flowin' right out of me and there's nothin' anybody can do about it. I'll never be yours.

I have a name. My name is ... what are you lookin' at ... my name is ... what are you lookin' at ... my name is ... what are you lookin' at ... my name is ...

Lights Out

The ALIENiation of Lizzie Dyke

1994

Written and performed by
Liz Pickard

The ALIENiation Of Lizzie Dyke

ACT ONE

The set for act one is all white. There is a large 8 foot X 12 foot X 3 foot platform. It is stark and bright against the black curtains which cross the stage. Trapdoors have been cut into the top of the platform. There are two square shaped trap doors; one in the centre, another at the back stage left corner and one equilateral triangle downstage right. The trap doors are used to denote set changes and time jumps and often are opened to reveal props or pictures of places. They can be lit different colours. The centre trap opens flat and the other two are rigged to stand up perpendicular to the platform. They are big enough for LIZZIE to go down through. A great deal of activity takes place under the platform where people are needed to set and change props, to provide a pair of elegantly gloved hands, to play a bass line on electric guitar, etc.

The platform functions as the main playing space for most of Act One becoming, among other things, an oversized bed, a spaceship, an operating table, a cabaret stage, a slum. There are stairs on either side of the platform, so LIZZIE can use the main stage to tapdance or walk down a dark Paris street. At the top of Act One, the setpiece is covered with a giant white satin sheet, under which LIZZIE sleeps as the audience get seated. There are three pillows for LIZZIE to rest her head.

There is a ten foot pillar at each end of the platform, at the back. A long piece of white or off-white fabric drapes from the top of the stage left pillar and across the side of the platform on to the floor. It is long enough for LIZZIE to wrap around herself and use as a prop / set piece. A two-sided full-length mirror is hidden under the fabric. There is a 10 foot x 10 foot filmscreen stage centre rising directly behind the bed.

There is a small, white, two by two foot platform far downstage right. It functions as a jail cell cinderblock and a tiny stage for 'Lizzie Dyke Clay.'

Hanging above the set piece there is one large, bare tree branch. A small globe of the moon hangs just stage left of this.

Lights go to black and come up on the moon.

Soundtrack, Opening Sequence, spacy, ambient music.

The ALIENiaton of Lizzie Dyke 371

A blue light comes up to reveal "Old Lizzie Dyke" asleep under the sheet. The light becomes more intense and she stirs. She rises, shrouded, and reaches towards the light. She is ancient.

LIZZIE: Hello ... is that you? Darling?!
(LIZZIE peers with sightless eyes. Pause.)
Hum. Oh my. Sometimes I don't know what dreams are real, and what are only dreams. But what does it matter, really, it's all the same thing.
(LIZZIE lies back down. Sound and lights fades out. Opening credits music comes in. The opening credits play on the film screen. In the original performance, the opening credits read as follows):
Resource Centre for the Arts Theatre Company Presents
The ALIENation of Lizzie Dyke
Written and performed by Liz Pickard
Directed and designed by Teri Snelgrove
Lighting by Flip Janes
Soundscore by Lee Tizzard
Costumes designed and created by Janis Spence and Mercedes Barry
Stage Management by Barry Newhook with Kelly Jones
Props designed and created by Elly Cohen
Dramaturged by Lois Brown
With music by The Lizband and Rene Flynn
Credits finish.
(There is the sound of something being sucked away as the satin sheet disappears down a small hole. Lights up on Young Lizzie Dyke, dressed in a red evening gown with pink satin gloves and a round red hat. She is wearing the "labia outfit", a long red tight fitting gown with a richly textured pink flare at the bottom. This costume is designed to be very flexible. It can be stretched up over LIZZIE's head and, employing the round "clitoris hat", made to look like LIZZIE is encased and then being born from a beautiful velvet vagina.

LIZZIE yawns and stretches on the pillows as the soundtrack of piano music, and babies' crying fades in. The piano is playing the simple cabaret tune for "Je M'Apelle Lizzie Dyke". LIZZIE gets up, takes centre stage, performs the labia dance and then sings, in the best French accent she can muster:)

LIZZIE: Je m'apelle Lizzie Dyke
qu'elle age et moi?
pourquoi je vingt
et pour le petit déjeuner
je mange le pain
le tea et deux ouefs baby
Je m'apelle Lizzie Dyke

ecouter moi, ecouter moi
je chanter pour le toute le monde
dans la rue de l'amour
dans la rue
de l'amour baby
tu connais Marcel Martin?
mais oui nous sommes
de bon copain
dupuis longtemps
dupuis longtemps dupuis
dupuis longtemps baby

(The babies' crying becomes increasingly louder and LIZZIE has to stop, embarrassed. She shouts to the audience, blowing kisses.)
LIZZIE: Excusez moi, Paris!!! Merci, mon amis, merci!!! Merci Pareee!!! Je t'aime, tu est tres belle!! Je suis sincere!
(She scurries "Backstage" and moves the pillows as the lights reveal three little bundles squirming on the bed. These are Lizzie's triplets. They are life-size baby dolls in sleepers with movable arms and hands. They are attached to each other so they can also be worn. One of the babies has a bluish tinge to her skin. As she speaks to them, the babies quiet down.)
LIZZIE: What are you all crying about? I had them eating out of the palm of my hand! Why is it that when one of you wakes up, you all wake up? I guess it's the great disadvantage to having three babies at the same time. Well, that and breastfeeding.
(LIZZIE nurses then burps the babies.)
LIZZIE: Come on then ... ah ... ah ... baby. I suppose I'll get down to naming you one of these days. It's just such an awesome responsibility, to give you names that you'll have to bear for the rest of your little lives. I can't decide. Good strong Goddess names ... you should have good strong Goddess names ...but...
(To blue triplet.)
How am I supposed to find the right name for you? You are so strange ... hardly ever make a sound. Just that sweet little hummmm. Where on earth did you get such a big head. And those eyes *(Shiver.)*, not from my side of the family. You don't look like me, you don't look like either of your sisters, and you certainly don't look one bit like that no good for nothing bum who abandoned us in a foreign country. *(Aside.)* As soon as he heard the word 'triplets' he skipped town. But do you know what, my little darlings? I never liked him anyway. We are much better off this way. Norman was a jerk.
Come on then babies, let's rock.
(She picks up the babies and arranges them so that one sits on her shoulders and the others hang and perch on either hip. It is

The ALIENiaton of Lizzie Dyke

a bit of a production. When everyone is in place she calls offstage.)
Bon nuit, Celeste!
(LIZZIE heads down the stairs and out onto the dark Paris street, humming the tune of "Je M'Appelle Lizzie Dyke". She is distracted by a noise. To Paris pervert.)
What are you looking at? Oh yeah, well, suckle this, buddy.
(LIZZIE sprays breast milk across the stage and then she hurriedly walks away.)
Pervert! Paris must be the pervert capitol of the world, I swear. I have never seen so many perverts in long coats before. And I went to a Catholic school!

Oh, babies, what are we going to do? I can't seem to save a franc. I don't know how I'll ever get us home. It seems so long ago now, since I was home. It seems like it was twenty years ago, and it's only been two. I was just a kid back then. Norman and I set out in search of the real world together. Didn't have any idea how phantasmagorically real the real world really was.

Now I'm stuck here, all alone in Paris, France, having to scrape together a living singing cheesy songs in sleazy cabarets on the Rue de L'Amour, because no matter how hard they try, the French just don't know how to rock and roll.
(Slow, moody piano music fades in as LIZZIE, still laden with three babies, jumps up on platform and uncovers the two-sided mirror. A small, choreographed piece begins in which LIZZIE spins and plays with the mirror and the images of herself, the babies and the audience that reflect there. She sings the following blues song.)

> It's funny kind of spin
> on the axis of the world
> when the town that you're in
> is so cold
> It's a heavy kind of scene
> for me a
> non-ordinary girl
> see, I'm really just eighteen
> but I feel so old
> Oh, hold on tightly
> I'll catch you if you fall
> me and you forever, girls
> me and you against them all
> I'll get us where we're going
> I'm just lost on the way
> But that's alright, it's okay

(The piano music continues as LIZZIE waltzes to the down-

stage trap door and opens it. She places the mirror so that when she gets down into the hole she can sit on a stool with her back to the audience and see them in what has become a dressing room mirror. LIZZIE lays the babies down. As she names then, she puts them to bed down in the hole.)
Well, the triplets are almost out of diapers, but I have finally settled on three names. I name you, my oldest daughter, Andromeda, because your head is so round, and for some bizarre reason, that makes me think your name should begin with an "A".

And you I name Electra, because you have so much energy, it's like there's electricity running through those veins.

And you, my littlest baby, my strange almost blue baby, I name you Persephone, because I like the way it rolls off the tongue, and you seem so silent and so full of secrets. Andromeda, Electra and Persephone. Andy, Elly and Percy for short.

(The piano music fades out. LIZZIE settles down into the hole. Underneath the platform she changes her clothes, all the while talking to the audience through the mirror.)
I must confess, I would have rather waited until they were old enough to pick out names for themselves. I mean, they called me Lizzie. Dyke. Lizzie Dyke. Can you believe that? Luckily, I grew up on a deserted island. It's true. Well, for a while, anyway. My father, Charlie Dyke, was a lighthouse keeper.

My mother was an immigrant. Her country had been invaded by the Capitalist Armies when ... well, it was a long time ago. It was a heavy scene. The b'ys literally just walked in, razed everything to the ground and began construction of their malls and complexes and vacation resorts.

Did you know ... my mother was a mail-order bride. Weird, eh? Weird but true. She said it was her only option. She, ah, had no other way out.

So, me and Mom and Charlie all lived together on a small island off the southern coast of Newfoundland for ... Well, until that fateful night, I guess. That fateful night when Charlie Dyke went out to re-light the lamps during a bad storm and never returned. It was concluded by the Company Inquiry that he had been swept from the rocks and taken out to sea. Poor Charlie Dyke.

(Soundtrack. A low, faintly Gregorian chant fades in.
The feeling is sinister.)
That's when my mother and I left our beautiful island and moved to the city. That's when the powers that be told us that I had to go to school.

(LIZZIE emerges from the hole dressed in a school uniform,
black tunic, white blouse, kneesocks and tap shoes.)
School. I had never seen school before. A low concrete building surrounded by a high chain link fence. All that was missing was

the barbed wire. My mother led me through the big front doors, (*The trapdoor closes with a bang.*), down the hallway and into the office of the head sister. The place smelled like disinfectant and discipline.

I met the nuns. I had never seen a nun before. My mother practically got down on her knees in front of them, my mother being from a family of charismatic Marion Catholics. They worship Mary in highly ritualized ecstatic ceremonies, and Mary holds a more lofty place in their hierarchy than even the high and mighty Jesus Christ, himself.

(LIZZIE is getting more and more distressed,
as intense music joins the chanting.)

So my mother starts chanting in her native tongue, too awe struck to even raise her eyes, clinging to the robes of one of the clerical nuns who was only trying to fill out a form. I could barely move. I remember only bone numbing terror at their humourless faces, and the way spit flew out of the head sister's mouth whenever she spoke.

If I'd had any idea what was about to befall me ... if I could have known about what twisted cruelty really lives deep inside the hearts of little girls, I would have bolted from that room and run as far away from "The Little Sisters of the Immaculate Heart Convent School for Girls" as my little legs would have carried me.

Instead, the head sister took me and silently led me through a series of dark passageways ... down, down, down into a labyrinth of underground catacombs, past a shrine to seven murdered priests, past the locked iron door that led to the sister's secret underground burial vault, then up, up, up an echoing stairwell, then weaving in and out of hallways, and finally into the classroom. The chasm opened, and I slipped into the void.

(The Gregorian chant speeds up to become the voices of children chanting in the school yard. LIZZIE is standing off by herself, hiding behind an upturned trap door which displays a photo collage of playground monkey bars.)

VOICES: Lizzie Dyke
got no friends
she's a big fat
lesbian

(Voices fade out)

LIZZIE: These are my new shoes. I just got them. Listen, (Tap Tap). My mother wanted to get me into ballet. She doesn't have a lot of money so she had to scrub and polish the floors at Madame La Footes Dance Studio in exchange for lessons. But then Madame La Foote said that there were no more openings left in ballet, so I had to settle for tap. At first I didn't like that. I had wanted to learn to be graceful. Mother says I am too heavy on my feet. She says I tramp around the house like an elephant.

They are all so snotty and stuck up. They make fun of my name and the way my mother does my hair. They say my mother is poor and doesn't have a husband, and they make up rhymes about me.

I don't even know what lesbian means, but it must be something really bad because when I asked Sister about it she made me stand out in the hallway all afternoon. Then she came out and told me never to say that word again for my whole life, and that I had better be sure to confess to Father Dickey.

They love to get me in trouble. Once, do you want to know what they did? Once they hung me upside down over the stairwell railing, so I was looking down over three flights of stairs.

(LIZZIE hangs over the edge of the platform.)

It made me so scared that I did it in my pants. Sister was really mad and made me go down to the Kindergarten class to find something in their costume box to wear. All I could find to fit me were a pair of leather pants with pictures of Indians with tomahawks all over them and big fringes running up and down the thigh. They laughed their heads off over that one. They called me "shitting bull" for weeks after.

I hate going to school with them. I hate eating lunch all alone in the cafeteria while they talk about their new oak bedroom sets and Barbie doll clothes. My mother won't let me play with Barbies. She says they are obscene.

They all think God is a man. Ha ha! Well, I saw God before and I know for a fact that they are wrong. I met God. It's true. She appeared to me in the woods when I was smaller.

(Angelic voices. LIZZIE takes the big piece of fabric and creates a path through the woods. She walks along it, picks up and ponders a rock when a beautiful blue light appears. LIZZIE is awed and gets down on her knees.)

She had fairy wings and beautiful eyes. Oh! You're not supposed to get down on your knees in front of God, She doesn't like that. *(To light.)* Sorry!

She told me that She would watch over me, always. God's mouth doesn't move when She speaks. I thought that was funny.

Oh, God, you are so beautiful.

*(LIZZIE gazes lovingly at the light until her
reverie is broken, she clears the stage.)*

Oh no, I have to do a dance at the spring concert. I didn't really want to do it. When sister was asking for suggestions for what we could do at the concert, Wanda Chafe raised her hand and said that I was taking tap and that I should do a dance. All the other girls thought so too. They just want a reason to make fun of me

some more. I'm afraid of getting up in front of all those people.
TEACHER'S VOICE: And now from the grade five class, please welcome young Lizzie Dyke.
(Tap dancing music, as played by a Catholic elementary school teacher begins and LIZZIE is pulled into the spotlight. She starts her little girl tap dance, mouthing the steps to herself. As the dance goes on the white spotlight becomes brighter and the music faster. LIZZIE becomes a whirling dervish as she undergoes a metamorphosis. She grows hips and breasts and is surprised by the changes. She looks down the front of her blouse and lets out a scream.)
I feel like a woman trapped in a little girl's uniform.
(She stops tapping and takes off the tunic. Then she removes and lays aside her tap shoes. This is the end of childhood. She admires her new body in a fourth wall mirror. (LIZZIE has a basic costume which is a silver spandex suit that covers her whole body and fits like a second skin.) LIZZIE puts on some lipstick and then drifts across the stage back to the platform as the piano music slows down to become the tune of "Stairway to Heaven". She is standing by the back wall at a high school dance. Slowly she begins to deflate as the music fades away. She takes a flask of lemon gin from somewhere and drinks from it. Darkly.)
LIZZIE: Wallflower. I am a fucking wallflower. Stuck here to this wall like glue. Been here all night. Didn't even get one dance. I even put lipstick on. Jesus. What a drag. Freddie Mooney was looking at me, but who wants to dance with a big, fat, slobbering pig like that?

I can't believe I kissed him. Blech. Well, more like I can't believe I nearly let him suffocate me to death. Freddie Mooney lures me outside, says he wants to talk to me. We sit on the grass by the path, and he's being real nice and the next thing I know, Freddie is on top of me with his disgusting snake tongue squirming around in my mouth. Drooling. I mean, the guy was drooling into my mouth. Wretch. Oh, Oh, Christ, it was so awful, I nearly threw up my guts.

Then he's on top of me, moving up and down and grunting like a rutting pig and I'm yelling "Get off me, you prick!" I'm gagging on his saliva, being crushed by his fat gut and then he rams his hand down the front of my skirt and into my underwear. *(Pause.)* That's when I looked into Freddie's little piggy eyes, undid the button of his GWG's, took down his pants ... and ripped his fucking balls right off!!! Ha ha ha hah!! *(Maniacal laughter.)*

I'll never forget the sight of him, stumbling away with his pants down, holding his bleeding balls, screaming, "You're a fuckin, Lizzie, Dyke, a fucking Lizzie ..."

Yeah, yeah, think up something original, Freddie. I was trying

to put a stop to that shit. Things were starting to calm down a little. My locker hasn't been vandalized in months and no one has written "Lizzie Dyke is a whore" on the bathroom wall since I beat the shit out of Wanda Chafe in the cafeteria that time.
(Lights down on LIZZIE as she takes a long drink.)
(Lights up on central trap door. LIZZIE produces a photograph collage model of her mother's tenement house. There are two figurines with the model. One is LIZZIE and one is her mother. LIZZIE is a customized Barbie doll and mother is a large Balkan type figure in a housecoat and kerchief.)
LIZZIE: This is my mother's house. This is my mother waiting up for me, reading her *True Crime* magazine. This is me trying to sneak home at two in the morning.
(LIZZIE starts to work the figurines. MOTHER has a very thick and bizarre accent.)
House looks pretty quiet. Oh, please, please, please, please, let her be asleep. Please... please.
MOTHER: Where in the blazes have you been??!! I'm sitting here worrying myself sick. It's two o'clock in the morning, where have you been, Lizzie?
LIZZIE: I thought you'd be asleep.
MOTHER: I knew it was strange, you going up to bed so early on a Friday night. I went in to see if you had enough air in your room, that room is so stuffy, and imagine the fright I got when I found out you weren't there. Where did you go?
LIZZIE: I went out.
MOTHER: Out. You went out! I hope you haven't been where I think you've been, because I don't know what I'll do. Did you go to that dance? That school dance which I forbade you to go to?
LIZZIE: Mother, everybody is allowed to go to the school dances. They're chaperoned.
MOTHER: What is that muck all over your face?
LIZZIE: It's lipstick. And it's not all over my face.
MOTHER: Where did you get it?
LIZZIE: Dee Dee gave it to me.
MOTHER: Oh, yes, Dee Dee. I knew she was a bad influence. She's vulgar and loudmouthed. Her father is a garbage man.
LIZZIE: He is not. He's a janitor. He's the school janitor.
MOTHER: Good Catholic girls don't parade around with lipstick all over their face. *(Sniff, sniff.)* Vas is das?
LIZZIE: Oh, mother, give me a break, please...
(They run around the house a bit. MOTHER nearly has a heart attack now.)
MOTHER: Liquor!!! Oh, sweet Sacred Heart of the Blessed Virgin, oh, dear Mother of God, you've been drinking liquor, the Devil's brew. Haven't you? You have been cavorting with Satan. Haven't you? Answer me.

LIZZIE: No.
MOTHER: You're lying to me, now. Now go and take that crap off your face. You look like a whore. You look like a tramp. That's what they will all be saying about you out in the streets. Lizzie Dyke is a whore!!
LIZZIE: Don't say that. Don't say it!!
(The situation is escalating.)
MOTHER: Oh, Sweet Mother of God, save me from this child.
LIZZIE: I wish someone would come and save me from you!!
MOTHER: How dare you raise your voice to me. You'll be damned in hell if you keep this up. You don't know what's out there, waiting for you. You don't know where your make-up and your short skirts are leading you. Asking for it, girl, you are asking for it.
LIZZIE: Asking for what, mother.
MOTHER: Oh, you'll find out well enough what happens to girls who strut around with make-up, wiggling their bums.
LIZZIE: Are you talking about sex, mother?
MOTHER: Don't let me hear you say that word in this house again.
LIZZIE: Sex, Sex, SEX, SEX. SEX!!!!
(MOTHER slaps her across the face, then proceeds to beat LIZZIE through the next sequence.)
MOTHER: You know nothing about it!! Now go in there and wash your face and then go into your room and get down on your knees and pray to God that your mother doesn't kill you!! Oh, Sweet Sacred Heart of Mary, forgive me, but you are a curse, Lizzie ... a curse ...
LIZZIE: I wish Daddy were here. He wouldn't let you talk to me like that.
MOTHER: He'd beat some sense into you, that's what he'd do. Stupid, stupid Charlie ...
LIZZIE: Don't talk that way about him...
MOTHER: Ah, Charlie was an ape...
LIZZIE: I don't want you to talk that way about him. Charlie was my father.
MOTHER: Charlie was not your father.
(Silence.)
You never knew your father. I was eight months pregnant when I arrived in this God forsaken place. Your father, Lizzie, was a Capitalist soldier. A pig. He dragged me off into the woods, and that's how I got pregnant with you.
LIZZIE: You're lying. You are a liar.
MOTHER: The nuns calling me up, telling me you're fighting in the school ... you display antisocial behavior. Father Dickey says you don't even go to mass, you stand out on the back porch and smoke cigarettes. Where are you going? You come back into this

house at once ... Lizzie!!! Lizzie!!!
(Lights change.)
LIZZIE: I didn't come home for three days after that. I don't even really remember where I went or what I did. I was dazed. I walked for miles and miles. There were barrens. I remember walking on the barrens. It was like I disappeared into my own mind, but I can't really remember it, you know. My mother was in the kitchen when I walked in the door, she was raving on and on about having the RCMP out looking for me, how she was nearly dead from a broken heart. I could barely look at her. I went to school. I smoked a lot of cigarettes. I ignored their taunts and jokes, I avoided eyes in hallways. And then. Well. Then I met Rosa.
(Sound. Rosa Music. Romantic Nun images.)
Sister Rosa Redempta was a young novitiate doing some practice teaching at our high school. She hadn't earned her habit yet, so she didn't look like the other crusty old hags who berated us from the front of the classroom. She had pale white skin, translucent, you could see her delicate blue veins tracing lines across her temple, and running down into hands that moved like they were made out of paper. There was something exquisitely fragile about her, yet when she spoke, her pale blue Virgin Mary gown against the blackboard, in a clear voice that almost sang, she commanded attention.

She quickly became the favorite sister in the school, all the girls clamoured around her for attention, wanting her input on their projects, seeking praise. I could hardly speak to her, I was so in awe of her beauty and her power, enamoured by the humour and flair with which she taught ancient history. I thought Sister Rosa Redempta was wonderful, just wonderful.
(LIZZIE picks up the fabric and plays with it, draping it around herself like a habit and robes.)
One day I was down at the Grotto of Our Lady of the Little Sisters. I often went there to avoid going home. It was May. Mary wore her crown of flowers. Then, down the path came sister Rosa. She stopped to talk to me, asking if she was intruding on something private. When I fumbled out a halting, "Oh, no, sister", to my lurching joy, she sat down beside me.

Sister Rosa Redempta was a human being. She made me feel at ease, and in a matter of moments we were conversing freely. Soon we were both giggling like girls making uncharitable remarks about Sister Helga Paul's elephant ankles, they spilled out of her shoes and down the sides. Sister Rosa felt badly afterwards and said she would have to confess that.

Then she asked me if I was troubled. She said I wasn't my usual saucy self. When I looked at her, struck between the eyes with her honest concern, her clear open expression, I couldn't even think of lying. It all came out in a torrent of tears and choking sobs. My life was miserable, I would never fit in, I didn't even want to fit in, anymore. Not only that my mother was a lunatic ...

Sister Rosa looked like she was going to cry herself as she held out her arms and wrapped me around in her robes. She tried to comfort me, reminding me there was only one more year of high school left, how she understood what I was going through, she knew what it was like to be different. She told me to pray to the Blessed Virgin. But I didn't want the guidance of the Blessed Virgin, being held there in her arms was comfort enough. We stayed there for a long time, in an embrace at the foot of the queen of the world.

We met there often after that. Sort of accidentally on purpose. We'd go for walks around the grounds of the convent and she would read to me from the book of the saints. St. Agnes was her favorite. While she read, I hardly heard a word, I was so busy gazing into her face, watching how the muscles moved around her mouth, her blemishless brow rising and falling with the passions that her stories evoked.

She talked about growing up in a small outport back when the supply boats only came once in the spring and once in the fall. How she had to wear the same shoes all year. She said she knew when she was very young that she wanted to become a nun. She promised herself to the Virgin Mary when she was seven years old.

One fateful day, she took me into the convent, which was strictly forbidden. Most of the other sisters were at chapel, so the place seemed deserted. I saw the kitchen where all the nuns ate their supper. They took turns cooking. Twenty wooden chairs around a big wooden table. Not a thing out of place. A perfectly kept kitchen in the house of God. But something made me uncomfortable. The convent smelled musty, like something fungal was growing all over the walls. It smelled like repression, like sex held in between closed legs. And sweat. The sweat of twenty nuns passionately praying on their knees for forgiveness of their unclean thoughts.

I only went into the convent that one time. Sister Rosa took me to her room and showed me the cot where she slept. She shared the room with three other novitiates. By the window there was a small statue of Mary. (*LIZZIE opens a trap to reveal a white veiled figure of Mary.*) Sister Rosa asked me to pray with her. We got down on our knees and I watched her pray, the sweat coming out in tiny beads on her forehead as she reached out to squeeze my hand with a beatific expression on her face. She opened her eyes for a moment and caught me looking at her. We both started to laugh ...

(*LIZZIE does the laugh.*)

... and then it happened. Nothing could stop it. We leaned in towards each other and our lips met. Tentatively at first, becoming more and more passionate until I surrendered completely and we were lying on the floor, her sweet body pressed against me, here sweet tongue wrapped around mine ... Oh, Rosa, oh, sister Rosa, I think I ... I think I ... Rosa stopped dead. I didn't realize what was happening at first. Then I saw it. The shadow in the doorway. The shadow of Mother Superior. (*Lights change. The ominous shadow of Mother Superior appears on the screen.*) Rosa jumped to her feet and then immediately to her knees in front of the Mother Superior.

"You," she pointed her finger at me, "to my office at once."

I ran out the door, looking back at Rosa, on her knees with her face in her hands. I waited for the Mother Superior like she was the executioner. She was one very feared nun. No one crossed the Mother Superior. I braced myself for the worst.

(*Soundtrack. Women's voices singing. During this next passage LIZZIE slowly blind folds herself with the veil from the statue and then turns in a full circle.*)

But Mother Superior's only concern was that I not tell ANYONE about what had happened. She said it would hurt everybody and I certainly didn't want that coming down on my head, now, did I. She didn't want any stories getting around. I asked what was going to happen to Sister Rosa. She told me that Rosa had led me astray, as she wasn't mature enough to handle her responsibilities. She hoped I could forget the whole incident. She said Sister Rosa would be punished appropriately. Then she told me I could go.

(*Sound out. LIZZIE takes off the blindfold.*)

I never saw Sister Rosa Redempta again. No one did. I spent many hours at the grotto, hopelessly hoping to see her coming towards me down the path. But she never came. I didn't really think she would. Once I thought I saw her watering the tomatoes in the greenhouse, but I couldn't be sure.

I didn't breath a word about what had happened to any one. Not even Dee Dee, who was the closest thing I had to a best friend. But one day after gym class, I heard Suzanne Murphy talking to Mary Beth Ryan in the shower room. She said that her mother told her that Sister Rosa had been taken out of teaching for having sex with a student. And that student was Lizzie Dyke. She said we had been caught in the confessional by father Dickey.

When they walked out of the shower room and saw me there, they simultaneously broke into an hysterical fit of laughter. After that, the story spread through the school like a wildfire out of control, getting bigger and more elaborate with each telling. My shame and humiliation knew no bounds. Then, one day, Dee Dee started ignoring me, too, and that was when I'd had enough. I

The ALIENiaton of Lizzie Dyke

said, I am finished with this. And I quit. Just like that.
After that day, and for many years to follow, I existed in a very murky world. Murky and strange.

*(Lights go down. Spot on LIZZIE.
Sung Acapella with a silly slide for each man.)*

LIZZIE: Norman was my first big love
but then I was too young.
to know what love was anyway
my life had just begun
so Norman hit the high road
and me I took the low
when I gave birth to triplets
who he will never know
oh men oh men, oh oh oh men men men
oh men, oh oh oh men men men men men...

Then I met Philippe
we really got along
we had alot of fun times
and so much in common
and I'd put on my coat tails
when he dressed up in drag
but the day came, and he came out
Philippe was a fag
woh men woh men etc.

(A slide of Chippendales dancers.)

A faceless string of strangers
waltzed in and out my door
I don't know just who they were,
but Oh, I was so bored
They only wanted the one thing
to get inside my pants
But I finally saved the money
and I got out of France
Woah Men Woah Men etc.

In Newfoundland I met a man
Cyril Rickets from Cow Head
he liked to drink and sleep in late
and screw around with my friends
he tried so hard to save me
"I'll take you home along the shore"
But the youngsters didn't like him
so I kicked him out the door.

Woah men woah men etc.

Me and Roger tried real hard
and he was good to me
but there was something I couldn't name
it got all in between
The day that he was leaving
he said I know what's wrong
I said, "I'm a dyke Roger"
he said, "You're a lizzie, Lizzie?"
I said, "I've known it all along".

(Slide of woman's beautiful body.)

Wo-men wo-men, wo wo wo men
women women ETC.

(The soundtrack of children's voices)
VOICES: Mommy, Mommy, come on, Mommy ...
Light changes and LIZZIE is now in her Welfare apartment putting her triplets to bed.)
LIZZIE: No, no, no, that is the very last story. I want you to go to sleep now. If I have to tell another story I will go mad! Your Mommy will go mad. It's very late, now, go to sleep.
(LIZZIE crawls into bed and covers herself up.)
LIZZIE: Finally. Oh, I am so tired. So tired I could sleep forever. Mmmmm, my beautiful bed. I love you, pillows.
(Arms come out of the pillows and hug LIZZIE.)
Yes ... yes ... oh, yes ... sleep, come to me, sleep ...
(LIZZIE quickly falls off to sleep. Moonlight spills in through the window. Off in the distance a low humming sound fades in. It gets closer and closer, something speeding in until it is very loud and hovering above LIZZIE's bed. Flashing lights and beeping sounds accompany the hum. The effect climaxes and LIZZIE awakens with a start, causing the lights to return to normal.)
LIZZIE: *(Jumping out of bed and running around.)* Ahhh ... what the fuck was tha-*(Exasperated.).* Oh, sweet sacred heart of the ever suffering mother earth!!! I finally get one frigging minute, one frigging minute to myself so I can sleep, and what happens? Nightmares!! Something comes for me, right at that moment when I'm about to drift into peaceful sleep. It rides in across the night and enters from the corner of the room. It stops and hovers over my bed. I don't know who or why or what ... I can't open my eyes or move a muscle. Some kind of swirling, whispering fear. The old hag. I know it's trying to get inside me, but I never let it in. When it finally speeds off through the wall, onto someone

else's nightmare, I scare wide awake. Oh. Oh. Oh. I'll be up all night now.
(LIZZIE gets back into bed and lights a smoke.)
Sigh. *(Pause.)* I wonder if there's enough food for the morning. Let's see, there's eggs out there. I have a couple of slices of bread left. This is the last smoke, though. I'll have to go through the furniture for change to get a couple of singles at Biddies.
(There is a small noise.)
Ahhh ... What was that? Hello. Hello! ... Mice, invading the kitchen again. *(The shadows of mice scurry across the film screen.)* They move in packs, I swear. Sure, come on in, eat up the last stain of food in the house. What can I do? I can't bear to kill them. They're the closest thing we've ever had to a pet. Jesus, it sounds like they're playing volleyball out there. *(The shadow mice play volleyball.)* Knock it off!! Knock it off!!

Last night I heard the walls crackling, right there above my bed. They are chewing up the wires in there. Something sinister moving behind the chintzy wallpaper.

Maurice doesn't care. Maurice, the slumlord. He doesn't care if the whole place falls down, so long as he gets his rent.

Well, at least he lets me play the Wednesday night slot at the Cock and Ball, his bar. Otherwise, I would never make it on the welfare cheque. I was a star in Paris, for goddessake!

I was a cabaret star on the Rue de L'Amour ... hmmmm ... a long time ago.
(LIZZIE is falling asleep. The dawn is just breaking. LIZZIE finally shuts her eyes and breathes deeply when ... Soundtrack of alarm fades in. LIZZIE jumps out of bed and starts hurrying around, picking up, doing dishes, putting bread in the toaster. It is a tightly choreographed chaos ritual. The trap-doors open and close as household items and toys are thrown into the air, appearing and disappearing.)

LIZZIE: Andromeda, Electra, time to get up for school. Come on, you've got to get ready. Go and brush your teeth. Stop fighting, you two. Andromeda, what have I told you about hair pulling? *(LIZZIE reaches into a trapdoor and rummages through the cutlery.)* Where are all the goddamned spoons. Why are there never any spoons? AHHHH. How am I supposed to function if they keep taking away my spoons.

What? Oh, nothing, honey, I am just trying to create something for breakfast and I don't have any spoons. Where's Persephone? Persephone! Persephone!!!!
(LIZZIE opens a door and a loud clanging is heard from within.)
Persephone, what are you doing in there? AHHH! Where did you get that blowtorch? Oh, I don't know where I got you from. Are there any spoons in there? Persephone!!!

(There is no answer, only more clanging. LIZZIE closes the door in frustration. The toast comes up black.)
I give up. That's it. I give up. I throw in the towel. I can't do this anymore. How am I supposed to live? No money. No spoons. Look at all those dishes. *(LIZZIE opens a trap to reveal a sink piled with dirty dishes.)* I am not doing them. Do you hear me, I am not doing the dishes, ever again!! Do you hear me, do you?!!

I told you to put it away when you were finished with it. That's why you can't find your lunchtin. I don't have any lunch to put in it, anyway.

(LIZZIE goes into a trance. All around her there is noise and motion. Frantic piano music plays. Household appliances switch on and off, eggs are juggled through the trap doors. The youngsters fight in the background. Suddenly, her trance is broken.)

Oh, no! It's ten to nine. Why is it always ten to nine? Come on girls, lets move it ... mitts, hats, scarves, boots!!! Let's go. Andromeda, you didn't eat any breakfast. Here, have some banana. Come on, it's yummy. Banana is yummy.

(The phone rings. The voice of Maurice, the slumlord, is heard.)

LIZZIE: Hello.
MAURICE: Where's my rent?
LIZZIE: Oh, get off my back, Maurice, I haven't got my cheque yet. You know Welfare doesn't send it until the first.
MAURICE: Well, I just want to make sure I get it.
LIZZIE: You'll get it. Is that all?
MAURICE: No, that is not all. I want to talk to you about that stunt you pulled in the bar last Wednesday night.
LIZZIE: What stunt?
MAURICE: I am talking about that homosexual crap you were spouting on stage the other night. I run a good clean business here, little lady ...
LIZZIE: Come on, Maurice, they loved it.
MAURICE: I don't want you playing lesbo music in my bar.
LIZZIE: Homophobia is a serious disease, Maurice. Perhaps you should hear the song before passing your lameass judgements. It was a song about identity, about discovering yourself.
MAURICE: Well, I don't want you discovering yourself on stage in my bar. Are you reading me, missy ...
LIZZIE: *(To PERCY, in the basement.)* Play along with me Percy, it's in B. *(To Maurice.)* It goes like this ...
(The lights change and a slow bass line begins. The telephone receiver becomes a microphone and LIZZIE begins to sing "I am a Lesbian". During the song, Maurice continues to interject.)

Through the years

I remained undefined
didn't take the cue
from my name
couldn't read the signs
all the answers
were locked inside
my own mind
until I looked into the light
and it burned away
my thin disguise
I long for a woman
I love my own kind
I long for a woman
to love me
like only a woman can
cause I
I know
I know who I am
I am a lesbian
I am
I am
I am

MAURICE'S INTERJECTIONS: Knock it off. Either you knock this off or I am pulling you from the Wednesday night slot. I don't want any homos frequenting my bar. Oh, Jesus.
(As the song ends, the lights return to normal. LIZZIE is standing with the receiver.)
MAURICE: I run a good clean business here. I don't want you messing around with my clientele. This is not a place for queers. Those two mafioso guys with the bald heads were in here looking for you again. They scare the hell out of the regulars. I don't need this shit.
LIZZIE: What two mafioso guys? I don't even know those guys. Besides, there's no Mafia in Newfoundland, Maurice.
MAURICE: I'm a busy man. I don't have time for this. Don't you forget who owns your arse. I gave you a place to live when you and your brood had nowhere else to go. All it will take is one phone call. One little phone call to the Department of Social Services ... and I had better not find out there is any weirdo lesbo sex going on in my building ...
LIZZIE: *(Now infuriated.)* Shut up, Maurice! Why don't you get off my back, you stupid motherfucker. You're making the youngsters late for school!
(She smashes the receiver a few times on the counter.
She slams down the phone. LIZZIE is shaken.)
LIZZIE: What, Oh, no, Mommy is alright! I just got a little bit

angry there, I ... It's alright. What do you say ... we take the day off? Maybe after breakfast we can go to the park or something. Do you like that idea?
(Lights up on the film screen. LIZZIE narrates the sequence from the stage. The images are of LIZZIE and the triplets at home, in the park, with an emphasis on PERCY and her differences. The apartment where they live is a slum. Shots of Andromeda and Electra playing in the park. PERCY is off by herself collecting soil samples. Her skin is brilliant blue.)
LIZZIE: We hide out in the park sometimes. Me and my girls. Andy and Elly seem to move pretty freely in the world. That makes me happy. It's Percy that I'm worried about. No one in the world can tell me what is wrong with her. Her skin is becoming bluer by the day, just like her mood. She has always seemed so preoccupied. Percy can't talk. She doesn't even have much of a tongue ... more like a useless flap of skin, really. It could be some kind of genetic thing.
(Shots of LIZZIE and PERCY waving goodbye to ANDY and ELLY as they leave for school.)
She's smart, though. They won't let her go to school. They wanted to send her to deaf school, even though she isn't deaf. I let her go once, but she refused to return. Now she just stays at home with me and memorizes the encyclopedias. I can't begin to imagine what goes on in that little mind.
(The camera walks up a flight of stairs and finds PERCY sitting on the top step with a huge book. There is an over-the-shoulder shot of the difficult physics problem PERCY is working on.)
The girls have some kind of unspoken communication with each other. It used to freak me out a little bit until I found out that was the way it is with twins and triplets. So Andy and Elly are always talking for Percy, interpreting for me ... *(Shot of LIZZIE at the stove cooking up hot dogs. The triplets file in and sit down.)* The other night it was all, "Mommy, Percy doesn't want to eat meat, anymore". Oh my. And me just after cooking up the big feed of hot dogs.
(Shot of LIZZIE and PERCY in the bathroom. LIZZIE is alarmed to find two wart-like growths on PERCY's back. She touches and worries over them.)
Last month strange growths started to appear on her back, right above the shoulder blades. They started out like little warty things, and now they are getting bigger and bigger and are turning into scaly protrusions. I don't know what I'm going to do. Sometimes I get afraid. The future is so uncertain.
(Shot of LIZZIE and the triplets in their pyjamas. They are sitting on the couch, watching "Star Trek".)
The girls insist on staying up late to watch all the space shows. I

The ALIENiaton of Lizzie Dyke

have become addicted to them. Space, the final frontier, or is it? I'm not so sure. If I could go out there, what would I find? Would it be the same as what I have found here on earth.
(Final shot of LIZZIE tucking the triplets into bed. Film screen goes black. Lights up on the tiny platform stage right. Prison bars are indicated with lights. LIZZIE sits on the platform in the jail cell.)

LIZZIE: Maurice, the slumlord's, made good on his threat. They've locked me away. They hauled me up in front of the judge for earning $150.00 a month at the Cock and Ball and not reporting it to the Social Services. The S.S. The S.S. came to the door and they dragged me away.

The judge said that single mothers were undermining the fabric of this great nation. I told him he'd been watching too much cable from the States. He said that because of single mothers the system was falling apart, the prisons were full to capacity and AIDS was running rampant. I said, "Oh, take a pill".

He reiterated over and over again the seriousness of the charge. In this day and age defrauding the government is a very grave offence, indeed. He said that despite my impudence he wasn't going to throw the book at me. Someone has to look after the youngsters and, as he so eloquently put it, "Seeing how you made the bed, you should be the one to lie in it."

He sentenced me to six consecutive weekends in the downtown lockup. It was the only alternative to being shipped off to the workfarm in Stephenville.
(An invisible guard lets LIZZIE out of jail. What follows is a tightly choreographed sequence where LIZZIE is arrested and escapes prison over and over again. The feeling is chaplinesque, the pace quickens as the piece proceeds.)
Thus began my notorious prison career. *(LIZZIE imitates the voice of the judge. After each conviction LIZZIE bangs a gavel on the platform and there is a flash of an unseen mugshot-taking camera.)* "Lizzie Dyke, you are charged with theft under $200 for stealing that Thanksgiving turkey from Dominion. Guilty!"
(LIZZIE goes into jail.)
I had my friend, Celine, take the girls out to her cabin in Salmon Cove to save them from the clutches of the state ...
(LIZZIE again gets let out of jail.)
"Lizzie Dyke, you are charged with illegal hackysack playing on our Veteran's War Memorial. Guilty."
(LIZZIE fights on her way into jail and gets thrown in. She tricks the guard.)
Ow ... my hand. I have hurt my hand. Guard, open the cage, open the cage ... It's hurt really bad. That's right, open it up, I need some help ... actually, I think it could be worse than I thought. You

had better go and get a doctor ...
> (*LIZZIE watches the stupid guard go for a doctor
> and she escapes.*)

"Lizzie Dyke, escaping confinement, resisting arrest and spitting on a public sidewalk. Guilty."
> (*LIZZIE struggles on her way in. She punches a guard. She
> gets thrown into the cell. After a moment of pacing she
> stops and thinks. She becomes inspired.*)

I am strong. I have the strength of two hundred Amazonian warriors. Let the goddess fill me with her power!!
> (*She strains and, with pure brute force, breaks
> through the bars.*)

"Lizzie Dyke, Guilty."
> (*LIZZIE is handcuffed and thrown in jail where she paces
> until ...*)

That's right, Percy, way to go, honey! Hold the blowtorch up a little higher. That's it. Now the cuffs, the cuffs.

"Dyke, guilty!"
> (*LIZZIE gets thrown in. She produces a tin plate
> and spoon from under the platform.*)

What do you call this slop. You expect me to eat this crap?!
> (*She throws the slop at the wall, but then picks up the spoon.
> She ponders it a moment. She soon proceeds to dig her
> way out as Mozart's "Flight of the Bumblebee" plays.*)

"Guilty!! Guilty!! Maximum Security."
> (*LIZZIE is led to her cell.*)

Yeah, yeah.
> (*LIZZIE is in for the final time. She is getting upset. The idea
> of maximum security is almost too much for her.*)

LIZZIE: Okay, get a hold of yourself. It won't be long until you're free again. They'll come and break you out ... (*She sings*), "I believe, I believe I am the Goddess."
> (*Voice of guard joins in.*)

WARDEN: "I believe, I believe you are obnoxious", now, shut up in there.
> (*LIZZIE begins to undergo a metamorphosis.*)

LIZZIE: (*Timidly.*) Fuck you.

(*She repeats this, becoming louder and louder and louder until
she is standing on the cinderblock, pounding her chest,
screaming.*)

LIZZIE: Fuck you ... fuck you ... fuck you and you and you!! Fuck the whole cocksucking, mother fucking, lot of you!!!

(*The lights change and jail cell bars disappear. Spotlights crisscross the stage as the opening movement of BUNG's "Bury it" blasts through the speakers. The cheesy announcer booms.*)

ANNOUNCER: Live, from the fornicatorium, in beautiful down-

town St. John's, where the elite come to meet, greet, beat and cheat. It's Lizzie Dyke Clay!!
(Sounds fade. Spotlight on LIZZIE, clad in leather and studs with magic boots. She has become the impenetrable radical feminist comedian "Lizzie Dyke Clay". She reaches into her pocket, produces a Zippo lighter, snaps it open and lights a smoke. She surveys her audience.)

LIZZIE: Alright. The building is sealed. You got that? No one gets out of this room during this performance. No cops get in. My personal Amazonian body guards are standing right outside the door, so I don't want any funny business. You got that, motherfuckers?

Yeah, that's right, I said motherfuckers. That is exactly what you all are. Motherfuckers. Fuckers of the mother. It doesn't take a genius to figure out what happens when you piss off mother nature, relentlessly, for generations. You're all are gonna get what's coming to you and you're gonna deserve every fucking plague and pestilence that she throws at you. And I am going to be sitting on my mountain top, laughing. I'll be laughing my fucking head off.

So, my inner child is lying in a pool of blood. Don't piss me off. Are their any men in the audience tonight? Well, just so you know, I'm a lesbian and, "SURPRISE!", I don't want to sleep with any of you. I'm not interested in sucking on your cock, so I don't want any assholes bothering me after the show. I don't care how much your cock throbs for me. I don't care if your collective cock explodes for throbbing for me. I don't want it.

That's so hard for most men to take. I hate that. I hate a lot of things. I hate those feminine hygiene ads that assault me from the T.V. screen. The ones proclaiming that women are supposed to be fresh and clean, to smell as sweet as a spring morning. Hey, you, yes, you, Sunshine! Smell this. What's it like? Sweet as the lily of the valley. As fresh as a new day? No. It smells like sweat. And that's what it is. It's my sweat. My own personal fragrance. Not powder fresh. Not pretty like a new day. It smells like sweat.

Now, let me get this straight. Women are all supposed to be clean and sweet and perfumed for what? In preparation for whom? The great dirty dick of the master, who only takes a bath about once a month and even then, I mean, Holy Cockcheese, Batman, don't you ever, ever wash this thing?!

The other night I was driving to the hideout in my Lizzie mobile, when I noticed the cherry of the pig on my tail. Before I had the chance to launch into turbo power, the dink pulls ahead of me and cuts me off. Alright, alright. I'll humour the asshole. I'm just hoping he isn't gonna recognize me from the posters they've got plastered all over the city. "Wanted, the Outlaw Lizzie

Dyke". Real crappy photo, too.
I try to be cool. I roll down the window.
"Yeah, what do you want, Pig?"
"Step out of the car, please."
"Don't lay any of your oppressive bullshit on me, Pansy Boy. Now, what's your problem? If I was speeding, just give me a ticket and get the fuck out of my face."
"You'd better step out of the car, now."
"Hey, fuck you, jerk man", I say, and I go to launch into turbo power, when his goony, scaly, pig hands reach in and pull me, struggling, right out through the window of the freaking car!
"Get your pig hands off me, oppressor!!"
He slaps me up against the hood of the car and starts to frisk me.
"What kind of a man are you, pulling women over on lonely roads in the middle of the night so you can fill a quota. Do you realize you were once your mother's baby, you were born in her pain, and she nursed you and rocked you and raised you up so you could become what? A power tripping motherfucker."
Then he cuffed me.
"Shut up, lady and come with me."
"Hey, I ain't no lady, (*Smack.*), so why don't you watch your mouth."
"Move it, Cunt"
I froze on the spot.
"What did you call me, motherfucker"
"I called you a cunt, now move along."
Well, that was it. I didn't have a choice, did I? I had to lay the boots to him.
"You call me a cunt, you hairy arsed motherfucker. You think that's a dirty word? Well, I have got news for you. No one takes the name of my cunt in vain. No one. My cunt is a fucking flow, a fucking poem. I've got more power in my labia minora than you could ever dream of your whole life. Do you read me, are you getting the idea ..."
I broke a couple of toes. It was pretty difficult driving with my hands in cuffs, but I managed it. The youngsters sawed the cuffs off when I got home. Percy, my youngest, is rather handy with the power tools. They thought my toes needed some medical attention, but I wouldn't set foot inside a hospital, no matter what you paid me.
Bunch of white coat pervos. Gynecologists, now they are the ones who really burn my bush. They are fascinated by the mutilation of the female genitalia and reproductive systems. They get turned on by it, you know. Let's face it. If you are a man and you dedicate your life to capitalizing on the mutilation ... of the female reproductive system, then you are a fucking pervert plain

and simple.
I've seen you, talking into your little dictaphone behind the doors of your million dollar practice up on Newfoundland Drive ...
"After a deep manual examination, I have discerned that this woman has a small growth on her right ovary. I recommend we open her up and go in there. Perhaps she will only need biopsy, possibly an ovary removed, or maybe we can go all the way with a complete hysterectomy. God, I love this job Hah hah hah hah hah ..."
Childbirth is a natural process, for fuck's sake. You want drums and tribal chants. But there they are at every turn, trying to shave you, stick things up your bum, cop a few feels and hook you up to their machinery. You are surrounded by a host of intrusive yuppy men, voyeurs in white coats, tampering with things they can't even begin to understand. Capitalizing on the birthing. Toll keepers at the gateway of life.
Labour is like this ...
OHHHHHHHHH .... AHHHHHHHHH ... MOTHER!!!!! ... AHHHHHHHHHH!!!
Hoards of white coats stand uselessly by, offering facemasks filled with drugs, narcotics by hypodermic. Birth is like this ...
UUUUUUUUUNNNNNNHHHHH ...
Your face turns purple, your legs turn purple, your eyes turn purple, fuck it, everything turns purple. Birth is a heavy duty purple experience.
(The lights change radically to purple and LIZZIE is pulled by some unseen force to the bed. Sound track of creepy 5th dimensional noises. LIZZIE seems to be going through a birthing experience, but is actually flashing back to an encounter with alien life forms aboard a spacecraft.)
Birth is a heavy duty purple experience. Birth is a ... where am I ... don't touch me, don't touch me with that thing ... *(LIZZIE is extremely disoriented.)* ahhh... get away from me.
(There is a sudden lighting change and LIZZIE Dyke Clay is back on the stage. She shakes herself off, does a fancy step and resumes her performance. She has obviously been thrown off.)
LIZZIE: Alright, alright .. what the fuck are you looking at? Huh? I'm Lizzie Dyke Clay and I've got a clitoris the size your head, buddy. Hah. I'm Lizzie Dyke Clay and I want to fuck with your head, for a change.
(Sound FX fade in. Sirens and booted feet running up the stairs. The lights are becoming red and distressful. The cops are at the door. They are pounding on it. There is the voice of the Police Sergeant.)
Lizzie Pyke, Lizzie Pyke, we know you are in there. Come out with your hands up. We have the building surrounded. Lizzie Pyke, come out with your hands up!!!

(LIZZIE is running around the stage looking for a way out.)
Oh, no, the pigs. Don't anyone move. Don't anybody move. Is there a back door to this place?
SERGEANT: We has the building surrounded. There is no way out, but our way, Lizzie Pyke. You cannot escape, you cannot resist. Come out with your hands up.
LIZZIE: The roof, maybe???
(The sound of helicopters fades in. S.W.A.T. teams are mobilizing outside.)
LIZZIE: You'll never take me alive, motherfuckers. I have hostages. I want a million dollars and my own helicopter on the roof, NOW!
SERGEANT: There will be no negotiations. Come out with your hands up. You have one minute before we beat this door down.
LIZZIE: Oh, fuck, I'm cornered. I'm snared like a rat in a trap. I'm ready for you. I have the fearlessness of an Amazonian warrior ... *(She is breaking down.)* I'm ready for you. I'm ready for you. Come and get me. Remember folks, you saw it here, you saw it live, you saw it first ... Come on, COME ON!!!!
(The battering ram starts at the door. LIZZIE is standing waiting for them. Above the commotion a low hummm fades in. The lights are joined by purples and blues as the voice of MAG is heard. MAG's voice is a harmonized, processed sound. It is ethereal, melodious, uplifting and gorgeous. The voice of an angel.)
MAG: Lizzie Dyke. I have finally found you.
LIZZIE: Hello? Who is that. Can you hear that?
MAG: I am Magenta Illuminous from the planet Karundia which spins deep in the Galaxy of Lesbos. I have been searching the stars for you ... I am now circling the Milky Way and can remove you from this rather pressing situation.
LIZZIE: Remove me? Well do it. DO IT!!!
MAG: As you wish, my friend ...
(There is a sudden lighting change. LIZZIE is floating in a column of light as the sound of the cops and commotion fade away.)
LIZZIE: Where am I? Where am I going? Hello? Hello? HELLO?!
(Lights snap to black.)
SERGEANT: This is Constable Cooney of the RNC. We have reason to believe that the outlaw Lizzie Pyke is still on the premises. Would you kindly leave the theatre while we conduct our search. Thank you.

End of Act One

ACT TWO

The set for Act II is expansive and vast. Curtains have been moved away to reveal a massive backdrop, rich in texture and warmth–the opposite of the confining white platform of Act One. (The textured effect can be achieved by hanging lengths of paper which have been moulded and enhanced with the application of a malleable substance, such as paper and glue or papier mache) By using lights and the projection of slides, this surface can be made to look like a sheer face of rock, space, time, moonscape, etc.

The platform from Act One remains intact and is now joined at the back to a four foot high, two foot wide, runway which covers the width of 40 feet of stage. The rest of the set from Act One has been struck.

At the very centre of the backdrop, the texture has been manipulated to form a vortex. Inside the vortex is a 10 ft x 10 ft film screen.

Stage right there is a stairway ascending to the sky. Stage left of the runway a huge swing is concealed. Standing on the runway, stage left, is a microphone on a stand.

A large globe of the earth hangs in the sky near the vicinity of the staircase. It is filled with salt. Throughout Act Two a small, steady stream of salt runs from a tiny hole in the bottom of the globe.

Eerie space music plays. Lights up on the filmscreen in the vortex. The disembodied head of MAG appears. She is beautiful and blue. Her head is bald. There is voiceover dialogue.

MAG: Even though I am travelling the speed of thought, it will take 1.15 to reach your island in the great vastness. You will be landing on the moon in fifteen seconds. I have projected a life support sphere and you will be safe until I regenerate the power to send you home. Brace yourself ...

LIZZIE: (*Offstage.*) Ohhhh.

(Lights up on the top of the staircase as LIZZIE lands on the moon with a thump. There is eerie silence and strange moon lights.)

Wow, I am on the moon. I don't believe it. Some radiantly beautiful space woman, she just has to be a woman, I just know it. She has lifted me up off the surface of my planet, flown me a few hundred thousand miles through space and dropped me on the moon. I sure would have liked to see the faces of those pigs when I disappeared into thin air like that. Ha, ha. Lizzie Dyke does it again. They will never catch me!!! Ha, ha, ha.

(Pause. LIZZIE is suddenly distressed. She searches the sky for the earth.)

... where is the earth. Where is the ... Holy mother, there she blows. A mystical vision. Oh, my sweet blue planet. Look at you. The

earth is so beautiful I could cry.
(LIZZIE starts to cry.)
Look at how she's all torn up there, scars and bruises around her middle ... Poor old mother earth, that's what they'll be saying. She was some sweet. She'd do anything for you. Give you the food right out of her mouth and the clothes right off her back. She was good as gold, as sweet as honey, gentle as rain, she was. She was the salt of the ...
... hey, there's Newfoundland. Wow. The girls won't believe this, guess what kids? Mommy went to the moon. I'm the mom in the moon. They will just go crazy. Ha hahah.
(LIZZIE laughs hysterically, then becomes paranoid.)
Am I really here? Is this an illusion? Have I been here before or was I dreaming? Magenta Illuminous. What a beauty. Her skin is my favorite shade of blue, like Percy's skin. Magenta looks a little bit like Percy, isn't that funny.

I've met her somewhere before. No. That can't be. Magenta Illuminous is an alien. An alien being. Wow. And so beautiful ... humm.. and I've only seen her head ... humm ...I've never been with an alien before. I wonder if she has a ... *(Pause.)* ...

(Demanding.) Magenta Illuminous!! Magenta Illuminous !!! Please show yourself. I want to talk to you ... Magneta Illuminous.

(Film of MAG flying through space. Now we see her whole body. Magenta Illuminous is all blue. There are crystals inlaid in her forehead. Magenta Illuminous has fairy wings. They are delicate, fine, and beautiful, like stained glass. She is naked but for her silver skirt, her silver gloves and her big silver power boots. She is a vision of strength and gorgeousness. LIZZIE is dumbfounded and not a little tongue-tied.)

MAG: Yes, Lizzie, we have met. Under very different circumstances.

LIZZIE: Really ... I can't place you ... so, are all the woman on Karundia as beautiful as you? ... I mean ... *(Uncomfortable pause.)* ... Uh, I just mean that you are very beautiful ... and that you are a woman, I wasn't sure at first and ... oh ...

MAG: All of the beings on my planet are women.

LIZZIE: Galaxy of Lesbo. Right!

MAG: We were not always an uni-gender planet. Our counterparts vanished from the face of Karundia during the Ion Age, about 200,000 revolutions past. A biogenetically engineered virus, lethal to the males of our species was released by the Reticuli.

LIZZIE: Reticuli?

MAG: You should know who they are, Lizzie Dyke. Hmmm. Perhaps your memory is blocked. Open your heart, I will plug into your receivers. Oh, oh, I am slowing down. I must end this transmission.

The ALIENiaton of Lizzie Dyke

(MAG film ends.)
LIZZIE: Wait Magenta ... Wait!!! Oh, no. She's gone. Gone. I don't know anymore than I did before. And is it ever quiet ...
(Eerie silence. Lights change and travelling music fades in. LIZZIE talks as she walks down the stairs, across the stage and up onto the platform.)
I wondered away the hours that night on the moon. I wondered about Magenta Illuminous' words. And her sweet face. I didn't have the first clue how to go about opening my heart, and the name Reticuli, although it seemed to mean nothing, struck a nerve somehow, and I was uneased by disquieting broken images of sharp edges and eyes watching from behind the black veil of night ...
As Magenta returned me to earth she transmitted one final image. It was a map of the northern peninsula of Newfoundland, with directions to a safe hiding place. Magenta was guiding us inland to await her arrival.
She brought me back pretty well the same way she brought me up, and she dropped me right outside of our hideout in Middle Arm. There I found my three daughters all sitting around the one channel, watching the "X Files".
I didn't tell them about what had happened. Not yet. First I had to get to the bottom of things. I didn't know how deep that bottom would turn out to be. I was dazed and confused and as time went on, I became more and more infatuated with my beautiful alien messenger. I poured over the map of Newfoundland to pinpoint the exact location of our next hideout.
(Slide of map of Newfoundland.)
I sent to town for books. I still had a few friends left at the Lesbian Woman's Collective, and Celine, goddess bless her radical heart, shuttled out all the information on alien involvement on earth that she could find. I don't think anything could have prepared me for what I was to discover. My perspective on reality widened about a hundred billion light years in the space of a few weeks.
(Face in book. Slide of hieroglyphic of Egyptian wall with eyes looking down from the sky.)
I didn't know the pyramids were built by aliens! So that's what all those huge eyes up in the sky are about. I always thought that there was something fishy about that "100,000 slaves pulled 15 million 1200 ton stones across miles and miles of desert on wooden rollers" theory.
Stir that soup for me, would you, Andromeda??
(Slide of the crowds at Fatima.)
Ah, yes, the miracles at Fatima, a typical example of an alien sighting, this one witnessed by thousands. Lights and geometric patterns in the sky, uh huh, ethereal being appearing to children. Sheesh!! A few extraterrestrials put a cheap light show together

and the human population goes mad. We are so easily fooled.
(Slide of the Pleiades star system.)
The Pleiades. The seven sisters. We have many relations in the Pleiades. They visit often. The people from the Pleiades are our ancient cousins. We were all made by the same race of master geneticist space creatures. Hmmm ...
(Billy Meir video [video of Alien spaceships.])
The Billy Meir case. A one armed Swiss farmer was approached by a group of people in a beamship from the Pleiades. They say, "Hey Billy, take footage of our ships, here are some metal samples for your scientists to examine." The ships are made out of a derivative of aluminum whose molecular structure no human scientist can yet understand. Will you look at that.
(LIZZIE is tired. She puts down her book and leafs through a copy of The Newfoundland Herald.*)*
Sigh. I wonder what is on TV tonight. "Full house" ... "The Price is Right" ... "Matlock" ... "Beverly Hills 90210" ... Oh, I wish I had cable...
(She continues to leaf through the Herald.*)*
"Prepare for the coming millennium. A dimensional shift is imminent." Dimensional shift? "Reconnecting the DNA is part of the transmutational process." My goddess, it's even on the back of the *Herald*!

"Planetary systems involved in covert operation on earth include: The Yahoos of Noomoo, the Arcturan Military, The Fairy Republic, Zeta One and Zeta Two Reticuli, the ..."

Reticuli?

(LIZZIE drops the Herald *and is pulled into another reality. Slide of the Reticuli star system. Sound FX. A spaceship coming in low over the land. Lights. LIZZIE walks along the back platform to the screen. Stars fill the stage.)*

I remember I was walking. I was walking down a lonely road. How did I get here? I walked here. I am walking on the barrens. Except, I don't think I am walking. I think I am floating.

There it is. I see it. The ship. It's coming for me. They told me to come here to meet them. But I don't want to go. I don't want to ... Oh, it's above me. There they are. Three of them. Horrible little grey things. Skinny little arms. Don't touch me, don't touch me with that...

(Spaceship sucks LIZZIE up. Lights change, scarier still.)

Little round room. Everything is grey. There's about a dozen of them now, swarming around me. What are they made of? They look like big plastic bugs, oversized heads and, oh, your eyes are awful. Black and shiny. Oh, no, here comes the head one with the painstick again. Ow ... they are trying to turn me.

(To Aliens.) Why don't you just ask me, I'll turn, I'll turn. Hahahahahah. ahah.

Oh, look, the hatch's opening, they are bringing in another prisoner. She's all blue. Where did she come from. She is unconscious, something is happening. They are all nodding together over in the corner. Their necks are double jointed. Ick.

(*To Aliens.*) Listen, I don't want to be here. I was just in the wrong place at the wrong time!! Ow. Oh, fuck, you are a cold bastard, anybody ever tell you that? I think they have put something in my belly. They have. There is something in there. They're doing something to the blue one. They are looking inside my belly. Oh, God ... He's got the stick again ... don't you touch me with that. Don't you put that in there. Don't touch my ovaries, you rat bastard!!

(*There is a strobe light and the sound of insanity ringing in the brain as LIZZIE yells and leaves the stage. Voice of ELLY is heard.*)

ELLY: Mom, I have to talk to you about all those alien books you've been reading. Mom, I hope you don't really, really, really believe in aliens. Percy is starting to think that she is an alien. She tried to do a mind meld on me this morning and I have had a really bad headache ever since. Not only that, but Andy is having nightmares about little grey bugs coming to take her in the night and ...

LIZZIE: (*Emerging in tap shoes with guitar.*) What? Andromeda is dreaming about what?! Okay, that's it. Girls, we are on the move again. Pack up your stuff and let's get the hell out of here. No buts about it, let's load up that van.

(*LIZZIE tap dances and sings the first verse.*)

> Oh, ever since I
> was a girl I
> didn't fit
> into this world
> on the outside
> looking in I
> built my castle
> I took my stand
> when the walls fell
> I seen it all
> caving in

(*Electric music comes in. LIZZIE taps to the microphone on the other end of the platform.*)

Ok girls, is everybody in? Here we go, out past Carbonear, out past Gander. Please girls! Stop fighting in the back!

> a long highway
> through the night

sleep my little darlings,
it's gonna be alright
I'm a hot nerve
out on the white line
got one headlight
and I feel just fine
I'm a rock hard
razor sharp
grown-up girl
and there's no fuckin' justice
in this fuckin' world

"They used me against my will for their genetic manipulation, their psychopathic investigations. Me! Lizzie Dyke!! The Lizzie Dyke. Nothing but a cosmic lab rat in the ever expanding laboratory of contrived evolution ..."
(She resumes singing.)

Ever since I
was a girl I
didn't fit
into this world
on the outside
looking in I'll
build another castle,
I'll take another stand
woah, oh
woah oh oh
lookin back across
that empty road behind me
I can't see who follows,
I got a light that is looking to guide me
thru all my black tomorrows
and it's
around the corner
around the bend
up the hill
down again
into the distant
horizon where
all my blue skies
all my beautiful blue skies
are waiting

*(Music stops and LIZZIE is at the hideout. She puts
her guitar away and sits.)*
It is late fall. Magenta Illuminous will not arrive for another 5

months. The girls complained endlessly in their very effective twelve year old way about not having a shack or even a school bus to hole up in this time. "A cave. Oh, great, Mom! Do you hear that, Percy? She says we are moving into a cave. Swashbuckling through the deep woods was a little much for us all, as well. Thank heavens for Percy and her power saw.

But the cave is wonderful. It's spacious and dry and the kitchen even has a sky light in it. There are several acres of land suitable for planting, just as Magenta said.

I still haven't told the girls the truth about Magenta. I can barely adjust to the colossal shifts in my own reality. I don't want to screw them up. They are already very suspicious and are asking too many questions, "Mom, when was the last time you had a check up?" "Mom, those things on Percy's back are getting really big. Don't you think she should see someone?"

It's true, Percy's wings are becoming rather obvious. I know I have to tell them. I am just waiting for the right moment. How can I tell them that, not only do I really, really, really believe in aliens, I gave birth to one. Percy is a biogenetically engineered half human, half alien being, and I just don't know how they are going to deal with that.

How can I tell them that hell is real. I know, because I have been there. Hell is a small dark place. Populated by monsters with long needles and insect eyes. It smells like cheese in hell. Cheese and burning cardboard.

Sometimes it's all too much. I get afraid. Andy isn't the only one having nightmares. Even though we are well hidden and protected by the deflector field Mag has surrounded us in, I feel vulnerable in the wilderness, miles from another living soul. And they are out there. Reticuli. An enemy bigger and more insidious than the CIA, the RNC, the Welfare Cops and Lesbian Thought Police put together.

When it comes time to get to bed, I push all of our mats together and we sleep in a big warm pile in the middle of the cave. Somehow I feel safer that way.

(The following scene appeared in it's full form on opening night of the original production, LIZZIE playing two of the triplets and the blue gloved hands performing the part of PERCY. During the course of the run this scene was edited out completely.)

Is everybody all tucked in there? Oh, Andy, your feet are freezing.

(Reading a "Brief History of Time".)

Wow, did you know that the entire universe is made up of the exact same elements that appear here on earth? You know, Hydrogen, Nitrogen, Carbon. Isn't that interesting?

(PERCY claps hands.)

Oh, yes, I know you know that, Percy, but I don't think Andy and

Elly do.
ANDY: And we don't care, either ...
LIZZIE: Andy, don't be so rude ...
ELLY: Well, it's just that you are driving us nuts with all this alien stuff. I really hope this is just a phase. But if you wanna know what I really think, I think Mommy has a girlfriend.
LIZZIE: I do not.
ELLY: Come on, Mom, come clean. All the signs are there. You're giggling and singing to yourself all the time. You've been tap-dancing around the cave. I don't know. Andy, what do you think.
ANDY: Come on, Mom, spill your guts. What is going on?
LIZZIE: Nothing. There is nothing going on.
ELLY: Who is she? I hope she isn't anything like that Helga you went mad over last year.
LIZZIE: Olga, Elly, here name was Olga. And Olga was sweet.
ANDY: Yeah, right. She was sweet, whenever you were around.
LIZZIE: Well, there is nothing going on, so stop tormenting your poor old mother. I was just about to tell you how big the universe is.
ANDY: Oh, brother.
(PERCY claps her hands.)
LIZZIE: See, Percy is all interested.
ELLY: Yeah, but Percy is weird. She thinks she's an alien, for one thing.
(PERCY does Vulcan "Live Long and Prosper" hand symbol.)
LIZZIE: You be nice to your sister. You know she's sensitive. Open your mind a little. You watch "Star Trek" all the time. What's so strange about thinking you might be an alien?
ANDY: Mom, "Star Trek" is a TV show.
LIZZIE: I know, but it isn't too far fetched an idea that somebody could be an alien. Every star we see in the sky is a potential sun to a solar system made up of the exact same elements as ours. All the stars we see in the sky are only a fraction of the millions and billions of stars in our galaxy. Our galaxy is only one in millions of billions of galaxies that expand out across a universe so big that we can barely conceive of it. The truth is ... the universe is full of life forms. And people and civilizations. Some just like ours. Some very different from ours.
ELLY: Yawn ...
ANDY: Un huh.
LIZZIE: The truth is, humans were made by space creatures with amazing abilities in altering reality at will. They made us and they are still messing around with us. They have sold a lot of ideas to the CIA. Control is a technology. A TV screen. A microchip. Jesus was a hologram.
ELLY: If Jesus was a hologram, who is God then?
LIZZIE: *(She searches momentarily in her book.)* God, God. Let me

The ALIENiaton of Lizzie Dyke

see, God, God ... Well, God is light, for one thing. God is a force so powerful, so bright and so in love with herself that no one, no entity, no life form anywhere in the universe has ever seen her .. Because, A) You would just explode or burn up coming in contact with the intensity of that emanation. You could never house the information of God in a puny three dimensional body, and, B) God is just too damned busy to be bothered with the likes of us. You see, the universe was created when the great sea of nothing, the great mother of emptiness, caught a glimpse of her own reflection on the curved mirror of time. It was love at first sight. Her desire to unite with herself became so strong that she turned herself inside out and from that union of herself within herself came the great explosion, the great cosmic orgasm which created all things. God had such a good time that she has been off playing with herself ever since, creating universes and moving on. Do you understand?

(The girls are snoring. Light fade.
Lights upon LIZZIE waiting, gazing skyward.)

Hey, what is that, there? Is that you? No, it's a bird. *(Pause.)* What about that? Is it? Could it be? Girls, girls, she's here. She's here! Oh, I knew you would come. I knew it.

(Lighting effect with musical humm. LIZZIE goes
to swing and unhooks it. LIZZIE swings
and delivers the following dialogue.)

She landed on the field on the 30th of June, at noon. The girls thought her arrival was the coolest thing they had ever seen in all their lives. She appeared first a blue speck on the horizon, speeding down past the clouds, then closer and closer, the light blazing through her wondrous wings until she touched down right in front of me. When I looked into her eyes I knew what I had suspected for a long time, ever since our meeting, long ago, on the moon, all through the long months of winter, through the planting time and up to that moment. It was love. Pure and simple.

(LIZZIE swings as the erotic video plays. The erotic video is a five minute, gentle piece, in which we see LIZZIE and MAG in love's warm embrace. The camera moves slowly with concentration on small, intimate details. The contrast between pink human skin and blue alien skin is luscious. The main idea is that sex between any two people who love each other is a beautiful thing. The soundtrack is a slow instrumental version of "Love Song to the Alien".
Video ends and LIZZIE is still swinging.)

Oh, I love her, I love her, I love her!! Mag can make the snow go away and she can light a fire in the thunderstorm. She has fertilized the fields with some kind of magic dust, and our crops are thriving. She has lined the walls of our cave with amethyst, to keep the invading eyes of Reticuli from seeing in, and she has hooked up the cable!! You wouldn't believe the channels we get. I got stuff from all over the galaxy coming across my TV set.

The more we find out about each other, the more incredible the connection becomes. Our names, for example, were both sources of torture to us as children. Mag got teased incessantly because her name was Magenta, even though she's blue. Mag's mother was colour blind.

Mag is an outlaw, too. On Karundia, most people don't know that they can use their wings to fly. They have been programmed to believe that their wings are only for decoration. Mag is the first person in recorded Karundian history to fly from the face of the planet and out into space.

Mag and Percy are off on the mountain. They are trying to unlock Percy's long-dormant telepathic abilities. The other day Percy transmitted her first image. It was Mag. The moment was rather bittersweet for me.

(Becoming meditative.)

Hmmmm. I am trying to reach another dimension but all I see are walls. Mag says that I have to wake up. Wake up to the multi-dimensional world where matter doesn't matter. She always laughs at that part, matter doesn't matter.

Mag has been buzzing out of this dimension and into the next for months, now. It happens mostly when she is tired. The first time it happened I was pretty freaked out, she was there on the bed and then gone. It took a couple of days to get over the fright. Sometimes she can only partly materialize and then she is just like a ghost.

Mag says we should expect that kind of thing to happen more and more as time moves forward. I'm not sure if I know what she means by that 'Time moves forward'. It has something to do with frequency, with what I am supposed to find inside my still mind. The girls are catching on, but I can't do it! Tomorrow I am going on a vision quest to the mountain.

(LIZZIE hikes to the staircase and struggles up the mountain.
She reaches the top, breathing hard. She takes a
yoga position and tries to still her mind.

Hmmm, hmmm. Stilling the mind, feel the vibration. Hmmm. Hmmm.)

(LIZZIE is frustrated easily.)

Oh, damn it, fuck!! Stilling the mind seems like such a waste of time!!

(LIZZIE descends the mountain.)

There is too much going on, my mind will not stop babbling. I can't stop thinking. Things are not looking good for human civilization. Cable has become something of a curse, I can see the deterioration growing vaster every day and sometimes I get so angry, I get so angry, I just want to ...

(Lighting change, MAG appears as a blue lighting effect through the triangular trapdoor, with bubbles. LIZZIE turns in a rage and addresses her.)
LIZZIE: Mag, I want to blow up some buildings.
MAG: That's terrorism, darling.
LIZZIE: I can't stand it. If the walls are falling, I am tired of waiting for it. Let's assist the process. Let's blow up the Senate. Those goddamned Americans, they ought to get what is coming to them.
MAG: Well, far be it from me to interfere with your karma, Lizzie, but I think you are being a little rash.
LIZZIE: Oh, stop it. How can we just sit here, knowing what we know. How can we just sit here and do nothing.
MAG: There is more going on here than meets the eye.
LIZZIE: But the carnage, the death, all those babies ...
MAG: Things are going to get much worse than that, I fear.
LIZZIE: Some heads gotta roll, baby. We know who the motherfuckers are, let's get to work.
MAG: It's not up to us to decide things for other people.
LIZZIE: Yes, it is.
MAG: I don't think it is, Lizzie.
LIZZIE: It is. How about we use some of your shazam to screw with their system. Let's send some messages. Let's interface with their system and interfere with their stuff. Come on, baby, please ... baby, please ... sweetiepie ... darling ... come on, I know you can do that stuff.
MAG: Lizzie ...
LIZZIE: Oh, come on. I just want to animate life a little. I am a performer, after all. What do you say? I promise no one will get hurt.
MAG: Do you know why you want to do this, Lizzie? Are you sure you want the responsibility.
LIZZIE: Responsibility? Responsibility, ha! Responsibility is my middle name.
MAG: Hah hah ha ha ... oh, darling!
LIZZIE: What is so funny. What are you laughing at?
MAG: I am laughing at you, braveheart.
LIZZIE: Why do you call me braveheart?
MAG: Because that is what you are.
LIZZIE: Oh, Mag. Come on, baby. I want you to do this for me. I want you to help me.
MAG: And so I will, my sweet pea. I will help you. Let's go out to the shed and brainstorm.
(MAG effect disappears.)
LIZZIE: We got to work and jammed all the TV signals of earth so that I could send my first message. The first of many.
(LIZZIE stands in front of the screen. It plays static.)

People of earth. This is Lizzie Dyke, coming at you live from my secret hideout. In case you are wondering how I have managed to jam all the TV signals of earth, it is because I have fallen in love with a woman from another planet and she has super powers. Ha ha, you can't catch me.

You have relations all over the universe, and they are coming. Watch the skies ...

(What follows is a montage of image and sound, as LIZZIE takes the world by storm. There are slides of natural disasters and places named in reports. Newspaper headlines are projected on both the film screen and across the whole backdrop. A lot of fun can be had with these.)

HEADLINES

"Dyke claims earth is a member of an intergalactic community"
"Lizzie Dyke re-routes Mississippi flood, thousands saved"
"Lizzie Dyke challenges Clyde Wells to a public debate, Wells resigns"
"Lizzie Dyke storms City Council, gives Andy Wells a wedgie"
"Notorious Dyke smokes Marijuana on Capitol Hill"
Enquirer "Lizzie turns Madonna down"
Lesbian Front "Lizzie Dyke, Woman of the Year"
Newsweek "Lizzie Dyke, criminal or saint?"
World Weekly News "I am Lizzie Dyke's illegitimate love child"
"Lizzie Dyke drops Peace Bomb on Middle East"

(There is a voiceover dialogue of reporters from all over the world, with a News Program Sting playing in between each report. There are the sounds of FAX machines and telephones ringing.)

"Dateline, Geneva: Lizzie Dyke shocked the world today by exposing 27 UN officials as alien conspirators from the planet Reticulum"

"Lizzie Dyke rocked the scientific community today with proof that Neptune has 10 moons"

"Lizzie Dyke appeared before the UN today and took them to task for their position on child care. Dyke, notorious criminal wanted in 27 countries, claims that since the Gorgons of Helio have achieved peace, earth ranks as having the worst child care system in the universe."

(A slide of the Whitehouse.)

"Washington D.C. was the site of another bizarre appearance by internationally wanted criminal, Lizzie Dyke. Witnesses say that Dyke appeared in a beam of light and stormed the US Congress during the afternoon session. While inside she somehow managed to force the entire Congress to remove their clothes as she applied clown make-up to the president and his men. When the Secret Service arrived on the scene, Dyke is reported to have levitated above their heads, shouting, 'choke on my dust, motherfuckers,' before disappearing in the same beam of light. The President

The ALIENiaton of Lizzie Dyke 407

remains locked in the Oval Office and is unavailable for comment."

(Slide of Sweden's map.)

"Lizzie Dyke is reportedly responsible for saving over 100,000 lives in Sweden today. At about 3 am today six Swedish cities were awakened as Dyke shouted warnings in the streets of a coming earthquake. 100,000 people were evacuated in an incredible two hours and located to a camp away from the danger site. At 6 am an earthquake measuring an astounding 9.1 on the Richter scale destroyed the villages of Uppsala, Linkping and Guttiberg ..."

(A slide of Buckingham Palace.)

"This is Fraser Uppityman of the BBC, live at Buckingham Palace, waiting on a sign of Lizzie Dyke, who, at tea time today, appeared in the Queen's chamber and took Her Majesty prisoner. They have been locked inside for seven hours. Palace officials report that many pots of tea have been ordered to the room over the course of today's tense hostage taking. The Palace seems to be surrounded in some sort of energy field that the authorities are unable to penetrate. Lizzie Dyke is wanted in twenty-seven countries on charges ranging from trespassing to industrial espionage. Oh, wait, something appears to be happening, there is some movement by the gate and ... here comes the Queen, thank heavens, she appears to be relatively unharmed. She is taking a microphone."

(Slide and voiceover of Queen Elizabeth.)

"Good people of the Commonwealth. I have just had tea with the outlaw, Lizzie Dyke, and over the course of the hours I have become a new woman. I hereby relinquish all claims on all Commonwealth lands not included within the confines of England. The wealth of the monarchy shall be distributed among the world's poor. That is where it all came from in the first place. I hereby dissolve the British monarchy. I abdicate the throne. I fire the government of Britain. Oh, and I am leaving you, Phillip. I am in love with Lady Hackery and we have been having an affair for the past twelve years. Oh, it is so good to be out."

LIZZIE: Mag, Mag, you have to see this. This is the best one yet!!

(MAG appears again, as a blue lighting effect with bubbles.)

MAG: Lizzie, we have a problem. Let's go outside.
LIZZIE: But it's after dark, it's dangerous. Reticuli ...
MAG: Just for a moment.
LIZZIE: Okay. Back in a minute, girls...
MAG: Lizzie, I think you should sit down.
LIZZIE: Okay.
MAG: I must tell you something ...
LIZZIE: What is it ...
MAG: There is something I didn't tell you. I kept it from you because I wasn't sure it was true. Lizzie, I think Percy has gone

into the metamorphosis trance. It, ah ... it is one of the initial stages of puberty.
LIZZIE: Puberty! Well, that is a relief. I was beginning to think she was never going to get there. Oh, Mag, is that what all this is about. Our little girl is becoming a woman?
MAG: No, Lizzie, you don't understand. The metamorphosis trance is the first stage of puberty in the ... the ... counterpart of our species.
LIZZIE: What counterpart?
MAG: According to myth, after sleeping the equivalent of four earth weeks, she will emerge from the metamorphosis trance with a fully grown erectile projectile.
LIZZIE: Erectile projectile, what is that?
MAG: Oh, Lizzie. It's a protrusion ... Lizzie, can't you see what all this means? Percy is a ... I mean she is ... well, she's not a ...
LIZZIE: She's what??
MAG: She is not a she. She's a ... he's a ... a boy. A malechild.
LIZZIE: You mean, our little girl is becoming a man? No. I do not accept that. I raised her from a baby, Mag, and Percy is a girl. A girl!!!
MAG: I don't know how Lizzie, but the Reticuli have really done a number this time. Lizzie we have to ...
MAG's voice becomes muffled. She is being abducted.
Strobe light. The film screen lights up with the image of three Reticulians standing around their control devices. They are whitish-grey insect–like beings with bald heads. They have a sinister disposition.)
LIZZIE: Mag!! Oh, no. Oh, no ... you bring her back. You bring her back !!!! Bastards! You bring her back.
(LIZZIE reaches for the Screen and then falls to the ground in despair. Film runs out. Transition. LIZZIE goes to PERCY and kneels down.)
We waited four weeks at Percy's side. Me and the girls. Those were dark days. Red hot emergency lights in my head, twenty-four hours a day. My love has been abducted. My daughter is a son.

And when Percy awoke, he was different. It was like he barely recognized us. When we told him about his transformation, he lapsed into an eerie mood. When we told him about Mag's abduction, he nearly went off his head, tearing the place apart, breaking up the furniture. He began to do very strange thing's like drinking the milk straight out of the carton, and every time we turned around he was playing with that erectile projectile of his. He couldn't keep his hands off it. He was off on the mountain for weeks. Then he started spending all of his time in the shed. How was I supposed to know that he was gonna build a spaceship and leave me, too.

I woke up one night to the sound of engines and light shining

on the empty space beside me, where she used to shimmer on the pillow. Then I heard Percy's voice, for the first time, he spoke directly into my brain..
(Sound. Spaceship.)
PERCY: So, I'm off, Mother. Into the great beyond ... to find Mag out there. Don't worry, now. Power discs on, life support ready ... Say goodbye to the girls for me. Don't go crying, now, mother. Lifting off ... one small step for ... may the force be ... Live long and ... Goodbye!!!
(PERCY takes off. LIZZIE is drunk, goes to platform and pulls out a disguise.)
LIZZIE: I can't stop drinking. Dressing up in these ridiculous disguises so I can move among the people again. I haven't been home in weeks. The girls must be worried sick. So they should be. Most nights I end up prostrate on the cold hard bathroom tile of some roadside Irving station, getting up every so often to cling to the cool sweating porcelain and heave up my woes in buckets. Nail me up. Nail me up on the cross, I am crucified ...

Oh, I'm sick. I got to lie down. Maybe if I lie down. I'll just get down here on the nice sidewalk ...
(She lies down.)
Oh no, gotta get up. The spins. The spins. Oh. Mag, remember when we were together. Me and you. We came together, intergalactic lesbian lovers. What more could a woman want than a lover who was telepathic? And you gave head that was out of this world, which I could never figure out, seeing how you didn't even have a tongue.

Bartender, bartender. Get me another drink. I want another drink. What does a person have to do to get a fucking drink around here!!
(Black-gloved hands appear with a glass of bourbon.)
Thank you.

Bastards. They came in the middle of the night and they took her. Bastards.
(She drinks.)
Mag used to say they were neither good nor evil. They were just reflecting what they saw. They were just people going through their thing. Go with the flow, that's what she used to say. Go with the flow. Ha. Fuck the flow, that's what I say. Fuck the flow. Ha ha. Prepare for the coming millennium, the end is near.

Oh, Magenta. I wrote a song for you. I'm gonna sing it. I'm gonna sing the song ...
(To invisible band.)
Gimme that microphone, boy. Now, go on, get outta here. Alright, play the song. It's in D. Play it. Play it!
(Soundtrack of band playing "Love Song to The Alien". She sings.)

> Where did you come from
> how far away
> how did you find me
> in this lonely place
> on my island
> turning in space
> you said you found me
> because my light
> shone like a beacon
> in the black of the night
> and from 200,000,000
> light years away
> you came, you came
> how many moons, love
> how many years
> I have waited in vain, love
> for you to appear
> on every horizon
> on the curve of the night
> I sit by my window
> and I scan the skies
> looking for you, oh
> where did you come from
> where did you go
> are you still mine, love
> how will I know
> the darkness of mourning
> dawns in my soul
> am I alone?

(LIZZIE breaks down.)
Oh I don't know, I don't care, I don't give a fuck anymore, about anything. I am crucified, the universe has crucified me ... Sob sob. I'm crucified.
(LIZZIE stumbles out into the dark street. She is raving.)
Nail me up!! Nail me up on the cross!! I'm crucified, I am crucified!!
(LIZZIE notices her hands, she is amused to see stigmata there. She laughs cynically to herself as she resumes walking, then falls down and passes out on the sidewalk. The voices of cops are heard.)
FIRST COP: Hey, Charlie, we've got us another vagrant.
SECOND COP: Heave him in the back.
FIRST COP: Jesus Christ, mac, we've landed us a Lizzie Dyke!! We'll get extra brownie points for this one.
(Lights fade into mental hospital film. The film is shot in black and white and is as dark as it can possibly be. LIZZIE is

The ALIENiaton of Lizzie Dyke

incarcerated in a mental hospital. There are shots of barred windows, hallways, bare lightbulbs, as we follow the route to LIZZIE's cell. The soundtrack is eerie and full of horrendous screaming. There is voiceover.)

FIRST DOKTOR: We've got a place all ready for you, Lizzie Dyke. Lizzie, I'm going to be straight with you, okay? I think we have a pretty clear cut case of schizophrenia here.

SECOND DOKTOR: So, on this planet that your alien lover comes from, there are no males at all, correct? They are all females. Uh huh. But what about the sperm, Lizzie, have you considered that? Where do they get the sperm? Everybody knows there has to be sperm ... has to be sperm ... has to be sperm ...

(The film now finds LIZZIE sitting on a cement floor in a straight jacket. She raves and drools and screams. The video ends with a close up shot of LIZZIE's screaming mouth.
Lights up on LIZZIE pacing in her cell. She is older. She has a shock of brilliant white hair. She is wearing a white prisoner's shift which has a bar code on the back. Soundtrack of thunder and extreme weather. Earthquakes and lightning.)

LIZZIE: Oh, wretched thunder, what do you want. Leave me alone. Incessant pounding !! Go away, go away.

(The sounds become more intense, until we hear a blast,
as the whole building blows apart.)

Oh. my head, my head is exploding.

(A shaft of light suddenly beams in. LIZZIE is momentarily
blinded. Sound effects continue.)

Oh, I'm blind!! I'm blind!! I..wait a minute, what is that? Is it? I can see the sun!! Ha ha. Is this real? I haven't seen the sun for years and years. Does this mean ... Ha ha ... could it be ... the walls have fallen. The walls have fallen!! Ha ha. I better get out of here.

(The sound of screaming mental patients fills the air.)

Don't worry, b'ys, I'm coming. I'll let you all out. The walls have fallen, just like we knew they would!! Hang on, Crazy Mary, I'm coming, Sledgehammer Grannie. Ha Ha. Don't worry, Hatchet Girl, I'll let you out.

(Sounds fade away.)

And that is how I came to be freed from the O.J. Simpson Memorial Franchise Confinement Facility for the Criminally Insane. A mudslide washed out the foundations and the walls just fell down.

I went on foot, across mile after mile of highway, all around me devastation greater than anything we had ever seen here in our cushy little corner of the western world. Cities and towns wiped out by the relentless superstorms, by industrial accidents and spills, by fire, tornado and flood. Global communications systems were down but reports of the same kind of thing were leaking in from everywhere. All the water was disappearing and with it went all the creatures of the earth. Except for the insects. The insects were taking over. Everywhere there was famine.

I worried about my girls. They would be women now. I had not seen them for many years and I didn't know if our little haven still existed in the wilds of northern Newfoundland.

When I finally made it to the edge of the Atlantic, I reached a standstill. There was no way to cross it. There had been so many tidal waves that there was not a boat left afloat. The Fairies were everywhere, looting and pillaging. A pesky race, those Fairies. People used to think that Fairies were sweet friendly people, but it didn't take long to find out that Fairies are actually quite cruel. They love to abduct babies, for example, so that they can all sit around in a ring and pinch them.

(Sound of Fairies engaged in mischief.)

Hey, you Fairies, stop tormenting that puppy. Why don't you pick on someone your own size, like a wasp or a hornet. Huh. Hey, watch who you are talking to. I am Lizzie Dyke and I am liable to come over there and squat you. Pesky bugs. Go on, get outta here.

I was beginning to think I was never going to find a way across the water to Newfoundland. I wasn't even sure if Newfoundland even existed anymore. One evening, as I was despairing, by a pier I saw a great light and a voice came out of the heavens ...

(The big, authoritative voice of God is heard.)

GOD: I am the lord, your god, you shall get down on your knees before me.

LIZZIE: Take a hike, bozo.

GOD: I am the lord, your god, how dare you speak to me in that manner, puny earthling.

LIZZIE: Don't pull that God crap with me. I know who you are.

GOD: You do?

LIZZIE: Yes, I do.

GOD: You do not.

LIZZIE: Yes, I do. You are an imposter. A hooligan. You, sir, are a poser.

GOD: I am not a poser. I am the lord, your god, and I shall make you taste my vengeance.

LIZZIE: I wouldn't try that if I was you, cheeseball. Let me tell you a little something about myself. I am an escaped mental patient from the O.J. Simpson Memorial Franchise Confinement Facility for the Criminally Insane. My home planet is in serious decline and I am not feeling very well today. So if you so much as count all the hairs on my head or try to fill my body with the holy spirit, I am going to rip you apart, molecule by molecule. Have you got that?

GOD: Uh huh.

LIZZIE: Good. You have to be a student. Let me guess. Sirius U.
GOD: Yeah, that's right.
LIZZIE: Major?
GOD: Philosophy.
LIZZIE: Ha ha ha ha ha. You philosophy students are always the worst. Where did you get such a cheesy line. I am the lord, your god. That is the cheesiest line I have ever heard. Trying to pickup a bit of skin, were you, boy? Well, there will be no skin for you here. Ever hear of the galaxy of Lesbos, motherfucker? Hey, you have spacecraft there, haven't you, haven't you?
GOD: Yeah.
LIZZIE: Listen, I need a ride and I need it bad. If you give me a shot up the northern peninsula of Newfoundland I will let you go without hurting you.
GOD: Okay.

(Flying music plays.)

Flying across the churning ocean and up the coast of my beloved, battered island was one of the biggest thrills of my life. I didn't even mind Dolbar's relentless babbling abut Migatorian theology and existential angst. I was simply overjoyed to see that she still stood there, fierce, proud rock that she was, braving the wild Atlantic.

Nothing could describe how it was to land in the meadow and come upon our little cave and find them there. Andromeda and Electra.

Our reunion was tearful and joyous. They had no idea whether I was alive or dead. Hey, who are these two guys? I was introduced to Kevin, "Hi, how are ya?" and Wayne, "Hey, how's it going?" two young fellas from the nearest community who were so at home in the cave that I soon realized they lived there. That would explain why my Andromeda was so round with child.

(Scene change. LIZZIE ages visibly. She arthritically reaches into a trapdoor and dons the Crone's Coat and the big round Crone's Hat and then she reaches for a large tree-branch which has been fashioned into a walking stick.)

LIZZIE: Oh, my camomile won't come up. One of the hardiest plants in the entire universe. My poor garden is deteriorating, it's fading away. The trees are holding on pretty strong, there, but I can't get anything to grow. No raspberries, no beautiful orange carrots, no precious flowers of any description. I don't even know what season it is. It looks like the end of winter. The air is warm, but there is no sweetness in it. Andromenda thinks it is June, Electra says it is September, but the climate has been wandering all over the place, and you never know when the night is going to fall early or not fall at all.

Any time, now, and Andromeda will have that baby. Of course, we have been saying that for ages. It's the longest, strangest pregnancy I've ever seen. It's been going on forever and the poor thing is absolutely huge. Longer, bigger pregnancies in the new millennia. Great!

Andromeda's belly is hot, too. Sometimes it glows. Touch your hand on it at the wrong time and—ssst—you burn yourself. Oh my, nothing surprises me anymore. She's very sensitive about the whole thing. Which is understandable. Andromeda is worried that she's gonna have an alien baby, which I don't see what the big deal is. I mean I had an alien baby. A long time ago. I had an alien baby.

And I lost him.

What I wouldn't give for a steaming pot of camomile tea. Or a good stiff bourbon.

(Lights start to change to purples and red. A trapdoor opens. A tribal drum beat fades in, accompanied by the low chanting of Kevin and Wayne.)

Come on, Andy, you're doing really well. It's almost here. Kevin, keep that drum beat going. Wayne, we need the hot water now. Okay, Elly, let's get ready to catch that baby! Just like I showed you. That's it, now, here comes another one, let's go, out with it. That's a girl! Wonderful! That's a girl, that's a girl. It's a GIRL. Ha ha ha. I think, yup, looks like a girl. Oh, my, Andy, she's beautiful. Okay, Elly, cut the cord. It's okay, it won't hurt, go ahead. Good work, Electra, good work.

(The Baby hums the tune to "Love Song to the Alien".)

You swallow down that ergot tea, Andromeda. Yes, I know it's gross, but it's very important you drink it. Andromeda, Wayne! Your baby is humming!! Listen. That means she's musical. Excellent!! That was a fine birthing. Oh, there's the whatchma callit. Have you got that bowl handy. That baby is still humming. Let me see. Does she look like me? May I please see the grandchild?

(Lizzie Fee is handed to LIZZIE through the trapdoor.)

Oh. Oh, look at you. My greedy arms would hold you forever, my little Lizzie Fee. I can't believe they've named you after me. My namesake. My progeny. And you do look like me. Thank heavens you got here safe. What took you so long, I wonder. Perfect, absolutely perfect. A perfect little creature, you are.

That's a song you're humming, I've heard it before. Are you trying to tell me something, darling? Are you, sweet thing?

(The Baby lights up.)

Oh my, oh my, oh my. You are a light baby. You are made out of light. Well, I will be fucked. A light baby. The human race seems to be evolving after all, huh, little one. Andromeda! Andromeda, she is a light baby.

(LIZZIE returns baby to Andromeda. Lights change. LIZZIE ages. During this next scene LIZZIE, with great difficulty,

covers the main platform with a huge black blanket. She is making her deathbed.)
Oh, my. I thought that Lizzie Fee had come to help the planet return. What a foolish old thing I am. I thought the light was trying to come back. Instead, Lizzie Fee came to lead the family into the next dimension. Except, I didn't go. You can't teach an old lady how to alter her molecular structure and what not, I can barely stand on my own two legs as it is.

But the children, they were ready to cross over. The days got shorter and shorter and shorter until the days ended all together, and darkness reigned over everything. They waited out the hours with me, but we all knew that the time was coming when they would have to go and I would have to stay. Then, the time came and Lizzie Fee dematerialized and did not return. One by one, they all went after her. One by one, they did not return.

Everything and everyone was gone. Except for me. One ancient Dyke. Staring out over the vacant landscape. (*She laughs gently.*)

Then the thunder began to roll and I looked up and watched as the stars fell down from the sky ... and then I was spinning and then there was nothing left but this blackness, this blackness which has taken over the earth and enveloped my soul.
(Everything fades away. LIZZIE slowly
gets under the blanket.)
I am taking to my bed.

I am taking to my bed and there I shall remain. I am tired and I want to sleep.

The distance between this universe and the next is only a dream.

Over there, they are all together. Andromeda and Electra. My girls. Percy has grown into a fine man. He was responsible for the Great Swarming which led to the transmutation of the entire planet of Karundia.

Across the great divide I can see my beautiful Magenta Illuminous. Her face has barely aged a day. Even as our universes pull apart, she remains here, with me. (*Hand over heart.*) Right here. A little fire I have protected in my heart. It will burn always. They are all right here.

I will die soon. I wonder what there will be when I am dead. I guess I will be a ghost. I will make a very good ghost. Whooo whooo. I'll gladly give my ghost to the poor dead mother earth. I'll gladly give her my bones. And on into the next universe, when they think of her, the great planet earth, as she was, they will be thinking of me.

(LIZZIE lies down and covers herself with the blanket as the Lizband song, "The Queen of Swords", plays. Black rain falls from the sky onto the bed. The last grains of salt fall from the

earth globe. LIZZIE dies.)

Oh she reigns tonight
in silence
keeping her secrets
falling to pieces
oh, it rains
upon the Lake of Aching
water breaking
filling up her bowl
inside me there's a desert
my heart's become a stone
how hard I cling to my hurt
all my gardens overgrown
my brain is bent on vengeance
my blade so true and sharp
my hand is raised and ready
to pierce your human heart

(The film screen comes up with the black and white image of an ancient LIZZIE lying on the ground. The LIZZIE on screen and the LIZZIE on stage simultaneously rise. The screen LIZZIE begins walking with her stick across a barren landscape. The onstage LIZZIE rises from the ground and slowly sheds her layers of clothes until she is dressed in only her silver skin. She ponders the LIZZIE on screen for a moment and then turns to walk with wonder to the staircase where she ascends into a cascade of stars. "The Queen of Swords" plays throughout and continues.)

I have spent the centuries
re-membering, re-membering
I have spent the centuries
re-membering my own
my own my own history
this fortress I have built
it is my home
me, by myself alone
I'm waiting til I'm wan
I'm so alone
This is not wisdom
my logic is destruction
de-struction is your
step by step by step instruction
so it don't matter, baby
if you're a non believer
cause the ax

the ax has fallen
see, these eyes have cried
a thousand bitter tears
these arms have held
every dying child
I gave you
the best two thousand years
of my of my of my life
I looked into your
bloodless eyes
and I named you
I named you liar
fuck the excuses
fuck the guilt
bury the sword
right up to the hilt
cause the truth is a bitch
and I am she
you call me by my rightful name
for I can't be contained
I can't be contained
I can't be contained
I can't, I can't, I can't, I can't

(The film continues to roll. The screen LIZZIE wanders and then, coming to the foot of a hill, she looks up as the film turns to colour and she sees MAG waiting with open arms. LIZZIE throws away her walking stick and her coat and runs to meet her.)

Paint the blood upon my face
I gave birth to the entire human race
the time is now, the time is here
I'm raging screaming rage
out into the biosphere
you were all born in blood
you were all born of she
her pain, her love her desire
only the truth will set you free
I give to you
The Bitch Goddess of Truth

(The film continues with closeup of LIZZIE and MAG, forever young, as they revel in their reunion embrace. Stars fill the stage. The song ends and the final image is a freezeframe shot of LIZZIE and MAG close and together. Lights down.)

End of Act Two